RESEARCH PAPERS:
A Guide and Workbook
Second Edition

Marian Arkin

LaGuardia Community College

Cecilia Macheski

LaGuardia Community College

Houghton Mifflin Company   **Boston**   **New York**

Marian Arkin would like to dedicate this book to her sister, Carol Abel, in memoriam.

Cecilia Macheski dedicates this book to her sister, Sylvia Macheski.

Publisher: Patricia Coryell
Editor in Chief: Suzanne Phelps Weir
Assistant Editor: Jane Acheson
Editorial Assistant: John McHugh
Senior Project Editor: Rosemary Winfield
Editorial Assistant: Jake Perry
Art and Design Coordinator: Jill Haber
Composition Buyer: Chuck Dutton
Manufacturing Manager: Priscilla Manchester
Marketing Manager: Cindy Graff Cohen
Marketing Associate: Wendy Thayer

Printed in the U.S.A.

Library of Congress Catalog Card Number: 2005920176

ISBN: 0-618-54978-1

1 2 3 4 5 6 7 8 9 – QE – 09 08 07 06 05

Contents

CHAPTER **4**   *Finding and Retrieving Sources*   **100**

CHAPTER **9**   *Documenting Your Paper in APA and Other Documentation Styles*   *242*

Preface

Good research skills are the foundation of every student's college education. Whatever major a student selects, he or she quickly discovers that being able to use the library and the Internet is essential. *Research Papers: A Guide and Workbook* is designed to help the beginning college writer to become familiar with the latest tools for locating information and, more important, to evaluate the articles, books, and Web sites that are located as a result of traditional and electronic searches. As students follow the steps, exercises, and practical guidance presented in this book, they progress from asking basic questions to pursuing thoughtful investigation. The hands-on workbook approach helps students acquire the confidence and skills to brainstorm, to inquire, to organize, and to avoid plagiarism. The text is directed both at students who have had little experience writing formal papers and those who have done research before but need to update and refine their skills.

Key Features

The unique approach of *Research Papers* is supported by an array of practical features, including the following:

- A step-by-step workbook format with numerous exercises for practicing and reinforcing concepts and skills.

- Facsimiles of research tools, including Web screens, library catalog screens, and facsimiles of primary sources.

- Checklists for completing key stages in the research process chapter by chapter.

- Detailed models and exercises for MLA and APA documentation styles.

- An annotated student research paper with a Works Cited page.

- Appendixes listing bibliographical sources and a glossary of research terms.

- Updated applications of research technology.

- *New:* A **Casebook** of readings, extending the guided workbook approach. Primary and secondary, factual and fictional selections provide material for launching research projects on five fertile topics. Two of these topics — Lizzie Borden and the *Titanic* disaster — link into the readings in the chapters, while the others are freestanding as jumping-off points for topic ideas.

- *New:* A **sample student paper** paired with that **student's research journal.** The paper and journal combine to offer a practical example for readers and a preview for the upcoming chapters. Marginal headings within the research journal correspond to topic headings within the later chapters and to a standard semester schedule on the front endpaper.

- *New:* Updates to the various approaches to learning with technology, such as electronic discussion boards and the ever-increasing number of licensed databases, e-books, and Web-based reference tools. Discussion of the perils of the digital environment also provides opportunities for increased and further-integrated discussion of avoiding plagiarism.

Approach and Organization

In *Research Papers: A Guide and Workbook,* students work inductively, starting with questions to be answered in a workshop-style series of exercises that are supported by explanatory material. At crucial stages, we highlight and reinforce essential skills for study, review, and easy reference in the form of Steps for Planning Your Research Paper. Central to our approach is the value of a staged research assignment, which evolves chapter by chapter as students engage in the process of writing their own papers while working with the models in the text.

A key strength of the book is versatility. All of the exercises can be used in class or as tasks for individual or online work. Practical suggestions for questions and topics are highlighted throughout the ten chapters in Part One:

- Chapter 1, What Is Research?, uses the unsolved 1892 case of Lizzie Borden to exemplify the crucial first steps: What is research? Why should you do it? When? How much? The open-ended Borden case encourages beginning researchers to see their task as a process, not a method of simply locating a right answer. Students work with primary sources that simulate the research process. Further readings and exercises help students to learn how important it is to ask the right questions.

- Chapter 2, Synopsis of a Model Research Paper, provides a model of what is ahead. A student paper, "40 Whacks," and an accompanying research journal written in conversational, accessible language invite students to join our model student in her research writing journey. A chronicle of the research writing process, including problems, frustrations, and successes, previews the lessons to be learned throughout the book.

- Chapter 3, Choosing a Subject and Narrowing to a Topic, helps students explore the first steps: selecting a subject, reading to find topics, and advancing toward a working thesis, a research plan, and finally a research proposal. Using excerpts from Edith Wharton's *In Morocco,* related sources in popular culture, and autobiographical pieces, this chapter introduces students to the tools for developing an original topic and a new perspective.

- Chapter 4, Finding and Retrieving Sources, guides the student through the steps of locating and acquiring sources both in the traditional library and electronically on the Web and in reference databases. Suggestions for using museums, professional sites, historical societies, archives, and other reference tools show the researcher how to seek a wide range of primary and secondary sources and to take advantage of the breadth of information currently available. Students are encouraged to assess their prior knowledge of the topic they've chosen as they begin evaluating what they find in their searches.

- Chapter 5, Evaluating and Recording Information from Sources, uses writings about the *Titanic* disaster to show students how to tell if sources are appropriate for the paper. In addition, students will find exercises and models for the crucial skills of paraphrasing, summarizing, and quoting correctly so they can avoid plagiarism and assemble a working bibliography. This chapter also illustrates the use of note cards and source cards and shows students how to read selectively on a topic.

- Chapter 6, Organizing and Outlining Research Material, introduces students to rhetorical strategies and helps them examine effective outline and development models, using excerpts from the autobiography of Frederick Douglass to illustrate these concepts. We conclude by asking students to develop and outline their own essays.

- Chapter 7, Writing the Paper, brings students to the synthesis stage, as they learn to arrange their notes and note cards and to integrate quotations and paraphrases into their writing. Students are shown model introductions and conclusions, and they review how to guard against plagiarism, a lesson they can never receive too often. The final goal of the chapter is for students to write a first draft of their own papers.

- Chapter 8, Documenting Your Sources Using MLA Style, and Chapter 9, Documenting Your Paper in APA and Other Documentation Styles, are designed to teach students the mechanics of MLA, APA, and other forms of in-text and final documentation. While many research paper textbooks provide sample entries of in-text and reference citations, *Research Papers* goes much further to help break the code of the machinery of style sheets so students learn to document intelligently. Students become able to see the link between their own research questions and the sources they use to support their investigations as they answer those questions. Chapter 8 includes an entire annotated research paper, with both in-text citations and a list of Works Cited, as an example for students to consult.

- Chapter 10, Preparing and Proofreading the Final Draft, takes students through the necessary steps for completing a neat, professional final draft of their work. We first teach students formatting and research mechanics and then offer various tools for reviewing the complete paper. Guidelines for proofreading, exercises for proofreading, and overall tips for producing an essay that a student can take pride in conclude the chapter.

Finally, Part Two's Casebook provides essays, documents, news articles, and literary selections for the students to use as inspiration for their own research papers. The five topics included in the Casebook are Lizzie Borden, the *Titanic* disaster, issues in war and peace, global health, and food controversies.

Ancillaries

The **Student Web Site** (at **http://college.hmco.com/english/**) offers additional material on the topics found in the book, including activities, forms and templates, advice on creating a research journal, and Web links. Students are encouraged to explore beyond the scope of the in-chapter readings and the Casebook and are given Web links to further readings and to a number of writing laboratories and research archives.

Instructors will find a wide array of suggestions in the online **Instructor's Resource Manual**. Each chapter includes discussion ideas, individual and collaborative activities, approaches to teaching the topic at hand, Web resources, and a Teacher's Journal describing the goals and methods of that chapter. The *Instructor's Resource Manual* is available on the instructor's side of the book's Web site.

Acknowledgments

We are grateful to the numerous reviewers whose suggestions contributed to this revised edition of *Research Papers:*

Arnold J. Bradford, Northern Virginia Community College
Peggy Brent, Hinds Community College, Mississippi
Adele Carpenter, Lewis & Clark Community College, Illinois
John Caserta, Ferris State University
P. J. Colbert, Marshalltown Community College, Iowa
Mary Cullen, Middlesex Community College, Massachusetts
Mary A. Fortner, Lincoln Land Community College, Illinois

Diane Gould, Shoreline Community College, Washington
Jaime H. Herrera, Mesa Community College
Kevin Jack Hagopian, University of Memphis
Marjorie Levenson, Massachusetts Bay Community College
Randall McClure, Minnesota State University
James T. McGowan, Parkland College, Illinois
David R. Miller, Glendale Community College, Arizona
Julie Nash, University of Massachusetts, Lowell
Christopher Orchard, Indiana University of Pennsylvania
Randall Popken, Tarleton State University, Texas
Kathleen G. Rousseau, West Virginia University
P. C. Scheponik, Montgomery County Community College, Pennsylvania
Tanya Slobodchikoff, DeVry University
Sylvia A. Stacey, Oakton Community College, Illinois
Judith B. Williamson, Sauk Valley Community College, Illinois

We would like to thank our colleagues in the English Department at LaGuardia Community College who helped us with suggestions and support, especially J. Elizabeth Clark, Daniel Lynch, Lenore McShane, and Leonard Vogt. We further wish to thank Eleonor Batchelder for precise proofreading. Our families and friends have continued to be patient and supportive. In particular, we would like to thank Anna Arkin-Gallagher, whose paper "40 Whacks" inspired us to make the Lizzie Borden case central to this book.

Also, we are grateful to the staff at Houghton Mifflin, especially Suzanne Phelps Weir, whose faith and continued interest in our project has enabled this revision, and Jane Acheson and Sarah Helyar Chester, who saw us through the editorial and technological processes with painstaking care.

PART ONE

The Research Paper Process

What Is Research?

■ Doing Research
■ The Research Process in Action

What is a research paper, or, more pertinently, what is research and why do we need to use it in preparing an essay? It does, after all, complicate the job of writing in college. Because doing research is much like solving a mystery, we've focused this first chapter on one of America's most famous mysteries: the murder of Mr. and Mrs. Andrew Borden, which happened in Fall River, Massachusetts, in the year 1892. We hope that by doing research about the crime, you can begin to answer those questions about why research is so important. When you finish this chapter, you should understand the basics of research, and perhaps you will have begun thinking about what kind of research paper you want to write.

Doing Research

Look at the photo that begins this chapter. Does this look like a murderer? Can this woman have taken an ax and hacked her mother and father to death?

Many of you probably recognize the rhyme accompanying the photo on page 3. Perhaps some of you know that it refers to a true story. A young woman named Lizzie Borden was accused of killing her mother and father. However, Lizzie was acquitted. People couldn't believe that she, a well-brought-up young woman, had committed such a heinous crime. According to law, she was not the wielder of that famous ax. But if not Lizzie, who did murder Mr. and Mrs. Borden?

The facts of the case are as follows: On August 4, 1892, Andrew Borden, a wealthy businessman, and his wife, Abby Borden, were found dead in their home in Fall River, Massachusetts. Both had been hacked to death. A week later Andrew's daughter Lizzie was arrested for the murders because it appeared that she was the only one who had both motive and opportunity. Her father was extremely wealthy, and she and her sister inherited an estate worth more than $300,000—a fortune at the time. When the trial was held nearly a year later, however, it was brief, and Lizzie was acquitted. During the past 100 years the case has attracted an enormous amount of attention; it has been the subject of numerous books and articles, all arguing different theories. Despite all this attention, the case has never been solved.

As we've seen on television, in movies, and in books, when detectives get a case, they begin by asking many questions; they do this to focus their searches. Writing a research paper is like being a detective, and the questions you ask and answer will help you to focus your subject—that is, to narrow it down to a topic you want to write about and can write about.

Starting with What You Already Know

EXERCISE 1.1	Freewriting Activity

Freewriting is a process that helps you "free up" your creative juices and find out what you might want to say about a topic. The steps in this freewriting exercise will acquaint you with this technique.

1. Write for five minutes on anything having to do with the Lizzie Borden case. When you write, do not stop; keep on writing even if you have nothing to say. (If that's the case, just write "I have nothing to say" or "Do wa do wa do wa.") Do not edit your writing for spelling, grammar, or vocabulary. Just write and let your ideas flow naturally.

Example of freewriting (about a minute's worth)

Lizzie Borden didn't kill her mother and father because she wouldn't do something that stupid. I mean how could she think she wouldn't be caught, anyway, why would she hate them that much? She wasn't a criminal, I don't think. She hadn't done things like that before, had she? She had no criminal record. So the whole thing doesn't make sense. I don't think a woman in the 1890s could have done this awful crime. To chop up your parents with an ax. How horrible.

2. Now read your freewriting, and make a list of what it tells you.

Example

Someone killed Lizzie's mom and dad.

The murderer killed them with an ax.

It happened in the 1890s.

I don't think Lizzie killed her mom and dad.

3. See whether you can add anything else you know about the crime to the list. Because you may know little more than we told you, even the simplest statements may be useful.

4. Now ask some questions about the crime.

Example

Did Lizzie kill her mother?

Did she leave any clues?

Did she hate her mother and father?

Had she done anything criminal in the past?

Was she a "good" person?

Were there any other suspects?

You have just begun to do research. You've found a topic that interests you. You've thought about what you know and what you don't know. You have questions that you can't answer and one big issue you need to resolve. Because you can't answer these questions by yourself, you must do research to answer them.

Doing Preliminary Research

EXERCISE 1.2   Beginning Research

Below is a newspaper article from the *New York Times* dated August 5, 1892, the day after Mr. and Mrs. Borden were found murdered. What information does it give you about the crime?

Lizzie Borden

"Lizzie Borden took an ax / And gave her mother forty whacks. / And when she saw what she had done, / She gave her father forty-one."

Excerpt from the original *New York Times* article.

BUTCHERED IN THEIR HOME

MR. BORDEN AND HIS WIFE KILLED IN BROAD DAYLIGHT.

He Was One of the Best Known Men in Fall River—No Clue to the Murderer, But the Police Suspicious of His Brother-In-Law—Story of the Crime.

1   Fall River, Mass., Aug. 4.—Andrew J. Borden and wife, two of the oldest, wealthiest, and most highly-respected persons in the city, were brutally murdered with an axe at 11 o'clock this morning in their home on Second Street, within a few minutes' walk of the City Hall. The Borden family consisted of the father, mother, two daughters, and a servant. The older daughter has been in Fair Haven for some days. The rest of the family have been ill for three or four days, and Dr. Bowen, the attending physician, thought they had been poisoned.

2   About 8 o'clock this morning Mrs. Borden received a note asking her to go and visit a friend who was ill. She left the house and shortly afterward her husband followed and walked down the street to one of the banks. He returned about 10:30 o'clock and sat on the sofa. In answer to a question from Bridget Sullivan, the servant, he said he was very well. Bridget then went outside the house to wash windows. In the meantime Miss Lizzie Borden, his daughter, arose from bed and walked down stairs, seeing and speaking to her father as she passed through the room. Supposing her mother was out, she went into the yard and stepped into the barn. While there she heard a cry of distress coming apparently from the house, and she ran in. Going directly to a sitting room leading from the main hallway in the house, she saw her father lying back on a sofa, lifeless and covered with blood.

3   She ran out again shrieking, and her cries attracted the servant and a neighbor. They made a hasty search for the mother and found her up stairs in a spare bedroom lying dead, face downward, on the floor. The women ran down stairs terrified and summoned Dr. Bowen, who lives opposite. He found both of the victims dead. Then the daughter and servant fainted. Patrolman Allen, who arrived early, became so excited that he ran at once with an incoherent story to the Central Police Station. Unfortunately, to-day was the date of the policemen's excursion, and one-half of the police force were at Rocky Point when the murders occurred.

4   A small posse of police surrounded the house, and in a short time they were busy in keeping back the crowd of business and curiosity seekers, who thronged Second Street. Medical Examiner Dolan found Mr. Borden's head hacked to pieces in a horrible manner, no less than seven long gashes being on his face and skull, some of them

an inch and a half deep through the flesh and bone.

5   When Mrs. Borden was first seen, her daughter and the others supposed that she had died from heart disease, to which she had been subject. A reporter first noticed blood in her train, but when the bed near which she was lying had been drawn away, it was seen that she, too, had been frightfully butchered about the face and skull.

6   The city is thoroughly excited over the murder and about a dozen different theories have been advanced by the police, who have as yet not the slightest clue to the murderer. One of the theories is that the murderer was concealed about the house when Mr. Borden came in. As soon as it became quiet it is supposed he went upstairs with the intention of murdering Mr. Borden. Before he could accomplish his purpose Mrs. Borden's attention was attracted. In view of the fact that Mrs. Borden made no outcry, it is thought she must have been killed first and instantly. The murderer probably followed her into a spare room and struck her from behind.

7   Everything was in perfect order in the room and this is evidence she was not aware she was being followed. The murderer probably went down stairs, where Mr. Borden had fallen asleep on the sofa, and there killed him. Robbery was not the motive of the crime, as no valuables nor money were missing. There were no bloodstains on the furniture coverings or floors, and these facts show how quietly the work was done. Two or three persons were arrested this afternoon, but none of them are believed to know anything of the crime.

8   Medical Examiner Dolan, assisted by other physicians, held an autopsy this afternoon on the two bodies. It was found that Borden sustained twelve cuts in the face and skull, varying in length 4 to 8 inches. He also suffered a fracture of the skull 2 by 4 inches and 3 inches deep. His wife's head and face was battered all out of shape.

9   The stomachs of both were removed and placed in alcohol. They will be sent to Boston to-morrow for analysis, to determine whether milk poisoning was attempted. The police are suspicious of John W. Morse, brother-in-law of Mr. Borden by his first marriage.

10   John W. Morse is fifty-five years of age and came here from Hastings, Iowa, two years ago. He became very intimate with Mr. Borden and the latter's daughter, and spent a great portion of his time with them. He came from New Bedford at noon yesterday and spent the night at the Borden homestead. He left there this morning at 9 o'clock and was next seen on the premises about twenty minutes after the bodies were discovered. The fact that so little ado was made by those who were most directly interested, and so little attempt was made at first to discover the possible murderer, is strengthening the police in the opinions they now hold.

11   At one time the police threatened to place Morse in custody, but it has been decided to keep him under close surveillance until further developments. The murder has caused the greatest sensation known here since the Granite mill fire.

12   Andrew J. Borden was born in this city in 1822. He was in the furniture business thirty-three years with William Almy, under the firm name of Borden & Almy, and accumulated a large amount of estate, valued at $350,000. He owns two farms in Swansea. He was a pattern of the old New-England type of industry, thrift, and conservatism, and was out-spoken in his advocacy of temperance and moral issues. He was President of the Union Savings Bank, a Director of the B. M. C. Durfee Safe Deposit and Trust Company, a Director of the Troy and Manchester Mills, and a Director of the Globe Street Railroad Company. He was twice married, his second wife being Miss Abbie D. Gray. Mr. Borden was seventy years old, and Mrs. Borden sixty-seven.

How many of your questions are answered by this article? Check them off and copy them below. Are there any questions raised by this article that were not on your original list?

_____

_____

_____

_____

Doing research is looking for material from outside your own personal experience to answer questions you may have about something and seeking facts and trustworthy opinions to support your viewpoints. By reading and asking questions based on your reading, you're doing research. But if you were writing your research paper on Lizzie Borden, you probably would still have unanswered questions. You would still have research to do, and your research would lead you to explore aspects of the case in much more breadth and depth than you would just consulting a single newspaper article.

Research as a Means of Discovery

As you will see when you continue the research process, the more you learn, the more you will want to know. Research is a way of asking questions and finding answers.

EXERCISE 1.3   Asking More Questions about Your Topic

Below are some basic questions about the Borden murder case. Put a checkmark next to those questions you can answer and an X next to those you cannot answer.

1. Who was Lizzie Borden?

2. What were the names of her parents?

3. What was the murder weapon?

4. Where did the family live?

5. What did Mr. Borden do for a living?

6. Did Lizzie dine regularly with her parents?

7. Was Lizzie ever charged with the crime?

8. Was Lizzie convicted?

9. Who killed Mr. and Mrs. Borden?

10. Why would Lizzie want to kill her parents?

11. How old was Lizzie when her parents were murdered?

12. Why wasn't Lizzie's sister a suspect?

13. Who else was suspected of committing the crime?

14. Were many people interested in the crime?

15. Did the Borden family members love one another?

If you had difficulty answering these questions, that may be because the one source that your research has turned up so far—the newspaper article—was not sufficient. You haven't done enough research yet.

EXERCISE 1.4   Answering Questions by Means of Research

1. Read the following extracts. Which questions from the list are answered? List them by number. (The first one has been filled in for you.)

From "What Made Lizzie Borden Kill?" by Marcia R. Carlisle

In the century since the trial, a number of authors have reopened the [Borden] case, finding new motives and new interpretations of the evidence. _____15_____

[Robert Sullivan] argued convincingly that Lizzie was guilty and that she was acquitted by the actions of the judge partial to her case. _____

From "A WASP Looks at Lizzie Borden" by Florence King in the *National Review*

On the day before the murders Lizzie joined Abby and Andrew for lunch for the first time in five years. . . . _____

From "Lizzie Borden Took an Axe" by Mary Cantwell in the *New York Times Magazine*

On August 11, 1892, Lizzie Borden was arrested for the murders of her father and stepmother. _____

On August 4, 1892, the younger daughter of [the Borden] house discovered a body sprawled on a settee in the sitting room. A short time later the maid and a neighbor found a second body face down on the floor of the guest room. Death in both cases came at the hands of a person, still officially unknown, wielding a small, sharp hatchet. _____

As you can see, some, but not all, of your questions were answered.

2. Read the article by Marcia Carlisle that follows. Does it help answer your questions? How many more questions can you answer?

_____

What Made Lizzie Borden Kill?

Marcia R. Carlisle

1   A century ago in Fall River, Massachusetts, a jury of twelve men deliberated about one hour before acquitting Lizzie Borden of killing her father and stepmother. Lizzie's innocence has not been so easily accepted by other people—either in 1892, when the murders were committed, or today. Since the trial people have continued to question evidence, police procedures, alibis, and strange behavior by members of the Borden household. Amateur prosecutors have put forward other suspects. Still, the evidence against Lizzie is strong enough to keep alive the speculation that she was the killer.

2   For many, the mystery hangs on motive. In the nineteenth century only two motives could explain her actions: jealousy and greed. Yet neither seems adequate to account for the extreme violence of the crime. Whoever killed Mrs. Borden knocked her down with the first stroke and then drove eighteen other blows into her back. Approximately ninety minutes later the murderer attacked Mr. Borden as he slept, chopping his face beyond recognition. Was this merely the work of a greedy, socially ambitious young woman?

3   Today, looking back across a century on the events of that stifling summer day, we would be likely to ask a somewhat broader question: Why would a woman kill her father and stepmother; what was wrong with that family? Of course, all the participants are far beyond the reach of our speculation, and hence, it can remain only that—speculation. But a growing body of literature on women and family violence has given

us a vantage point that simply didn't exist a hundred years ago, or even twenty years ago. And in examining distant events through the lens of the present day, we find an impressive body of circumstantial evidence to suggest, in that bloody morning's work, the awakening rage of the incest survivor.

4   Although nearly everyone can recite the rhyme, many people are unfamiliar with the details of the case. Andrew Jackson Borden, seventy, and his wife, Abby, sixty-four, were respectable residents of Fall River, a mill town divided into crowded working-class neighborhoods and a fancier section for the upper classes on "the Hill." Mr. Borden was a retired businessman who had made his considerable fortune through a combination of ruthless financial practices and fanatical thrift. With assets worth at least five hundred thousand dollars, he could well have afforded to live in the better neighborhood, but he chose to live downtown on Second Street. His wife Abby was the second Mrs. Borden. She had few friends and spent her days quietly in the home she shared with Mr. Borden's two unmarried daughters, Emma, forty-two, and Lizzie, more than ten years younger. Lizzie led a more active life than her sister, teaching Sunday school and doing volunteer work for local charities.

5   On Thursday morning, August 4, 1892, Mr. and Mrs. Borden and John Morse, a visiting relative, ate an early breakfast together. Around 9:00 A.M. Morse left to run errands and Mr. Borden went downtown, as was his custom, to take care of small business matters. Mrs. Borden went upstairs to make up the guest room and was killed there at about 9:30. Mr. Borden returned home and lay down for a nap on a couch in the parlor, where he died shortly after 11:00. Emma had gone to visit friends, and Lizzie and Bridget Sullivan, the domestic servant, were the only people around the house that day. Not long after 11:00 A.M. Lizzie found her father's body and called Bridget for help. They discovered Mrs. Borden's body a short time later. Medical examiners determined early that both people probably had been killed with an ax or a hatchet.

6   The Fall River police, working under considerable pressure from an outraged, frightened public, were hampered in their search for the killer by the absence of any witnesses. Every door to the house had been locked and double-locked, making it unlikely that anyone unfamiliar with the home could have gotten in without being seen. The absence of probable suspects encouraged frantic speculation: rumors circulated about a tenant who had a grudge against Mr. Borden; about a Portuguese farm laborer who had once been employed by the Bordens in nearby Swansea; about a poorly dressed man hurrying down the street on the morning of the murders, carrying what appeared to be a hatchet wrapped in newspaper. The Borden sisters offered a five-thousand-dollar reward for information. But as the August 5 edition of the Fall River *Herald* lamented, there wasn't a single theory "against which some objection could not be offered from the circumstances surrounding the case."

7   One story that surfaced would reverberate later. According to accounts in several newspapers, Mr. and Mrs. Borden and Bridget had suffered upset stomachs earlier in the week. Mrs. Borden had consulted Dr. Bowen, the family physician, wondering if someone might be trying to poison them. After questioning both Mr. and Mrs. Borden, Dr. Bowen attributed their symptoms to leftover food they had eaten for dinner the night before. Lizzie must have emerged early as a possible suspect, because in the same interview in which Dr. Bowen dismissed the allegations of poisoning, he denied the possibility that she could have been involved in the murder. "I do not believe a hardened man of the world," he said, "much less a gentle and refined woman, in her sober senses, devoid of sudden passion, could strike such a blow with such a weapon as was used on Mr. Borden and linger to survey the bloody deed." The police and many Fall River residents were beginning to think otherwise.

8   At the inquest early the following week, Lizzie was unable to maintain a consistent story about her activities on the morning of the murders. Pressed on her whereabouts at the time of her father's death, Lizzie first claimed she was in the barn loft seeking iron to make sinkers for a fishing expedition, then that she was up in the loft eating pears. Since the temperature that day stood in the nineties, it seemed unlikely that anyone would choose to spend time in the loft for any reason. Lizzie also testified that her stepmother had been called away by a messenger on the morning of the murders, but no corroboration of that story ever came to light. Even more damaging was testimony of a clerk in a local drugstore. The day before the murders, he said, Lizzie had come in shopping for prussic acid—a deadly poison. This, along with the illness in the family the week before, seemed to suggest Lizzie had attempted the murders more than once. Finally, the police produced what they said was the murder weapon—a hatchet they had found hidden in the basement, its wooden handle, which might have borne traces of blood, broken off.

9   All this evidence seemed to point to Lizzie, but the only motive anyone could come up with was simple greed; upon the deaths of her father and stepmother, Lizzie and Emma would come into a sizable inheritance. At the end of the inquest, Lizzie was arrested and charged with the crimes.

10   The following June Lizzie was tried in New Bedford's Superior Court. If convicted as charged, she would be the first woman to be executed in Massachusetts since 1778. Although many people in the eastern part of the state believed her guilty, some newspapers outside Massachusetts and fledgling feminist organizations across the country portrayed her as the innocent victim of incompetent police work. Much was made of her church activities and her Christian character.

11   The prosecution's case, which rested almost entirely on Lizzie's inquest testimony, was dealt a serious blow when the judge ruled it inadmissible as evidence because he felt she had not received adequate legal counsel at the time she gave it. He also declared the druggist's testimony inadmissible, since the purchase of poison did not prove that it was to be used to commit murder. Both these rulings were disputed at the time and continue to be questioned by legal scholars.

12   Lizzie's own lawyers poked holes in the prosecution's case, but they made no sustained attempt to incriminate anyone else; nor did they put Lizzie on the stand to defend herself. Emma testified, but she seemed oddly passive. She stood by her sister but didn't go out of her way to proclaim her innocence, saying simply that the prosecutor's case had not been proved. In short order Lizzie was acquitted.

13   In the century since the trial, a number of authors have reopened the case, finding new motives and new interpretations of the evidence. A kind of historiography of the Lizzie Borden murders has emerged, depending on who was writing and when. Lizzie has been recast as a woman who killed for love, as a woman who killed in an epileptic fit, and as a loyal sister who covered for Emma, the real killer. Others have turned suspicion on Bridget Sullivan, the maid, and John Morse, the visiting uncle, as well as on mysterious strangers in the neighborhood. Perhaps the most systematic and credible attempt to retry Lizzie was made in 1974 by Robert Sullivan, a Massachusetts judge. In *Goodbye Lizzie Borden* he argued convincingly that Lizzie was guilty and that she was acquitted by the actions of the judge partial to her case. Historians writing in the context of the burgeoning women's movement have accepted Lizzie's guilt but sought other explanations for her acquittal. Both Kathryn Jacobs, writing in *American Heritage* in 1978, and Ann Jones in *Women Who Kill*, published in 1980, argued that Lizzie was acquitted because she was a "lady" who, to a classbound age, simply *couldn't* have done such a thing. But for all the contention about whether Lizzie Borden did it, there has been little discussion of *why* she would have done it.

14   In the last thirty years much research has been done on family violence. In 1962 an article in the *Journal of the American Medical Association* documented a "battered-child syndrome." Not long after, the women's movement began to focus on the "battered-woman syndrome." This new focus on physical violence and neglect has turned up controversial but alarming data on the number of children who are sexually abused in the home and the impact of that abuse on their adult lives. Only twenty years ago the psychiatric community estimated that perhaps one person in two hundred thousand was a victim of incest. A well-respected 1985 study by the sociologist David Finkelhor put the figure at closer to one in five. Part of this almost inconceivable increase has come about because of a broadening of the definition of incest: today incest is often defined as sexual abuse by a relative or someone else— stepparent, baby sitter, family friend—whom the child would be expected to trust and obey. But current statistics also suggest the extent to which incest may have been underreported in the past.

15   The link between sexual abuse and parricide came forcefully into the public consciousness in 1982, when the sixteen-year-old Richard Jahnke killed his father after enduring years of physical abuse and witnessing the physical and sexual abuse of his mother and sister. According to Paul Mones, a lawyer who specializes in defending abused children who kill their parents and the author of a book on the subject, the Jahnke case was "the first parricide to attract intense national attention since Lizzie Borden." In 1986 a Long Island teen-ager named Cheryl Pierson paid a classmate to murder her father. When she was caught, Pierson told authorities that she had been abused by her father since she was eleven and that she feared he was about to turn on her younger sister. These two cases drew attention to abuse in respectable middle-class families, families in which the abusers, as Mones writes in his *When a Child Kills*, are "successful wage-earners, regarded by their peers as honest, hardworking people," people, in other words, "generally indistinguishable from the rest of us."

16   In the nineteenth century the connection between sexual abuse and homicide was simply not part of the public consciousness. A rare example came to light in Boston in 1867, when the seventeen-year-old Alice Christiana Abbott poisoned her stepfather. According to the correspondent for *The New York Times*, she claimed he had had "improper connection" with her from the time she was thirteen. She had told others about it, but most believed "something was the matter with her head." When her stepfather threatened to put her in a reform school if she revealed the abuse, she killed him. Her case came before the Suffolk County Grand Jury in August 1867. That body committed her to the Taunton Lunatic Asylum without further investigation. Buried in the records of the Magdalen Asylum, a home for "fallen women" in Philadelphia at the turn of the century, are other reports of women seeking refuge from their fathers. The administrators of the home told these women to work hard and to pray hard; little other recourse was available.

17   Sigmund Freud himself met with disbelief when he raised the issue of incest. In Vienna in 1896 he presented a paper suggesting that the hysteria in the women he was treating was caused by childhood sexual trauma. So outraged were his male colleagues that Freud recanted and constructed his seduction theory, incriminating fantasizing daughters instead of their abusive fathers. He did so, he told a correspondent, with a sense of relief. If he had been right the first time, he added, it would have meant that "perverted acts against children" were a general occurrence in society.

18   Recent work by historians suggests that they were. In *Heroes of Their Own Lives*, published in 1988, Linda Gordon analyzed the case records of one of the many child-protection organizations at the turn of the century. She identified one hundred cases of

incest. According to her sources, the average age of the victims at the time the incest was reported was ten. About one-quarter of the episodes took place in households in which the mother was absent. In another 36 percent of cases the mother was "weakened" by illness or fear of violence from the male in the household. Some of the victims resisted the abuse by running away. When they did, they entered the files of other social service agencies as "delinquent girls" or prostitutes.

19   In the early 1980s Denise Gelinas, a co-founder and co-director of a medical treatment center for incest victims in Springfield, Massachusetts, documented certain conditions under which incest is most likely to occur (although the conditions themselves are not causes of abuse). A father may turn on his children when the mother is unavailable and his sense of entitlement is strong or when he has sustained an important loss. Children between the ages of four and nine are particularly vulnerable because they are trusting, deferential to authority, and eager to please and because they cannot always distinguish between proper and improper actions. The likelihood of incest can also increase if there is a strong sanction against extramarital sexual activity.

20   All these signs of a family at risk were visible in the Borden family when Emma and Lizzie were growing up. Two years prior to Lizzie's birth, her mother bore and buried another daughter, "baby Alice." The first Mrs. Borden died two years after Lizzie was born. In the interim she suffered from a condition described on her death certificate as "uterine congestion," one of the unspecific female complaints that plagued Victorian wives. Its victims often took to their beds for long periods of time. This, coupled with the death of one child and the birth of another, might have made Mrs. Borden sexually unresponsive to her husband. Although there was a subculture of prostitution in Fall River, Mr. Borden, an intensely private and rigid man, might have been reluctant to turn to it. As provider and patriarch he may also have expected his needs to be met in his own home.

21   Emma might easily have been urged to take up her mother's role in a process therapists call "parentification." She was just thirteen when her mother died, and for the last two years of Mrs. Borden's life, Emma had cared for Lizzie. In the absence of other women in the home, Emma would have assumed responsibility for household tasks. Mr. Borden refused offers of help from other family members, including his sister. He chose to keep his household his own private domain, establishing a kind of family isolation well documented in the case histories of incest survivors.

22   As the result of a sense of entitlement and the absence of an appropriate sexual partner, Mr. Borden might have abused first Emma, then Lizzie. Research on serial abuse is sketchy, but it may occur in as many as 50 percent of all cases. The shift from one sibling to another often takes place as the older child begins to resist the abuse. In the Borden household the transfer might have taken place when Emma was about fifteen and Lizzie was about four. This would have coincided with the arrival of the second Mrs. Borden.

23   Shadows of the first marriage haunted the second. Most followers of the case agree that the Borden girls did not respond well to the arrival of a stepmother. There is no indication that Abby treated them badly, but from the first Emma refused to call her Mother. Lizzie never established a close relationship with her either, although she was young enough for Mrs. Borden to have assumed a mother's role.

24   Abby Borden might well have been expected to bear children herself; neither her age nor Mr. Borden's precluded a second family. The absence of children raises the possibility that Andrew Borden's second marriage was an asexual one.

25   Seven years into the marriage the family moved to the house on Second Street, a building that has been the source of much controversy about the Bordens as a family. Although it was a marked improvement over their old house, it still lacked many of the

amenities that others of Mr. Borden's position would have demanded. If the move was made, as some have argued, to enhance the Borden girls' chances for matrimony, it was unsuccessful. Lizzie and Emma were average-looking girls with a more than average inheritance due them, but neither was ever engaged nor married.

26   If, however, the house was purchased to allay Abby's suspicions, the choice was a sound one. The building was a long, narrow, two-family dwelling. When the Bordens moved in, they made only minor changes, leaving the structure essentially divided. Mr. and Mrs. Borden's upstairs bedrooms, for instance, were not accessible to Lizzie's and Emma's bedrooms except by coming downstairs and going up another flight of stairs. The doors connecting several upstairs rooms were kept locked and blocked with furniture. The house effectively separated Mr. Borden from his daughters. As time went on, the family divisions grew even deeper, and by the time of the murders, the Bordens did not regularly eat together at a common table.

27   Apparently, little affection passed between any of the family members with one exception: by all accounts Lizzie and her father had once been very close. Mr. Borden always wore a gold ring she gave him when she graduated from high school. He was wearing it when he died. This affection between a teen-age Lizzie and her father would not be inconsistent with a past history of sexual abuse. Whatever passed between her and her father was her only experience of parental love. She did not know her mother or love her stepmother. She had been her father's "special girl." Confused feelings would be expected, too, if Lizzie had successfully repressed her memories of abuse, as many incest victims do today. A powerful chronicle of another special girl who repressed abuse is Sylvia Fraser's *My Father's House*, published in 1988. Fraser, a Canadian journalist and novelist, created an imaginary "twin," another self who experienced her incestuous relationship with her father and the guilt that accompanied it. The presence of the twin enabled Fraser to live a normal teen-ager's life loving her father.

28   No single disorder is enough to make a case for a family at war with itself. But viewed as a pattern, the long-time absence of a wife-mother, the ages of the girls at the time of their mother's illness, the autocratic father, the isolation of the family, the failure of the family to bond as a unit when the new Mrs. Borden moved in, the timing of the move to the new house, the structure of the house, the special relationship between Lizzie and her father, the tensions between both daughters and the stepmother—all these together suggest long-standing structural flaws that could have led to family violence and to the murders. Even the way in which the killings were committed seems telling. All the hatchet blows directed at Mr. Borden were aimed at his face. As the prosecuting attorney described it in his closing argument, the hand that held the weapon was "not the hand of masculine strength. It was the hand of a person strong only in hate and the desire to kill."

29   What drove Lizzie to murder, according to the prosecution, must have been greed. The evidence for this assumption was a previous family squabble that became public at the trial. In 1887 Andrew, normally frugal to a fault, had bought Abby a house for her sister to live in. Both Emma and Lizzie were upset at what they saw as favoritism; Lizzie's anger was later interpreted as selfishness. But arguments about property and money are often about position in family structure as well. This disagreement may even have triggered memories of other moments when Mr. Borden's affections were sought by both Mrs. Borden and Lizzie.

30   The awakening or surfacing of memories about incest is a slow and unpredictable process. Sometimes a woman who has repressed her victimization for years will remember what happened as she becomes a mother herself. This phenomenon, well

known to clinicians treating incest patients, made national news recently when Eileen Franklin-Lipsker, twenty-nine years old, suddenly remembered that her father had raped and killed her childhood friend. She was eight years old at the time. Her father had told her that no one would believe her if she reported what happened, and for two decades she had repressed the memory. Then, one day, prompted by a look on her daughter's face, the memory surfaced. Psychologists call such awakening of memories "delayed discovery." Children deliberately forget as a way to distance themselves from the guilt and shame they feel. Once they remember, they must not only believe themselves but ask others to believe them as well. Recent research on delayed discovery has prompted lawmakers to extend the statute of limitations for prosecuting sexual assaults against children. The most liberal of these laws allows a victim twenty-two years after his or her eighteenth birthday to file charges.

31   Delayed discovery can have what Gelinas describes as a "time-bomb quality." When such an awakening happens today, a skillful therapist can guide the survivor through the tangled morass of feelings. Dr. Judith Herman, a leading authority on father-daughter incest, helped one group of adult women through the healing process recently. The median age in the group was Lizzie's at the time of the murders, thirty-two. The majority were white, educated, and unmarried and had suffered some degree of amnesia about the incest. Many were engaged in the "helping professions," today's counterpart to the church activities that were important to Lizzie in the 1890s.

32   But in the 1890s the silence around incest could not be broken in a healing fashion. Women who remembered were left alone to bear the hurt, the anger, and the sense of worthlessness and guilt that can emerge. Some women acted strangely, became neurotic without knowing why. Lizzie herself reported confused feelings to her friend Alice Russell the night before the murders. "I feel depressed . . . as if something was hanging over me that I cannot throw off, and it comes over me at times, no matter where I am. . . . When I was at the table the other day . . . the girls were laughing and talking and having a good time and this feeling came over me, and one of them spoke and said Lizzie, why don't you talk?"

33   Victims in the nineteenth century who did talk were not believed or were labeled crazy. As recently as 1934 the legal scholar John Wigmore argued in his definitive classic *Treatise on Evidence* that women and children were not trustworthy witnesses in sex offense cases because they were likely to bring false charges against men of good character. He even discounted medical evidence corroborating their testimony if he was in any way suspicious of the stories they told. Even today, when incest victims take matters into their own hands and kill their abusers, they are frequently portrayed as crazy by the media. People are disturbed, in particular, because they don't seem to experience remorse for what they have done. Psychologists explain this absence of feeling as a defense. As Mones writes, incest victims are "forced to numb their real emotions for so long, by the time of the parricide they have no tears."

34   Parricide is the most extreme, the rarest response to incest. Why some victims kill their abusers and others do not is, of course, a mystery embedded in the deepest layers of human character, and it is here that speculation must become most tentative. Today most women Lizzie's age who experience delayed discovery are living outside the family home. Many of them experience homicidal rage, but they don't have to face their fathers every day. Lizzie was still under her father's roof. With no means of earning a living and no prospect of marriage, she would have been trapped there as the memories surfaced.

35   Why did she kill Abby too? Perhaps because her stepmother had known about the incest and had been unable to stop it, or worse, had blamed Lizzie for it. What about Emma? She must have known Lizzie had committed the murders and why. Otherwise her eerie calm in the face of violent death is almost inexplicable. The day of the murders both Emma and Lizzie stayed in the house with the bodies laid out on the dining-room

table. They stayed there until the funeral, which was held in the room where Mr. Borden was killed. Is it possible that either woman would have done so if she thought some unknown killer had entered the house and committed the crimes?

36   In the months and years following the trial, Lizzie changed. She began calling herself Lisbeth; she moved to a stately new house she named Maplecroft. She began buying things for herself and living the life she felt she had been denied. She struck up a close friendship with a Boston actress. Lisbeth's new way of life wore on her sister. In time Emma left Maplecroft and Fall River, where children were still chanting the insidious rhyme. The two sisters never saw each other again.

37   In a rare interview twenty years after the crime, Emma defended Lizzie and stressed the duty she felt toward her sister. She had promised her mother that she would take care of Lizzie. "I am still the little mother," the old, graying woman said, "and though we must live as strangers, I will defend 'Baby Lizzie' against merciless tongues."

38   Today the Borden double murder is remembered as bloody hatchet work. We all nod in recognition when a television anchor reports that a Senate committee did a "Lizzie Borden" on a piece of legislation. But if that same newscaster were reporting the Borden murders today, it is far from inconceivable that he or she would, a few days later, return to the subject with an even darker side to the story.

_____

This is research: seeking information about a topic. You won't find all your information in a single source. You have to keep searching until you get enough information. And the exciting thing about research is that if you have chosen well—that is, if you have found a topic that truly interests you, you will want to keep searching, because you will realize that only with research will you discover your answers. (See Chapter 4 for work on figuring out how much research is enough.)

The Research Process in Action

Following is an article from a book about female murderers. It is filled with information about the crime and the people involved in the crime—the family, prosecutors, judge, and defense. See whether it can help you form a thesis about the Lizzie Borden case.

EXERCISE 1.5   Reading "Laying Down the Law"

Read "Laying Down the Law" from *Women Who Kill*, and answer the questions that come after it.

_____

Laying Down the Law
Ann Jones

1   Bordens were among the very first settlers of Fall River. Wisely, they grabbed up the water rights in what was destined to be a mill town; and God rewarded their foresight with riches and power. By the late nineteenth century, when Fall River had become the largest

cotton manufacturing center in the United States, the mills and banks and shipping lines were all Borden. And one of those Bordens was Andrew Jackson, Miss Lizzie's father. His father, Abraham, was one of the poor relations who attach remotely to even the best of families—a fish peddler at the end of the Borden coattail. But Andrew, by dint of hard work and parsimony and an impeccably dour face, had won his rightful Borden place in the town. He sat on boards of directors at some of the Borden mills and the new Fall River street railway, he officiated at several local banks, and he owned a good deal of real estate, including the new, massive red-brick "Borden Block." He was worth more than a quarter of a million dollars.

2   You wouldn't have known it, for Andrew Jackson Borden was the perfect capitalist. He made money—lots of it—for the sake of making money. Yet, as a Christian, Andrew Borden knew that money could be the root of all evil—if one took pleasure in money and used it as a source of enjoyment. The trick then, for a good Christian capitalist, was to make money but to enjoy it not at all. And that skill Andrew Borden had perfected.

3   His second daughter, Lizzie, had not. She complained a good deal, mostly about money. But there was more to it than that. Since Andrew Borden, held back by his meager beginnings, had taken longer than his luckier cousins to make his mark, his every move seemed, by the standards of his fellow entrepreneurs, just a little late, a little short, perhaps flawed by the unshakable caution of a man who started poor and didn't want to finish that way. Andrew's success was impressive, if imperfect, and it apparently pleased him; but it left his daughter mired in might-have-beens. Lizzie Borden might have lived, as her name and money entitled her to, among the society people on the hill, but Andrew, when he left his father's homestead, moved only a few blocks to "the flats" near the business district, below the hill. And the house he bought was not even a proper house, but two apartments gerrymandered into a one-family residence. Miss Borden might have visited on the hill, but for that a proper lady needed a private carriage, a luxury Andrew Borden had no use for. And a proper lady needed a chaperone, a position that Andrew's second wife, Abby, for all her grand old Durfee blood, could never fill, for she too was a poor relation, the daughter of a blacksmith, and for a time herself a "tailoress." Lizzie was acquainted on the hill; most of her cousins lived there. She had even persuaded Andrew to send her with some of them on a European grand tour, but Lizzie was no Consuela Vanderbilt or Jennie Jerome; she returned reluctantly without a lord.

4   At the time, thanks to a half-century battle for woman's rights, women could do more than marry or go into society. The Fall River *Daily Globe*, which Lizzie read every day, reported that women were graduating from medical school in New York, running for public office in Wyoming, voting—at least in school elections—right there in Fall River. And Lizzie had several friends (she planned to go off to a house party at Marion with them soon) who were single, self-supporting, working women: teachers, school principals, bookkeepers. But Lizzie herself, born just a little too soon to join the fashionable Fall River daughters going off to the new women's colleges, was not trained for any work. She taught some classes in the Sunday school now and again, but mostly she stayed at home. With her stepmother, her older sister, Emma, and the Irish servant all keeping house for one old man, there wasn't much to do in that small house. She tidied up her own bedroom, mended her own dresses, ironed her own hankies. She kept the treasurer's records for her church group. She read magazines and the newspaper and sometimes a letter from a friend. . . .

5   On the morning of August 4, 1892, just before eleven o'clock, widow Adelaide Buffinton Churchill, returning from market to her home on Second Street, saw the Borden family's

servant Bridget Sullivan "walking fast" toward the house of Dr. Seabury Bowen across the street. It was not a day for hurrying; the heat wave continued and already the temperature was in the nineties. "Someone at the Bordens' must be sick," Mrs. Churchill thought. She went into her house, put down her bundles, and looked out at the Borden house next door from her kitchen window. Later, in court, Adelaide Churchill described what she saw and what she did:

> *Miss Lizzie Borden was standing inside their screen door, at the side of their house. I opened the window and said, "Lizzie, what is the matter?" She replied, "Oh, Mrs. Churchill, do come over. Someone has killed father." I went over and stepped inside the screen door. She was sitting on the stair. I put my hand on her arm and said "Oh, Lizzie!" Then I said, "Where is your father?" She said, "In the sitting room."*

Mrs. Churchill went through the kitchen to the sitting room. There on the horsehair sofa lay Andrew Jackson Borden, apparently stretched out for a nap, except that where his face should have been was only blood and pulp. The coroner would find the marks of ten hatchet blows.

6   Before running to summon help, Mrs. Churchill put two more questions to Lizzie Borden. The second—"Where is your mother?"—was answered later when Mrs. Churchill and Bridget Sullivan, searching upstairs at Lizzie's suggestion, found Mrs. Borden huddled on the guest-room floor, her skull battered in. But the first question—"Where were you when it happened?"—has never been satisfactorily answered, although Lizzie Borden, like Bridget Durgan before her, pulled a story together. Sometimes she had to shave it here or puff it out there to make it fit; but finally, unlike Bridget Durgan, she drew the line and held it.

7   She had been in the barn behind the house, she said, for ten minutes or fifteen or twenty—in any case, just long enough to miss her father's murder. She had been looking for lead to make some sinkers for her fishline, although she hadn't gone fishing for five years; or she was looking for a piece of screen to repair a window. And she had eaten some windfall pears, perhaps two or three, while standing up in the hayloft looking out the window, or perhaps not looking out the window. In any case, after some time she walked the few yards back to the house and heard a grating noise, or her father groaning, or nothing at all. The kitchen screen door was wide open, and her father lay dead upon the sofa. As for her stepmother, Lizzie had not seen her since shortly after nine o'clock when the old woman went upstairs to make the bed in the guest room. Lizzie, who spent the entire morning in the kitchen reading an old magazine and perhaps eating a cookie, thought that her stepmother had gone out in response to a note from a sick friend. Lizzie had told that story earlier to the servant; she had told it to her father when he returned from the morning round of his business interests and prepared for a nap on the sofa before midday dinner; and she repeated it again and again although, curiously enough, all the investigators on the case were unable to find the note, the woman who sent it, or the boy who delivered it.

8   Later, as the police questioned the family and friends, Miss Lizzie told of her father's quarrels with laborers at his farm and with a prospective tenant. She told of mysterious men she had seen lurking about the house, of vandals breaking into the barn, of family sickness that Abby Borden feared to be poisoning, of a strange ransacking of Abby's desk the year before, a robbery that Andrew had reported to the police and then asked them to forget. All the murder suspects Lizzie suggested either had sound alibis or proved to be phantoms; but Lizzie clearly had been worried all along. On the evening before the murders she recounted her fears to her best friend, Miss Alice Russell, who repeated them in court: "I feel depressed," Lizzie had said. "I

feel as if something was hanging over me that I cannot throw off, and it comes over me at times, no matter where I am. . . . I feel as if I wanted to sleep with my eyes half open—with one eye open half the time—for fear they will burn the house down over us. . . . I am afraid somebody will do something; I don't know but what somebody will do something." The next day somebody did something, and it seemed strange that Miss Lizzie should so clearly have seen it coming.

9   The murders took place on Thursday morning. Saturday morning, while Lizzie attended her parents' funeral, the police vainly searched her closet for a bloodstained dress. That evening the mayor, paying a condolence call, told Lizzie that she was suspected. On Sunday morning, when Lizzie's friend Alice Russell entered the Borden kitchen, she found Lizzie, in Emma's presence, burning a dress in the stove. "I'm going to burn this old thing up," she said. "It is covered with paint."

10   On the following Tuesday, Wednesday, and Thursday, Lizzie testified at the inquest—circling, evading, contradicting, revising her story as she went along, scorning the badgering of District Attorney Hosea Knowlton. Accounting for some twenty minutes spent in the barn loft, Lizzie told of slowly eating two or three pears. But Knowlton remembered that she, like her parents and Bridget Sullivan, had been nauseated the day before and unable to eat breakfast that morning. The story of her eating pears in the barn loft—improbable on the face of it—became doubly suspect, and Knowlton tried to pin her down.

Q. *You were feeling better than you did in the morning?*

A. *Better than I did the night before.*

Q. *You were feeling better than you were in the morning?*

A. *I felt better in the morning than I did the night before.*

Q. *That is not what I asked you. You were then, when you were in that hot loft, looking out of the window and eating three pears, feeling better, were you not, than you were in the morning when you could not eat breakfast?*

A. *I never eat any breakfast.*

Q. *You did not answer my question, and you will, if I have to put it all day. Were you then, when you were eating those three pears in that hot loft, looking out of that closed window, feeling better than you were in the morning when you ate no breakfast?*

A. *I was feeling well enough to eat the pears.*

Q. *Were you feeling better than you were in the morning?*

A. *I don't think I felt very sick in the morning only—Yes, I don't know but I did feel better. As I say, I don't know whether I ate any breakfast or not, or whether I ate a cookie.*

Q. *Were you then feeling better than you did in the morning?*

A. *I don't know how to answer you, because I told you I felt better in the morning anyway.*

Q. *Do you understand the question? My question is whether, when you were in the loft of the barn, you were feeling better than you were in the morning when you got up?*

A. *No, I felt about the same.*

11   Lizzie Borden was not easily pushed around. When she claimed not to know whether Bridget had actually been washing windows that morning, Knowlton asked in

exasperation, "Do you think she might have gone to work and washed all the windows in the dining room and the sitting room and you not know it?"

12   "I don't know, I am sure," replied Miss Lizzie, "whether I should or not. I might have seen her, and not know it."

13   That was too much for Hosea Knowlton. "Miss Borden," he said, "I am trying in good faith to get all the doings that morning of yourself and Miss Sullivan, and I have not succeeded in doing it." He asked her directly, "Do you desire to give me any information or not?"

14   "I don't know," said Miss Lizzie. "I don't know what your name is." Miss Lizzie, after all, was a Borden. But Hosea Knowlton—who was he? On Thursday afternoon, August 11, one week after the murders, Lizzie Andrew Borden was arrested for the murder of Andrew Jackson Borden. But she never weakened. And by the time her trial was all over, unknown Hosea Knowlton, prosecuting attorney, would seem to be—like the judges—on the side of Miss Lizzie Borden.

15   When Miss Lizzie took her seat in the middle of the courtroom, just in front of the railing that separated the public section at the rear from the judicial bench, she was wearing a simple black crepe dress trimmed with rows of black velvet piping. Her new black snubnosed shoes were more practical than stylish. Her hat, a black straw "poke shaped" style featuring a blue plume and blue rosettes, was "of no existing fashion." Black cotton gloves concealed her hands. Halfway through the trial, Miss Borden appeared in a new dress—a dress that even to the untrained eyes of male crime reporters was obviously expensive: black silk overlaid with black lace in a cape effect, much more stylish than the old-fashioned shirred basque in which she made her courtroom debut. But with the new dress appeared the old hat and the old black cotton gloves—an ensemble distinctly out of the contemporary fashion, which called for a medley of colors in the costume. Of course, she was in mourning, but at her throat she wore a large enameled pansy pin, which even reporter Julian Ralph of the New York *Sun*, who so admired Miss Borden; considered "rather loud." Her ignorance or defiance of the rules of fashion marked her as no mere fashion plate but a true lady. Indeed she had about her, as reporter Ralph put it, "that indefinable quality which we call ladyhood." . . .

16   Only one thing troubled the reporters, most of whom were, like Ralph, sympathetic to Miss Borden. Her calm self-possession, appropriate to a lady, seemed too tightly controlled. Shortly after the murders, the Fall River *Daily Globe* observed that Lizzie showed "no other feeling than that of a disinterested party."

17   For the first two days of the trial she scarcely altered the posture she assumed on first taking her seat. In the morning she rested her chin on her left hand, in the afternoon on her right. The journalists, who described her as "a graven image," agreed that Miss Borden was possessed of an extremely "phlegmatic and undemonstrative" nature. And everyone knew, for it was widely reported, that she had not been seen to shed a tear since the death of her father and stepmother—and a woman who did not cry was surely an unnatural creature. Then, after a long, tense debate among the attorneys, a crucial point of law was decided in Lizzie's favor—and she began to cry. To reporters like Ralph, it made all the difference. "Miss Borden's womanhood," he wrote, "was fully established when she burst into tears. . . . " During the following days of the trial Lizzie was sometimes in great distress: she called for water, she asked to be excused, she leaned heavily for support upon the railings behind and in front of her, she sniffed her smelling salts, she wept, and more than once she fainted dead away. The sympathetic journalists reported these incidents with detailed flourishes. Miss Borden, it seemed, was not only a lady, but a true womanly woman.

18   As such, she was conspicuously out of place in the courtroom that resembled nothing so much as an old boys' club. Ralph reported that "the Judges, the lawyers, the Sheriff, and most of the attendants were in the main a white-haired, aged lot of citizens." All three judges were thin-lipped "grey beards." The jurors, all men, were chosen deliberately by the defense because they were at middle age or beyond. The foreman was a prosperous landowner, and another juror managed an iron works; the rest were farmers or artisans of modest means. Miss Borden was represented by a panel of attorneys well respected among the "grey beards." Andrew Jennings was a prominent citizen who for many years had been Andrew Borden's attorney. Melvin O. Adams, an experienced Boston trial lawyer, impressed the jury with his big-city manners and waxed mustache. And George D. Robinson, at fifty-nine, a stately, imposing gentleman of the old school, had served three times as governor of the Commonwealth.

19   The attorneys for the prosecution were somewhat less impressive. Arthur Pillsbury, attorney general of the Commonwealth, whose duty it was to prosecute, dropped out pleading ill health rather than face the undignified work of prosecuting a lady. "No lawyer who could have his choice would care to try a woman for her life," commented the Fall River *Daily Globe*. The task fell to Hosea Knowlton, district attorney of Bristol County, who had already had enough of Miss Borden at the inquest. He too tried to get out of the job—a thankless one politically—and when he couldn't shirk the task, he performed it with conspicuous lethargy. He was assisted by William Moody, district attorney for the eastern district of Essex County, at thirty-eight the youngest man in the courtroom and thoroughly eclipsed by the posturings of his elders. . . .

20   In this courtroom, thickly carpeted and amply furnished with spittoons, Lizzie Borden, a lady in sensible shoes, fanned herself while William H. Moody delivered the opening arguments for the prosecution.

21   The government's case, as Moody presented it, was based upon three propositions: that Lizzie was predisposed to commit the murders, that she did in fact commit them, and that her behavior since the murders indicated her guilt. Many witnesses testified to the hostility within the Borden household: to locked doors and silences and squabbles over property and Lizzie's persistence in addressing her stepmother of twenty-five years as "Mrs. Borden." Medical experts agreed that the murderous blows were well within a woman's capability. Other witnesses established that Lizzie had the opportunity to commit the murders while other possible suspects, such as her uncle John Morse, her sister Emma (who was away), and Bridget Sullivan, did not.

22   Miss Lizzie's defense team offered no opposing theory of the crime but attacked the prosecution's case by discrediting witnesses, casting doubt on their memory or credibility. Then they effectively created a smoke screen, ignoring real issues as if they had never been raised, arguing as central issues points that were at best tangential. It was a clever if devious defense. As prosecutor Moody said of one of Governor Robinson's torrents of irrelevant oratory, "It is magnificent, but it is not law." Central to the defense was the sanctity of Lizzie's relationship with her father, as described by Governor Robinson.

> *He [Andrew Borden] was a man that wore nothing in the way of ornament, of jewelry but one ring, and that ring was Lizzie's. It had been put on many years ago when Lizzie was a little girl, and the old man wore it and it lies buried with him in the cemetery. He liked Lizzie, did he not? He loved her as his child; and the ring that stands as the pledge of plighted faith and love, that typifies and symbolizes the dearest relation that is ever created in life, that ring was the bond of union between*

the father and the daughter. No man should be heard to say that she murdered the man that so loved her.

This evidence that Andrew was fond of Lizzie was construed by both sides to mean that Lizzie was fond of Andrew.

23   That a woman should kill her father, to whom she was attached even in a pre-Freudian era by so many Freudian strings, was simply *unthinkable*. Particularly must it have been so to Chief Justice Mason, who had three daughters, all about Lizzie's age; to Judge Dewey, whose three daughters were only a few years younger; and to several of the jurors who had been carefully chosen by the defense especially because they had daughters of nearly Lizzie's age. In his summation Governor Robinson reminded them: "You are out of families, you come from firesides, you are members of households, you have wives and daughters and sisters and you have had mothers. . . . " When the trial was over these men would go home, as Andrew Borden had, to be greeted by their daughters. A jacket would be hung, a pair of slippers fetched, a pillow puffed and placed beneath the head—if Lizzie Borden were guilty as charged who among them would ever feel the same about such domesticities?

24   The defense asked, "Where is the motive for this crime?" as though coming into a half-share of a quarter of a million dollars is not motive enough for murder. To prove that Miss Lizzie was a well-to-do young woman who could not have wanted for money the defense asked her older sister, Emma, to testify to Lizzie's holdings at the time of her father's death. Two thousand dollars in one bank, $500 in another, $172.75 in a third bank, $141 in a fourth. In addition she held two shares of the Fall River National Bank and nine shares of the Merchants' Manufacturing Company. That Miss Lizzie, at the age of thirty-two, possessed almost $3,000 in her own name was considered evidence that she had all a woman could want. "What is the use of talking about that?" Governor Robinson asked the jury. "Did she want any more to live on in comfort?" If she *did* wish for more, it was ever so tactfully suggested, she had only to wait a few years until her father died. The Fall River *Daily Globe* pointed out that, according to Massachusetts law, if her father died before her stepmother, Abby would inherit at least one-third of Andrew's estate as her widow's dower, but nothing whatsoever was made of this point at the trial by either the prosecution or the defense who got on so curiously well with one another. And no one alluded to those intangible things a woman with enough money might buy: independence, self-determination, a larger life.

25   Everyone pretended that women do not care about money. On the Sunday following the murders the Reverend W. Walker Jubb, Lizzie's minister and supporter, asked the Central Congregational Church: "Where is the motive? When men resort to crime it is for plunder, for gain, from enmity, in sudden anger or for revenge. Strangely, nothing of this nature enters into this case, and again I ask—what was the motive?" Interviewed a few days later by the *Daily Globe*, Jubb quoted Emma Borden as saying to him: "Lizzie is innocent. . . . I cannot see the slightest motive she might have, either in the way of money or revenge, for of the first she had all she needed, and of the latter there was no reason." And in an early interview granted the *Daily Globe* two days after the murders, Andrew Jennings, referred to in the article as Andrew Borden's attorney, said, "A most outrageous, brutal crime . . . and absolutely motiveless—absolutely motiveless." Months later, at the trial, Jennings was still of the same opinion. Opening for the defense, he said: "The Government's . . . claim . . . is that whoever killed Abby Durfee Borden killed Andrew J. Borden; and even if they furnish you with a motive on her part to kill the stepmother they have shown you absolutely none to kill the father."

26   The defense also made a good deal of Miss Lizzie's godliness—calling various ministers and wizened ladies to testify to her character—and of her cleanliness immediately

after the discovery of the bodies. Mrs. Churchill, Miss Russell, Bridget Sullivan, Dr. Bowen, Mrs. Bowen—all testified that immediately following the murders, as they comforted and fanned Miss Lizzie, they saw no sign of blood upon her; but the defense argued that the killer must have been drenched in the blood of *his* victims. In fact, all the medical experts agreed that the assailant need *not* have been spattered with blood. Reporters who first viewed the bodies had found the absence of blood one of the most remarkable features of the case; and the first doctors who examined Abby Borden's body concluded from the lack of spattered blood that she had merely fainted. By the time of the trial, however, when Governor Robinson ranted on about the "blood flying all over the walls and the furniture, on the bed and everywhere," the tidy scene of the Borden murders and the person of the "unknown assailant" were thought to be awash in a "sea of blood." But not Miss Borden. Except for a tiny blood spot near the hem of her white petticoat—a spot which at the inquest she attributed to fleas—she was immaculately clean. That single speck of blood was discussed briefly at the trial. Professor Wood, who examined it, swore that it came from the outside, but the defense quickly, delicately, and improbably explained it away as a trace of Miss Borden's "monthly sickness" which had ended Wednesday evening before the murders. And that was the end of it. Because she was a woman, Lizzie Borden was used to disposing of bloody cloths; but because she was a lady, it could not be discussed.

27   During menstrual periods, women of the time, in the days before disposables, wore fairly heavy cloth napkins or towels, which could be laundered and reused. That is what Lizzie did; and she kept the used, blood-soaked napkins in a pail under the sink in the cellar. Thursday night—after the murders and presumably twenty-four hours after Lizzie stopped menstruating—she made two trips to the cellar, both observed by Officer Joseph Hyde stationed outside. She went down first with her friend Alice Russell, who was staying with her, to empty a slop pail in the water closet. Miss Russell, obviously nervous, held the lamp with a trembling hand. Later Lizzie came down again alone, carrying a lamp, and for about a minute stooped over the sink. Officer Hyde couldn't see what she was doing.

28   Governor Robinson quickly dismissed Hyde's testimony as meaningless; and Julian Ralph wrote that it was off-limits. "That is, it was without significance," he wrote, "as it seemed that the prisoner's second visit to the cellar had to do with a certain pailful of towels that was in the cellar and which *both sides have agreed not to discuss during this trial.*" . . . The men of the Borden court could not discuss menstruation without inviting the charge of indelicacy and the argument that women must be judged by their peers to protect them from such offenses to their sensibilities. So the Borden prosecutors, who might have made *something* of spotless Lizzie's pail full of bloody towels, used Hyde's testimony only to argue that Lizzie's midnight solo trip to the spooky cellar of the murder house required extraordinary nerve of a naturally timid female. "I do not care to allude to the visit to the cellar," said prosecutor Knowlton as he summarized the case for the jury. "And all the use I propose to make of that incident is to emphasize from it the almost stoical nerve of a woman, who . . . should have the nerve to go down there alone, . . . and calmly enter the room *for some purpose that had I know not what connection with this case.*"

29   Connections often seemed obscure or missing because behind the conduct of the Borden trial was another level of meaning so powerful that it became more decisive than mere physical evidence. Even as the attorneys debated and the judges and jurors decided, all of them seemed caught up in a drama far more encompassing and profound than the facts of the case would suggest. They played their parts as surely as if

each had been handed a script, acting—as Julian Ralph noted—in curious concert. It is no wonder that Lizzie became a legend to subsequent generations, for her trial itself was the ritual reenactment of a very old legend: the embarrassingly trite tale of the damsel in distress.

30   It is true that at age thirty-two the stolid, plain-faced Lizzie was miscast as a fair damsel. But the habitual practice in the United States of referring to adult women as "girls" distorted perceptions then just as it does today. Throughout the trial, Lizzie—a full-grown, ablebodied woman—was referred to by prosecution and defense alike as "this poor girl." Often she was "this poor *defenseless* girl" for she had no parents (particularly no father) to protect her from harm. That she probably was, as Alexander Woollcott quipped, a "self-made orphan" was beside the point. The force of legend is not to be deterred by facts.

31   At least Lizzie *was* a lady. No one champions a lower-class woman; and many commentators on the case, then and now, would pin the crime on Bridget Sullivan with the same alacrity that made the hanging of Bridget Durgan such a festive event.

32   District Attorney Knowlton spoke directly of these class differences in his summation:

> One [woman, namely Bridget] is poor and friendless, a domestic, a servant, uneducated and without friends, and the other [Lizzie] is buttressed by all that social rank and wealth and friends and counsel can do for her protection. . . . supposing those things that have been suggested against Lizzie Borden had been found against Bridget Sullivan, poor, friendless girl. Supposing she had told wrong stories; supposing she had put up an impossible alibi; supposing she had put up a dress that never was worn that morning at all, and when the coils were tightening around her had burned a dress up that it should not be seen, what would you think of Bridget? Is there one law for Bridget and another for Lizzie?

The answer, of course, was and still is "Yes." During the inquest Bridget trudged more than a mile every day to the hearing from the house of the friend who had taken her in, while Miss Lizzie was driven the few short blocks from her house in a closed carriage dispatched at public expense. The Fall River *Daily Globe* commented on town gossip: "Open statements are made that if Lizzie Borden were a poor and unfortunate woman, she would not be treated as she has been."

33   Once Lizzie caught on to the role expected of her as a lady, she played it to the hilt. The tears that dissolved her sullen immobility of the first two days may have been genuine, but at times alert reporters caught her playacting. Julian Ralph noticed that whenever the prosecutors mentioned blood, Lizzie hid her face in her hands, but when her attorneys talked of it, she listened brightly. Oddly enough, this artifice counted in Lizzie's favor; like her tears, her dissembling—one of the "arts and ways of femininity"—was proof of her feminine nature. Later in the trial—about the time she donned her new, more fashionable dress—Lizzie began carrying flowers into the courtroom: one day a little nosegay of pansies, another day a single white rose.

34   How convincing it must have been when Robinson, falling back heavily and comfortably on old notions men shared about ladies, exhorted the jury: ". . . you *must* say such acts are physically and morally impossible for this young woman. It is a wreck of human morals to say this of her."

35   The role of villain in the courtroom drama fell naturally to the Fall River police department, and although most officers seemed more bumbling than sinister, they all finally appeared to be persecutors of Miss Lizzie. Three months before the Borden murders, the Fall River *Daily Globe* reported as "a matter of common notoriety that the

police force is in a more or less demoralized condition." Individual officers were accused of dereliction of duty and indifference to discipline; and the whole department was charged with "rottenness." And on the very day of the murders, when the alarm came into headquarters, most of the officers were out of town, attending the annual department picnic. Within days of Lizzie's arrest, the *Daily Globe* reported that "three-fourths of the New England papers were sneering at the police and expressing a belief in Lizzie Borden's innocence." . . .

36   In his summation at the trial, Governor Robinson reminded the jurors that "you do not get the greatest ability in the world inside a policeman's coat." He was being charitable; and he could afford to be, for he had earlier made fools and worse of the Fall River officers. "When they come upon the witness stand," he remarked, "they reveal their weakness. . . . They knock their own heads together. They make themselves, as a body of men, ridiculous. . . ." Indeed they did.

37   State Police Officer George Seaver, giving physical evidence for the prosecution, read off a list of the bloodstains: five spots on the mopboard, eighty-six above the head of the lounge, forty on a picture over the lounge, the highest spot six feet one inch from the floor, the most distant spot nine feet seven and one-half inches from the lounge—and so on, listing the tiniest pinpoints of blood in both murder rooms. Then in cross-examination Robinson forced him to admit that after taking the measurements he had lost his notebook and had written down all the data again *from memory*. Officer Harrington testified that the window in the barn loft was shut; Robinson read his previous inquest testimony, saying that it was open. Some officers who searched the Borden closet said the dresses were covered with a sheet; others said they were not. Several officers saw the head of the so-called handleless hatchet, the suspected murder weapon, but only one said that the handle was found right along with it. One officer said he wrapped the hatchet head in a pocket-sized package; another said he wrapped it in a large bundle. And some officers seemed to have learned their testimony by rote.

38   Governor Robinson played the discrepancies in the officers' testimony for full theatrical effect, and he began to interpret such carelessness and bungling as signs of sinister conspiracy. Commenting on the case later in the *American Law Review*, Professor John H. Wigmore, one of the country's foremost legal scholars, noted the defense's suggestions throughout the trial that "the testimony of *all* the officers was *wilfully* false." Robinson cast even standard police procedures in a bad light. Although it is hard to imagine how the police could have proceeded without looking over the Borden premises and interviewing the person who discovered the crime, Robinson denounced their harassment of Lizzie: "And there [Assistant Marshal Fleet] was, up in this young woman's room in the afternoon [on the day of the murders], attended with some other officers, plying her with all sorts of questions in a pretty direct and peremptory way. . . . Is that the way for an officer of the law to deal with a woman in her own house? What would you do with a man—I don't care if he had blue on him—that got into your house and was talking to your wife or your daughter in that way?" Reporters lamented that the "unfortunate maiden" had been "ten months in the custody of [these] witch burners."

39   Dr. Dolan, the chief medical examiner, explained in court that before the Bordens were buried, their stomachs were removed for chemical analysis and their heads were cut off and stripped of tissue so that the skulls might be exhibited and the wounds examined. He testified that this grisly procedure was carried out under police order and without notifying the Borden daughters. At that moment, wrote Julian Ralph, "nearly all eyes were turned upon the lonely girl in deep black as she sat listening with her calm face. A new bond of sympathy was created for her in every sympathetic heart, and for

her sister also, who had not been told what dismemberment followed the mutilation of the bodies of their father and stepmother." No matter who was guilty of the murders, it was the police who had dismembered the bodies.

40   Luckily for Miss Borden, the unfortunate damsel beset by this squad of villains, she had her champions. Ralph described Andrew Jennings's opening argument for the defense in these terms: "For an hour he championed her cause with an ancient knight's consideration for her sex and herself. It must have been a strange sensation to that girl to hear, for the first time in ten months of agony, a bold and defiant voice ringing out in her defense. She wiped her eyes furtively a few times, but the tears came so fast that she had to put up her handkerchief." Strange indeed that the "girl" should be both the accused and the romantic heroine.

41   But Jennings and Robinson were more than simply knights-errant impaling police dragons in defense of a fair maiden; for both men also stood as surrogate fathers to her—Jennings by reason of his long friendship with her father, and Robinson by reason of his age and public position as a leader of the Commonwealth. The newspapers commented again and again that her attorneys treated Lizzie in the manner of "kindly fathers." The ritual courtroom drama was complicated by this dual role of Lizzie's attorneys, for they were both patriarchs and champions, both fathers and lovers. This double role of the father/protector to the young woman, with all its incestuous implications, runs as a sinister undercurrent throughout the trial and surfaces only rarely, as in Robinson's maudlin references to Lizzie's ring that Andrew wore at his death and that was buried with him, as though he were not father but spectral groom. . . .

42   Ritual drama is always oversimplified, for its purpose is to reduce human ambiguity to unitary, straightforward statements that can be acted out. So in this courtroom drama of the distressed maiden, there are only two male parts: champion-*cum*-lover played by Lizzie's attorneys, and villain played by the police. But other men were intimately involved with the case—the prosecuting attorneys, the judges, and the jurors. As discreetly as possible, they aligned themselves with Miss Borden's champions; and in doing so these "grey beards" carried out the task entrusted them by the "public" (that is, other men), the defense of the patriarchy and of themselves. They could scarcely have been expected to do otherwise. Julian Ralph, who saw mythic symbols everywhere, described the flowers on the judges' bench: ". . . the deep red carnations that typify bloody guilt and the gentle pink ones that stand for maidenly suffering. A change in the carnations was noticed. The guilty ones were drooping and their heads hung down around their vase. The others, emblematic of distressed maidenhood, were erect." How was a mere man to remain disinterested in a drama in which even the flowers were thought to take sides?

43   Prosecutor Hosea Knowlton, unfortunately, found himself on the wrong side; and from the time of Lizzie's arrest, he explained every time he got a chance that he was only doing his duty as district attorney. Apparently he was convincing, for the Fall River *Daily Globe* stated with approval that "District Attorney Knowlton was prejudiced On Miss Borden's Side from the first. It did not devolve on him to support the local police in their views. . . . he never performed a harder duty than when he was forced to order Miss Borden's arrest." Knowlton had good reason to try to protect himself; Judge Josiah Blaisdell, when he bound Lizzie over for the grand jury, was heavily criticized for the harsh words he spoke against her—words that had served as the standard form of criminal complaint in Massachusetts for 150 years. But in the last stages of the trial, in his summation to the jury, Knowlton was still going on about his "painful duty." He said, "The prisoner at the bar is a woman and a Christian woman . . . of the rank of lady, the equal of your wife and mine, of your friends and mine, of whom such things had never

been suspected or dreamed before. I hope I may never forget, nor in anything that I say here today lose sight of the terrible significance of that fact."

44   Nevertheless, it remained Knowlton's duty as district attorney to prosecute, and he cautioned the jury to "face this case as men, not as gallants"; judgment must be based strictly on facts, not on "fealty to the [female] sex," he said—after agreeing with the defense attorneys not to discuss the delicate topic of Lizzie's bloody towels. He simply couldn't bring himself to judge her in the same terms that he would apply to men. Labeling her resentment of her stepmother as "petty," he continued: "Nay, if it was a man sitting in that dock instead of a woman, I would characterize it in more opprobrious terms than those. I trust that in none of the discussion that I engage in today shall I forget the courtesy due from a man to a woman; and although it is my horrible and painful duty to point to the fact of this woman being a murderess, I trust I shall not forget that she is a woman, and I hope I never have." He never did—and he never let anyone else forget it either.

45   For Lizzie had committed patricide. There lay the "terrible significance" Knowlton saw in the case. The murder of Mrs. Borden hardly counted. Verbally re-creating the crime, Knowlton said: "I have left the dead body of that aged woman upon the guest-chamber floor in the room where she was last at work, and am now asking you to come down with me to a far sadder tragedy, to the most horrible word that the English language knows, to a parricide." Strictly speaking, the murder of Abby Borden was also a case of parricide—that is, the killing of a father, mother, or other revered person. But to Knowlton, Abby was simply an old woman who had "served her husband for thirty years for her room and board." Andrew's death was what mattered. Knowlton continued:

> *There may be that in this case which* saves us *from the idea that Lizzie Andrew Borden planned to kill her father.* I hope she did not. I should be slow to believe she did. *But Lizzie Andrew Borden, the daughter of Andrew Jackson Borden, never came down those stairs. It was not Lizzie Andrew Borden that came down those stairs, but a murderess, transformed from all the thirty-three* [sic] *years of an honest life, transformed from the daughter, transformed from the ties of affection, to the most consummate criminal we have read of in all our history or works of fiction.*

46   Knowlton argued that Lizzie, the daughter, hated Mrs. Borden, planned to kill her, and carried out that plan; but when Lizzie, the murderess, came downstairs and saw her father, it occurred to her that he probably would discover what she had done and disapprove of it. So, on the spur of the moment, she had to kill him too, even though she hated to do it. "But it is a *grateful relief* to our conceptions of human nature," he said, "to be able to find reasons to believe that the murder of Andrew Borden was not planned by his youngest daughter, but was done as a wicked and dreadful necessity, which *if she could have foreseen she never would have followed that mother* up those stairs. . . ."

47   Knowlton's argument gave the jurors an out. They could convict this "consummate criminal," for she was not a lady after all, and not a *real* patricide. And if the jury returned a conviction, Knowlton's argument provided rationalizations for the patriarchy which otherwise would have to deal with a certified female father-killer. Significantly, Knowlton's argument rests on the assumption that a woman who could plan and carry out a murder couldn't think ahead to what she would do next. If that notion of female intelligence was taken seriously by the men in the courtroom, it is no wonder Lizzie Borden terrified them. "And so I leave that [argument] there," Knowlton said, "not as a matter of proof—oh, no, oh, no—but to relieve my mind of the dreadful

necessity of believing that there is a deliberate parricide yet living in America." The jury didn't want to believe it either.

48   Neither did the judges. In earlier rulings on the admissibility of evidence, the three justices had given a decided advantage to the defense. First, in the most important evidentiary decision of the trial, the court ruled that testimony Lizzie gave at the inquest could not be read in court and entered as evidence. Three days later the justices ruled out the testimony of Eli Bence and two other clerks from Smith's Pharmacy who were prepared to swear that Lizzie Borden had attempted to purchase prussic acid from Bence on the morning before the murders. This testimony, which the prosecution hoped would clinch its argument that Lizzie was predisposed to murder, was ruled out largely on the grounds that the attempt to purchase poison was not relevant to murders committed with a hatchet. All the precedents cited by prosecutor Moody in his thoroughly documented argument—including the most authoritative works of Wigmore on *Evidence* and Warren on *Homicide*—were defied by the court; what the justices and Robinson kept referring to as "common sense" prevailed over the law. The renowned Professor Wigmore himself later attacked both these evidentiary decisions, but the immediate damage to the prosecution's case had been done. And as the trial neared its end, *The New York Times* noted: "On every legal point the prosecution has been defeated, and this has greatly lessened the strength of their case."

49   After Robinson's final four-hour theatrical performance for the jury and Knowlton's apologetic summary, Justice Dewey dealt the final blow to the prosecution's case: his charge to the jury amounted to a directive for acquittal. He began by explaining that state statute required him to instruct the jury on certain matters of applying the law, but not on matters of fact. The statute, he explained, "was intended to prevent the judges . . . from expressing any opinion as to the credibility of witnesses or the strength of evidence." Dewey then proceeded to do exactly what the statute forbade. He discredited prosecution witnesses, including one woman whose testimony he discounted altogether because she had used "the language of a young woman" instead of what he considered to be the "real meaning" of words. He suggested that the five medical-expert witnesses had been irreconcilably at odds with one another when in fact they had agreed unanimously on every substantive point. He raised issues that had not been brought up in the testimony, and he ignored matters—such as the dress burning—which the prosecution considered significant. . . .

50   The most remarkable passage of his address occurred as he cautioned the jury not to count Lizzie's failure to take the stand against her.

> *It is a matter which the law submits to her own discretion and to that alone. You can see, gentlemen, that there may be cases where this right to testify would be valuable to a defendant. It may be able to afford the jury some further information or give some explanation that would help the defense. In another case where there was no doubt that an offense had been committed by someone, he might have no knowledge as to how or by whom it was done, and could only affirm under oath his innocence, which is already presumed. The defendant may say, "I have already told to the officers all that I know about this case, and my statements have been put in evidence; whatever is mysterious to others is also a mystery to me. I have no knowledge more than others have. I have never professed to be able to explain how or by whom these homicides were committed."*

Lizzie had never said anything of the sort. In effect, the judge was testifying *for* her. "As you have the right to reason from what you know of the laws and properties of matter," he advised the jurors, "so you have a right to reason and judge from what you know of the laws and property of human nature and action." Dewey said, in effect, that if the evidence in the case conflicted with the jurors' preconceived notions about the nature of ladies, the jurors were free to vote their preconceptions. Certainly Judge Dewey had made his own preconceptions clear. The Boston *Globe* headlined its report of his address: JUDGE'S CHARGE A PLEA FOR THE INNOCENT.

51   Judge Blaisdell, in announcing his verdict of "probably guilty" at the preliminary hearing, had said, "Suppose for a single moment that *a man* was standing there [in the dock]. He was found close by the guest chamber which to Mrs. Borden was a chamber of death. Suppose that *a man* had been found in the vicinity of Mr. Borden and the only account he could give of himself was the unreasonable one that he was out in the barn looking for sinkers, that he was in the yard, that he was looking for something else. Would there be any question in the minds of men what should be done with such a man?" But the prisoner was not a man; the prisoner was, as even prosecutor Knowlton said, "a woman, one of that sex that all high-minded men revere, that all generous men love, that all wise men acknowledge their indebtedness to. It is hard, it is hard," said the district attorney to the gentlemen of the jury, "to *conceive* that woman can be guilty of crime." What's more, she was a lady; and that made all the difference. For the men of the Borden court shared—in addition to a common host of fears—a body of beliefs about true womanhood. Lizzie Borden owed her life largely to those tacit assumptions: ladies aren't strong enough to swing a two-pound hatchet hard enough to break a brittle substance one-sixteenth of an inch thick. Ladies cry a lot. Ladies love to stay home all the time. Ladies are ceaselessly grateful to the men—fathers or husbands—who support them. Ladies never stand with their legs apart. Ladies cannot plan more than a few minutes ahead. Ladies' conversation arises from ignorance, hysteria, overenthusiasm, or the inability to use language properly, and in any case, is not to be taken seriously.

52   None of these generalities about "women" applied to Irish servants. . . . And had Bridget Sullivan been tried for the Borden murders on evidence similar to that raised against Miss Lizzie, the result would certainly have been different. As lower-class women, the Bridgets were thought ignorant and sluggish, prone to filthy habits, petty thievery, and perhaps more serious crime; they were almost never suspected of giddiness, physical weakness, gratitude, or innocence.

53   The twelve "stout-hearted men" of the Borden jury who shared the assumptions of the attorneys and the justices marched off to the jury room, voted Lizzie's acquittal on the first ballot, sat for an hour to avoid the appearance of undue haste, and returned to the courtroom. Before he was asked the question, the eager foreman blurted out, "Not guilty."

54   Lizzie dropped into her seat like a stone and wept as loud cheers went up in the courtroom. Mr. Jennings, almost in tears, shook Mr. Adams's hand, saying in a breaking voice, "Thank God." Mr. Adams was unable to speak. Governor Robinson turned to the jury and "gleamed on them with a fatherly interest in his kindly eyes. . . . " District attorneys Moody and Knowlton crossed the room to shake hands with the defense counselors—and with Miss Borden. Judge Dewey's eyes flooded with tears, and "Judge Blodgett's face contorted with the violence of his effort to repress his strong emotion." Sheriff Wright, whose duty it was to maintain order, was crying too much to try. His daughter Isabel had been a childhood playmate of Lizzie Borden.

55   As the cheers continued, Lizzie retired to an adjoining room and sent for Julian Ralph and other reporters to thank them for their support. But the journalists were not quite finished. *The New York Times*, which had been relatively restrained in its trial coverage, printed a long editorial condemning the villainy of the police—"of the usual inept and stupid and muddle-headed sort that such [small] towns manage to get for themselves"—and "the legal officers who secured the indictment and have conducted

the trial." *The Times* took the acquittal of "this most unfortunate and cruelly persecuted woman" as "a declaration, not only that the prisoner was guiltless, but *that there never was any serious reason to suppose that she was guilty.* . . . We do not remember a case in a long time in which the prosecution has so completely broken down, or in which the evidence has shown so clearly, not merely that the prisoner should not be convicted, but *that there never should have been an indictment.*" The editor fell back on the myth of the distressed damsel: "The Fall River police needed a victim . . . and the daughter was the nearest and most helpless." Fortunately for Miss Borden, as a jubilant Julian Ralph wrote: ". . . it took only an hour for the jury to decide that witches are out of fashion in Massachusetts and that no one is to be executed there on suspicion and on parrot-like police testimony." The Boston *Globe* even printed an interview with Judge Dewey. Although it was highly irregular for a trial judge to publish his opinions, Dewey professed to be "perfectly satisfied" with the verdict. "I was satisfied when I made my charge to the jury," he said, "that the verdict would be not guilty, although one cannot always tell what a jury will do."

56   Just before the preliminary hearing, the Reverend Dr. Mason, visiting from Brunswick, Maine, had reassured the congregation of the Fall River Central Congregational Church that God the Father was "with that poor, tried tempest-tossed girl" and would "make her glad. . . . The Father is over all," he intoned. "He will vindicate, and raise and glorify." And sure enough, he did.

57   Banker Charles Holmes, his daughter Anna, and Emma Borden took Lizzie by train to Fall River and arrived in a carriage at the Holmes Pine Street residence about eight-fifteen that evening, Wednesday, June 20, 1893. Several friends called during the evening to offer congratulations; and Lizzie told a United Press reporter that she was "the happiest woman in the world." Her friends, she said, had agreed not to discuss "the subject." Just before ten o'clock a band stopped in front of the Borden house on Second Street and played "Auld Lang Syne." But Lizzie and Emma, not long afterward, sold that house and bought a much finer one, a spacious Victorian with indoor plumbing, on the hill; they had the name *Maplecroft* carved into the stone steps out front. Lizzie changed her name to Lisbeth, bought a horse and carriage, and hired a coachman who drove her about, mostly alone. After the grand charade of the trial, most of her townspeople—who knew she had got away with murder—turned against her; though perhaps they would have been kinder if she had not flaunted her victory so. Years later even Emma left her in what was rumored to be a quarrel over property. Miss Lisbeth Borden continued to live in the big house on the hill, taking occasional excursions to Boston, until she died in 1927 at the age of sixty-six, leaving a good bit of the legacy she had received from her father to the Animal Rescue League. Then she passed into legend. . . .

58   Other American women have murdered their fathers without passing into folklore. Who today remembers the name of Alice Christiana Abbott, who poisoned her stepfather in 1867 because he repeatedly raped her and threatened to commit her to an asylum if she told? Even at the time her charges were regarded as "singular" and best forgotten. And there have been many other ax murders. Right there in Fall River, even as the Borden jury was being selected, José Corierro struck down a woman with an ax; but he was a man and a lower-class Portuguese immigrant—just the sort of person to commit brutal homicide. But Lizzie's crime, with its "masculine" motive (money and independence) and its "masculine" weapon, raised all sorts of anxious questions that cluster about the difficult issue of woman's place.

59   Lizzie Borden herself was connected with women's groups, including the prosuffrage Woman's Christian Temperance Union, but her affiliation with women was mainly

social and religious rather than political; and it was, at best, sporadic. Still, women rallied to her support. Shortly after Lizzie's arrest the Fall River Woman's Union, a philanthropic social club, passed a resolution of support:

> *We offer our profound sympathy to Miss Lizzie A. Borden in the sad and painful bereavement which has befallen her in the recent tragic deaths of her parents. We would also declare our unshaken faith in her as a fellow-worker and sister tenderly beloved, and would assure her of our constant and earnest prayers that she may be supported under the unprecedented trials and sorrows now resting upon her.*

60   The Christian Endeavor Society and the Fruit and Flower Mission of the Congregational Church—Lizzie's chief interests—passed similar resolutions; and Henry Brown Blackwell, husband of Lucy Stone, reprinted them in *The Woman's Journal*, the organ of the American Woman Suffrage Association. Lucy Stone used the occasion to write again about the need for women jurors (without voicing any opinion in Lizzie's case); and Mary Livermore, the abolitionist and suffragist then in her seventies—the same Mary Livermore who had argued in *What Shall We Do with Our Daughters?* that all young women should be trained for jobs so they would not be dependent upon men for their happiness—went to visit "the girl" in Taunton jail and wrote a passionate, misguided article on her innocence for the Boston *Post*. Feminists were concerned, quite correctly, that Lizzie Borden would not get a fair trial from a jury of men—although they did not foresee that the unfairness would swing in her favor. Suffragists must also have been somewhat embarrassed by the possibility of her guilt, for they had won supporters to the cause of suffrage recently with the elitist argument that votes of well-educated, morally superior ladies were needed to offset the votes of ignorant, lower-class men. A lady ax murderer could do the cause no good.

61   The support Lizzie Borden received from religious and social women's clubs and from people like Stone, Livermore, and Blackwell, who had been leaders of the suffrage campaign for so long, must have amplified the fears men already felt as husbands, fathers, patriarchs. Society seemed to be coming unglued. And all this talk of woman's rights—where would it lead? Only a few years later an analysis of New York City crime rates provided an answer at once alarming in its implications and comforting in its foolish conventionality: women's emancipation produces women criminals. The rate of women's crimes seemed to be increasing even faster than that of men's crimes. Overall arrests of women were up from 412 in 1886 to 722 in 1896. Only 8 female burglars had been arrested in 1886; a decade later the number had doubled. In 1886 only 8 women were arraigned for homicide; in 1895 the number was 19, an increase of over 100 percent. Like the 1690s, which produced the Salem witch trials, and the 1840s, which produced both the Seneca Falls Convention and a whole body of literature about evil women, this was an anxious time. And it is hardly surprising that in another anxious time, just after World War II, when women liberated by wartime jobs and independence were shoved back into the sculleries and bedrooms of America, antifeminists should pry Lizzie Borden free of her own history and resurrect her as a "feminine vigilante," a lesbian marching out of the kitchen with a bloody ax, a sort of Nat Turner of the women's movement.

62   Of all the latter-day revisionists of the Borden story, however, Agnes DeMille came closest to the bone of Lizzie Borden's existence when she created her ballet *Fall River Legend*. "Lizzie's life," she wrote, "consisted mainly in things . . . that didn't happen. And how does one put inaction, lack of dynamics, the maintenance of status quo into dance? . . . How does one express boredom on stage?" Like the courtroom myth of true womanhood, the modern theories—whether of true love, lesbianism, violent "feminism," repressed sexuality, or incestuous desires—constrict woman's life, a life already

passed in too narrow a house. Lizzie Borden the lady was pronounced innocent and sent home; Bridget Durgan the maid was hauled drunk into the street and hanged in the middle of a prayer. At the time, according to the social fathers, these two women had nothing in common. And today the laws and the continuing legends of a man-made society are still unwilling to acknowledge that they were both women, that they shared a life consisting mainly in things that didn't happen.

1. What do you learn about Lizzie's character from this article?

   _____

   _____

2. Where did Jones get this information?

   _____

   _____

3. What do you learn from the article about the crime that you didn't know before?

   _____

   _____

4. What do you learn about attitudes toward women in the late-nineteenth century that you didn't know before?

   _____

   _____

5. What do you learn about attitudes toward class?

   _____

   _____

6. Why was Lizzie exonerated?

   _____

   _____

_____

Research as a Way of Supporting a Thesis

In this essay, Ann Jones is writing not only about Lizzie as a woman murderer but also about how society constructed the idea of female in relation to crime. As this is not an article in a scholarly book, she doesn't include citations and so we don't know precisely where she got the information she did. In writing your research paper, you must methodically conduct your research to establish and explain your thesis and then you must show your reader where you got this information. This is called documentation. See Chapters 8 and 9 for information about how to document your sources.

EXERCISE 1.6	**Using Research to Support a Point of View (Thesis)**

What kind of evidence does Ann Jones offer to convince us that Lizzie was probably guilty? On the lines that follow, make a list of facts she uses to support her point of view, or thesis. State the thesis first.

Thesis:

_____

_____

_____

_____

_____

_____

The Research Process

When you are assigned a research paper, you are, in a sense, expected to be a detective. You may be assigned a general subject, but you need to find, within that subject, a topic that interests you. Within that topic you need to find a question that needs to be answered. Once you have settled on a major research question, you need to answer it. The process of methodically finding the answer to your research question and writing it up correctly, in an acceptable format, is called the **research process,** and because it is a complicated (though thoroughly satisfying) process, it is the subject of an entire book.

An Overview of the Research Process

1. *First, you need to find and narrow your topic.* If you are doing this paper for a specific subject area course, the paper will certainly be related to the subject of the course. If you are writing this paper for a composition or research paper course, you may have more latitude. Your teacher may let you pick a subject or may assign a general subject, such as twentieth-century immigration, and ask you to find a topic related to that subject. Let's say you pick immigration from the Caribbean. Your job is to narrow that topic, perhaps to Jamaican immigration, and then to ask a question about it. To do so, you need to consider what you want to know about Jamaican immigration. You next form an early answer to your question, which may be called your hypothesis. After you have completed your research process, your hypothesis becomes a thesis (unless you are doing certain kinds of science and social science projects in which students may be asked to do research and to explain this research and its outcome in report form).

2. *Your next task is to find your sources*—the material written and researched by others that will help you defend or explain your hypothesis. This is not as easy as it sounds. In order to find sources, you need to know how to use the library—to search for books, magazines, journals, CD-ROMs, and listservs. In addition, you need to know how to conduct research on the Internet. You need to be able to evaluate these sources to make sure they are reliable and pertinent.

3. *Once you find sources, you must read and record them.* This takes skill. You need to know how to read selectively, how to copy relevant information into your notes, and how to paraphrase and summarize your notes in such a way that you don't plagiarize when you integrate them into your paper. **Plagiarism,** the theft—even the inadvertent theft—of someone's work, is a major pitfall in college writing, and avoiding it is essential to writing a successful college research paper.

4. *When you have recorded all your sources in your research notes, you are ready to organize your material and to make an outline.* This outline should show how

you plan to support your main idea, how you will classify and arrange your topics to do that, and what developmental models you are considering.

5. *If you have prepared yourself well, writing the first draft of the paper, which is the next step, should not be too difficult.* You will need to introduce your essay, integrate your quotations and paraphrases into it, develop your ideas, and conclude.

6. *The documentation method you use will depend on what your teacher requires.* MLA and APA are the two forms most utilized in research papers, although there are others, such as CBE and *The Chicago Manual of Style.* These methods are quite intricate. You must know which form to use and when, and you must be precise in your documentation.

7. *Finally, you must revise and proofread your paper.* You must also put it in the proper format—that is, the format required by your instructor—and make sure it is correctly and persuasively written.

Your Equipment

There was a time when a pen and a pad were all you needed to write your research paper. The pad gave way to the typewriter, and it is still possible to complete a good research paper with only a pad or a typewriter, but it is harder. Technology has advanced and has given us tools to "expedite" the process of writing—not do it for you. A personal computer (PC) with Internet capability will help you to write and revise more easily. A laptop is more mobile than a PC, and thus you can take it to the library or some other quiet area to work. A network card will enable you to go online from many locations. Many campuses are networked for this; even some coffee shops and eateries have access to the Internet for a small fee.

Many colleges use a course management tool such as Blackboard that allows faculty to post syllabi, materials, and assignments and offers a discussion board so students can talk to one another in small groups or as a class.

CHECKLIST   THE RESEARCH PROCESS

❑ Have you found a suitable topic? (Chapter 3)

❑ Have you narrowed your topic? (Chapter 3)

❑ Have you formed a research question? (Chapter 3)

❑ Have you formed a working thesis? (Chapter 3)

❑ Have you found your sources? (Chapter 4)

❑ Have you read through all your sources? (Chapters 4 and 5)

❑ Have you evaluated your sources? (Chapter 5)

❑ Have you taken notes on your sources? (Chapter 5)

❑ Have you made working bibliography cards of your sources? (Chapter 5)

❑ Have you organized your research into an outline? (Chapter 6)

❑ Have you written your first draft, synthesizing and integrating your sources into your essay? (Chapter 7)

✔

CHECKLIST   THE RESEARCH PROCESS (continued)

❑ Have you documented your research, using an appropriate citation method? (Chapters 8 and 9)

❑ Have you prepared a Works Cited list according to MLA or other guidelines? (Chapters 8 and 9)

❑ Have you revised your paper, taking care to respond to the suggestions of your peers and teacher? (Chapter 10)

❑ Have you proofread your paper for grammar, spelling, and mechanical errors? (Chapter 10)

CHAPTER 2

Synopsis of a Model Research Paper

Student Paper

Forty Whacks

by Anna Davis

Lizzie Borden took an ax

and gave her mother forty whacks,

And when she saw what she had done,

she gave her father forty-one![1]

On August 4, 1892, Andrew Borden, a wealthy businessman, and his second wife, Abby Borden, were found dead in their home in the small city of Fall River, Massachusetts. Andrew Borden was lying on the living room couch with his face hacked to pieces. Abby Borden was upstairs in the guest bedroom, face down with nineteen blows to her face and the back of her skull. The Fall River Police Department searched for suspects for nearly a week before arresting Andrew Borden's thirty-one-year-old daughter Lizzie.

1. This famous children's rhyme encapsulates the crime that Lizzie was charged with and found not guilty of.

Davis 2

Lizzie was arraigned in November, and on June 5, almost a year after the murders were committed, the trial began. The trial was brief, lasting a mere fifteen days, after which the jury found Lizzie innocent of murdering her parents. While many people agreed with this decision, others believe that while she did commit the crimes, and her actions could never be said to be justified, they were certainly explicable. Still, most, to this day, believe that she was a cold-blooded murderer and a look at some of the voluminous research that has been done on the case makes a convincing argument that Lizzie was guilty.

Some family background may help us understand why Lizzie may have been driven to commit the crimes. One important aspect to consider is Lizzie's social position. Lizzie came from a prominent family in the town of Fall River. The Borden family had come to this country in 1638 and, settling in New England, owned many businesses in the area. While Andrew wasn't born wealthy, he worked his way up to become president of Union Savings Bank, director of First National Bank, director of Durfee Safe Deposit & Trust Company, director of Globe Yarn Mill Company, director of Troy Cotton & Woolen Manufacturing Company and director of Merchants Manufacturing Company and his estate, valued at $300,000, while ample now was a veritable fortune at the time. Abby had been obese for many years and was a semi-recluse; Andrew was not particularly interested in society. ("He had not led a public life," the *New York Times* reported [14 August 1892:8].) Lizzie, on the other hand, had a few friends whom she saw on occasion. Lizzie wasn't extremely social, but much more so than the rest of her family. She went to Europe once with her cousins. And she sometimes taught Sunday School and kept the treasurer's records for her local church. Despite all this, as a middle-class woman in the late nineteenth century, there was not much for her to do. As Ann Jones writes, "Lizzie had several friends . . . who

Davis 3

were single, self-supporting, working women. . . . But Lizzie herself, born just a little too soon to join the fashionable Fall River daughters going off to the new women's colleges, was not trained for any work" (Jones 211).

Another important point in the Borden family background is Mr. Borden's known "tightness" with money, and this is an important aspect of the case. "A retired businessman who had made his considerable fortune through a combination of ruthless financial practices and fanatical thrift," writes Marcia Carlisle in her article "What Made Lizzie Borden Kill?," he moved the family to diminished quarters in the downtown, working-class area of Fall River rather than the upper-class area on the hill. The *New York Times* called him a "pious skinflint" (14 August 1892:8) and Victoria Lincoln tells us: "When he was an undertaker, he cut the feet off the corpses so that he could cram them into undersized coffins that he got cheap"(Lincoln 35). Lizzie often complained, it was reported, that she didn't get enough money from her father and was particularly distraught when her father purchased a home for Abby's sister five years previously. This apparently angered both Lizzie and Emma, who "were upset at what they saw as favoritism" (Carlisle 71). Moreover, it can be conjectured that Lizzie wanted to move up the social ladder in Fall River society and felt her father's penury wouldn't allow for this (Jones 210). It is, thus, interesting to note that after her acquittal, Lizzie moved to a fashionable house and changed her name to Lisbeth, a more "distinguished" name.

Yet another persuasive thread in Lizzie Borden's background is the lack of closeness in the family. Lizzie Borden had been living together with her older sister Emma, her father and stepmother and their servant Bridget Sullivan in this small cramped house for ten years when the crime took place. Because the house was originally built for two families, it remained divided; Andrew and

Davis 4

Abby lived on one side and Lizzie and Emma on the other. All connections between the two sides of the house were blocked up so that if Lizzie wanted to visit her family she had to go downstairs, exit, and reenter through the door to her parents' side of the house. The family rarely ate together and the two women spoke of their stepmother with distance. Neither Emma nor Lizzie accepted Abby as a maternal figure in their lives, although they had lived with her for nearly thirty years and although "there is no indication that Abby treated them badly . . . from the first Emma refused to call her Mother"(Carlisle 70). Lizzie reported at the inquest: "She isn't my mother. My mother died when I was an infant" (*New York Times* 7 June 1893:2).

It is important to note the details of the crime itself in order to understand the arguments against Lizzie. On the morning of the murders Lizzie claimed that Mrs. Borden had gone out to see a sick friend. That morning, Andrew Borden was out attending to some business; when he came back, he fell asleep on the couch in the living room. Lizzie said that the last time she saw her father was on the way out to the barn, when she had a short conversation with him. While she was in the barn, she claimed to have heard moans and cries for help from inside the house. She said that she ran inside the house, found her father lying dead on the couch, and called up to Bridget, who was sleeping in the attic, telling her that Mr. Borden had been killed. She ran out and got help from a neighbor, Mrs. Churchill. Then she went upstairs, and she and Mrs. Churchill found Mrs. Borden dead as well. At first they thought that she had died of heart disease, a condition she suffered from, but later a reporter pointed out that she had blood on the train of her dress, and when she was flipped over, it turned out that she, too, had been hacked in the face beyond recognition.

Davis 5

The murder scene was horrid. As reported in the *New York Times*, Medical Examiner Delan describes Mr. Borden as follows:

> One gash went straight down through the nose, the eyes, and chin; another extended from the eye to an inch below the angle of the lower jaw; another was on the left side of the forehead, taking out a piece of the skull across the eyeball, splitting the cheekbone and stopping at the left angle of the mouth. . . . All were crushing wounds. (26 August 1892:1)

Mrs. Borden was equally mauled:

> The body of Mrs. Borden was lying . . . face downward. . . . The arms were thrown around the head, so that no part of the face was visible. Several wounds were in sight, all on the head, and all but four were on the right side. Fourteen of them were in a small square on the top of the head. . . . Part of them [sic] were through the skull and entered the brain. . . . The body was lying in a pool of blood, and the front of the clothing was soaked with blood.
> (26 August 1892:1)

Strangely enough, although both the victims had been hacked to death, there was very little blood on the victims nor was there much in either room in which the victims had been murdered. The *Times* reporter wrote, "It was as if the life current had been retarded and partly congealed from other causes before the murderous blows were struck" (14 Aug. 1892:8). At the trial there were several theories about this. One is that Mrs. Borden fainted before she died and Mr. Borden was asleep when hacked (Jones 220); others involved the placement of the bodies in the room (Sullivan 182–3), but how these theories would result in an absence of blood is not clear.

Davis 6

Lizzie was not the first to be suspected of the murders, although the police quickly began focusing on her. John W. Morse, Borden's brother-in-law by his first marriage, was questioned, since he had been at the house that morning. A Portuguese immigrant who had once worked for the Bordens was sought but quickly eliminated. Soon the police narrowed their search to Lizzie, and her "alibi" was confusing and not very convincing. She told the police several different stories about what she had been doing on the morning of the murders, but ultimately she insisted that she had been in the barn eating some pears and looking for iron to make a sinker for a fishing trip she had been planning at the time that her father was murdered. Since the weather was unusually hot that day, it is hard to believe she would choose to stay in the barn longer than necessary. Ann Jones tells us, "Accounting for some twenty minutes spent in the barn loft, Lizzie told of slowly eating two or three pears. But [District Attorney] Knowlton remembered that she . . . had been nauseated the day before and unable to eat breakfast that morning" (213–4). At the inquest, Lizzie kept dodging the questions [about her appetite] and finally said that she was not sure whether she had been able to eat breakfast or not (214).

The police also had questions about the clothing Lizzie was wearing at the time of the murders. After the murders had been discovered, Lizzie told Emma and a few neighbors that she had burned a dress that day because it had red paint on it and she thought she would never wear it. Why would she do this after discovering her father and mother had been brutally murdered unless she was trying to cover up her crime? The police also had questions about where Lizzie was in the house at the time of the murders. Because the Borden house was once a two-family residence, it was impossible to get from one section to another

Davis 7

without first going downstairs and then going up the stairs on the other side of the house. Bridget Sullivan testified that Lizzie and Emma rarely went up to their parents' side of the house, but on the morning of the murders Bridget was having trouble closing the many locks on the front door, and she heard Lizzie laugh from the top of the stairs on her parents' side of the house where she normally never went (8 June 1893:8). At the time that Mrs. Borden was murdered, Lizzie (conveniently) had sent Bridget Sullivan outside to wash windows. It would have been hard for someone else, some unknown murderer, to enter the house without being seen by Bridget, especially since the front and back doors were locked, leaving the side door as the only possible entrance to the house. It also would have been strange for a murderer to kill one person, leave the vicinity, and then come back and murder the second person 90 minutes later. Doing this, the murderer would have to risk being seen twice, which would double his or her chances of being caught. For Lizzie this would not have been a problem. She could have murdered her stepmother, and then simply performed her normal daily routine until her father returned home. Another area the police investigated had to do with Lizzie's purchase of the poison, prussic acid. There is evidence that Lizzie might have tried to poison her parents before she settled on using the famous ax to kill them. Two clerks at different drug stores in Fall River testified that Lizzie Borden had come into each of their stores and asked to buy prussic acid, a drug that is fatal if ingested (7 August 1892:1). Also, it was said that Mr. and Mrs. Borden and their maid Bridget Sullivan had upset stomachs that week (5 August 1892:2) and that Lizzie had, indeed, bought prussic acid at a nearby pharmacist's (19 June 1893:1).

Then and now, Lizzie's story seems very feeble. When the loft of the barn was examined, no footprints were found in the thick

Davis 8

dust of the floor of the loft (19 June 1893:1). Lizzie said that on the morning of the murders Abby had received a note calling her out of the house to go and visit a sick friend. When all the scraps of paper in the trash can were pieced together, this note could not be found and Lizzie claimed she didn't know the neighbor and thus couldn't give her name. This woman was never located (14 August 1892:8). In any case, Lizzie said that Mrs. Borden had been out all morning, but the autopsy showed that Mrs. Borden had been killed "at least an hour" before Mr. Borden, placing her time of death at around 10:00 (19 June 1893: 1). After much searching, the police found a hatchet in the basement of the Borden house, but as the handle had been broken off, no blood stains could be traced. However, the blade seemed to fit the wounds of the victims and Lizzie was arrested and tried in New Bedford's Superior Court the following June (Carlisle 68).

There are many reasons why Lizzie Borden would have wanted to kill her parents. The prosecution's argument, and that of most modern critics, was, simply, that Lizzie wanted the money. Andrew Borden had moved the family into an inferior house in an inferior location, in Lizzie's opinion. He had used his money to buy a house for their stepmother's sister. Carlisle conjectures, "Both Emma and Lizzie were upset at what they saw as favoritism; Lizzie's anger was later interpreted as selfishness" (72). Moreover, when Andrew died, Abby would get at least one-third of his money by Massachusetts law. In fact, Andrew could leave all his money to Abby if he chose to, effectively disinheriting his daughters. Only if Abby and Andrew died at the same time would Lizzie be sure to get her half of the inheritance, sharing it then with her sister Emma. In the 1800s it was hard for women to earn a living, and without money how could they live on their own? By killing the Bordens, Lizzie

Davis 9

would ensure that she got the money that she both wanted and (arguably) needed.[2]

The Lizzie Borden case wouldn't still be considered a mystery if the prosecutors of Fall River, Massachusetts, had proved, beyond a reasonable doubt, that Lizzie Borden had killed her stepmother and father. Ann Jones reports that the jury decided on her innocence on the first ballot, and waited an hour before returning to the courtroom, just to make it appear as if they had deliberated thoughtfully (232). If so much is wrong with Lizzie's story, why would the jury acquit Lizzie Borden, and so quickly?

Several possible answers emerge for why Lizzie was acquitted. One can be found in nineteenth-century attitudes towards women. No woman had been executed in the state of Massachusetts since 1778, and Lizzie knew it would be difficult for her neighbors to convict her. Women were not murderers. They were supposed to be sweet and innocent and Lizzie promoted that image incessantly, bringing flowers every day to court, asking to leave the courtroom on several occasions and even fainting to show her delicacy. How could such a sweet and innocent young woman wield an ax against her parents? Furthermore, women were supposed to be emotional, confused and unreliable. Lizzie's testimony at the trial was confusing and unreliable. She told the police several different stories about what she had been doing on the morning of the murders, but ultimately she insisted that she had been in the (very hot) barn, eating some pears and looking for an iron fishing sinker

---

2. Marcia Carlisle has a very different thesis, which she develops in her article "What Made Lizzie Borden Kill" in the July/August 1992 *American Heritage Magazine*. She believes that Lizzie may have killed her parents to get revenge for sexual abuse. Carlisle contends that Lizzie may have recovered her memory of the abuse shortly before she killed her father. Why both of them? Carlisle says: "Perhaps because her stepmother had known about the incest and had been unable to stop it, or worse had blamed Lizzie for it" (Carlisle 72). It is impossible to know if this is true or not, but Carlisle says there were many telltale signs of incest.

Davis 10

for that upcoming fishing trip. Lizzie claimed that she had not seen Abby since the early morning when Abby went to see that sick neighbor (who was never located). Lizzie claimed that she and the rest of her family got on well, but she was demonstrably upset when asked about her "mother," saying that her father's second wife was *not* her mother. All this contradictory evidence was deemed inadmissible at the trial because of improper counsel. As a result, the jurors never heard the conflicting evidence in this early testimony.

Shoddy police work further assisted Lizzie in escaping conviction by weakening the prosecutor's case. The District Attorney claimed that he had been the first person to enter the barn after the murders, and he said that there were no footprints but his own in the inch or more of dust on the ground. However, other witnesses testified that they had seen other police officers entering the barn before the District Attorney, and that the dust was not in fact thick enough to retain clear imprints of either the DA's shoes or anyone else's (19 June 1893:1). As has been mentioned, at the time that Mrs. Borden was murdered, Bridget Sullivan claimed she had been sent outside to wash windows, though it seems an odd task to undertake on a scorching hot day. If she were outside, though, it would have been hard for someone, particularly a stranger, to enter the house without being seen by her, especially when the doors at both the front and back were locked (and why was Bridget having trouble with the locks—had Lizzie, perhaps, jammed the locks to get more time?). This left the side door as the only available entrance to the house. However, neither the prosecutor nor Lizzie's lawyer seems to have asked Sullivan if she saw Lizzie enter or leave by this side door during the time she claimed to be in the barn. There were also problems with the prosecution's investigation of the clothing Lizzie was wearing at the time of the murder. As has been discussed, on the

Davis 11

morning of August 4, after the discovery of the murders, Lizzie told Emma and a few neighbors that she was going to burn a dress, because it had red paint on it, and apparently she did burn a dress. Bridget Sullivan said that she had seen Lizzie wearing that dress, or at least one similar to it, that morning, but the prosecutor couldn't tie the dress to the murders. The fact that Lizzie had no blood on her person led some people, including her own attorney during the trial, to speculate (facetiously, that is) that she may have committed the crime in the nude. He suggested at the trial, "I would not wonder if they are not going to claim that this woman denuded herself and did not have any dress on at all when she committed either murder" (Lincoln 281). Such an assertion, even if sarcastic, was unthinkable for a woman of Borden's social position at that time, and people must have been shocked at the implication. The suggestion that police procedures were careless no doubt influenced the jury to discredit much of the police testimony. Ultimately, the defense prepared a much better case than the prosecution. As the *New York Times* reported:

> The utter absence of any other explanation was the sole support of the suspicion against the daughter. In spite of the circumstances that made it look dark for her, there was as complete a lack of direct evidence against her as of any kind of evidence against anybody else. If circumstantial evidence is a chain only as strong as its weakest link, we have presented here an attempt to make a chain out of wholly disconnected links, which has no continuity or binding strength at all. (17 June 1893:4)

After the trial and her acquittal, Lizzie Borden lived a quiet life. With the money she inherited from her father, she moved up to "the Hill," to a much grander house than the one in which she had lived with her parents. For some years, she shared this house with

Davis 12

her sister Emma, but they had a fight which caused Emma to move away. From that time on, Lizzie lived virtually alone, having only a few friends and seldom seeing Emma. In 1926, thirty-four years after the murders, she underwent surgery from which she failed to recover. Upon her death, her estate was valued at $1,000,000, a very great sum given the value of the dollar in 1926. Emma Borden died about a week after Lizzie. Both sisters left large sums of money to the Animal Rescue League.

Even today, the Lizzie Borden murder case excites interest and debate. New books are published frequently, the house in Fall River is a tourist attraction, and the infamous rhyme appears on Borden Web sites and other popular culture resources. The particularly gruesome nature of the murders grabbed the public's attention in 1892 when the idea that a white, middle-class woman could butcher her parents seemed unthinkable. It's a wonder that with crime shows and serial killers crowding each other for space on television and in the movies, the Borden case remains fascinating, perhaps because the crimes of matricide and patricide still stir our blood. Maybe we have all, at one time or another, wished for the death of a parent. Or maybe we simply want a final answer, a convincing solution to an unsolved case.

Davis 13

Works Cited

"Bridget Sullivan a Witness." <u>New York Times</u> 8 June 1893, 8.

"Butchered in Their Home." <u>New York Times</u> 5 Aug. 1892, 2.

"The Fall River Mystery." <u>New York Times</u> 7 Aug. 1892, 1.

Jones, Ann. <u>Women Who Kill</u>. Boston: Beacon Press, 1996.

Lincoln, Victoria. <u>A Private Disgrace: Lizzie Borden by Daylight</u>.
     New York: Putnam, 1967.

"Lizzie Borden in a Faint." <u>New York Times</u> 7 June 1893, 2.

"Lizzie Borden's Hearing." <u>New York Times</u> 26 Aug. 1892, 1.

"Lizzie Borden's Triumphs." <u>New York Times</u> 19 June 1893, 1.

Sullivan, Robert. <u>Goodbye Lizzie Borden</u>. New York: Penguin, 1989.

"Story of a Great Crime." <u>New York Times</u> 14 Aug. 1892, 8.

"Will It Remain a Mystery?" <u>New York Times</u> 17 June 1893, 4.

Anna's Research Journal

Week of 9/15: Beginning the Research Assignment

Today we began talking about the research assignment. Our professor suggested we keep a Research Journal to help us think through what we want to say and to keep track of the many and varied aspects of research writing that we'll be learning.

Defining Your Purpose

The assignment for the paper is to take a popular legend from American history and reexamine it using a variety of primary and secondary sources.

Identifying a Possible Subject

At first nothing came to me, but as we discussed the topic in class, I thought about a rhyme I knew from grade school and started wondering who Lizzie Borden was and why she murdered her mother and father. Here's the rhyme: "Lizzie Borden took an ax and gave her mother forty whacks and when she saw what she had done, she gave her father forty-one."

Narrowing the Subject

I did a Google search of the case and came up with the following details. I want to know more about this. If Lizzie didn't do the crime, who did? If she did, why did a jury find her innocent?

On August 4, 1892, Andrew Borden, a wealthy businessman, and his second wife, Abby Borden, were found dead in their home in the small city of Fall River, Massachusetts. Andrew Borden was found on the living room couch with his face hacked to pieces. Abby Borden was found dead upstairs in the guest bedroom, face down with nineteen blows to her face and the back of her skull. The Fall River Police Department searched for suspects for nearly a week before arresting Andrew Borden's thirty-one-year-old daughter Lizzie. Lizzie was arraigned in November, and on June 5, almost a year after the murders were committed, the trial began. The trial was brief, lasting a mere fifteen days, after which the jury found Lizzie innocent of murdering her parents. While many people agreed with this decision, others, to this day, believe that she was a cold-blooded murderer. Still others believe that she did commit the crimes, but while her actions could never be said to be justified, they were certainly explicable.

Choosing Your Topic

I decided to write about whether Lizzie Borden was guilty or not. I know that's a big topic but it is the one that interests me the most.

Forming a Research Question

My first research question was "Did Lizzie Borden kill her mother and father?" However, when my professor warned the class not to ask a research question with a yes/no answer, I changed it to "What is the evidence that Lizzie killed her parents, despite the acquittal; and, if she did kill them, why did she do it?"

Formulating a Working Thesis

My first working thesis, the answer to my preliminary research question, was as follows:

> While we will never find out for certain if Lizzie did give her stepmother and father forty whacks, we can learn a lot by looking at some of the voluminous research that has been done on the case and perhaps be in a better position to make up our own minds.

We discussed these questions in groups in class and my group suggested I needed to focus the thesis more. Looking at my research question again— Why did Lizzie Borden kill her mother and father?—it is obvious that I must commit myself to an answer and not to a restatement of the problem.

> After a review of original sources and recent interpretations I argue that Lizzie was guilty.

This thesis both answers the research question and will guide me in structuring the rest of the paper. Below is the calendar I worked out. I've given myself the most time to look for sources, take notes and write the first draft. It's still daunting. There's so much to do.

My Calendar

9/15 Select topic, form research question, form working thesis
9/22 Write proposal
10/3 Find, evaluate, and retrieve sources, make source cards, prepare working bibliography
11/3 Take notes
11/17 Make an outline
12/1 Write first draft
12/8 Prepare Works Cited list
12/15 Revise paper
12/22 Hand in final draft

Week of 9/22: Writing a Research Proposal

My teacher has asked for a written proposal in the first week of the term. She wants a one-page summary of what I plan to do in the paper. Following the plan in <u>Research Papers</u>, here is my proposal:

Research Proposal on Lizzie Borden

I've been fascinated with the subject of Lizzie Borden ever since I heard my next-door neighbor recite the little poem: "Lizzie Borden took an ax and gave her mother 40 whacks. When she saw what she had done she gave her father 41." I wondered whether Lizzie were a real person and, if so, what kind of a person would kill her mother and father. It didn't occur to me to ask whether Lizzie Borden killed her mother and father until I did some preliminary research and found out that Lizzie was found innocent. How interesting. So my research question is Why did Lizzie Borden kill her mother and father?

My working thesis is that I believe Lizzie Borden did kill her mother and father. This thesis is based on my preliminary research, which shows how weak Lizzie's alibi was and how strong a reason she had for disposing of her parents. I've read some newspaper articles from the time of the murder and also an article about the case written ten years ago. I plan to see if there are some more recent articles by going to the Web and also looking on some library databases. I know there is a very good Web page about Lizzie called "Lizzie Borden Unlocked." It has a fairly current bibliography.

My audience is the class and my teacher and I hope to convince them as well as to show how Lizzie's story is tied to economics and gender and that, perhaps, not enough has changed.

Week of 9/29: Finding and Retrieving Sources
Gauging Existing Knowledge about a Subject

As Research Papers suggests, I've made a list of questions about the subject. I have found that until I do further research I know very little. Here are my questions:

Who was Lizzie Borden?
Where did she live?
Who else was in her family?
What did her father do?
What kind of home did she live in?
Did Lizzie have any friends?
When did Lizzie live?
What was she doing with an ax?
Were Lizzie's parents mean?
How old were they?

I have no answer to any of these questions.

I figured that the next step was a trip to the library. But then I remembered that I can log on to our college library from home by going to the library's homepage, just like it looks in the library. But where do I start? The homepage has a dozen icons for things I'm not sure how to use. What's EBSCOhost, for instance? I decided to start with what I know, the books. I did a keyword search for Lizzie Borden, and found that the library has five books. I wonder if that's enough? I printed out the list so I can look at them in the library. And I see <u>Research Papers</u> explains how to use EBSCOhost to find articles.

Then I talked to the reference librarian about how to get more information. He suggested that I should look at primary sources—that is, firsthand accounts or materials written during Lizzie's lifetime. The best way was to start with newspaper accounts. Unfortunately, our library doesn't subscribe to the <u>New York Times</u> online, except for current papers, so I had to use microfilm. But it paid off. There was the headline for the day of the crime, August 4, 1892: BUTCHERED IN THEIR HOME! The print is a little hard to read, but I made a copy, which made it easier to read, and now I can keep it in my folder of sources. I must admit, I spent quite a bit of time reading other parts of the paper, like news items and ads for clothes. A nice dress only cost $2.00 then. That made me realize that if Lizzie inherited even a thousand dollars, she would be very rich in her day. I think she inherited far more. Evidence of guilt?

I also looked at the <u>Encyclopedia Americana</u> to get some background. (We're encouraged not to use them as secondary sources as they are not considered "academic.") The shelves were nearby, so I found the <u>Americana</u> and looked under "B" and right away I recognized her picture. There was quite a lot on her. I skimmed it and took some notes, but since it's in the reference section, I can't take it out. The encyclopedia helped me answer several of my questions, at least the factual ones. I feel like I have a basic understanding of the case now. Progress!

Next, the librarian helped me use an online source hosted by the Fall River Historical Association. It had some really good material. Particularly useful were the pictures and lists of books.

By the time I left the library, I had a fair amount of material. I made sure I had all the dates on the newspaper copies and the page numbers so I can put them in the Works Cited later.

Week of 10/3: Finding Specialized Sources

Online and digital libraries
Museums and expert sites
What to copy down about specialized sources

My visit to the library was very successful. Today I'm going to see what I can find using the Internet. I did a Google search and a lot of sites came up, but was confused at first because many were not really what I wanted. I did find one that seems good, the LB Virtual Museum and Library at www.lizzieandrew borden.com. They have many links. (I need to remember to evaluate it: who runs it, and so on.) But what I liked was it had links on Resources and Research. The Resources led me to a really long list of all kinds of work on the case, divided by primary and secondary, and then by books, fiction and nonfiction, articles, and even music! There is so much material! How do I decide what to use? I need to think about what I want to do in my paper, I guess, and choose what can help support my point. I can't read everything! I decided to print the list. Then I can check which ones are available in my college library. I found another site that seemed good, but when I got to it, it turned out to be by a student. Even if it's a good paper, I'd rather rely on experts. I'm going to read her paper, though, just to see what she has to say.

I also found that there is a site for the Fall River Historical Society; Fall River is the town where the murder happened, and the house where the murder took place is now a bed and breakfast! I bookmarked these so I can go back if I need to. I wish I could go to Fall River; that would be a good primary source. One site lets me take a virtual tour of the murder scene. Maybe if I do this I can use the plan of the rooms to try to understand the case better.

Week of 10/10: Retrieving Sources

I took my list of sources to class, and showed it to my professor. She told me about some databases that have whole articles available online, so even if our library doesn't have the paper copies, I might be able to read them. She suggested that before I go any further, I should return to RP and read more of the sources in there on the Lizzie case. Then I should go back to *my list* of questions and sketch in the answers and revise the list by adding new questions that came from the readings. In the meantime, I can now download the sources I sent to myself from the Victorian Women's Project.

So far, I have found several kinds of sources, but it's taking a lot of time.

Our instructor told us to bring all the sources we have so far to class on Wednesday. So far I have the following:

New York Times from 1872 and 1873
Marcia Carlisle's article, "What Made Lizzie Borden Kill?"
Victoria Lincoln's book A Private Disgrace
Sullivan
Evan Hunter's novel Lizzie
Edmund Pearson's chapter on Lizzie Borden in the book Unsolved:
Classic True Murder Cases
http://curiouschapbooks.com
www.crimelibrary.com (put out by Court TV)
Lizzie Borden Virtual Museum and Library at
www.lizzieandrewborden.com
Fall River Historical Association site: www.lizzieborden.org
Ann Jones, chapter on Lizzie Borden in Women Who Kill

Need more?

Week of 10/13: Evaluating and Recording What You Have Found

Evaluating Sources

Guidelines for evaluating sources

I went through the list of Guidelines for Evaluating Print Sources in Research Papers. This is what I found: "Is the source necessary, useful, and appropriate for my research topic?"

Below are my sources so far. All of my sources meet that guideline except the novel I found based on the Lizzie Borden story, Evan Hunter's Lizzie, and the opera Fall River, since they are fiction.

New York Times from 1872 and 1873
Marcia Carlisle's article, "What Made Lizzie Borden Kill?"
Victoria Lincoln's book A Private Disgrace
Sullivan
Evan Hunter's novel Lizzie
Edmund Pearson's chapter on Lizzie Borden in the book Unsolved: Classic True Murder Cases
Ann Jones, chapter on Lizzie Borden in Women Who Kill

Need more?

Is the Source Reliable, Authoritative, and Dependable?

The article by Marcia Carlisle (see above) has a very strong point of view but I think I'll include it since I think it's important to have multiple viewpoints. The author has a good reputation; it was published in a reputable magazine (I checked with my teacher since I had never heard of it). The Times is considered "the paper of record," and thus has authority. Lincoln, Pearson and Jones have good reputations as journalists.

Is the Source Long Enough to Develop Accurate and Complex Ideas?

I have used all newspaper and magazine articles and chapters from books. I did not use any quotations from other sources.

Guidelines for Evaluating Web Sources

I looked at four Web sources, but of course looked at the following Guidelines for Evaluating an Electronic Source in Research Papers. The sites are Lizzie Borden Unlocked, www.curiouschapbooks.com; the Fall River Historical Association, www.lizzieborden.org; Crime Library, www.crimelibrary.com; and the Lizzie Borden Virtual Museum and Library, www.lizzieandrewborden.com.

Who Sponsors the Site?   The ".com" after Curious Chapbooks tells me it is a commercial site, but the site of a small press, Tulip Press. This site sells books published by the press, many of which can be read in whole or part on the site as well. The Lizzie Borden paper was available free in toto on the site and was also offered for sale. Crime Library is sponsored by Court TV, which is not at all academic. However, it does seem to have real photos of the event. The Fall River Historical Association is an organization sponsored by the town of Fall River, Mass. Finally, the Lizzie Borden Virtual Museum and Library is sponsored by a small publishing company, Pear Tree Press.

What Is the Sponsor's Point of View or Purpose?   I would think that since two of the sponsors are small presses, they want to sell their books. But they also want to convince people that they are serious. That's why they have a very full bibliography on works written on Lizzie Borden and the LB Virtual Museum hosts a journal, The Hatchet. So they aren't trying to tell us that they are the only source. The FR Historical Assoc. is a legitimate historical organization to promote and research the city. Court TV wants viewers, I guess. So gruesome pictures are appropriate.

Who Is the Author?   For Chapbooks and the Lizzie Borden Virtual Museum the author of the book and editor of the journal both have academic credentials. I couldn't tell who was authoring the other two sites but I assume a historical society is composed of historians and Court TV of TV writers, etc.

Formulating a Working Bibliography

OK. This is when I begin to choose among the works I've found, which I'm going to use to write my paper and which I'm going to throw out. I've decided not to use the Carlisle article in the paper itself. That incest stuff is really dated and you could never prove it anyway. But I want people to know about the theory so I'm going to put it in a footnote. I am NOT going to use Evan Hunter's novel Lizzie. It doesn't meet the criteria of necessary and reliable. Just long. But it's fiction. I don't think fiction is appropriate for this project. I'll probably use everything else for now.

Creating Source Cards   Research Papers tells us that if we don't have our sources recorded from the beginning, we may be in danger of not being able to find them again to do the documentation correctly. Our professor wants us all to do source cards, with information on the books, articles, and Web sites that we use and a suggestion of what the article is about. And she wants the information on a certain kind of card (5 inches by 7 inches lined) and in a certain order (Author, Title, Publisher, etc., as in Research Papers) so that we can easily use it for our Works Cited list. That's why she's making us hand in a sample card early on. Here's one I gave her that she didn't like.

<u>New York Times</u>, June 7, 1893
Page 2

Lizzie doesn't like her stepmother.

She told me to put in the author and title and where I got it. Here is my revision:

No author
<u>New York Times</u>, June 7, 1893
Page 2
"Lizzie Borden in a Faint,"
Lizzie doesn't like her stepmother.
New York Times archives online.

Reading Sources Selectively

I made a list of questions when I began this paper. So when I read my source material, I am trying to read with a focus so that I can answer these questions. Here were my questions:

1. Who was Lizzie Borden?
2. Where did she live?
3. Who else was in her family?
4. What did her father do?
5. What kind of home did she live in?
6. Did Lizzie have any friends?
7. When did Lizzie live?
8. What was she doing with an ax?
9. Were Lizzie's parents mean?
10. How old were they?

Here's where I found the answers. Nos. 1–5, 7, and 10 were background questions. I didn't feel I had to document where I found the information, since it's factual. Nearly all of my sources gave this information, but since some of the information varied, I used what was most recent (e.g., Lizzie was 32, not 31).

The other questions were more subjective and needed documentation. The question on whether Lizzie had any friends, for example, was unanswered as of yet. I had no documentation for it and realized I need it. For question #9, however, I did have several sources. The <u>Times</u> talks about it, as do Lincoln and Carlisle.

It's an important point and will come up later when I discuss motivation for the crime, so I'm happy I have a lot of documentation there.

I have to admit that since these books and articles were fascinating, I got a little involved and forgot for a while what I was looking for. I loved especially reading firsthand accounts from over 100 years ago reported in the <u>Times</u> about how everyone looked and their exact words. I spent more time than I should have but then I looked at my calendar and realized I was not on track so I checked my list of questions and that was when I began reading more selectively.

Taking Notes on My Research Question

Now that I have a working thesis I need more research questions. When I made the first list I didn't really know what I needed to know. Now that I've done some preliminary research and think I have a thesis, I know I need to find more answers. So, following the instructions in <u>Research Papers</u>, I generated the following eleven questions:

1. Why did they suspect and indict Lizzie?
2. What did the crime scene look like?
3. What are the exact details of the crime and were any of these details especially important in the case?
4. What were the other members of Lizzie's family like socially?
5. How important an issue was money—to Lizzie, to the others?
6. How important was social class?
7. How did the people in her family feel about one another?
8. Were there any other suspects?
9. Why do I think she did it?
10. Why was she acquitted?
11. Why is the world still interested in the case?

Now that I have a lot of—I hope not too many—questions, I can start reading and taking notes. But first I had to decide how I will take notes. The book suggests several different ways: note cards, a research journal, electronic notes, and photocopies. Right away I'm eliminating photocopies as the "sole" means of taking notes because it isn't a way of taking notes. You still have to take notes on your photocopies and I can email electronic sources to myself. I still want to photocopy the most important articles, and pages from books, because I know from previous papers that I might need more information and it will be a lot easier to have the photocopies right there than to have to go back to the library and get the sources again. (But I will make Source Cards for all of them.) I decided to try note cards, since it looked like a good way of organizing my paper after I finished taking all my notes. I actually did a few cards before I realized that I would have too many note cards to keep them straight. I'll continue to use note cards for my sources, but not for my notes. I never even considered doing electronic notes. I don't type quickly enough and I love the idea of a research journal. (In fact, I've been doing a research journal without calling it that.) I like to do journals. It helps me think through my ideas. I planned to get a really pretty book, something that actually looks like a journal, hoping it would inspire me. Then my teacher reminded me that if I wanted to use the notes to help me organize, I would want a journal in which I could easily tear out the pages, either one with serrated pages or a loose leaf. I'm using a loose leaf so I can include my earlier journal entries. That was easy to find.

Avoiding Plagiarism

Today our professor gave us a very serious lecture about plagiarism and told us that we would fail the paper if we "committed" this crime. I must say, at first I couldn't understand why she was making such a fuss. What is the big deal about using a few words or even a paragraph from another published work? But then she explained how serious many people think plagiarism is and gave examples of people (some well known) who had, she used the word "stolen" other people's words, taken credit for them, that is, by not clearly telling the reader of the text who had written these words. She also showed us how easy it is to plagiarize without meaning to and that many students don't mean to do it but are just sloppy and don't take their notes carefully and thus don't even realize they are using someone else's words. The important thing, from what I can tell, is copying down all the bibliographic details from every source I think I may use AND making certain to document my paraphrases and summaries AND to quote accurately.

Paraphrases   We practiced paraphrasing today in class. It's a lot harder than I thought. We each had to pick a paragraph from a document that we wanted to use and put it into our own words. I chose the following sentences from the New York Times, August 14, 1892.

> "Borden was a rich and pious skinflint aged seventy-six years, whose probity was equal to his thrift. He had not led a public life, he had no known enemy who, it could be conjectured, would go to the extent of killing him, much less his wife, and when the mutilated bodies of the couple were discovered, in their own house, shortly before noon on Aug. 4, the police and the public were utterly at a loss for motive, and in the intense excitement that overwhelmed the community they turned to one another in helpless astonishment and horror."

My first try was not very good; it was returned by my professor with certain words in boldface, meaning that they were plagiarized.

> Lizzie's father was a very rich, upright, and **pious** citizen of the town but a real **skinflint**. Since he hadn't **led a public life** there were **no known enemies** that might have wanted to kill him, so when the cut up bodies of him and his wife **were discovered in their** home on Aug. 4, everyone in the town was upset and no one could figure out why anyone would want to murder them.

I didn't realize that even simple words like "pious," "skinflint," and "public life" had to be quoted and documented.

Here's my revision:

> Lizzie's father was a prosperous, "upright" citizen of Fall River, but was considered a "skinflint." He didn't hold public office and, thus, no one was known to have wanted to kill him. The discovery of the bodies in their home on Aug. 4 upset everyone in town for the hideous damage to the bodies but also because they were mystified as to the murderer.

This was better, she said, but I have to work on not following the order of ideas in the original and, literally, making the work my own.

Summarizing   According to <u>Research Papers</u>, summarizing is different from paraphrasing in that a summary is an outline of a written text without the details. Sometimes we use summaries to move an argument along. Again I used the above sentences from the <u>New York Times</u> to practice.

> Andrew Borden was a wealthy and prominent member of Fall River society but people thought he was a "skinflint." He didn't hold public office so no suspects were apparent. His wife was killed also.

My professor faulted this summary for omitting the detail of his miserliness, an important detail in the argument against Lizzie that I want to make in the paper. Also, there are details I can conflate. Here's my revision:

> Andrew Borden, a wealthy and prominent (albeit a "skinflint") citizen of Fall River, Mass., and his wife Abby, were brutally murdered. No suspects were immediately apparent.

This works and in only two sentences!

Quoting　In practicing paraphrases and summaries I understand that there are certain words that really cannot and should not be put into other words. The word "skinflint" is a really good example because its use by the <u>Times</u> is "authoritative." We are asked to believe that after journalistic research at the time of the event this is the conclusion the reporter came to. One of my classmates suggested I put an explanation of the word in brackets since she, at least, didn't know what the word meant. Thus I might say, Lizzie's father was a prosperous, upright citizen of Fall River, but was considered a "skinflint" [a miser]. Perhaps I should also have quoted the word "mutilated" as being somewhat terminological. It's certainly more precise than the words I used in my paraphrase, "hideous damage."

We also talked about using the ellipsis properly. Some students use quotations that are much too long. A paper shouldn't be all quotations; it should mainly be my argument. The trick in using the ellipsis, however, is not to change the meaning of the quotation. Here's my first attempt:

ORIGINAL: "Borden was a rich and pious skinflint aged seventy-six years, whose probity was equal to his thrift. He had not led a public life, he had no known enemy who, it could be conjectured, would go to the extent of killing him, much less his wife, and when the mutilated bodies of the couple were discovered, in their own house, shortly before noon on Aug. 4, the police and the public were utterly at a loss for motive, and in the intense excitement that overwhelmed the community they turned to one another in helpless astonishment and horror."

WITH ELLIPSIS: "Borden was a rich and pious skinflint aged seventy-six. . . . He had not led a public life, he had no known enemy. . . . When the mutilated bodies of the couple were discovered, in their own house . . . the police and the public were utterly at a loss for motive."

It can be argued that I don't need the part about his "public life" and do need the part about how upset the community is, but it seems to me that's apparent by what is already in the quote about how surprised they were by the event.

Week of 11/17: Organizing and Outlining Research Material

Understanding Outlines

I'm trying to learn how to outline. I haven't done it with other papers, because they've been shorter and seemed more manageable and I could keep them in my head as I went along. But there is so much detail in this paper, and the documentation, and it's longer, so I think it would be a good idea to do an outline.

First, I'm outlining what I'm reading (a running outline, it's called) so I can keep track of the authors' main ideas; I want to list the important events of the case as I read the articles in the newspapers:

August 1892: The murders take place
August 1892: First round of testimony at the inquest
September 1892: LB indicted and sent to prison
June 6, 1893: The trial begins
June 21, 1893: LB acquitted

This helps. But it's not an outline of my paper so that I know which material supports the thesis, and where quotes belong. Maybe I'll begin with something short and simple, like listing the main ideas. Once I've done more reading and am ready to start writing a draft, I can begin a formal outline, like they have in RP. I'll need to go back to my thesis, look at all the source material, and begin to shape the argument, or plan. Since I want to make a case that Lizzie Borden is guilty, I have to decide what to select from the sources that will best support my position. My outline can help me think through why I believe Lizzie is guilty:

One Possible Outline

Lizzie's main motives

I. Hate: Lizzie hated her stepmother and missed her natural mother

II. Greed: Lizzie felt her father did not give her enough money, even though he was rich

III. Possible incest: Lizzie may have been an incest victim and wanted revenge on her father

IV. Social position: Lizzie had no training for a job, and needed to secure her future if she was to maintain her position in Fall River as a social superior

Eventually, I can take my notes and line them up with the points in this outline so I know where I am going to use each of the quotes or theories I found in my reading. I can pencil in a corresponding number from the outline on each note to keep track of where I am going to use each source in the paper. Now I see what my instructor meant when she urged us to use individual notes or cards: it's much easier to get the draft organized this way.

I guess I could also arrange the essay by motives, reasons for the crime, breaking down why the testimony was not enough to convict her: her father's status, Lizzie's role as a woman along with Victorian attitudes toward women and lack of women on the jury; inability of the police to present solid evidence. As I write and think, I can go back to the outline and add subheadings under each Roman numeral to flesh out the main point as I did here:

III. Incest as a possible motive

    A. Introduce Carlisle's article suggesting father-daughter incest motivated the crime

    B. Find a succinct quote from the article as evidence

    C. Analyze (or create "sandwich") linking quote to my thesis about Lizzie's guilt

    D. Evaluate whether or not I think incest is a motive

In the essay, this outline led to the following paragraph (which wound up in a footnote):

    Marcia Carlisle has a very different thesis, which she develops in her article "What Made Lizzie Borden Kill?" in the July/August 1992 <u>American Heritage Magazine</u>. She believes that Lizzie may have killed her parents to get revenge for sexual abuse. Carlisle contends that Lizzie may have recovered her memory of the abuse shortly before she killed him. Why both of them? Carlisle says: "Perhaps because her stepmother had known about the incest and had been unable to stop it, or worse had blamed Lizzie for it" (Carlisle 72). It is impossible to know if this is true or not, but Carlisle says there were many telltale signs of incest.

In thinking about how I am going to shape all of this into a coherent paper I decided that since many of my readers (my classmates) will not know much about the Borden case, I think it might be necessary to provide a long introductory section that presents the "facts" of the case, based primarily on the newspaper accounts of 1892, and later sources, and then to present my thesis that Lizzie is guilty with the reasons why I have come to believe this. So, adding background, my outline for the essay now looks like this:

Outline

Working thesis: Lizzie Borden killed her mother and father.

    I. The Bordens didn't have many friends.

        A. Mr. Borden "had not led a public life."

        B. Mrs. Borden was obese and a semi-recluse.

        C. Lizzie was the only one who had some social life.

II. Mr. Borden was tight with money.

    A. He moved the family to a poor neighborhood.

    B. Lizzie complained she didn't get enough spending money.

    C. Lizzie and Emma were upset when Andrew bought a house for their step-mother's sister.

III. The family wasn't close.

    A. They lived in a literally "divided" house.

    B. They rarely ate together.

    C. They wouldn't call Abby "Mother."

IV. Lizzie's alibi was inconsistent.

    A. She gave the police several different alibis.

    B. One alibi had her eating pears in a 90 degree loft.

    C. She said at two different times that she was and was not too nauseated to eat breakfast.

V. The police had serious questions about several different matters.

    A. Lizzie burned the dress she was wearing that morning.

    B. Her maid said she had gone up to her parents' side of the house, even though she and her sister never went there.

    C. No one else could have entered the house.

    D. Lizzie purchased a poison shortly before the murders.

VI. Lizzie's case falls apart

    A. The loft

    B. Her stepmother's visit to a sick friend

    C. The hatchet is found.

VII. Why Lizzie wanted to kill her parents.

    A. Greed

    B. Hatred

    C. Incest

VIII. Why Lizzie was acquitted.

    A. Nineteenth-century attitudes toward women

    B. Lizzie's conflicting testimony was deemed inadmissible.

    C. Shoddy police work

    D. Better defense

IX. Lizzie Borden today

    A. Parallel cases

    B. Books, films, etc.

Now I need to make sure the thesis in paragraph 1 is supported in the essay.

Week of 12/1: Writing the Paper

Before I Write

I'm sure there are some people out there who anticipate a writing project with all the joy with which they anticipate an evening out with their friends. I, however, would much rather be doing anything else—talking on the phone, working out at the gym, even doing laundry. This negativity evaporates after I get into the paper, but beginning is so hard I have to give myself a few days just to work off the tension. The book recommends certain actions to make the writing process easier, and I plan to try them.

My Writing Space and Tools   I'm going to write my paper in the library. There are some quiet areas with Ethernet accessibility where we can use our laptops. I will not tell anyone where I am! One of my roommates doesn't have a computer and wants to handwrite his paper so he's decided to write in the apartment, after our other two roommates have gone out. We talked it over with them and we all agreed to stay out of the living room until he finishes a first draft. One of my classmates who doesn't have a computer is using the computers available in the school library. There's a real advantage to using a computer. First of all, many of the original sources are online and can be found or checked easily. Also, the computer has software which will do footnotes, bibliographies, even a works cited and will check for spelling and grammar (although our teacher tells us we must double check as the grammar program is often wrong and the spelling program can't check for homophones—"to" and "too" will both be correct although only one is correct in context). The computer will number pages, put in running heads, and even check for repetition. Our professor insists that we hand in a typed copy and I find it much better to get my first draft on computer, so that I can make changes more easily, than to have to copy it from a handwritten draft.

Freewriting   Our professor suggested we read through our notes and "freewrite" before we start. This will help to get us started—it will produce writing—and will help us to see what our research has uncovered. Here is the freewriting I produced:

> There seems to be a gap between Lizzie as we see her today, from a distance, and how they saw her and the case then. Frankly I can't see why they ever acquitted her. It seems so obvious that she's a cold-blooded killer and that should have been obvious to the jury. It will be my job to get over my prejudice and to argue the case as if there is another point of view. That means I need to lay out the background really carefully and give a lot of details about the case. I think I have a lot of details but, I don't know, I'm worried. Maybe I'm using too much from the <u>Times</u>, but the stuff is so good. I think my outline will keep me in shape.

Arranging Notes Here is my working outline. The book tells me to try to arrange my notes according to the major and minor headings. Here's where using note cards and note sheets comes in handy. Thankfully, our professor had us practice sorting the notes in class to make sure we understood how to arrange them according to our outline. I chose the paragraph I used to practice paraphrasing, etc., since it's already saved on my disk and all I have to do is copy and paste it. Here it is again:

> "Borden was a rich and pious skinflint aged seventy-six years, whose probity was equal to his thrift. He had not led a public life, he had no known enemy who, it could be conjectured, would go to the extent of killing him, much less his wife, and when the mutilated bodies of the couple were discovered, in their own house, shortly before noon on Aug. 4, the police and the public were utterly at a loss for motive, and in the intense excitement that overwhelmed the community they turned to one another in helpless astonishment and horror."

Obviously part of it belongs in II. Mr. Borden was tight with money. But part of it belongs in IA. The Bordens did not have many friends. Mr. Borden "had not led a public life."

My notes will look as follows:

> IA, public life
> <u>New York Times</u>, "Story of a Great Crime," p. 8
>
> "He had not led a public life, he had no known enemy who, it could be conjectured, would go to the extent of killing him, much less his wife, and when the mutilated bodies of the couple were discovered, in their own house, shortly before noon on Aug. 4, the police and the public were utterly at a loss for motive, and in the intense excitement that overwhelmed the community they turned to one another in helpless astonishment and horror."

II, "skinflint"
<u>New York Times</u>, "Story of a Great Crime," p. 8

"Borden was a rich and pious skinflint aged seventy-six years, whose probity was equal to his thrift."

Reviewing Your Source Material for Quantity   After I laid out all my notes I found that I didn't have enough about the poisoning (VD) or about the hatchet (VIC or VIIIC).

Reviewing Sources to See That They Are Appropriate   I also had some great sources that didn't support my argument. These I will, regretfully, save for a future project. Here's an example:

<u>New York Times</u>, 11/13/1892, p.15

"Miss Borden appears to be suffering no inconvenience and shows no anxiety respecting the Grand Jury hearing. She is outwardly the same cool and composed woman who entered Taunton Jail so many weeks ago. During the day, when she desires, she takes exercise in the corridors of the women's apartment, and she spends much of her time in the hospital room above, where Mrs. Wright has given her two windows of flowers to look after. She is very fond of them, and in their care appears for the time to forget that she is a prisoner. Her health continues good."

While this is really interesting, it does not fit into my outline.

Evaluating Quotations   It's so tempting to use a whole quotation but I know I should cut most of them down by paraphrasing or summarizing. Here's an example of what I originally had:

Marcia Carlisle wrote:

"What drove Lizzie to murder, according to the prosecution, must have been greed. The evidence for this assumption was a previous family squabble that became public at the trial. In 1887 Andrew, normally frugal to a fault, had bought Abby a house for her sister to live in. Both Emma and Lizzie were upset at what they saw as favoritism; Lizzie's anger was later interpreted as selfishness. But arguments about property and money are often about position in family structure as well. This disagreement may even have triggered memories of other moments when Mr. Borden's affections were sought by both Mrs. Borden and Lizzie."

Obviously I don't need all that. If I am using this quotation to support the idea that Lizzie murdered her parents because of greed, I can eliminate a number of the sentences by paraphrasing and summarizing them. Here's what I did:

Marcia Carlisle summarized the prosecution's case in one word, "greed" on Lizzie's part. Andrew had purchased a house for Abby's sister and the sisters were jealous. "Both Emma and Lizzie were upset at what they saw as favoritism; Lizzie's anger was later interpreted as selfishness."

I eliminated the rest of the argument because it's about the incest argument and I don't think I'm going to use it in the paper. I only took two sentences from the original quotation because these sentences were Carlisle's opinion while the first two sentences were summaries of factual information.

Incorporating Source Material into Paragraphs: Making a Sandwich
This part sounds more "fun" than it is. A sandwich, great, I'd love to take a sandwich break. Instead, it's a way of making quotations fit smoothly into my argument. My professor told me that the above paragraph from Carlisle was a good example of a sandwich. All I had to do was add the other slice of bread. So I did. The professor asked us to show how our sample paragraphs conform to the model. Here are the sentences in my paragraph:

TOPIC SENTENCE (I'll put this in when I've gotten further along in the writing of the paper.)
INTRODUCTION TO THE SOURCE (This is the top slice of bread in the sandwich; notice that I've used the word "summarized" as my introductory word): Marcia Carlisle summarized the prosecution's case in one word, "greed" on Lizzie's part. Andrew had purchased a house for Abby's sister, and the sisters were jealous.

DIRECT QUOTATION OR PARAPHRASE (This is the meat in the sandwich): "Both Emma and Lizzie were upset at what they saw as favoritism; Lizzie's anger was later interpreted as selfishness." COMMENTARY ON THE SOURCE (This is the bottom slice of bread in the sandwich): She felt that all of her father's money should go to her. CITATION: (71).

Writing Out Your Paper

Writing the Introduction   OK. This is it. I have to begin the paper. I'm going to try to write a really good introduction because I know if I do the rest of my paper will follow more easily. Anyway, I know that whoever reads it will respond to my paper better if I make them interested in my topic. Here is my first try:

> Everyone has heard the children's rhyme: "Lizzie Borden took an ax and gave her mother forty whacks and when she saw what she had done she gave her father forty-one." Did you ever wonder what the real story is, whether there was a Lizzie Borden and if she did give her parents 40 and 41 whacks successively? Would it surprise you that there was a Lizzie and she was tried for murder and found innocent? While many people agreed with this decision, others, to this day, believe that she was a cold-blooded murderer. Still others believe that while she did commit the crimes, and her actions could never be said to be justified, they were certainly explicable. A look at some of the voluminous research that has been done on the case makes a convincing argument that Lizzie was guilty.

I showed this to my research group and they thought it was good but could be more dramatic. After all, it was a very bloody crime. Here's my second try:

> On August 4, 1892, Andrew Borden, a wealthy businessman, and his second wife, Abby Borden, were found dead in their home in the small city of Fall River, Massachusetts. Andrew Borden was lying on the living room couch with his face hacked to pieces. Abby Borden was upstairs in the guest bedroom, face down with nineteen blows to her face and the back of her skull. The Fall River Police Department searched for suspects for nearly a week before arresting Andrew Borden's thirty-one-year-old daughter Lizzie. Lizzie was arraigned in November, and on June 5, almost a year after the murders were committed, the trial began. The trial was brief, lasting a mere fifteen days, after which the jury found Lizzie innocent of murdering her parents. While many people agreed with this decision, others, to this day, believe that she was a cold-blooded murderer. Still others believe that while she did commit

> the crimes, and her actions could never be said to be justified, they were certainly explicable. For a look at some of the voluminous research that has been done on the case makes a convincing argument that Lizzie was guilty.

I will still use the rhyme, but at the very beginning of the essay.

Reexamining Your Working Thesis   Now I'm ready to begin writing. But my professor urged us to look at our working thesis first and make sure it works now that we've done our research. This is my working thesis:

> While many people agreed with this decision, others, to this day, believe that she was a cold-blooded murderer. Still others believe that while she did commit the crimes, and her actions could never be said to be justified, they were certainly explicable. For a look at some of the voluminous research that has been done on the case makes a convincing argument that Lizzie was guilty.

Looking at it again, it really doesn't reflect my research. Most of the research shows that she was probably guilty. I need to emphasize that point. Here's my revision:

> While many people agreed with this decision, others believe that while she did commit the crimes, and her actions could never be said to be justified, they were certainly explicable. Still, most, to this day, believe that she was a cold-blooded murderer; and a look at some of the voluminous research that has been done on the case makes a convincing argument that Lizzie was guilty.

Writing the First Draft   I can't believe I'm writing. Now all I have to do is follow my outline. Ha! I have two other papers due next week, but they don't involve any research, just my opinions. The important thing to do is to keep on track and to ask my professor questions when I run into problems.

Writing the Conclusion   Since the assignment was to put the topic into a modern context, I'm going to finish up by exploring what people think today. Here's what I came up with:

> Even today, the Lizzie Borden murder case excites interest and debate. New books are published frequently, the house in Fall River is a tourist attraction, and the infamous rhyme appears on Borden Web sites and other popular culture resources. The particularly gruesome nature of the murders grabbed the public's attention in 1892 when the idea that a white, middle-class woman

could butcher her parents seemed unthinkable. It's a wonder that with crime shows and serial killers crowding each other for space on television and in the movies, the Borden case remains fascinating, perhaps because the crimes of matricide and patricide still stir our blood. Maybe we have all, at one time or another, wished for the death of a parent. Or maybe we simply want a final answer, a convincing solution to an unsolved case.

I have listened to the book's advice and did not start a new subject.

Reviewing for Plagiarism   Our professor has again asked us to assure her that we have checked for plagiarism. I've reviewed my notes and checked to make certain I documented both quotations AND paraphrases AND summaries. And that I've quoted correctly and accurately. But she wants us to use the computer to check. She says our library owns Turnitin.com and we can submit our papers and make sure we haven't messed up by mistake. First, though, she said we can do a Google search and submit any phrases or sentences we're unsure of.

Documenting Your Sources Using MLA   So now I'm getting close to the end. I have my draft revised, and I have to finish the last step: the Works Cited list (since I'm using MLA documentation). The hard thing about it is that it follows a formula and you have to be really precise, something like doing an e-mail or a Web address. I don't tend to be very precise—I miss small details—so I'm going to have to be really careful and proofread a lot. Mostly I used the articles from the newspaper, the New York Times, and then I used books. I guess I can also list some Web sites I browsed; I think I'll ask my instructor whether I should do this.

First I looked at the research paper called "Child Labor" in the book as a model. I looked at the Works Cited list, and then I flipped to the section that shows models. If I want to include a book in my Works Cited, I look for the section on books. But since not all books are the same, I next have to match the book I have with the various models and find the ones that are closest to my sources. I guess I'm lucky, because my sources in this area are books with only one author. So I studied how the example was broken down, and then I made my first try:

My book was by Ann Jones; she's the author: Jones, Ann.
Next is the title of the book, which gets underlined: Women Who Kill.
The city where the book was published (not the state or the country) is Boston.
The publisher was Beacon Press.
The book was published in 1996.

So all I have to do is line these items up in the order they appear in the model and add the punctuation:

> Jones, Ann. <u>Women Who Kill</u>. Boston: Beacon Press, 1996.

If I do the same for all my book sources, I'll put them in alphabetical order, and then I'll have that part of the list. It's not hard, but it just has to be accurate. If the entry is incorrect, and my instructor or another reader needed to find and read one of the sources I used, they wouldn't be able to, unless I do it really accurately. They might even think I was plagiarizing because they won't find the source.

Since they're pretty easy to do, I did all the books first and then went back and added in the other sources. So far my Works Cited list looks like this:

> Jones, Ann. <u>Women Who Kill</u>. Boston: Beacon Press, 1996.
> Lincoln, Victoria. <u>A Private Disgrace: Lizzie Borden by Daylight</u>.
>   New York: Putnam, 1967.
> Sullivan, Robert. <u>Goodbye Lizzie Borden</u>. New York: Penguin, 1989.

Next is trickier: I read the article by Marcia Carlisle in <u>Research Papers</u> that begins on page 6, but then I decided to go to the original article to see if there were any pictures or other materials. So I cited the pages not from the textbook but from the original:

> Carlisle, Marcia R. "What Made Lizzie Borden Kill?" <u>American Heritage</u> July/August 1992.

Today I realized I forgot to copy the page numbers and thought I would have to go all the way back to the library. Then I realized that I could do a search on the library's database and see if the article is listed. Then I'd have the right pages.

I could have used the version of the article that's in <u>Research Papers</u>, and cite the pages there, but then I would have had to go back to the in-text citations and fix them so that they match the pages in the book. If I did that, then I have to change the citation, since it is a source quoted in another source. Now I know why our instructor kept reminding us to be really careful. If I have to use the version in <u>Research Papers</u>, my citation in the essay becomes:

> (qtd. in Arkin and Macheski 6).

Then I'd have to add the textbook to my Works Cited, using the model for a book with two authors:

> Arkin, Marian, and Cecilia Macheski. <u>Research Papers: A Guide and Workbook</u>. 2nd ed. Boston: Houghton Mifflin, 2006.

This way, a reader could locate the textbook and find the article on page 6. But I'd rather cite the original source. It doesn't look "academic" to cite the textbook.

In class, we each went to the board and wrote out one of our entries so everyone could look at it and we could discuss any errors. Homework was to bring in two different kinds of Works Cited entries to our research group for criticism. I brought in the following two citations:

> Victoria Lincoln. <u>A Private Disgrace: Lizzie Borden by Daylight</u>. Putnam, 1967.
> Carlisle, Marcia R. "What made Lizzie Borden Kill?" <u>American Heritage</u> July/August 1992: 66–72.

Jeff reminded me that I have to reverse Victoria Lincoln's name so that the last name is first. I had it right before, but I messed it up when I typed it. Also Maureen noticed that I forgot the city where the book was published and that I need to capitalize the word "Made" because it's in a title and isn't an article or preposition. I knew that. Just bad proofing. This is going to be slow going.

Now I can do the newspaper articles, which are my primary sources. I noticed that how I cite these depends on whether I got them from microfilm, or from the newspaper's online archive. I'm a little confused because there is no author on these, but they are all from the <u>New York Times</u> so once I figure one out, the rest should be easy.

The headline is "Story of a Great Crime." It was on page 8 of the paper that I read on microfilm. Since there is no author, I guess I begin with the headline as title but I'm not sure about the punctuation, since I don't have the book handy.

> Story of a Great Crime. The New York Times August 14, 1892, p. 8.

I showed this to Tracy who wrote back and told me that I had a mistake; in fact, a few. She reminded me that the title of the article has to be in quotation marks, and the newspaper gets underlined. She said drop "the" from the name of the paper.

> "Story of a Great Crime." <u>New York Times</u> August 14, 1892, p.8.

Maureen noticed that the date has to be done like they do in Europe: 14 August 1892, 8. I don't need the "p." So now I have a model for the microfilm versions of the paper:

> "Story of a Great Crime." <u>New York Times</u> 14 August 1892, 8.

I can do the rest quickly since I have the pattern. I need to alphabetize the list, and remember not to alphabetize by "The" or "A" since they are articles.

> "Bridget Sullivan a Witness." <u>New York Times</u> 8 June 1893, 8.
> "Butchered in Their Home." <u>New York Times</u> 5 Aug. 1892, 2.
> "The Fall River Mystery." <u>New York Times</u> 7 Aug. 1892, 1.
> "Lizzie Borden in a Faint." <u>New York Times</u> 7 June 1893, 2.
> "Lizzie Borden's Hearing." <u>New York Times</u> 26 Aug. 1892, 1.
> "Lizzie Borden's Triumphs." <u>New York Times</u> 19 June 1893, 1.
> "Story of a Great Crime." <u>New York Times</u> 14 Aug. 1892, p.8.
> "Will It Remain a Mystery." <u>New York Times</u> 17 June 1893, 4.

Not exactly exciting, but it's done. Now I need to go back to the essay and be sure the in-text citations are all correct. I'm not sure if I use the date or the title, but it would seem to make sense if I use both ("Butchered" 2) according to the example in the "Child Labor" paper in the book, since he uses the author's name and the page. Since I have no author, I have to do the citation according to what is first in the entry, so a reader can find it. I better remember to ask in class tomorrow.

In the meantime, I can go ahead and cut and paste my Works Cited list. I forgot I have to add in the other sources alphabetically.

> "Bridget Sullivan a Witness." <u>New York Times</u> 8 June 1893, 8.
> "Butchered in Their Home." <u>New York Times</u> 5 Aug. 1892, 2.
> "The Fall River Mystery." <u>New York Times</u> 7 Aug. 1892, 1.
> Jones, Ann. <u>Women Who Kill</u>. Boston: Beacon Press, 1996.
> Lincoln, Victoria. <u>A Private Disgrace: Lizzie Borden by Daylight</u>.
>   New York: Putnam, 1967.
> "Lizzie Borden in a Faint." <u>New York Times</u> 7 June 1893, 2.
> "Lizzie Borden's Hearing." <u>New York Times</u> 26 Aug. 1892, 1.
> "Lizzie Borden's Triumphs." <u>New York Times</u> 19 June 1893, 1.
> Sullivan, Robert. <u>Goodbye Lizzie Borden</u>. New York: Penguin, 1989.
> "Story of a Great Crime." <u>New York Times</u> 14 Aug. 1892, 8.
> "Will It Remain a Mystery." <u>New York Times</u> 17 June 1893, 4.

I wonder if I should include some pictures? I could get these from the Web sites. How do I cite those?

Week of 12/15: Preparing and Proofreading the Final Draft

Formatting the Final Manuscript

Well, I'm done but not quite. I've finished all the researching and writing and now it's time to put it all together in the correct format. This means it has to look neat and professional, and all of the sources have to be identified using the MLA documentation style. My professor told us to follow Chapter 9 in Research Papers: "Just follow it carefully," she said. "This is not the time to be creative! Think of it like using an e-mail address: one letter wrong, and the mail doesn't go through."

I'm going to select 12-point font in Times New Roman (it's what I always use), set the format for double-spacing, select for page numbers in the upper-right-hand corner. I'm including my last name with the page number as a header: Davis 4. Look at the title page (p. 33) to see the results.

I will save all of my notes and photocopies and downloaded source materials until after the paper is graded. This way, if the instructor has questions, I can pull out the sources and show her where I got my quotes and facts from. Then I'll review all items under "Research Mechanics," checking that I used quotation marks correctly and did the underlining right. Did I spell all the names right? Did I underline book titles? There's still a lot to do.

Working in Groups to Prepare the Final Draft

My instructor arranged the class into work groups of four students. We each had to bring four copies of our draft, one copy for everyone in the group. We gave each other copies of the papers, and as group members read, we pointed out problems with organization and clarity if we noticed any on the paper. (It's funny how much easier this is to do on someone else's paper than on your own!) Next, we returned the drafts to the writers so they could have all the comments.

How Much Research Is There—Too Little, Enough, Too Much? How Do You Know? Then, with a highlighter we each went through our essays and highlighted all the quoted material. It looks like about 20 to 30 percent is highlighted in mine; not bad. Jeff had about 60 percent, which meant, we thought, that he had too much. Over half the paper was not his in own words. We called over the instructor, and she agreed with our assessment of Jeff's paper. She explained that it was not a good strategy to have too much quotation and too little analysis or argument, since the paper would only be a cut-and-paste job and not very original.

Check for Research Mechanics Using the section in the book on MLA documentation we went over the Works Cited list to be sure every entry followed EXACTLY the model for that kind of source. We discussed when to underline, when to use quotation marks, when to capitalize, which abbreviations are used and which are not. In one paper with foreign language sources we checked accent marks, and whether the citations were complete if the paper included statistics, graphics, photographs or artwork taken from a source like a government document or a Web site. I was thinking of including a few photos of the Borden family and maybe of the murder scene, so I made sure to pay attention to this part. It seemed easiest to just have the book opened to the MLA section and find the model for the source I was using, like a book with one author, and then to put my entry right under it and check that they match—author last name first with a comma in between and a period at the end, book title underlined with the caps in the right place, etc. At first it was pretty tedious, but eventually I started to see that these things are like a code. You just have to copy exactly. If you do it wrong, the reader won't know whether the source is a book or a poem, or whatever.

Week of 12/17: Using Technology to Present Your Research

The professor had each of us do a PowerPoint presentation of our papers based on our outlines. Mine went very well since I jazzed it up with lurid details and pictures.

Week of 12/18: Reviewing for Style

Audience and Purpose

Since my audience is primarily my classmates and the teacher, I have to think about the way I write the paper with them in mind. I am not writing for specialists, as I would be if I were a forensic pathologist who was preparing a scientific report on Lizzie's DNA, say. Still, I don't think that means I can use slang. But I also have to be careful not to borrow too much jargon from the sources, like legal terms I wouldn't be familiar with myself. If they are really necessary, then I have to define them. My purpose is to introduce readers to the case, to show why it has remained unsolved and fascinating, and mainly to present my case for Lizzie's guilt. I can't be too casual since the instructor is a reader, too, and says I should aim for the educated, general reader.

Voice and Tone

This is MY paper, so it has to sound like ME, but a more formal me. My job is to be informative, polite, well-prepared, like at a job interview. The best thing I can do is get my group to read it, and make sure I sound like I should. Our instructor asked us to post our papers to one person in our research group on our Blackboard discussion board. This group member will be responsible for suggesting final areas we may want to change. I exchanged papers with Tony Diaz, who wrote on Joe Hill. It was a fascinating paper, very well written. But he never mentioned the song. We used to sing it in camp all the time. When I mentioned it to him, he decided to use it to preface his paper. He liked my paper too, but said I sometimes repeated words and phrases too much. Luckily I have a software program that checks for repetition. I just have never used it. It made this aspect of the revision much easier.

Revising the Paper

Once I get the paper all together, and I've critiqued it with my group in class and made whatever changes seem needed, I can do a final revision. This means I have to check the content and the form. For content, I can compare the paper to the outline, and see if all the paragraphs are where they belong. The thesis—my main idea that Lizzie is guilty—has to be supported all the way through. Is it convincing? I need to check that my sources are all used correctly, that the Works Cited page has all the sources I used, and that the sources are in correct MLA form.

Week of 12/20: Proofreading the Final Version

At last—I'm nearly done! And I'm two days ahead of schedule. This is great, because I think I need to just get away from the thing for a day and get some distance.

Now I can come back and proofread really carefully for all the little stuff—the spelling, the punctuation, run-on sentences. I'm going to use the spell-check program in my computer. I know I can't rely on it since it often tells me words are correct that aren't (homophones), but it's a start. I'll use the grammar program too even though I know it's very limited and not very reliable. It's a starting point! Then I'm going to try what the book suggests and read it backward, and with a piece of paper so I can concentrate line by line. After all this work, I don't want the paper to have typos.

Week of 12/22

Done! It's ready to turn in. I'm going to prepare the title page and print the whole thing out. Farewell, Lizzie!

Choosing a Subject and Narrowing to a Topic

In this chapter, you will explore some of the first steps a writer takes in conducting research. After completing this chapter, you should have a research topic, a tentative thesis, and a research proposal, and you should be ready to head for the library to begin preliminary research on your own topic.

Choosing a Subject

Generally, the subject is a broad area about which the researcher begins to ask questions. If you consider Morocco, a fascinating country in North Africa, as a possible subject because you are planning a trip there, you might want to investigate the best time to travel, the currency rates in relation to the U.S. dollar, the availability of "study abroad" opportunities at local colleges, or the size and quality of beach resorts. Another researcher running an interior design business might need to know about import and export regulations on carpets. He would probably select different books from those you were reading, and he might continue his search in the areas of business and economics after a while. A third researcher might be working on an essay about the role of Morocco in World War I. A quick survey of the travel guides would fail to provide the appropriate books for her search, so she might then look at books on history. All these researchers share the same subject, Morocco. Each researcher, however, is moving toward a different topic within that subject.

Getting Ideas about a Subject

There are many techniques you can use to help you begin your preliminary exploration of a research subject. Going to a library or bookstore and wandering among the shelves will give you a quick overview of what kinds of subjects are available. Another method available to computer users is to visit the home page of a large book dealer such as Amazon.com or Barnes and Noble online. Using the "search" box, you can type in a possible subject and begin to browse through the brief descriptions of books. There are other ways to explore subject areas, both with and without a computer. Read on.

Your class may be using an electronic discussion board (DB) such as Blackboard or another course management system. If so, your instructor may have posted the syllabus and course description and assignments on the site as well as links—that is, addresses that can take you directly to sites. If you have this server capability, now would be a good time to start discussing your research project with your fellow students.

Brainstorming

This simple method for finding a subject requires only a pen and paper. You can do it anywhere. The idea in **brainstorming** is to relax and, using a clean sheet of paper, scribble down words in whatever order they occur to you. Simply make lists or jot down words in random order as your mind wanders from one phrase or clue to the next. Don't try to select or edit the results. For instance, if you started with the word *Venice*, you might get these results:

Example

VENICE: Italy. Canals floods water bridges, paintings by Caneletto and Tiepolo and Titian, glass making, lace making, food, music, gondolas, Woody Allen married there, movies, film festival, Katharine Hepburn in <u>Summertime</u>, romantic, Lido, beaches. Also Venice, California. Cool place. Roller blades. Leo DiCaprio as Romeo. Modern Shakespeare. <u>Merchant of Venice</u>. Jews in ghettos. Shylock. Stereotypes.

This is a brief list, but it got the writer through a wide range of subjects—from Venice, the city in Italy, to the city in California named for it, and then to literature—by a form of associative thinking. The writer might now use another technique called clustering to try to make some sense out of this disorganized list.

Clustering

Clustering, or rearranging the brainstorming results into groups, helps you relate or connect ideas to your theme or subject. You can fill in links as you arrange the words.

The list on Venice might be clustered in several ways:

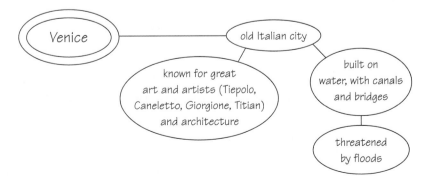

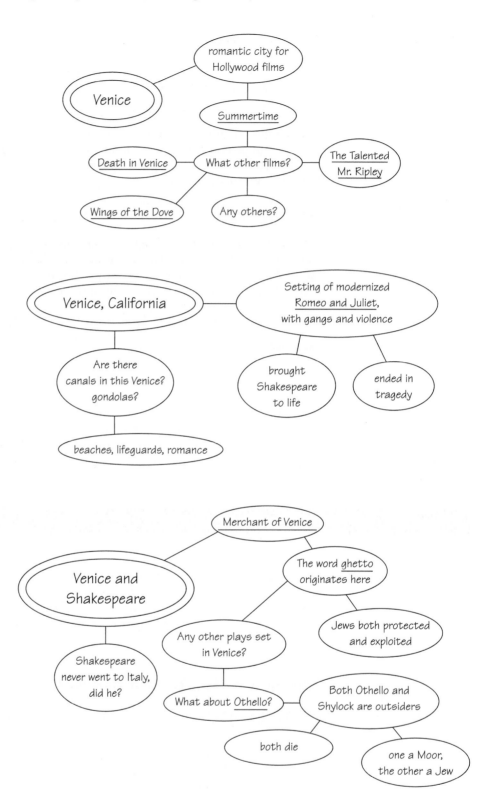

EXERCISE 3.1   Brainstorming

Using one of the following words or phrases, try a brainstorming session of ten minutes, timing yourself. See how many different things come to mind.

murder   *Titanic* sinking

travel   slavery

immigration

EXERCISE 3.2   Clustering

Using the results of your brainstorming, experiment with clustering by putting the words into small groupings linked by subject or theme.

Perhaps you have been given a very general subject as a research assignment, or maybe you have been told that you can pick your own subject. Either way, another good method to help you begin thinking about what you want to explore is a technique called listing. **Listing** is similar to brainstorming in that you start with the general, or large, subject and then write down at least 20 smaller, related subjects. Don't be too fussy about whether these subjects are "good"; just add each one to the list. If you have a general subject to write about—let's say "Italy" or "animals"—simply make a list of everything you can think of under the heading of your choice, and this very process will start you focusing on an aspect of your subject that you might enjoy writing about and exploring through research.

Step 1	IDENTIFYING POSSIBLE SUBJECTS

Use one or more of the techniques described above: brainstorming, clustering, and listing. If you have been given a general subject by your teacher, then make a list of subjects that interest you, you have read about, or people have been talking about. Give yourself 10 minutes, or make yourself a list of at least 20 subjects. The point is to let yourself go and give your imagination free rein. Go over the list yourself and see whether you can find a preliminary subject for your research paper.

Using the Web to Find Subjects

Once you have begun looking for a subject, you can go to the World Wide Web and explore with search engines. These are tools that help you locate information. One popular search engine is Google. If you type the address www.google.com into the address line and "go" there, you can begin a search. Type in "Venice Italy," for example. Or you might look back over your clustering and head to "Venice California" instead. Perhaps you might try "Shakespeare plays Venice" and see what you get.

From here, you use links—words or phrases that are highlighted so that if you activate them (by putting the cursor on them and clicking), you can explore related aspects of your subject. The search engine helps you locate related material by giving you these links. Clicking on a link helps you explore new or related subjects. If you get lost, use the Back command (on the menu bar at the top of the screen) to start again. While this is an acceptable place to start, you will discover as you read and research further that results from a commercial site like this one, or Vivisimo (www.vivisimo.com) or Yahoo (www.yahoo.com), need to be evaluated carefully. These commercial results are ranked by popularity, rather then by their validity or accuracy or quality. They are supported by advertisers and thus subject to bias.

Choosing a Topic within a Subject Area

One of the keys to success in research writing is the ability to narrow the subject to a manageable size. Too often, students stake out a vast general territory, such as slavery or music, because they think this will be easier to write about than a topic that is more narrow, such as marriage ceremonies among slaves in Georgia or political protest in gangsta rap. However, once they begin to use a library or the Internet to find information, beginning researchers realize that a narrow or specific topic leads to more efficient, successful, and exciting work.

From General to Specific

One subject that is too general, for example, is "writers." This subject is very broad. It includes all writers, from all countries, during all time. To write on this huge subject would require a vast amount of research, as well as skills in every written language! The wise researcher would create a narrower subject, such as "American writers." This is smaller but still too big, unless you are writing a large reference book.

Let's try again with "African American writers." Now we are moving toward a more specific topic, but we need to go farther. One direction would lead us to a specific writer, such as James Baldwin, Toni Morrison, Frederick Douglass, John A. Williams, or Zora Neale Hurston.

To make the topic even more specific, we can focus on one aspect of one writer's work. Perhaps you have read the short story "Sonny's Blues" by James Baldwin. If you have, then you might consider this story as the subject of your research essay and create the final topic accordingly: jazz in Baldwin's "Sonny's Blues," perhaps, or sibling rivalry in "Sonny's Blues." Or maybe you saw the film of Toni Morrison's novel *Beloved* after you read the book. Your topic could be a comparison of the two versions, or it could be an examination of the importance of spirituality in *Beloved*. That is the difference between general and specific.

EXERCISE 3.3 **Listing from General to Specific**

Examine the following list. Number the items from 1 (most general) to 4 (most specific).

architecture _____

Edith Wharton's house, The Mount _____

American architecture _____

American houses preserved as national landmarks _____

Now try this longer list, using numbers 1 through 7.

Newland Archer's plans for adultery _____

books _____

Newland Archer, a character in *The Age of Innocence* _____

novels by Edith Wharton _____

novels _____

Wharton's novel *The Age of Innocence* _____

Newland Archer's marriage to May Welland _____

Narrowing the Subject: Going from General to Specific

EXERCISE 3.4 **Narrowing the Subject**

For each general term listed below, provide increasingly specific topics. Include in the list any subjects you may be considering for your own research.

Example

Music—classical music—eighteenth-century classical music—Mozart's music—Mozart's music and the film Amadeus

Food

_____

_____

World health

_____

_____

Women writers

_____

_____

Famous crimes and criminals

_____

_____

Travel

_____

_____

Talk shows on television

_____

_____

War

_____

_____

Reading to Discover Topics

The most important and exciting way to discover workable and valuable topics within your subject area is to read. Whether you read books, magazines, or electronic sources, reading broadly and frequently will increase your background knowledge of the subject area and help you select a better topic. What you should read depends on what you want to know. For example, researching a possible career as a travel agent might require you to learn more about geography, the leisure market, such recent trends as eco-travel and adventure tourism, and such specialized markets as gay couples and handicapped travelers. No single book is going to help you gain mastery of this subject. You need to explore magazines published by the travel industry as they come out every month. You need to visit local travel agencies to investigate popular vacation spots. You need to visit Web sites posted by local tourism boards and by advocacy groups like AARP. You need to read articles in the *Wall Street Journal* that analyze trends in the marketplace. As you can see, this kind of reading to discover ideas takes time. That is why most teachers want you to start your research paper early in the semester and plan your steps carefully so you have enough time to find, absorb, and process all that you read.

What to Read

The traveler to Morocco who in our earlier example was exploring subjects on foreign countries might begin his or her research by reading an entry in a travel guide or by looking at a general travel Web site like Orbitz (www.orbitz.com) or Frommer's (www.frommers.com). Reading such general information can be quite helpful in determining whether you are interested in a particular subject. A general source can also raise some interesting issues about the subject that might spark a researcher's curiosity.

After reading the travel guide description, the traveler may decide not to go to Morocco after all, or he or she may be eager to find out more. If this were your research subject, you might decide to continue investigating Morocco or to explore another topic. It is important to explore several broad resources on a subject to determine your level of interest and your need for further research.

General resources for background reading include the following:

An Encyclopedia

Encyclopedias are a good place to begin your reading, but they are not recommended as sources for research essays because they are too broad. Try a traditional text in your library, such as *World Book Encyclopedia* or *Encyclopaedia Britannica*. You can also try an online encyclopedia like *Encarta*. These reference tools arrange topics alphabetically, so use the volume that covers "M" in the paper version, or search "Morocco" in the electronic source.

An Atlas

An atlas is a collection of maps. Maps may show various aspects of a country (location, size, population, topography, and availability of public transportation routes), but specialized maps also reveal religious and language groups, political territories, earthquake faults, historical boundaries, and so on. Explore a number of atlases and compare the information. There are atlases published by National Geographic, the American Automobile Association, Rand McNally, and many other organizations and publishers.

Travel Guides

Many publishers issue guide books aimed at a wide variety of readers. Popular guides include the Eyewitness series, Fodor's, Frommer's, Lonely Planet, Let's Go, and Michelin guides. Most have related Web sites. A survey of these will introduce you to the highlights of Morocco from differing vantage points; some, such as Eyewitness, feature art, culture, and history through glossy illustrations. Others, such as Lonely Planet, provide information on the cheapest places for students and backpackers to stay. Michelin is favored by drivers and those who are searching for historical sites abroad. Browsing through a few of these guidebooks will provide you with visual and verbal clues about your subject.

Tips for Reading

If you collect five or six reference books on your subject, you should not try to read each one from cover to cover. Use the books as tools. If you are using a library book, do not highlight, underline, or otherwise mark the book! Either take notes or use paper bookmarks to identify important pages. Explore the table of contents, the illustrations, and the index to survey the subjects covered in the book. Sample the sections that arouse your curiosity. You may also make photocopies of useful pages, but remember to check rules about copyright for proper use of such materials. These rules may be posted near photocopiers; they should also be available from librarians or your teacher.

EXERCISE 3.5	Reading for Topics about Morocco

Let's begin our exploration of Morocco. Edith Wharton, a nineteenth-century writer, traveled to Morocco in 1919, during World War I, and wrote a book called *In Morocco* describing what she experienced. Read the following paragraph from the chapter "Harems and Ceremonies." The selection describes Wharton's visit to the harem of a dignitary.

We had been invited, one day, to visit the harem of one of the chief dignitaries of the Makhzen at Fez, and these thoughts came to me as I sat among the pale women in their mouldering prison. The descent through the steep tunnelled streets gave one the sense of being lowered into the shaft of a mine. At each step the strip of sky grew narrower, and was more often obscured by the low vaulted passages into which we plunged. The noises of the Bazaar had died out, and only the sound of fountains behind garden walls and the clatter of our mules' hoofs on the stones went with us. Then fountains and gardens ceased also, the towering masonry closed in, and we entered an almost subterranean labyrinth which sun and air never reach. At length our mules turned into a cul-de-sac blocked by a high building. On the right was another building, one of those blind mysterious house-fronts of Fez that seem like a fragment of its ancient fortifications. Clients and servants lounged on the stone benches built into the wall; it was evidently the house of an important person. A charming youth with intelligent eyes waited on the threshold to receive us: he was one of the sons of the house, the one who had "studied in Algeria" and knew how to talk to visitors. We followed him into a small arcaded *patio* hemmed in by the high walls of the house. On the right was the usual long room with archways giving on the court. Our host, a patriarchal personage, draped in fat as in a toga, came toward us, a mountain of majestic muslins, his eyes sparkling in a swarthy silver-bearded face. He seated us on divans and lowered his voluminous person to a heap of cushions on the step leading into the court; and the son who had studied in Algeria instructed a negress to prepare the tea.

Edith Wharton, *In Morocco*

EXERCISE 3.6 **Writing Your Paragraph**

After you read Wharton's paragraph, write a brief paragraph of your own in which you tell about anything you discovered while reading.

Step 2 **READING GENERAL SOURCES**

Now that you have explored some general sources on Morocco, you are ready to begin to search for sources on *your* topic.

Using the brainstorming and clustering techniques, create a tentative subject, a smaller subject, and a topic for your own research assignment.

Using the topic you have chosen, consult the library and the Internet to locate the following. Be sure to write down the complete title and author of each print source, as well as the library call number you used to locate the source. Check that the complete Internet address (URL) is visible on any printouts.

1. a general reference article from an encyclopedia

2. a visual source (map, photograph, chart, or the like)

3. a Web site with general information on the topic

Defining Your Purpose and Choosing a Topic

Considering Your Purpose

As we saw earlier, the three researchers studying Morocco have the same subject, although each would be investigating a very different aspect of Morocco with a different purpose behind his or her work: the tourist to plan an exciting vacation, the businessperson looking for lucrative opportunities, and the historian seeking to understand the role of Morocco in World War I. Each researcher might use some of the same library materials to get information, but their different purposes in conducting the search would result in different topics.

Defining the purpose of the search helps the researcher guide and narrow the search. If you are planning a vacation in North Africa and are aiming to find the least expensive hotel and the cleanest beaches, you do not want to waste your time reading statistics on land use for agriculture, literacy rates, names of political parties, and the rate of growth of industrial production. However, the businessperson might want exactly these statistics, all of which are readily available at www.cia.gov/cia/publications/factbook/mo.html on the Internet. The historian, whose purpose is to understand events in the past, might not be interested in reading about today's hotel rates or the prices in modern restaurants but would be more interested in Wharton's visit because it took place during World War I. All of the researchers would need the same background information: where Morocco is located, a brief history of the country, information on religious practices there that might affect travel, business, or history, and so on. But each individual topic would lead the researcher to different sources, depending on the purpose of the investigation. "Why am I doing this research?" is a fundamental question each researcher keeps asking. Real-life answers direct you to the purpose: the tourist needs to uncover correct behavior in a mosque; the businessperson needs to find out what role women play in the economy; the historian needs to find out where the documents were signed; the traveler wants to know what is the best beach resort. Purpose, then, is a map guiding the researcher to the right sources.

Choosing a topic usually means deciding to focus on one aspect of the subject to narrow the field of investigation. Some possible topics on the very broad subject of Morocco are:

1. import and export regulations on Moroccan carpets shipped to the United States

2. travel in Morocco for a tourist

3. the importance of Morocco in World War I

Once you have settled on a subject, it is important to consider your purpose for doing research before deciding on a possible topic.

Discovering a Topic

In Chapter 1, we practiced freewriting. Freewriting is a good method to use after you have collected and read a few general sources, examined a Web site, or studied a map or photograph, because freewriting will help you to discover what you already know about a topic.

EXERCISE 3.7   Freewriting

Skim through some of the articles in the Casebook. Choose one that interests you and do a freewriting based on that subject.

Step 3   SELECTING YOUR TOPIC

1. On the basis of what you have read in the Casebook, or another subject you might be considering for your research paper, freewrite on a separate sheet of paper for ten minutes. (Time yourself.)

2. When you have finished, read over your freewriting and see whether you can find five other topics that might work well as the focus of a research paper. Make a list of your results.

3. Review the list and consider the various topics you produced. Which is most interesting to *you*? Which would be most interesting to a general audience?

4. Check out Anna's freewriting on page 61. How did it help her find her topic?

5. Write two sentences explaining the difference between a subject and a topic. Give an example to support each definition.

Forming a Research Question

Another way to choose a good topic is to think about what question you want to answer. A writer usually sets out to do research in order to answer a question or several questions. As the writer of a research paper, you will use these questions to help you choose a topic that can develop into a working hypothesis—what you think may be the answer to your research question. Framing a **research question** is a way of focusing the main direction of the research; it expresses what you want to find out. Once the question is prepared, the writer is ready to go in search of answers. To put it simply, a research question is what results when writers ask themselves exactly what they are trying to find out or what they want to learn.

Identifying Research Questions

Wharton was particularly curious about the local way of living in Morocco, so she did some research. She visited a harem. Her purpose was to record what she learned in order to bring information to other travelers. (In the era before radio and television, audiences depended on such written reports as we would now rely on the Internet or television to provide a picture of a foreign country.)

The following is another excerpt from Wharton's book, in which she recounts a conversation she had with the women in the harem.

1 My hostess received me with the utmost amiability, we seated ourselves in the oriel facing the view, and the interchange of questions and compliments began.

2 Had I any children? (They asked it all at once.)

3 Alas, no.

4 "In Islam" (one of the ladies ventured) "a woman without children is considered the most unhappy being in the world."

5 I replied that in the western world also childless women were pitied. (The brother-in-law smiled incredulously.)

6 Knowing that European fashions are of absorbing interest to the harem I next inquired: "What do these ladies think of our stiff tailor-dresses? Don't they find them excessively ugly?"

7 "Yes, they do." (It was again the brother-in-law who replied.) "But they suppose that in your own homes you dress less badly."

8 "And have they never any desire to travel, or to visit the Bazaars, as the Turkish ladies do?"

9 "No, indeed. They are too busy to give such matters a thought. In *our country* women of the highest class occupy themselves with their household and their children, and the rest of their time is devoted to needlework." (At this statement I gave the brother-in-law a smile as incredulous as his own.)

10 All this time the fair-haired interpretess had not been allowed by the vigilant guardian of the harem to utter a word.

11 I turned to her with a question.

12 "So your mother is French, *Mademoiselle*?"

13 "*Oui, Madame.*"

14 "From what part of France did she come?"

15 A bewildered pause. Finally: "I don't know . . . from Switzerland, I think," brought out this shining example of the Higher Education. In spite of Algerian "advantages" the poor girl could speak only a few words of her mother's tongue. She had kept the European features and complexion, but her soul was the soul of Islam. The harem had placed its powerful imprint upon her, and she looked at me with the same remote and passive eyes as the daughters of the house.

16 After struggling for a while longer with a conversation which the watchful brother-in-law continued to direct as he pleased, I felt my own lips stiffening into the resigned

smile of the harem, and it was a relief when at last their guardian drove the pale flock away, and the handsome old gentleman who owned them reappeared on the scene, bringing back my friends, and followed by slaves and tea.

Below are some examples of possible research questions that Wharton may have pursued. Asking questions like these leads researchers in search of answers. Wharton's research involved gaining access to several harems, interviewing the women who lived there, and observing the surroundings carefully. She also read books on Moroccan history and culture before she started her trip.

1. What is life like in a Moroccan harem?

2. Who lives in a harem?

3. Who controls life in the harem?

4. How do the women feel about living in a harem?

5. What do harems look like?

EXERCISE 3.8   Developing Research Questions Based on Reading

What other research questions about harems in Morocco can you think of? What questions might we ask today, almost a century after Wharton, that she would not have asked? Make a list of ten questions.

Research Questions and Point of View

A good way to formulate a research question that reflects what you think about a subject is to look at several points of view on the same issue. Your **point of view** is your opinion on the topic, or what you want to say about the topic, or how you see or think about the topic. Sometimes the writer uses a particular strategy to develop and organize the paper. Your point of view will be used to shape the kind of essay you write. Some common viewpoints or strategies are:

argument or persuasion: The writer proposes a position and defends it.

information: The writer provides a more objective statement of the topic.

analysis: The writer's primary job is to understand critically and explain the topic.

description: The writer presents very specific details (sight, sound, texture, and so on) to bring the topic to life for the reader.

Sometimes, depending on the topic, these can be combined within the same essay.

EXERCISE 3.9   Exploring Point of View

Examine the following illustration from *Harper's* magazine, January 1900. Imagine that you can hear the conversation between the European woman and the Arabian woman. Each would have a different point of view on what it is like to be a harem member. Examine this illustration closely, and then list five statements about harem life that you can imagine each woman making. Pretend these women were featured on a modern television talk show.

Harem woman

1. _____

2. _____

3. _____

4. _____

5. _____

European woman

1. _____

2. _____

3. _____

4. _____

5. _____

EXERCISE 3.10 Considering Point of View

Using the following four points of view, write a sentence in which you show how each one could be used to shape the harem scene in a different way.

1. persuade: _____

_____

2. inform: _____

_____

3. analyze: _____

_____

4. describe: _____

_____

_____

Remember that Wharton is only one observer of harem life. Moreover, she is an outsider, from another culture. Read the following short excerpt from the book *Dreams of Trespass: Tales of a Moroccan Girlhood* by Fatima Mernissi. Mernissi grew up in a harem and writes from a very different point of view about the world within the walls of a harem. After reading the selection, answer the questions below.

I was born in a harem in 1940 in Fez, a ninth-century Moroccan city some five thousand kilometers west of Mecca, and one thousand kilometers south of Madrid, one of the dangerous capitals of the Christians. The problems with the Christians start, said Father, as with women, when the *hudud*, or sacred frontier, is not respected. I was born in the midst of chaos, since neither Christians nor women accepted the frontiers. Right on our threshold, you could see women of the harem contesting and fighting with Ahmed the doorkeeper as the foreign armies from the North kept arriving all over the city. In fact, foreigners were standing right at the end of our street, which lay just between the old city and the Ville Nouvelle, a new city that they were building for themselves. When Allah created the earth, said Father, he separated men from women, and put a sea between Muslims and Christians for a reason. Harmony exists when each group respects the prescribed limits of the other; trespassing leads only to sorrow and unhappiness. But women dreamed of trespassing all the time. The world beyond the gate was their obsession. They fantasized all day long about parading in unfamiliar streets, while the Christians kept crossing the sea, bringing death and chaos. . . . But since then, looking for the frontier has become my life's occupation. Anxiety eats at me whenever I cannot situate the geometric line organizing my powerlessness.

Fatima Mernissi, *Dreams of Trespass: Tales of a Moroccan Girlhood*

EXERCISE 3.11   Comparing Opposing Points of View

1. In what way is Mernissi's point of view different from Wharton's?

_____

_____

2. Does reading Mernissi make you want to change your impression of Wharton's attitude toward the harem women? Why?

_____

_____

3. What does the author mean by "boundaries" and "powerlessness"?

_____

_____

4. What do you think Mernissi would have thought of Wharton's description of the harem?

_____

_____

_____

Getting to the Right Question

After reviewing some general information about a subject and determining any prevalent points of view, you will probably have some interesting questions already in mind. It is important, however, to make sure the research question you choose to pursue is appropriate for your purpose and will lead you to the information you hope to discover.

What Makes a Good Question?

The key factor that makes a question good is that *you want to know the answer*. In addition, a good question has to be "the right size." If it is too broad, your research will take too long. If it is too narrow, you will not have enough material. Here are some common problems to avoid:

- *Avoid a question that can be answered simply "yes" or "no."* A good question requires a complex answer; it asks why or how or develops a critical inquiry.

- *Avoid questions whose answers are purely factual*, unless your teacher has assigned such a topic. An interesting question leads to the interpretation of facts, not just to an accumulation of facts. Thus, although you can report factually that Morocco has a population of about 30,000,000, an infant mortality rate of 52.99 deaths per 1,000 births, and an average life expectancy rate of 68.51 years, according to the online *CIA Factbook*, you would not have much to say about these facts until you create a research question that digs into their possible meanings or applications. Is the infant mortality rate high or low compared to that of the United States, and is the cultural attitude toward women in any way responsible for the difference in rate? When you find other facts, that 43.7 percent of the total population is literate and that 56.6 percent of males and 31 percent of females are literate, you might begin to see a real question emerging: Why is the rate of literacy so much higher for men than for women? Is this disparity in any way related to the history of women's lives in harems?

The purpose of a good question is to lead the researcher to a synthesis of information. This means that the researcher gathers information from a variety of sources—often sources that contradict one another or take differing points of view—and brings it together, along with his or her own thinking, to a new formulation that suggests a new question.

Distinguishing between Different Kinds of Research Questions

Even though we want to avoid research questions that produce only factual answers, we do need to ask some factual questions to give us background information about our overall question. Knowing the difference between fact and opinion is essential for research, and will come up later when we discuss documentation.

EXERCISE 3.12   Fact and Opinion

Return to the illustration from *Harper's* magazine (page 86). Look at it carefully, and then answer these factual questions as best you can on the basis of what you observe:

1. What is the woman on the left wearing? Where do you think she is from?

_____

_____

2. What is the woman on the right wearing? Where is she from?

_____

_____

3. What is in the hand of the woman on the left?

_____

_____

4. Where does this scene appear to be taking place? How do you know?

_____

_____

The answers to these questions convey factual information.

EXERCISE 3.13   Moving beyond Facts to Analysis

Now let's try some more probing questions that might lead to our research hypothesis.

1. The illustration was made for a Western audience. In what way is this important to how we interpret it? How might the picture be different if it were intended for a non-Western audience?

2. Which woman has the better life? What do we mean by "better"? How do we judge? On the basis of your brief readings by Wharton and Mernissi, how do you think each woman would answer the question?

3. Morocco was a French colony until 1956. How important is this fact in helping us interpret Western attitudes like Wharton's toward Moroccan culture?

You have not done a lot of reading about Morocco, so you can try this another way. Imagine the same picture with a Native American on the right—for example, a Navaho. Change the setting from a harem to the American Southwest. Think of the woman on the left as an Easterner migrating to California in 1849. Now ask questions about the conversation and the attitudes of the two figures.

_____

Ideally, a research essay tries to find out something new or to establish a position that has not been readily understood. Using facts as a starting point, the researcher interprets these facts to answer the research question.

Let's try another subject: Western films about Morocco. Here are the titles of four films set in Morocco:

Casablanca (1943)

Outpost in Morocco (1942)

Morocco (1930)

The Sheltering Sky (1990)

Perhaps you have seen at least one of these films. If you were to watch all of them, you might begin to ask research questions such as these:

1. Why is Morocco so popular with Western filmmakers?

2. In what way is the political history of Morocco reflected in the films?

3. Why has the film *Casablanca* remained popular for more than 50 years?

4. Why was Morocco so attractive to writers such as Paul Bowles (author of the novel *The Sheltering Sky*)?

5. What would Edith Wharton, who traveled in Morocco in 1919, think of the country as it is portrayed in *Casablanca*, filmed in 1943?

RESEARCH QUESTIONS

A good research question

- avoids a simple yes-or-no answer

- avoids predictable or "worn out" topics that have been too frequently the subject of recent media exploitation (such as child abuse, abortion, capital punishment, and gun control) unless you have a fresh new approach or material

- synthesizes different points of view

- limits the scope so that the question can be answered reasonably well in the assigned number of pages (say, five to 10 double-spaced pages)

- leads the researcher toward a clear purpose: to find out why or how something happened, to pose a rational argument, to interpret a text or idea

- uses factual information from sources but applies the facts to the writer's point of view

- excites curiosity in the researcher and the potential audience

Step 4   FORMING YOUR RESEARCH QUESTION

From among the topics you listed in the freewriting exercise on page 83 choose the one that you are most interested in and that you think will be of most interest to a general audience. Write your topic at the top of a sheet of paper and brainstorm for 10 minutes on questions you have about the topic. If possible, ask a fellow student, friend, or family member to help you think of more questions. Try to give yourself enough time to "live with" the question so that you will find one you genuinely want to answer. Review all the possible questions, and select the one that you think best fits the criteria listed above.

Formulating a Working Thesis

Once you have a list of questions, you can begin the next step: formulating a hypothesis. Many writers believe this is the most important step in organizing a successful essay or research paper: a good thesis creates the plan or map of everything that will follow in the paper. However, as you begin, you should think of the thesis as a hypothesis or working thesis. You haven't yet done the research necessary to collect information to answer the question or help you interpret the subject, so you should *not* have a final answer. If you did, you wouldn't need to do the research! The research should shape the thesis; the thesis should not control the research. Although your working thesis may prove accurate, the most exciting discoveries occur when you let the research lead you to new territory. As with Lizzie Borden, whom you read about in Anna's paper "Forty Whacks," there may be no sure answer to the mystery, but the sources can be interpreted reasonably to support a number of different thesis statements. The writer of "Forty Whacks" used her resources to support *her* position that Lizzie was guilty, for instance. Just check the library to see how many books have been published on this unsolved case to see how many different thesis ideas are possible! If your research leads you to a document you did not know about before, you might have to revise the working thesis completely. For example, if you had the hypothesis that Lizzie Borden definitely killed her parents, and then as you did research, you found a previously unknown letter from Lizzie's sister confessing to the murders, you might have to reconsider your thesis. Is the letter authentic? Why was it lost until now? All sorts of new questions would have to be asked, and these would lead you on a new path. At first you might be tempted to ignore the letter, because acknowledging it means you will have to change your comfortable ideas. But to do so would be dishonest and irresponsible. Once you included the mysterious letter, you would probably find that the search became much more exciting—and the revised thesis both original and easier to prove.

The research question provides the starting point from which students can begin to ask further questions, brainstorm ideas, and prepare an outline.

Thesis

A **thesis** has two parts: the topic and your point of view on the topic. For example, Edith Wharton's topic is "Harems in Morocco." Her hypothesis could be

> Harems are romantic enclosures where women are protected from violence.

However, after interviewing a member of the harem in Fez, she might revise her hypothesis on the basis of the information she received:

> Harems in Morocco oppress women, who are like prisoners in these gloomy palaces.

The difference between a topic and a thesis is the writer's point of view. Another visitor to the same place might have proposed a different hypothesis:

> Harems are beautiful spaces and, as museums of Islamic art, are important to an appreciation of Arabic culture.

Using the same topic, these writers have developed very different "maps" or hypotheses, and as a result, each will pursue different sources and end up with a unique essay.

EXERCISE 3.14   Writing Thesis Sentences

Read each of the following topics, and then develop it into a thesis by adding a point of view.

Example

> Topic: Hollywood films set in Morocco
>
> Thesis: Hollywood distorts the realities of life in Morocco in order to create a romantic or barbaric entertainment setting for its films.

1. Topic: movies set in Los Angeles (or another city of your choice)

   Write a thesis: _____

   _____

2. Topic: turning a novel into a movie (select a specific novel and film you know)

   Write a thesis: _____

   _____

3. Topic: portrayal of African Americans (or Latinos, or Asian Americans, or Italian Americans, or any other ethnic group) in films

   Write a thesis: _____

   _____

4. Topic: influences of international music on American musicians (select a specific example you are familiar with)

   Write a thesis: _____

   _____

5. Topic: ethnic restaurants in your region

   Write a thesis: _____

   _____

_____

How a Research Question Becomes a Working Thesis

Another way to understand the importance of the working thesis is to think of it as an umbrella. The thesis must cover the entire essay, so that each paragraph is "under the protection" of the thesis. Each paragraph, each page, and each source referred to must "fit" under the umbrella of the thesis.

Audience

In addition, the writer has to think about who is the intended audience. For most beginning writers, the audience is *general:* classmates, family, friends, and teachers who are not necessarily experts or specialists on the subject. For more specialized situations, a writer could be aiming at an audience of experts: a group of travel agents, all of whom have been to Morocco, or historians who already know a great deal about the events of World War I. Identifying the audience is important in helping you decide how much and what kind of material to include. In addition, determining the audience will help you gauge the levels of vocabulary and language that are appropriate. It will also help you avoid plagiarism because you will not want to use words that are inappropriate for your audience even though they "sounded good" in the source you read.

FORMING A THESIS

A successful working thesis should

- identify the narrow topic the paper will explore

- state the writer's opinion

- label the writer's point of view, or "angle," on the topic

- suggest the method or direction the research will take, with reference to who the audience will be (general? specialized or expert?)

- be flexible enough to change in response to information and ideas gleaned from sources

Step 5   FORMULATING YOUR WORKING THESIS

Now is the time for you to develop your own working thesis.

EXERCISE 3.15   Developing Your Working Thesis

Using the examples as a guide, answer each of these five questions until you reach your own working thesis in question 6. You can list several responses and create two or even three possible thesis statements, but eventually you will have to select one to give your essay organization and focus.

1. What narrow topic will your paper explore?

_____

_____

Example

Morocco as portrayed in Hollywood films, especially <u>Casablanca</u>

2. What is your opinion so far?

_____

_____

Example

Films like <u>Casablanca</u> ignore the local culture, religion, and history of Morocco and instead create a romantic desert where the "natives" are inferior to the Westerners.

3. What is your point of view or "angle"?

_____

_____

Example

Although <u>Casablanca</u> is a memorable film, one of the classics in American film history, it has distinctly Western perspectives on Moroccan life. How would the film be different if it were told "from the other side," by a Moroccan filmmaker? How would a Moslem opposed to the use of alcohol, for instance, react to all the drinking Bogart does as the famous saloon keeper of Rick's Café?

4. What method will you use? (Or in what direction do you plan to go?)

_____

_____

Example

I'll watch at least four films by Western directors set in Morocco. I'll look for scenes that seem to portray Western culture as superior to Arabic. I'll read reviews of the films and books on cinema history and technique. I might focus on one aspect of these films, such as the use of military characters or the lack of women, to show how narrow the cultural perspectives are.

5. What might you have to be flexible about?

_____

_____

Example

I might discover that the more interesting issue is the use of these films as wartime propaganda or the portrayal of Morocco as a place for people whose lives have reached a dead end (Rick, Foreign Legion soldiers).

6. What is your working thesis in a single sentence?

_____

_____

MAKING A CALENDAR

Use your planner or an academic calendar to sketch out the key dates. When is the final version of the paper due? Start here, at the end of the project, and work backward.

Let's say you have 12 to 14 weeks to complete the research assignment. A possible calendar or schedule might be

- Steps 1 through 8: two weeks

- Steps 9 through 12: two weeks

- Steps 13 and 14: one week

- Steps 15 and 16: two weeks

- Step 17: one week

MAKING A CALENDAR (continued)

- Step 18: two to three weeks
- Steps 19 through 21: two weeks
- Step 22: one to two weeks

Creating a Research Plan

As you work, you will have a better idea of how long each step takes. For most beginning researchers, the steps take *much longer* than they anticipated! Start early, and work at a consistent pace. You probably will have fewer deadlines from other classes earlier in the term. Also, libraries are less crowded early in the semester, and you can find more sources and get more sympathy from busy librarians if you begin your project early.

The key to success with research is *planning*. As you can see from your working thesis, you do not always know what kind of reference materials you will find or how long it will take to pull your material together into the final thesis. As you begin to consider your plan, therefore, it is important to use the calendar to be sure you have followed all of the necessary steps and to allocate enough time for finding materials, reading them, and developing the final essay.

Step 6 — MAKING YOUR RESEARCH PLAN

The following seven-step research plan will help you determine exactly where to go next with your research.

EXERCISE 3.16 Planning Your Research

Below is an example of a research plan that reviews some of your earlier steps and prepares you to move on to the final step in this chapter, writing a research proposal. Review the example in each question as you fill in your own plan.

1. What is your research subject?

Example

Women writers

_____

2. What source (book, article, or Internet site) did you use to find this subject?

Example

Edith Wharton's <u>In Morocco</u>

_____

3. To what topic have you narrowed your subject?

Example

Wharton's Westernized viewpoint, her prejudice against non-Western culture

_____

4. What is the research question you are posing?

Example

Does Wharton's upper-class social position permit her to understand sympathetically the position of Islamic women?

_____

_____

5. Indicate what sources (library, Internet, interview, museum, other) you will use to answer this question, and for each source, explain why you will need it.

Example

Biographical materials on Wharton, travel guide to Morocco for general background, book on role of women in Islam, interview with Islamic classmate on attitudes toward women in Islam and wearing the veil today, encyclopedia for background on colonial and postcolonial Moroccan culture

_____

_____

_____

_____

6. Who is your audience most likely to be?

Example

Classmates and faculty in an American college curious about different perspectives on other cultures, but not too knowledgeable about Moroccan history or culture

_____

_____

7. What is your working thesis?

Example

Edith Wharton's travel book, In Morocco, reveals that she feels herself superior to non-Western women.

_____

_____

_____

Writing a Research Proposal

Once you have completed Steps 1 through 6, you are ready to synthesize your work into a proposal. The **proposal** is a brief written statement in which you explain to your teacher your goals for the research assignment. Students are often asked to hand in their proposals early in the semester so that the instructor can check that they are headed in the right direction. The proposal is like a letter of commitment, or a contract, demonstrating that the student has been thinking about the topic and preparing to write the paper. The proposal is also designed to prevent procrastination.

The length of a good proposal usually depends on what the final length of the paper will be. For a paper of 1,000 to 2,000 words, the proposal might be one double-spaced page (about 250 words), or it might be one concise paragraph. For a master's thesis of 60 to 80 pages, the proposal might be close to 10 double-spaced pages. For an extended work such as a doctoral thesis or a full-length book, the proposal could be much longer.

The proposal functions as a map for the research paper. It presents a brief introduction to the subject, leads up to the thesis, and shows the direction in which the writer plans to go to answer the research question and support the thesis. The writer must have done some preliminary reading, Internet surfing, or film viewing to provide the information a good proposal offers.

A GOOD PROPOSAL

The ingredients for a good proposal are

- a clear subject, with brief background information

- a narrow topic

- a working thesis

- awareness of the level of the audience

- a map, or plan, for locating the appropriate sources

Sample Research Proposal

Here is a student's first draft of a proposal based on the examples in Step 6. Read it, and then use the questions to evaluate the work:

George Smith

English 103 Writing the Research Paper

October 1, 2004

Professor Hudson

Research Proposal

Everyone loves to travel. Today, we can go into a bookstore and find a wall filled with vivid photographs and travel tips to help plan

Smith 2

our trips. Early in the twentieth century, however, travel was not so common or so comfortable, especially for women. Thus when Edith Wharton visited Morocco in 1919 and returned to write a book, *In Morocco,* about her adventures, she was quite a pioneer.

Wharton, an upper-class, recently divorced American living permanently in France, was invited by a French military official to tour Morocco, then a French colony. Because she had been active in war work, especially in helping refugees in Paris, and because she had established a reputation with several novels and many short stories and magazine articles, Wharton was a logical candidate to visit war-torn North Africa and report on her findings.

I propose to examine how Wharton's position as a privileged member of society, however, biased her view of what she saw. Focusing on her visits to Moroccan harems, I will argue that the American's point of view was that Western civilization is superior to that of the Islamic world. This assumption or value shapes and twists her story. I will try to identify the cultural assumptions that are behind Wharton's harem chapters.

By reading more about Wharton's life, I plan to place her in the society of her day. I will use several Web sites such as the one hosted by the Edith Wharton Society. By reading descriptions of Morocco by other writers at this time and looking at some Islamic art in a local museum, I will try to appreciate a contrasting view of life in the harem and of Moroccan culture in general.

EXERCISE 3.17   Analyze a Research Proposal

1. This proposal consists of four paragraphs. Identify in your own words the goal or purpose of each paragraph.

   _____

   _____

   _____

2. Do you think this is a successful proposal? List three reasons why or why not.

_____

_____

_____

_____

Step 7   WRITING YOUR PROPOSAL

After reviewing the ingredients for a good proposal, write a proposal for your own research topic. Before you begin, review all of your work in Steps 1 through 6. Do not create a title, an outline, or fancy computer graphics. Make this a clear, effective, single-page, businesslike document. Follow guidelines provided by your instructor, or follow these suggestions for the format:

1. Put your name, the date, the course name and number, and the instructor's name on the page in the upper-left corner.

2. Label the page Research Proposal.

3. Double-space, and add page numbers.

4. Indent each new paragraph five spaces.

5. Aim for at least 250 to 300 words.

6. Proofread carefully for errors in spelling, grammar, and sentence length.

CHECKLIST   CHOOSING A SUBJECT AND NARROWING TO A TOPIC

❑ Have you found an appropriate topic by exploring your subject via brainstorming and clustering?

❑ Is your topic specific enough?

❑ Have you read some general sources to help you find a topic?

❑ Do you know the purpose for the intended topic?

❑ Is your topic interesting to you, and will it interest readers?

❑ Do you have a good research question (or several questions)?

❑ Do you understand the differences between fact and opinion?

❑ Does your topic idea reveal your own opinion?

❑ Have you begun to analyze your topic?

❑ Do you have a working thesis?

❑ Have you used your semester calendar and the course syllabus to prepare a research calendar?

❑ Have you written a research proposal that is a legitimate statement of your intentions for the research paper?

Finding and Retrieving Sources

In Chapter 3, you practiced choosing and narrowing a subject, forming a research question, formulating a working thesis, creating a research plan, and, finally, writing a proposal. This chapter will cover the next phases of research: finding and retrieving your sources.

Gauging Existing Knowledge about a Subject

A good way to start is to find out how much you already know about your topic. Testing knowledge on a topic means that the writer assesses or measures how much he or she knows about the subject. Through brainstorming, clustering, and freewriting, you have begun to make this assessment. Now you will begin to organize your preliminary explorations into a map for finding sources to expand your knowledge. Assessing how much you already know will help you decide which sources are the ones to read first. If you already know a lot, you can skip the most basic sources and begin at a more advanced level. If the subject of your research is completely new to you, however, you will need to begin with basic tools like encyclopedias.

Step 8	TESTING YOUR KNOWLEDGE

In your research group ask group members three questions each about their subjects. Read their questions to you, and try to answer them. What if you did not know the answers to any of these questions? You can still write about this subject—or any subject—by conducting *research*. In fact, even someone who could answer all the questions would have to do further research to write a good essay. Why? Because academic research requires the writer to identify and evaluate sources carefully. Thus, even if you know a lot from your personal experience, you'll need to use sources to support your own knowledge.

| **EXERCISE 4.1** | **Ten Questions to Gauge Someone's Knowledge** |

Using the subject from your own research proposal, write a list of ten questions you think would gauge someone's knowledge about that area.

_____

Books

Books can be located by using the library's catalog—an online system—and are arranged in terms of either Dewey Decimal or Library of Congress codes that label the subject of each book. Libraries contain many kinds of books:

- *Reference books* are used to get background, or facts, or to learn where other sources might be found. Reference books include encyclopedias, dictionaries, directories, guidebooks, and so on.

- *Reserve books,* in college libraries, are usually the texts assigned in current courses and other books put on reserve by an instructor for a particular class. These do not circulate.

- *Fiction* consists of works of the imagination, such as novels.

- *Nonfiction* books are based on fact or intellectual inquiry. They include such areas as biography, statistics, geography, history, architecture, religion, science, technology, and all of the other academic disciplines.

Periodicals

Librarians identify *magazines, journals,* and *newspapers* as "periodicals" because they are issued daily, weekly, monthly, twice a year (semiannually), or once a year (annually).

- *Magazine* is a term used to identify the more popular periodicals, such as *Time, Newsweek, Cosmopolitan, Sports Illustrated,* and the many other titles familiar from home subscriptions (or the dentist's waiting room).

- *Journals* are another form of magazine, but these more academic publications are specialized. Their content is reflected in such titles as *Sociology Review, Parabola,* or *Chemical Review.* Journals are designed to be read by experts in the field or by researchers looking for more detailed and extensive information. Whereas a magazine might run a two- or three-page story about a crisis on the California-Mexico border, with many color photographs, a journal article on the same subject would be much more substantial—20 or more pages, perhaps— and would contain an in-depth analysis of what happened and why.

- *Newspapers* cover daily or weekly current events. With the Internet, researchers now have access to both international and national papers online. Some libraries carry local newspapers, as well as national ones, but traditional papers are hard to store because they take up so much space, and the paper ages and falls apart quickly. Major newspapers such as the *New York Times* and the *Los Angeles Times* are made available on microfilm, a medium we will discuss shortly. Working online, researchers can now have access to hundreds of local, national, and international papers. Newspapers are particularly useful if your subject is current, but archives (collections of historical papers available online) give researchers the opportunity to read papers that were published in the 1800s, too.

Specialized Reference Tools

The library's reference section contains encyclopedias and dozens of other books with more precise or specialized subject areas. Walk through the shelves of your library's reference area and familiarize yourself with what is available. The following books are some of the most useful reference tools:

American Heritage Dictionary

Random House Dictionary of the English Language

Bartlett's Familiar Quotations

Essay and General Literature Index

Reader's Guide to Periodical Literature

National Geographic Atlas

E-books

More and more, universities and libraries are making texts of important books available as electronic books, or e-books. This means that if you want to read Shakespeare's play *Macbeth*, for instance, you can now go to a site, locate the book online, and either read it or print it off the site. The Guttenberg Project has undertaken the immense task of sponsoring this kind of work, as have many libraries. Most make the e-books available at no cost to readers. You can find e-books at www.ebrary.com, as one example. Most college and public libraries have links on their home pages that will quickly link you to e-books. You can also go to the Internet Public Library, www.ipl.org, for many titles. These electronic texts can also be found on professional sites that focus on a writer or a subject. The Edith Wharton Society site, www.edithwharton.org, for instance, provides links to full-text versions of most of Wharton's fiction online.

The Internet

Researchers can visit thousands of sites to gain access to complete books, recent journal articles, newspapers, visual images, music, museums, and historic sites. Universities sponsor valuable sites for research on a wide variety of subjects across the disciplines; sites focus on people, places, themes, questions, or professional interests and organizations. The problem is that there can be too much, especially if you are a relatively inexperienced researcher. It is easy to get overwhelmed and select sites that are quick to find, rather than to search patiently for the best sites. Unfortunately, many Internet sites are set up by private individuals or lobbying groups, and the user may have trouble determining whether the material posted on the site is reliable.

While most Web surfers are inclined to use a search engine like Google (www.google.com) or Vivisimo (www.vivisimo.com), most college students should begin not with these familiar pages, but instead with databases from their own college library home page. By using these sites, you are much more likely to find reliable academic sources that have been reviewed by experts in each field. Databases such as EBSCOhost, LexisNexis and ProQuest—available in most public and college libraries—are dependable and provide access to thousands of articles you would not find on the commercial search engines.

Museums and Other Sites

Nonprint sources can help you answer questions about your subject if they are dependable and authentic. These sources include photographs, recordings, documentary films, interviews on tape, museum collections, professional organizations and academic societies, knowledgeable people, art, architecture, historic sites, and monuments (battlefields, national parks such as Ellis Island).

Interviews and Questionnaires

To complete an interview you need to find an expert, set up an appointment, design the interview and prepare questions, and then conduct the interview. Questionnaires can be prepared and distributed and then collected, reviewed, and analyzed.

Finding and Evaluating Primary and Secondary Sources

As you explore these sections of the library and the Internet, you will learn how to identify two essential kinds of sources: primary and secondary.

Primary sources are *first,* or *original.* For example, documents that are primary for a historian include the Declaration of Independence, John F. Kennedy's letters, and photographs taken by Matthew Brady of Civil War battlefields. **Secondary sources** are those that derive from a primary source; they rely on primary sources but represent someone's interpretation or application of the primary source. A biography of Thomas Jefferson might interpret the Declaration of Independence, for example, in trying to understand Jefferson's political philosophy. A theorist seeking causes of the JFK assassination might read Kennedy's letters looking for clues. A Civil War buff would look at Brady's photos in order to learn exactly how soldiers were dressed and what kinds of rifles they carried.

Places can also be primary sources. An example for a paper on immigration is the large room at Ellis Island where immigrants waited to hear the verdict of the customs inspectors. Statistics collected in 1905 by passenger line companies are primary documents that help historians and others assess the number of arrivals at Ellis Island. An interview with a recently arriving immigrant would be primary as well. Secondary sources include documentary films that interpret historical events, like Ric Burns's *Coney Island,* about how immigrants spent their leisure time at the famous amusement park in the early part of the twentieth century. A study by a sociologist, historian, or anthropologist *about* the era is also a secondary source.

The following can also be primary sources:

• Manuscripts (diaries, letters, unpublished material such as first drafts of poems, early books painstakingly written by hand in the days before the printing press, and other special handwritten documents)

• Government documents (census reports, maps, tax records, property deeds, wills, Bureau of Statistics listings, and other documents)

• Photograph collections

• Sound recordings

• Film, television, and radio archives (original records of events)

• Artifacts (items in museum collections)

Artifacts can be useful clues to understanding a subject. For instance, a building (a tenement inhabited by immigrants or a mansion decorated by an art collector) can help us interpret the life of a subject. Blueprints for Thomas Jefferson's house at Monticello help us understand the tastes and talents of America's third president. Beadwork designs on Sioux deerskin clothing help us study Native American life.

EXERCISE 4.2   Distinguishing between Primary and Secondary Sources

On your own or in a group with other students, check which of the items listed for each possible research project are primary and which are secondary. If you are not sure, enter a "?" and write a sentence explaining why the source is difficult to categorize.

Research project subject: A critical essay on the New York Yankees

Sources	Primary	Secondary
a. a book called *The House That Ruth Built*	_____	_____
b. the original blueprints for Yankee Stadium	_____	_____
c. a program for the May 16, 1997, game	_____	_____
d. a documentary film on PBS about the Negro Leagues	_____	_____

Research project subject: A paper on Polish immigrants in Chicago

Sources	Primary	Secondary
a. an interview with a waitress in a Polish restaurant in Chicago	_____	_____
b. Polish-American characters in a novel called *Tunnel Vision* by Sara Paretsky	_____	_____
c. figures from the 1990 U.S. Census	_____	_____
d. a collection of nineteenth-century letters at the local historical society	_____	_____

Research project subject: A paper on the African American writers of the Harlem Renaissance

Sources	Primary	Secondary
a. Zora Neale Hurston's novel *Their Eyes Were Watching God*	_____	_____
b. a sound recording of Langston Hughes reading his poem "Harlem"	_____	_____
c. a documentary film about writer James Baldwin called *The Fire Next Time*	_____	_____
d. a radio interview with poet Claude McKay taped in 1953	_____	_____

Research project subject: A paper on the roles of women during the Gold Rush of 1849

Sources	Primary	Secondary
a. the diary of a woman who traveled with her family in a covered wagon from Philadelphia to California	_____	_____
b. an episode from the television series *Little House on the Prairie*	_____	_____
c. a woman's dress and shoes from the 1840s at the Wright County Museum in Iowa	_____	_____
d. Willa Cather's novel *O! Pioneers*, from the 1920s	_____	_____

Research project subject: An argument on the effect of immigration law on the Texas-Mexico border

Sources	Primary	Secondary
a. an interview with a migrant farm worker	_____	_____
b. U.S. government statistics on the costs of border patrols	_____	_____
c. a newspaper article on changing patterns of worship based on ethnicity in El Paso churches	_____	_____
d. a school principal's speech to the PTA on bilingual education	_____	_____

Primary sources are often difficult for the student researcher to obtain or use. Many originals are rare or fragile, and often they are in distant places, with restricted access. You can visit Jefferson's home in Virginia, because Monticello is now a museum. But unless you are a qualified NASA engineer, collecting soil samples from Mars is impossible. To read Edith Wharton's diary in manuscript form requires a trip to the library in Austin, Texas. With the Internet, some primary sources, like manuscripts and letters, are now easily available, as are "virtual" visits to museums and historic sites. Nevertheless, most student researchers depend on secondary sources for much of their information. Secondary sources are more widely available because they usually exist in multiple copies.

Sometimes the differences between primary and secondary can be confusing. Remember that a twentieth-century reprint of the Declaration of Independence is still a primary source; it presents the original text, even though it is not on the original paper or in Jefferson's handwriting. A 1999 paperback of Zora Neale Hurston's novel is still a primary source, because we are reading the original text. On the other hand, an analysis of the meaning of the Declaration by Jefferson biographer Fawn Brodie is a secondary source; she is using the original (primary) but offering an interpretation of it. Likewise, a review of Hurston's novel by Alice Walker is a secondary source; the more recent novelist is writing *about* the work of another writer. A scientific paper analyzing soil samples from Mars is a paper using secondary sources.

Commonly used secondary sources include the following:

• **Printed books** History books, biographies, literary criticism, manuals, and the like all depend on primary sources.

- **Articles in magazines, journals, and newspapers** Whereas blood from a crime scene is a primary source, an article by a DNA expert would be secondary. Researchers often refer to critical articles, which offer a *critique,* or interpretation, of primary sources.

- **Film, television, and radio** Documentary films and news programs interpreting or commenting on current events are secondary because they depend on the primary events. Of course, film that actually records an event, such as footage of a space shuttle launch, can be a primary source.

- **Reviews** Reviews are published or recorded evaluations of sound or film recordings or of books. Reviews are secondary because a critic is using the primary source (novel, play, poem, song, or film) and writing or speaking about it.

A successful researcher investigates both primary and secondary sources. The goal is to read as many sources as possible to avoid taking too narrow a view. Each researcher must find the sources best suited to his or her own investigation. A paper on jazz in the 1920s would require sound recordings, whereas a paper on migrant farm laborers might require looking into regulations on workers' rights and interviewing workers, border patrol officers, and farm laborers.

| Step 9 | USING THE LIBRARY TO FIND YOUR SOURCES |

Most general libraries have similar materials organized in a similar fashion, whether you visit the local public library or a large university facility. The following basic elements can be found in most libraries:

- information desk

- circulation desk

- library catalog: also called public access catalog (PAC) or online public access catalog (OPAC)

- reference section

- book-shelving area (stacks)

- periodicals section

- reserve desk

- microform area (microfiche, microfilm, and machines for reading microforms)

- nonprint media area (films, sound recordings, CD-ROM stations)

- Internet stations

- special collections or archives or rare books (in some libraries)

- a quiet study section with tables, desks, or individual work areas

- seating areas with wireless access or electric plugs and modular jacks for using your laptop

Most libraries provide a map or printed library guide to help you familiarize yourself with the arrangements. Spend time exploring on your own, or ask the librarian for a map of your library, and inquire about when tours are given so you can become familiar with the location of the materials you are going to need.

Step 10	GETTING TO KNOW YOUR LIBRARY

No matter what their size, libraries can be imposing and confusing—so much so that some people are afraid even to enter them! Maybe such people believe they will look stupid if they cannot find something right away, or maybe they do not know where to begin. As a result, they put off doing research much longer than they should. The only way to make a library friendly and familiar is to plunge in, get lost if necessary, and figure out how it works. In this chapter we will focus on how to locate information about books and articles.

The Library Catalog

Searching for Books

A library catalog contains a comprehensive listing of all the books in a library. They are arranged in several ways: by author, title, and subject and, for online catalogs, by keyword, or word. In the past each work was listed on an index card, which was then stored in a file drawer called a card catalog. Card catalogs have largely been replaced by online catalogs. The one you encounter may be called PAC (public access catalog) or OPAC (online public access catalog).

Beginning to Use an Online Catalog to Search for Books

Find the online catalog in your library. Most of the time, you'll start with a welcome screen. It might look like this:

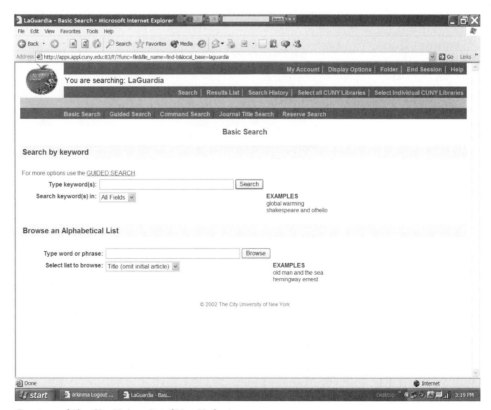

Courtesy of The City University of New York.

If you type the search term "Lizzie Borden" in the keyword search box and click on "search," the next screen will list the books available:

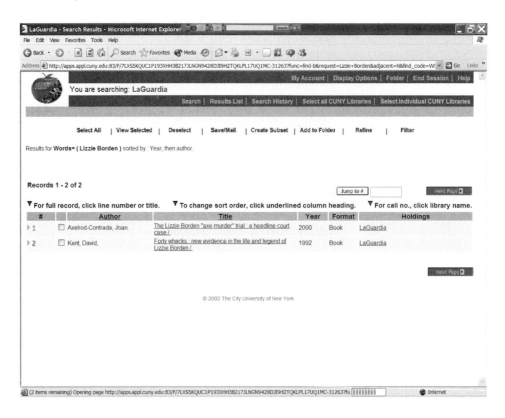

There are only two books. If you click on the title of the first one, or click on the small box next to the 1, you will get details on that book:

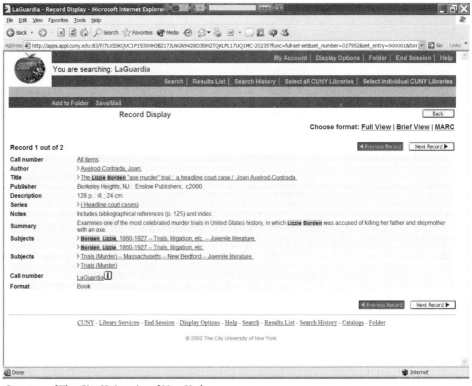

Courtesy of The City University of New York.

While your library may have a different style for presenting the information, you should find that the basics are the same: a title, an author, and a place for locating a call number.

The most important item is the **call number,** because it tells us where the book is located in the library stacks. Let's try a search by returning to our topic of Edith Wharton and Morocco from Chapter 3.

EXERCISE 4.3   **Finding Sources about Edith Wharton in Your College's Online Catalog**

1. Using the author search, enter the name Edith Wharton. How many items does the catalog list?

2. Now use the subject search and try the same entry: *Edith Wharton.* How many entries does the catalog list?

3. Are they the same or different from the results of the author search?

4. Now begin a title search. Use the title of the Wharton book you read from, *In Morocco.* Does your library own the book? If so, what is the call number? Has the book been taken out? How do you know? (If there is no entry for this book, try the book *The Age of Innocence,* also by Wharton.)

5. Try a keyword search. Enter the code for keyword or word as instructed by the menu screen, and type in *Wharton Edith* and press "Enter." Then try the same search with the word *Morocco.* Are any of the titles the same in the two results?

6. What kind of book do you find if you search by author? by subject? by keyword?

7. If you are starting to search for an assignment, which technique is the best to use? Why?

Types of Searches

The **author** command presents books and library materials by the name of the writer. Use this search only if you know the name of the writer of the book you want. Edith Wharton wrote many books, so libraries list them alphabetically by title within the entry for *Wharton.*

The **title** command is useful only if you already know the exact title of the book you want. If you have read paragraphs from *In Morocco,* or if you have a list of specific books that you need, this is the right type of search. Most of the time, however, this command is not useful because you do not already know the titles of the books you need. When using this command, drop *the, a,* and *an* from titles to speed up the search.

The **subject** command can be confusing. Because you are looking for the subject or topic that appears in your research proposal, you might expect the database to recognize any word you type in. However, in most libraries *subject* has a specialized meaning: It refers to words or specific subject headings prepared by the Library of Congress. These lists are mainly for the use of librarians or advanced researchers. The words you decide to use—say, "Black writers"—may give you "0" results. Common sense tells you this is not accurate. What happened? The "subject" heading in the database is "African American writers." The machine cannot guess that these are related terms. Unless you put in the label that appears in the database, nothing will turn up. Because this can be frustrating, we suggest that beginning researchers avoid the subject search until they have more experience.

Using a **keyword** can be the best way to begin a search. This approach is versatile and helps you explore your subject more easily. A keyword locates the word you enter in *any* location, whether it is in the title of a book, the author's name, or the subject. Keyword searches may result in a fairly long list at first, because the search will be for all the words you enter ("Edith Wharton's *In Morocco*" will yield sources for both Edith Wharton and Morocco), but at least you do not need to know an exact word. If you enter "Black writers" you will get results, and you will get similar results by entering "African American writers."

You can expand your keyword search further by using the terms AND, NOT, and OR. Here are some examples of what is known as a **Boolean search:**

Immigration AND Puerto Rico

Here you would search for sources that contain both terms, so you would eliminate sources on immigration in Norway, Korea, Ukraine, and so on. Using AND in this way narrows the search and gets you to sources closer to your own subject.

Immigration OR Puerto Rico

This is a way to broaden your search. OR asks the database to give you all the sources on Immigration *and* all the sources on Puerto Rico, so you would get a very large list of sources.

Immigration NOT Puerto Rico

This search would lead you to the sources on all other immigration topics, but *not* those on Puerto Rico.

EXERCISE 4.4   Using the Catalog for Keyword Searches for Books

Perform each of the following searches.

1. Execute a keyword search using the term "multiculturalism."

2. Do a second search with "multiculturalism and America."

3. Try a third keyword search, this time using "multiculturalism and Japanese and California."

You should begin to see how the use of *and* helps to narrow the search and shorten the results so that the list is more closely related to exactly what you need.

EXERCISE 4.5   Doing an Online Search with Boolean Connecting Words

Do an online keyword search on the following topics. Use at least two AND connectors in each one (such as "Wharton AND Morocco AND travel"). Try several Boolean searches, experimenting with the use of OR and NOT.

1. literature by Native American women writers

2. drug use among Olympic athletes

3. role of Chinese immigrants in building railroads in nineteenth-century America

4. ethnic diversity in community colleges in the United States

5. power of health-care lobbyists in Washington, D.C., to influence policy decisions

EXERCISE 4.6   Using Keywords to Search Your Research Topic

1. Make a list of five keywords or words connected with *and* based on your own research proposal.

_____

_____

_____

_____

_____

2. Use the online catalog to search each of the entries you developed in Question 1.

_____

These results should suggest that there are some guidelines to keep in mind as you proceed to your own search:

- Do not give up too easily.

- Be sure all your spellings are accurate.

- Try a variety of words if your first search gets "0" results. Also try synonyms.

- Narrow the search with *and* as much as possible.

- Do not hesitate to ask the library staff for help.

How many entries did you locate? If you found thousands, then your search is still too broad. If you found "0," then your search is too narrow. Ideally, a list of about 10 titles is a good start. If you found more than that, narrow the list to the 10 that seem closest to your own topic.

What to Copy Down about Book Sources from the Online Catalog

When you are at the computer, be sure to copy down or print out information that will help you locate the book; this information will also be necessary later for identifying the source if you use it in your research paper. For each book you wish to examine, be sure you have the following information:

1. all authors' names

2. the names of editors or translators, if any are listed

3. the full title and subtitle of the book

4. the publishing company and its address

5. the date of publication

6. *most important:* the complete call number (otherwise you won't be able to find the book on the shelves in the stacks)

EXERCISE 4.7   Identifying Call Numbers

Make a list of the call numbers of the books you want. With these numbers, you can move away from the computers and toward the bookshelves in the stacks.

_____

How to Use Library Call Numbers

Once you have copied down the call number and other information, you will be ready to find the book. Most college and university libraries use what is called the Library of Congress system to organize books. However, some libraries, especially smaller public libraries, use the Dewey Decimal system.

The Library of Congress (LC) system uses letters and numbers, usually a four-line code plus the year of publication, to identify a book. A typical call number would look like this:

PS 3534.H16 Z595 1994

In the LC system, each book has a distinct number. PS tells us the book falls in the category of literature, and the further numbers indicate a particular literary biography, a book about the life of Edith Wharton called *No Gifts from Chance*. If it were classified by the Dewey system, the same book would have this code:

B
Wharton

However, this code would also be used for other biographies of the same subject, so you would have to look more closely (at the actual books) to determine which you wanted. The LC system is more precise and specific, so it has been adopted by most large libraries. We will use it as our example.

In the Library of Congress system, each book has a unique call number. No matter which library you use, the book will be shelved according to its number. The first line, such as PS, tells you the general subject area—in this case, literature and fiction. A single letter, such as P, might be subdivided into sections PA, PB, PC, and so on. The first line is important because it tells you in which section of the stacks to begin looking for your book. Stacks have labels on the side identifying which letters are held on those shelves. For example, a stack might have a sign that says "PR-PS." The book PS3534.H16 Z595 1994, because it begins with PS, would be on these shelves.

Once you locate the "PS" shelf, look at the next line. There are many "PS" books, and they are now lined up according to the second number: PS 1, PS 2, PS 3, ... all the way to PS 999 and beyond. Our book is "PS 3534," and we would follow the PS books until we got to that area.

Now look at the third line. In this case it is .H16. Again, each PS 3534 will have a third line and a fourth line arranged numerically or alphabetically. Keep narrowing the search until you locate the exact book you want.

The last number in this example, 1994, tells the year in which the book was published.

Once you have the number, you will be able to retrieve the book, But before you leave the computer, let's look briefly at what else you can find there.

Searching with Electronic Resources for Articles

Searching with Electronic Databases

Databases are the newest way to locate articles in magazines, journals, and newspapers. In the past, a researcher would have to search for information in large, heavy, printed indexes and then move to the library stacks to find the actual articles. Today a great deal of what the college researcher needs may be located using electronic tools exclusively. However, since there is so much available, you need to know how to focus and narrow your search, or you will find yourself overwhelmed by the sheer volume of material. Fortunately, librarians have redesigned library home pages to make the searching easier and more effective. Here is the home page, for example, from a community college library:

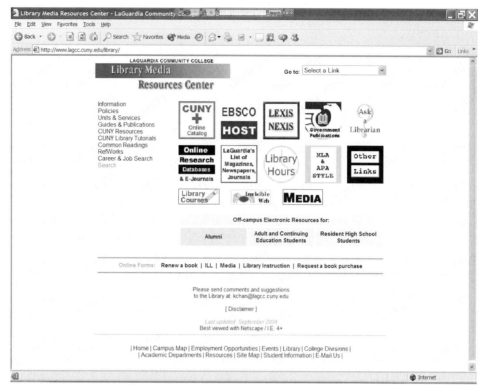

Reprinted by permission of La Guardia Community College.

While at first it may look confusing, the page is like a table of contents to the electronic sources available to students. Each link, or icon, represents one source for finding materials. You have already seen the online catalog, here available as "CUNY+Online Catalog." But the other links are equally valuable, since they take the user to thousands of articles from journals and other periodical publications. Many of these licensed databases are available nationally, and so are likely to be in your own library, if the librarians have decided to order them. Once you learn how to search in one, you'll see that you can apply the same skill to using many other databases.

EBSCOhost and LexisNexis are two widely used databases found in most college libraries. These huge collections organize information and allow you to locate the information you seek with several kinds of searches. In most cases, when you are planning your paper you will want to search by keyword. This means you want to locate articles about your topic; you do not know the titles or authors of articles, and you do not know where they are published. If you click on the icon for EBSCOhost on the library home page illustrated above, you will be able to select from a long list of databases. Here is a sample page:

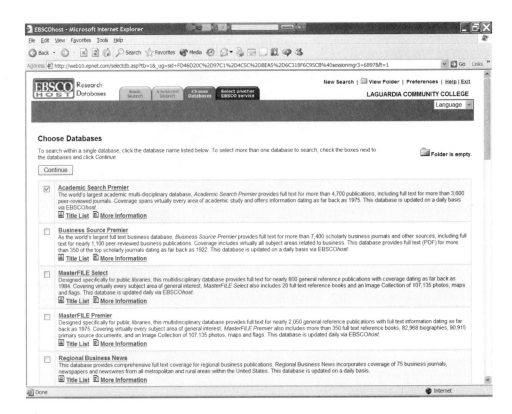

If you then click on the box next to one of the databases that relates to your topic, or if you select a general one that covers fields like Academic Search Premier, as we did in the following example, you can type in the subject of your research paper and see what you find. Here is the first page of the results for the request for articles on "Edith Wharton":

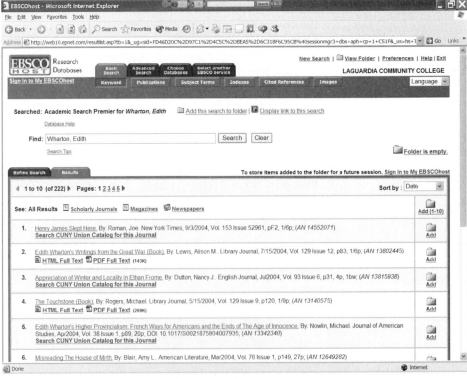

This page begins the list of scholarly journals—that is, articles by experts on literature published in professional or specialized sources. If you look at the six entries on this page, you will see that there are several choices in each source box. The first one provides the title of an article, "Misreading the House of Mirth." It also indicates that you would have to "Search the CUNY Union Catalog for this journal." This means that there is no electronic way to read the article. If you wanted this particular study of Wharton's novel *The House of Mirth*, you would have to continue to search with the link to find which library has the journal *American Literature* and go there to read it. You might be able to get it through interlibrary loan as well. However, if you look at entry 3 and entry 4, you will see that for these articles, electronic versions are available. You can click on the "PDF Full Text" or "HTML Full Text" or "Linked Full Text" links and read the article immediately. You can also e-mail the file to yourself for later reading.

Clearly, the databases are a valuable tool. You have to select articles that are appropriate to your topic, of course, but as you are in the early stages of your research, it is often helpful to browse quickly through a number of articles to get an overview of a subject. (It is not good practice to ignore an article just because it is not available electronically, but we will discuss this later, when we review how to evaluate a source.)

Another widely available database is LexisNexis. There is a specific database within this software for Business subjects that is widely used by lawyers and corporate researchers, but there is also an academic database, which led to some recent articles on Lizzie Borden after a keyword search:

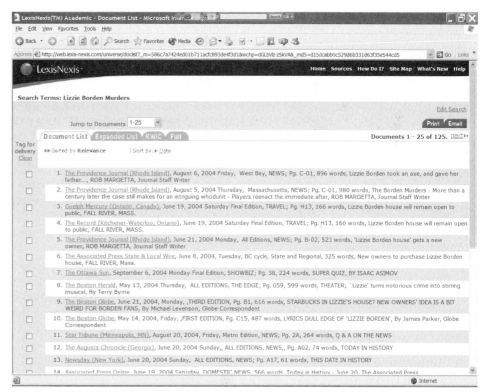

Reprinted with the permission of LexisNexis.

This list contains recent articles from newspapers from across America on the Borden murder case that can be read if you "tag" or mark the box next to the article by clicking on it. Tag each article you want to read. There is a "How Do I?" link at the top of the page to help you use the information and e-mail it to yourself for later reading.

EXERCISE 4.8   **Finding Databases in Your Library**

1. Using the home page of your college library, find and list below three general research databases that are available to users.

_____   _____   _____

2. Using your own research topic, use these databases to locate articles from magazines, newspapers, and journals. E-mail the articles to yourself, and post what you found on your discussion board.

_____

Electronic Sources for Historical Newspapers

Most of us read newspapers. In the days before the Internet, newspapers were meant to be current and were read only by a limited local audience. Therefore, when a researcher wants to locate and read an article from a paper several months or years old, it is not easy to find the original paper copy. Local libraries or historical societies will preserve as much as they can of these impermanent forms, but to use a newspaper for a research essay, most of us are dependent on **microfilm.** Photographs are taken of each page of a newspaper; these are reduced to the size of a postage stamp on a reel of film. Thus several weeks of a daily newspaper can be stored on a single reel. A library can store the *New York Times,* for instance, with every page from 1851 to today, in a filing cabinet.

One limitation of online resources is that they have only limited holdings, containing articles published in the last 10 years or so. Each one is different, and you need to check the information about the holdings to find out what is included. To pursue the research for the essay "Forty Whacks," then, online databases such as EBSCOhost or LexisNexis might not be very helpful. If your library were licensed to offer ProQuest, you could search the link to historical newspapers and locate the original 1892 *New York Times* articles, as Anna did for her paper.

However, in many cases researchers still rely on microfilm. Especially if you want to read local newspapers rather than national ones like the *Washington Post* or the *Los Angeles Times,* you will need to use this medium. To read the articles, the user has to locate the spool of film for a given issue; these are usually stored by date in a file cabinet in the library. You then take the spool to a microfilm reading machine, which allows you to enlarge, read, and print the page.

Keep in mind, though, that it is often difficult to locate articles unless you know the date of the event you are investigating, since not all newspapers have a subject index. Because Anna knew that the Borden murders took place in August 1892 and the trial continued through 1893, she could use the microfilm to locate articles fairly quickly. Some newspapers, like the *New York Times,* produce massive subject indexes in book form, published annually for microfilm users. You could look up a subject in each annual volume, make a note of the date on which the article was published and the page number, and then use the microfilm machine to read the article.

Additional Reference Works

Print Encyclopedias

Another source is an encyclopedia. These are available both in paper and online. Let's look at the paper ones first. If you locate the area in the reference section where encyclopedias are shelved, you will see that most sets have one volume for each letter of the alphabet or a group of letters that identify the first and last entries in the volume. These letters are printed on the spine of the book, usually near the bottom. You have to decide which volume to use. If your subject is "Norwegian immigration to the United States," for instance, you could try the "N" volume, look up "Norway," and see whether, in the article on Norway, there is a section about immigration to the United States. Alternatively, you might try "I" and find an article on "immigration." Don't give up. Try several possible words and volumes until you locate what you need.

Encyclopedias can be found on the shelves of the reference section, on CD-ROM, and online. Some general encyclopedias are:

Collier's	*Encyclopedia Americana*
Encyclopaedia Britannica	*The World Book*

EXERCISE 4.9   Locating Encyclopedias

In the reference section of your library, find the shelves where the encyclopedias are located. Which of the four encyclopedias listed above are available in your library? List three other encyclopedias you find.

1. _____

2. _____

3. _____

Online Encyclopedias

There are several encyclopedias available online. *Encyclopaedia Britannica* is one that many libraries subscribe to, for example. These are quicker to use than the paper volumes because the material is alphabetized in the database, and users can simply enter the word or words they want to search. They are usually located in Online Reference links on most library home pages.

EXERCISE 4.10   Using Online Encyclopedias

Find an electronic encyclopedia in your library's online reference tools. Search for an article related to your topic. Print out the article. On the page, be sure to write down which source you used to obtain the article.

Printed Bibliographies

Printed bibliographies are books that contain lists of books and articles by subject. Many of these are now available online, but researchers may still need to use the paper versions because not all libraries have these resources online. Depending on the subject you are investigating, one or more of these sources will help you locate articles or books on your subject.

We will use as an example an entry from a well-known bibliography of literary studies, the *MLA Bibliography*. This is an enormous and intimidating work, and its use is generally more appropriate for advanced researchers than for beginners. However, if you were working on an essay about Edith Wharton, you could consult this tool to find academic articles published about Wharton by going to the "W" section of the annual volumes. These volumes are updated each year, so a researcher using the paper versions has to consult each year's volume to check for articles.

If you found an article in the *MLA Bibliography* that was related to your essay subject, you would copy down the *entire* entry on a notecard or pad or on your laptop (see Chapter 5). Then you would have to go to your library's online catalog to see whether the particular journal referred to in the entry was available. As you can see, using a bibliography is just a first step in finding a source. It indicates where to find articles but does not contain the articles themselves. As you will see by comparing the two, RGPL directs the user to popular magazines, whereas MLA is a scholar's tool for locating articles in specialized academic journals. RGPL is easier for the beginner to use, but academic researchers working in language and literature depend on the more advanced articles available through MLA.

There are hundreds of bibliographies available, on every subject you might need. Once you understand how a bibliography works, you will be able to use any one of them. See Appendix B for a list of some of the most commonly used printed bibliographies.

What to Copy Down about Periodical and Reference Sources from the Online Catalog

Just as you did with books, you must copy down important information for each periodical source you investigate. Use one card per source, or make a list on a notepad or your laptop. Copy

- all authors' names

- the exact title of the article, including subtitles or headlines

- the exact title of the magazine, newspaper, or journal in which you found it

- the complete date: month, day, and year (newspaper or weekly); month and year (monthly); other date information for quarterly or semiannual publications (for example, Autumn 1997)

- the issue or volume number, if there is one

- the pages on which the article appears

- for a print encyclopedia, the name of the encyclopedia, the title of the article you found, the date when the edition of the encyclopedia was published, the volume, and the pages; for an online encyclopedia, the URL

EXERCISE 4.11   Finding Sources in Online Databases

Select an ethnic group you want to learn more about—Chicano, Norwegian, Chinese, Jewish, Polish, Italian. (Alternatively, you may choose to complete this exercise on the subject you have chosen for your research.) Then go to the reference section of your library and find the following sources. Write down what you find and tell how you found it. Include the mistakes you made, how you got lost, and how you finally found your source. For each source, record the information about the article, following the guidelines above.

1. Find an entry for a newspaper article in LexisNexis.

2. Find an article in a popular magazine. Print it, and be sure that it includes the title, author, date, and page information.

EXERCISE 4.12   Retrieving Sources

1. List the steps that you would follow if you wanted to find a book called *No Gifts from Chance* by Shari Benstock. This is a biography of the writer Edith Wharton and has the call number PR 3549, .H16 Z595 1994.

   _____

   _____

   _____

2. If you were looking for books with the following four call numbers, in which order would you find them on the library shelf? Put 1 under the first, 2 under the second, and so on.

   PR3509   PC4999   PN1691   PR1897

   _____   _____   _____   _____

3. Suppose you found an article about the murder of Lizzie Borden's parents that was listed in the *New York Times Index* for August 2, 1892. What other information would you need before you could retrieve this article?

   _____

   _____

4. Where would you look for this same article in an online format?

   _____

   _____

5. You think that the film *Coney Island* by Ric Burns might be useful for a paper on immigration in the early 1900s. Does your library have a copy of this documentary on DVD or VHS?

   _____

   _____

6. For a paper on jazz in the novels of Toni Morrison, you want to listen to some music from the 1920s and 1930s. Where would you look in your college library to locate this music if it is available? How would you find a print copy of Morrison's novel *Jazz*?

   _____

   _____

EXERCISE 4.13   Retrieving Sources for Your Topic

Retrieve one book, one article from a newspaper or popular magazine, and one Web site, using the notes you took from the online catalog or other reference tools such as online databases.

   _____

What If You Can't Find a Source?

Often you will have many sources in your notecards or source list that you would like to consult, but when you try to find them in your library, these books are not on the shelf. There are several steps you can take:

1. Go to the circulation desk to verify that the book has been checked out or placed on reserve. Sometimes books are lost or stolen, and you need to know whether the book will be returned soon or is permanently lost.

2. Check with the reference librarian to verify that you have the right call number or other source information and that you are looking in the right place.

3. If the book is not available at your library, check with the library staff to see whether it is available on interlibrary loan. Keep in mind, however, that borrowing from another library can take up to four weeks, and you may not be able to wait that long for the book. If the other library is close to your campus, it might take less time to go there and obtain the book yourself.

4. Continue to look for other sources; don't get obsessed with the one you can't find unless you are sure it is essential to your subject.

5. See if there is an e-text version of the book.

Finding What You Need on the Internet

Most students today are becoming familiar with the Internet and the World Wide Web. The technology of the computer has become increasingly valuable for shopping, e-mail correspondence, games, chat rooms, information retrieval, and many other purposes. However, most beginning researchers doing academic work are not familiar enough with the special sites available, hosted by dependable and reputable Webmasters at universities, libraries, museums, government bureaus, and other sponsors. Our purpose in this section of *Research Papers* is to start you on the path to finding these valuable electronic sources. As you become familiar with the basic techniques for finding the kinds of sites appropriate for college-level work, you will be able to explore the vast networks that are expanding rapidly. For most researchers, the problem with the Internet is that it seems too big and too confusing. Let's focus on the basic steps in using the Internet to find what you need, without getting overwhelmed by the enormity of its resources. Although the Internet offers an exciting, dynamic wealth of material, not everything on the Internet is authoritative, and some of it could be risky as a source. We will discuss the issue of how to evaluate sources in Chapter 5. Here we will begin with techniques for the first step, finding sources on the Internet.

Search Engines

Most users access information on the World Wide Web through search engines, commercially supported sites designed to help a user begin a search. Keep in mind that because they are supported by advertising, search engines are user-friendly and readily available, but they are not always the best tool for getting to good academic Web sites. As a starting point, however, they can be useful as long as you do not depend entirely on what they provide. They tend to lead a user to the most popular—but not necessarily the best—academic sources.

If you subscribe to an Internet service provider (ISP) such as AOL or MSN, the welcome screen of your ISP will suggest additional ways to search.

There are also educational sites for finding information, and these are usually more efficient for the types of subjects that college students need to investigate.

Search engines change rapidly. Popular ones have been Google (www.google.com) and Yahoo! (www.yahoo.com). However, less well-known but more powerful tools exist for academic research. The site Beaucoup (www.beaucoup.com) helps you find Web sites through subject links. Another site that helps you search more thoroughly is www.infopeople.org/search/tools.html. Likewise, www.highbeam.com guides you to specialized databases and local newspapers; www.alltheweb.com and www.gigablast.com are further competition for the more familiar sites and deserve to be explored. You should also become familiar with www.lii.org, the Librarians' Index to the Internet, which helps you find reliable sources.

Step 11   FINDING YOUR ELECTRONIC SOURCES

Set aside at least an hour to explore the resources available on the Internet. If you have never used the Internet before, use a computer in the library so that you can ask a librarian for help. Ask if your college holds workshops in using the Internet and the library's databases, too.

1. Make a list of at least 10 possible key words related to your own proposal.

2. Select three different search engines from the list above.

3. Do a search for your key words on each of the search engines, and print the results.

4. Compare the results: how many hits did each give you? Which results look more closely related to your interest?

5. Keep a list of the best sites, and if you are working on your own computer, bookmark these sites.

6. Go to your library's home page. Use a database such as LexisNexis or EBSCOhost and do another search using the same keywords you used with the search engines. Examine at least three of the articles that you get.

7. Compare the results from the search engines and the databases. Post a comment to your discussion board about what you found.

How to Use a Search Engine

A **search engine** is a device that tells the computer to narrow down the huge database, or collection of available material, to the specific topic you want. It is, in fact, just like doing a search in the online catalog, but the search starts with a much bigger collection of data, and the engine has to search through more material to find something. Unlike the library catalog, the search engine results can help you locate **links,** which are electronic addresses you can go to in order to continue the search. You will see that it is not always easy to get to exactly the site you want right away, just as you had to know how to modify the library search with keyword or title or author to direct the online catalog inquiry.

When you click on the icon for "Internet Explorer" or "Netscape Navigator," you are starting to use a browser that will help you with the search. The browser will either present you with one search engine or give you a choice of several. If your browser leads you to only one search engine, you can still access others by typing in the address, or URL (uniform resource locator)—for example, www.google.com.

Once you have selected the search engine, find a box and a search command such as "go" or "submit search." Type one or more keywords in this box. Click on "go."

Always use the Back command to return to the previous page. This is usually an icon such as an arrow pointing left on the upper-left-hand part of the toolbar. You risk losing your site if you do not work this way.

If you find a site you like and may want to return to, and you are working on your home computer, use "bookmark" or "favorites" to have the address placed in your computer's memory, where you can later find it easily. Look in the toolbar at the top of the screen for a command for "bookmark" or "favorites." Pull down the command, and click on the box for "add." When you later want to locate the source, you pull down the same bar and go to the list of favorites indicated. Without using this technique, it can be difficult to return to a site you found on an earlier search.

Hyperlinks are the key to using the Internet, for these are connections to other sites that are related to the first one. When you are at a Web site, the lists of other sites you can go to in order to locate more information are highlighted in blue or another color. These are links, and when you click on them, they bring you to a related site. They are a means of cross-referencing, or finding similar or related topics. You can move back and forth from link to link, "surfing" until you find just what you need. Use the Back and Forward (scroll) arrows to move this way.

EXERCISE 4.14   Using Search Engines

Let's look further at the kinds of information a site can provide. This time we will use the search box and enter the author's name, Edith Wharton, and click "search" or "go."

1. How many sites did you find?

2. Choose one site by clicking on the hyperlink or colored text for that site.

3. Look carefully at the first Edith Wharton page you selected, and answer the following questions:

   a. Is there a chronological list of Wharton's publications, starting with *The Touchstone* in 1900? Do some of the titles say "online" whereas others do not? Click on the hyperlink to one that says *online text* if you can find one on your site. What appears on the next screen?

   b. Which link would you select if your topic were Wharton's life (or biography)?

   c. Does the site list a bibliography or a "hypertext bibliography"? If so, click on this list. What is the result?

   d. What other information about Wharton does the page help you find?

   e. What is missing from this site that you expected to find?

   f. Return to the first screen by clicking on the Back icon several times until you reach the screen with the list of search results. Try another link, and answer the same questions.

   g. Now compare the two sites. Which do you think would be most useful if you were using Wharton as your subject for a research assignment? Why?

Once you have clicked on the Search command, the search results will be listed, usually at the bottom of the screen. Use the scroll arrows to pull up the results, one by one. You can usually maximize the screen (make the image bigger) by clicking on another icon in the toolbar. Sometimes you will find a site that seems to be exactly what you want; other times you will have to try several searches to get the best results. Remember that, just as with the library online catalog, it helps to be specific. One important difference is that in the online catalog, you can link related keywords with "and" to narrow the search. On the Internet, leave out the "and." For example, in the library catalog, you might search for "multiculturalism and America." On the Internet, you would try "multiculturalism America." Experiment to see which techniques get results for your subject, however. The speed with which the search engines work makes it easy to try many searches in a short time, so you can explore rapidly.

EXERCISE 4.15   Finding Web Sites with a Search Engine

1. Make a list of three search engines.

2. Go online, and for each search engine, in the "search" box, type in a keyword from your own research proposal. Try using the same keyword or words that you used for your library online catalog search if you are not sure how to get started. Click on the Search command.

3. On the next screen, scroll down and select a site. Point the cursor to it with the mouse, and click.

4. Keep going until you have reached a site that looks as though it might be useful or interesting for your paper.

5. Try searching with other keywords.

EXERCISE 4.16   Finding Sources with Two Different Search Engines

1. Using your own research topic, go to the Internet Public Library, www.lii.org, or use another tool to find sources. Be sure to print out promising results or to bookmark these pages so that you can return to them later.

2. Look carefully at the results of all the searches. Which engine did you find the most useful? Why?

3. What differences did you observe between Yahoo! and Google, for instance, in terms of what kinds of sites you were able to access or what the screens looked like? Are the results from lii.org similar to or different from the others? How?

Set aside at least an hour to explore the resources available on the Internet. If you have never used the Internet before, use a computer in the library so you can ask questions of a librarian if you have trouble. If possible, use a computer with a printer attached so you can keep track of your results.

1. Make a list of at least 10 possible keywords related to your own proposal.

2. Use a search engine and try out the keywords. Persist until you find three Web sites you think will help you learn more about your topic. Print out the home page, or bookmark the sites for future reference, if you are working on your own computer.

3. Using the same words, search a database such as EBSCOhost or LexisNexis. Follow the same process as in the previous step.

Finding Specialized Sources

Locating and Using Specialized Libraries

In addition to the general libraries that most students use, researchers sometimes need more specialized materials not available in their local public library or college collection. Although for most beginning researchers the home library is both adequate and easier to use for an undergraduate assignment, you should be aware that as your skills advance, you may want to explore further. Here are some examples of particularly good Web sites:

> www.nypl.org (New York Public Library)
>
> www.ipl.org (Internet Public Library)
>
> www.loc.gov (Library of Congress)

Your own college library's home page probably offers you links to other libraries, as well as reliable databases and Web sites.

EXERCISE 4.17 Exploring Specialized Libraries

Using links on your library's home page or one of the Web sites above, find specialized libraries that would be of interest to researchers working on the following subjects. List the name of the library and the Web address.

1. architecture

   _____

   _____

2. music

   _____

   _____

3. agriculture

   _____

   _____

4. law and criminals

   _____

   _____

5. science and technology

   _____

   _____

6. politics and government

   _____

   _____

7. psychology

_____

_____

8. African American studies

_____

_____

9. engineering

_____

_____

10. health and medicine

_____

_____

How can libraries in other cities—or even other countries—be helpful to you?

_____

Online Catalogs

Browsing the catalogs of other libraries—which you can do online through the libraries' home pages—helps you find the titles and authors of books and articles on your subject. You can then go to your local library and try to find these. In addition, you can ask your librarian whether it is possible to have books from another library sent to you via interlibrary loan, as mentioned earlier.

Digital Libraries

Many libraries, especially very large and specialized collections, are making the full texts of books available online. In other words, you can locate a library, determine whether it has a digital collection, and then search the titles. If something interests you, you can click on the full-text icon and the entire book or document will appear on your screen. Some libraries allow you to download these sources so you can either transfer them to a disk or print the text for home use.

For example, if we go to the New York Public Library Digital Library Collection and highlight "Browse the collection," we obtain a menu listing additional choices. If we highlight "Digital Schomburg" and "African American Women Writers of the 19th Century," we enter a digital full-text library.

Expert Web Sites

Additional sources may be found on Web sites that, like journals, are aimed at experts in a particular field. These may be too specialized for a beginning researcher, but it is nevertheless important for you to know that they exist if you want to explore your subject in greater depth or if you cannot find sources in other places.

- **Academic societies**   Within each academic discipline, such groups enable experts to meet and exchange ideas and information via meetings, newsletters, journals, and listservs. In literary studies you might locate the Edith Wharton Society, the Jane Austen Society, and the Emily Dickinson International Society, whose members focus on the life and works of their chosen author. Biologists have societies for those who study spiders or birds; astronomers have societies devoted to new theories on black holes. Such societies exist in every academic discipline. As a start, ask a professional in the subject area of your proposal what some of the most respected societies are. Use a search engine or other search tool such as Academic Info to locate a group in your subject area. The Web site will lead you to lists of books and articles, as well as help you become familiar with your subject through illustrations and links to other sites.

- **Professional organizations** Teachers, lawyers, engineers, police officers, architects, doctors, and virtually all other professionals have a society devoted to defining and maintaining the goals and ethical values of the profession, to serving as a conduit for information, and to defining the requirements for entry into the profession. The American Medical Association, the Modern Language Association, the American Institute of Architects—these are all professional organizations. Locating the organization for your subject can help you find professional journals, specialized libraries or archives, the names of prominent members who might be contacted, issues in the profession that might be important to your topic, and so on. Professional organizations are generally larger than academic societies and serve a national or international membership. They publish journals, hold conferences, issue press releases, and are responsible for many other aspects of the profession they represent. Use a search engine to locate the group that represents the field you are investigating by searching for the subject (sociology, for example) and the words "professional organization." You can also ask a professional in the field to help you locate the URL, or address, that you need.

Museums and Other Resources

Sources for research may not always come in the form of words. As we have noted, artifacts can also be a valuable source of information. Museums exist to collect and identify artifacts. Local history societies are designed to collect the documents, photographs, and objects that record a community's past. You can have access to large world-class collections such as the British Museum in London, which holds everything from mummies to manuscripts. Museums can be valuable places to go to expand your knowledge as you are trying to locate sources. Never overlook the opportunity to draw on resources such as the following:

1. A local museum (check your local phone directory for the hometown Web site for listings of museums, historical societies, historic sites or monuments, and house museums)

2. A museum outside your own region, online

3. A site related to a famous individual or celebrity

Archives

Archives are special collections of historical documents and artifacts. The National Archives in Washington, D.C., for instance, houses such rare and important documents as the original Declaration of Independence. Many colleges and libraries have archives that feature local history and biography, such as the LaGuardia and Wagner Archives at LaGuardia Community College in New York City. This collection contains thousands of letters, maps, trophies, medals, photographs, and personal memorabilia of New York's mayors. Like many archives, this one is a rich source of photographs, many of which are available online. Many large corporations and even some smaller businesses have archives of their own history. For research on a business topic, such corporate archives can be helpful.

EXERCISE 4.18   **Finding Sources in Expert Web Sites, Societies and Organizations, and Museums**

1. Using your local phone directory or Chamber of Commerce listing, identify five sites that might be useful for researching immigrants in your community. Alternatively, you can locate sites related to your own research topic.

2. Examine the Web site for the academic society AAALS, www.australianliterature. org. Explain how you might use this page to locate sources for a project on the history, culture, or literature of Australia.

3. Using a search engine, locate Web sites on the immigrant museum at Ellis Island. How many sites can you find? Which one seems most useful for a student who wants to learn about the history of immigrants in the 1890–1910 period? Explain how you made your choice.

4. Using the subject of your own research paper, use the Internet to find the name of at least one professional organization that represents experts working in that field.

On notecards, on a notepad, or on your computer, create a list of all the sites you located.

What to Copy Down about Your Sources

The list of information you must record about book sources appears on page 111. Review the list, and copy down all the necessary information so you will be prepared to retrieve all of the sources you have found.

Retrieving Sources

In this chapter you have learned how to find a variety of sources (including books, periodicals, and newspapers) in the online catalog. You also explored some applications of the Internet to college research. Now, after you have thoroughly searched the catalog and reference room and carefully recorded the source information for the materials you would like to consult, the next step is to actually find the works and see whether what you have found so far is the best material for your research paper.

Books

Books that are not located in the reference section are found in an area known as the stacks. Some libraries allow patrons to enter the stacks, find the books they want, and check them out. Others have closed stacks. In these libraries, patrons must fill out a piece of paper known as a **call slip** in order to request a book. You will need to write on the call slip the same information you copied when you found the book in the online catalog: author, title, publisher, year, and (most important) call number. You submit the slip at a service desk, and the library staff will go into the stacks and retrieve the book for you. In most libraries that use this system, the researcher is provided with an identification number. When your book has arrived at the service desk, the identification number is announced or posted so that you can return to the desk and claim the book. If the book is marked "reserve," it does not circulate, and must stay in the library.

Periodicals (Print Version)

The word *periodical* refers to popular magazines, newspapers, professional magazines, and academic journals. Whereas a popular magazine or newspaper article written by a journalist may give you a more general account of your subject, a journal usually has articles that are longer, treat the subject in more depth, and are written by academic experts. Thus, although it is acceptable to begin learning about your subject through popular magazines and newspapers, you must be prepared to investigate further once you have a basic understanding of the subject. Academic journals should be part of your research.

To retrieve a periodical, you must have with you the notes where you recorded all you need. Check to see that your library subscribes to the periodical by looking in the online catalog. Start with the title of the magazine and the exact date. Find the copy, or volume, or appropriate spool of microfilm. Once you have the right magazine, use the rest of your notes to find the precise article by the page numbers you copied down. The article you find should have exactly the title and author indicated in your notes. If you think the article will be useful, you can make a photocopy. Be sure to record all the information on the photocopy so that you know where the article appeared: title of the magazine, author's name, title of the article, complete date, issue or volume number (if there is one), and pages on which the article appears.

Web Sites

Retrieving information from Web sites requires fewer steps than retrieving print materials, because once you have accessed a Web site, the links will take you directly to the material on the computer. What is important about retrieving Internet material is getting to the best Web sites. Web sites can be found through search engines, by means of links, or directly via a URL (an address). You can retrieve the information by using the "download" command to transfer the page or pages you need to your own computer, if you are working at home; print it if the library terminals are equipped with printers; or send it to yourself by e-mail if there is a tool for doing this on the site. Note that you will need to record the URL if it is not already on the printout.

Radio and Television

It can be useful to consult programs on radio and television for topics about science, nature, music, history, and especially current events. The limitation is that unless the program has been recorded and saved either by you or by the library, using it will be difficult because you will not have the exact wording of the commentator with information for your bibliography. For radio programs, you might try using the Web site of National Public Radio, www.npr.org. Here, programs from this not-for-profit network can be retrieved and replayed; printed transcripts are sometimes available, although you may have to pay for this service. If you can record a television program you have seen and label the cassette with the name of the program, the date it was taped, and the channel on which it was presented, using the program will be easier. Check your library catalog of films and radio recordings that are available either in the library's own collection or through interlibrary loan.

Film, Video, Photographs, Paper Ephemera, and Music

Media of all kinds may be helpful in sparking ideas on your subject. Just remember that even these sources have to be included in the Works Cited list at the end of your essay, so be sure to label each source and identify where it came from. Then you will have the information you need later on. Films and videos can be retrieved by using a number of reference books and then checking with your library's online catalog. *The International Directory of Film and Filmmakers, The Film Encyclopedia,* and *The Film and Video Finder's Complete Guide to Videocassette Movies* are among the tools available.

Photograph collections are often held in museums, as well as in libraries, and you can explore the collections of both on the Internet to locate what you need. Many libraries and museums are putting their photographic collections online. The Smithsonian Museum in Washington, D.C., for instance, has thousands of photos of nineteenth-century America posted to their site. Local museums and historical societies have photo archives for regional topics. Generally, you can search for photos the same way you searched specialized libraries and then retrieve the photos by means of the Web site. In addition, ask your librarian whether your college library has a photo archive, or collection.

Paper ephemera are printed materials that, until recently, some libraries did not consider worth saving. Advertisements, labels, posters, and the like were frequently discarded, but now they tend to be saved as evidence of popular taste or trends in business. Check whether your library has a paper ephemera collection, just in case your subject leads you to such artifacts.

Pamphlets, Flyers, and Newsletters

These "disposable" publications from local civic agencies, organizations, churches, associations, businesses, and schools are generally not cataloged by libraries, but some libraries collect them in a "vertical file," or filing cabinet, where they are grouped by subject. Although these may be good starting points, remember that they are frequently very brief and are not always produced by dependable sources. It can be hard to identify when a pamphlet was published, because often they are not dated or labeled, and as a result the information is not always easy to evaluate. (We will discuss evaluation of sources in Chapter 5.)

Microfilm

Libraries store documents on microfilm to save space. As we saw earlier, newspapers are usually filed as microfilm, as are popular magazines and many journals. Retrieving from microfilm can be done easily if the microfilm reader is connected to a printer. Once you have found the spool with the article you want and have had the librarian help you load it onto the reader, you can print a copy by inserting coins into the printer, which works like a photocopy machine. (Note that not all readers have printers attached. If you can, use a machine that is equipped in this way so that you have the option to print.)

CHECKLIST FINDING AND RETRIEVING SOURCES
- How much do you already know about your topic? a lot? some? not much?
- Do you know the difference between primary and secondary sources?
- Do you know how to search for a book in an online catalog?
- Do you know how to use a database?
- Can you identify a reliable search engine?

CHECKLIST   FINDING AND RETRIEVING SOURCES (continued)

❑ Have you explored the Internet using Web sites?

❑ Have you explored traditional library sources, such as books and print journals?

❑ Have you explored electronic resources such as InfoTrac and LexisNexis?

❑ Have you found a museum or professional organization for your topic?

❑ Have you looked at other sources such as radio programs, video, or micro-film articles?

CHAPTER 5

Evaluating and Recording Information from Sources

Evaluating What You Have Found

Guidelines for Evaluating Print and Online Sources

One of the most important steps in writing a research paper is evaluating sources, especially when you are using the Internet. Evaluating or assessing means that you have to decide several matters:

- Is the source necessary, useful, and appropriate to my research topic?
- Is the source reliable, authoritative, and dependable?
- Is the source long enough to help me develop accurate and complex ideas?

Usefulness

One way to evaluate the usefulness of a source is to ask, "Am I using the source to shape my topic, or am I letting the source dictate how the paper is developing?"

Is the source about your topic? Will it help you? One way to find out is to read it. If it is an article, read the entire piece. If it is a book, at least read the table of contents, scan the index, and read the appropriate sections of the book that relate to your own subject. You can also survey other sections, such as any preface, introduction, and appendix or notes, to find further reference to your particular area of interest. Is your topic mentioned? If it is not, try rephrasing your subject by using a variety of keywords. If your subject is African American writers, you might also check black authors or (if the book was published earlier in the century) Negro writers. Lizzie Borden's case might be included under her name, but it could also be identified by category: unsolved crimes, women and murder, or parricide. After you have surveyed the source, skim through it. Look for words or phrases you recognize as potentially useful. If you are uncertain, ask your instructor or librarian. Is the level appropriate? Is it too simple? too specialized?

Reliability

Is your source objective or does it support a personal or political bias? This is a harder question for a beginning researcher to answer. Because anyone can create an Internet site, it is imperative that you look carefully at who has created a Web page before you accept it as a source. Books and traditional printed materials, however, must also be evaluated for reliability. Here are some tips:

- Who is the author? Does the author have credentials or a reputation within the field? You can check a directory like *Who's Who* or *The Dictionary of American Scholars* to begin evaluating the writer. If you are using a printed book, there should be a brief biographical blurb about the author either on the dust jacket or at the very end of the book. For an online source, check to see whether the author is associated with an institution such as a university, government department, museum, or other recognized agency. If not, does the page offer you any clues to who the author is and why he or she has authored this Web site? Does the site end in .com or .org or .edu? Is the author a professional or a student? You might want to read a student's Web page to gather general knowledge, but a college research paper should refer to more established sources. If your subject is one that requires interviews or witnesses, then you might be able to use a personal Web site, if you can be sure that the author has the credentials he or she claims.

- Is the source up-to-date? Facts and opinions are continually being reassessed and revised. Check the date of the source, especially if your topic is on current events. If the source is historical, such as an 1892 newspaper article about the Lizzie Borden murder case, consider how reliable an article in a nineteenth-century periodical could be, especially if the reporter was writing before the trial and without the benefit of live press coverage.

- Does the piece have a strong point of view? If so, does the author admit to bias and/or does the author balance the viewpoint in the source by comparing it to other positions on the subject? For example, if you are reading an editorial on the achievements of a Republican mayor, was the article written by a Republican or a Democrat? If you were reading a news article about the Civil War published in 1863, you would need to know whether the writer was an abolitionist, a slave owner, or a visitor from France observing the scene for a Paris newspaper. On the Internet, bias may be more difficult to evaluate. Track down the writer's links to any organizations or publications that might offer clues to his or her point of view. (See the section "Evaluating Web Sites" later in this chapter.)

- Is it a primary or a secondary source? Review the guidelines in Chapter 4 on this topic.

Thoroughness or Range of Sources

Have you collected a mixture of types of sources? Primary and secondary, scholarly and journalistic, books, periodicals, nonprint sources—a mixture is necessary for a well-balanced paper. Do not depend on only one source, even if you think it is excellent. This will result in a book report or book review, not a college research paper.

Completeness of the Article or Summary

Have you read a complete source or an excerpt or selection from a longer source? Some reference books, such as *Contemporary Literary Criticism,* are designed to help the user locate other sources. They provide a summary or a sample of an article, but then the user is expected to go to the complete article to read and evaluate the source. Relying entirely on the excerpt in the reference book could lead to an incorrect or incomplete result. Likewise, some databases provide summaries while others link to a full-text version of the source. It is better to use full-text articles. Do not depend on summaries to give you enough information.

EXERCISE 5.1   **Evaluating Sources**

Read carefully the following material on Lorraine Hansberry, which is part of the entry about this twentieth-century African American playwright that appears in *Contemporary Literary Criticism* (*CLC*).

Lorraine Hansberry (1930–1965)

American playwright.

During her short career, Hansberry seemed destined to become an important force in American theater. With the success in 1959 of *A Raisin in the Sun,* Hansberry became the first black woman to win the New York Drama Critics Circle Award for the best American play. This, her first play, was also the first by a black woman to be produced on Broadway. It told the story of a black family living on Chicago's South Side, struggling to hold together and to get ahead in a forbidding world. Although a few critics charged her with sentimentality, the sincerity and realism of her perceptions along with her effective use of staging earned the play much acclaim. The film version, adapted by Hansberry, was not as well-received critically, although it was still a popular success.

Her second play, *The Sign in Sidney Brustein's Window,* closed after 101 performances on the day Hansberry died. Among her unpublished papers, however, she left a few partially finished plays. Some of this material has been edited and revised by her ex-husband and literary executor, Robert Nemiroff, *Les Blancs* being the most notable of these plays. He also produced the pastiche of her plays, letters, and journal entries called *To Be Young, Gifted and Black.* All her works are revived in their original form on occasion; they and their adaptations continue to please audiences. Most recently, *A Raisin in the Sun* became the highly successful musical *Raisin.* Due to their unfinished state at Hansberry's death, perhaps, none of the posthumous works has the same coherence and drive of her early work. However, her plays are often acknowledged for their expressive, compassionate view of people who transcend the limitations of their lives. (See also *Contemporary Authors,* Vols. 25–28, rev. ed.)

Brooks Atkinson

"A Raisin in the Sun" has vigor as well as veracity and is likely to destroy the complacency of any one who sees it. . . .

"A Raisin in the Sun" is a play about human beings who want, on the one hand, to preserve their family pride and on the other hand, to break out of the poverty that seems to be their fate. Not having any axe to grind, Miss Hansberry has a wide range of topics to write about—some of them hilarious, some of them painful in the extreme.

You might, in fact, regard "A Raisin in the Sun" as a Negro "The Cherry Orchard." Although the social scale of the characters is different, the knowledge of how character is controlled by environment is much the same, and the alternation of humor and pathos is similar.

If there are occasional crudities in the craftsmanship, they are redeemed by the honesty of the writing.

[Honesty] is Miss Hansberry's personal contribution to an explosive situation in which simple honesty is the most difficult thing in the world. And also the most illuminating.

Source: Brooks Atkinson, "The Theater: 'A Raisin in the Sun'," *New York Times*, March 12, 1959. Copyright © 1959 by The New York Times Company. Reprinted by permission. Also reprinted in *New York Theater Critics' Reviews*, vol. 20, no. 7, March 16, 1959, p. 345.

First, you notice a heading that gives the author's name and her dates of birth and death. This is followed by two paragraphs that summarize the main points of Hansberry's career. After the biographical summary, there is a heading with the name of a theater critic. Below it are remarks that Atkinson made about *A Raisin in the Sun.* At the end is a citation, telling where this piece of criticism was originally published. Read the entry and then answer the following questions.

1. Why are there quotation marks around the five words just after Brooks Atkinson's name? What kind of material is this? Is it primary or secondary?

2. Is this the entire article or book that Atkinson wrote? How can you tell?

3. If you wanted to use this article for your research paper, what would you do to obtain the complete article?

4. Which would be the better source to use in your research essay on Hansberry, *Contemporary Literary Criticism*, or Atkinson's article from the original source? Or both? Why?

Next, read the following entry on Lorraine Hansberry from *The Bloomsbury Guide to Women's Literature.* Then, using the guidelines for evaluating sources that appear at the beginning of this section, answer the questions that follow.

Hansberry, Lorraine (1930–1965)

U.S. dramatist, journalist and essayist. Hansberry was born in Chicago, Illinois, to middle-class African-American parents. She studied at the University of Wisconsin, Roosevelt College, and the School of Art Institute of Chicago. In 1950, she worked for *Freedom,* a radical African-American newspaper, in New York City, which brought her into contact with black intellectuals such as Paul Robeson, Langston Hughes, and W. E .B. DuBois. She continued to write and speak on both race and gender issues, for example, her speech "In Defense of the Equality of Men," which is published in *The Norton Anthology of Literature by Women,* edited by Sandra M. Gilbert and Susan Gubar.

With *A Raisin in the Sun* (1959), Hansberry became the first African-American woman to have a play produced on Broadway, and the first black dramatist ever to win the New York Drama Critics Circle Play of the Year Award. The play celebrates the African-American struggle for freedom and equality. Racism has consigned the Younger family to life in the ghetto until the death of the family patriarch offers an opportunity for the family to overcome their oppression. The mother uses his legacy to buy a house in an Anglo-American neighbourhood. The family confront Anglo-American racism with pride and dignity when they are offered money to stay out. The play addresses issues of racism and the tension between racial assimilation and separatism. Her play *The Sign in Sidney Brustein's Window* (1964) focuses on a Jewish intellectual, and challenges assumptions about appropriate subjects for African-American writers.

Other works include: *The Movement: Documentary of a Struggle for Equality* (1964), *To Be Young, Gifted and Black: Lorraine Hansberry in Her Own Words* (1969), and *Les Blancs: The Collected Last Plays of Lorraine Hansberry* (1972). Bib: Bond, Jean Caron (ed.), *Lorraine Hansberry: Art of Thunder, Vision of Light,* a special issue of *Freedomways* magazine.

Claire Buck, ed., *The Bloomsbury Guide to Women's Literature*

1. Is this an in-depth source, adequate for use in a research essay? _____

2. Does the entry provide fact or opinion on Hansberry? _____

3. Is this a primary or a secondary source? _____

4. Near the end, the entry says "Bib:." What do you think this means? How can this article lead you to other sources for your research paper?

_____

Look again at the entry from *Contemporary Literary Criticism* on Lorraine Hansberry to help you compare the sources you locate.

1. What is the major difference between this entry and the one from the *Bloomsbury Guide?*

2. Does *Contemporary Literary Criticism* provide you with the complete article on the writer? How do you know?

3. What seems to be the purpose of this reference book?

4. Which of these critical articles is taken from a book about Hansberry? How do you know?

5. Which of these articles appeared in a magazine or journal? How do you know?

6. If you wanted to read a primary source by Hansberry, what would you read?

EXERCISE 5.2   Evaluating Primary Sources from Print Media

Read the following excerpt from James Baldwin's *Notes of a Native Son.*

Harlem, physically at least, has changed very little in my parents' lifetime or in mine. Now as then the buildings are old and in desperate need of repair, the streets are crowded and dirty, there are too many human beings per square block. Rents are 10 to 58 per cent higher than anywhere else in the city; food, expensive everywhere, is more expensive here and of an inferior quality; and now that the war is over and money is dwindling, clothes are carefully shopped for and seldom bought. Negroes, traditionally the last to be hired and the first to be fired, are finding jobs harder to get, and, while prices are rising implacably, wages are going down. All over Harlem now there is felt the same bitter expectancy with which, in my childhood, we awaited winter: it is coming and it will be hard; there is nothing anyway one can do about it.

All of Harlem is pervaded by a sense of congestion, rather like the insistent, maddening, claustrophobic pounding in the skull that comes from trying to breathe in a very small room with all the windows shut. Yet the white man walking through Harlem is not at all likely to find it sinister or more wretched than any other slum.

James Baldwin, *Notes of a Native Son*

On the basis of this reading, what conclusions can you draw about this writer? List at least five assumptions you can make on the basis of this description. Next to each assumption, indicate which words in the paragraph support this assumption.

1. Could you use this primary source to draw conclusions about the writer's ethnic background?

2. Could you use this primary source to draw conclusions about the years in which he grew up—1850s? 1940s? 1970s?

3. Where would you go to read the complete work?

4. Does Baldwin's work seem to be a useful source for a paper on the Harlem Renaissance, a literary movement? Explain.

5. Does Baldwin's point of view come across clearly? Explain.

6. Does James Baldwin seem to be a reliable witness to life in Harlem?

EXERCISE 5.3   Evaluating Point of View

Read the following excerpt from Jacob Riis's book *How the Other Half Lives.*

Between the tabernacles of Jewry and the shrines of the Bend, Jos has cheekily planted his pagan worship of idols, chief among which are the celestial worshipper's own gain and lusts. Whatever may be said about the Chinaman being a thousand years behind the age on his own shores, here he is distinctly abreast of it in his successful scheming to "make it pay." It is doubtful if there is anything he does not turn to a paying account, from his religion down, or up, as one prefers. At the risk of distressing some well-meaning, but, I fear, too trustful people, I state it in advance as my opinion, based on the steady observation of years, that all attempts to make an effective Christian of John Chinaman will remain abortive in this generation; of the next I have, if anything, less hope. Ages of senseless idolatry, a mere grub worship, have left him without the essential qualities for appreciating the gentle teachings of a faith whose motive and unselfish spirit are alike beyond his grasp. He lacks the handle of a strong faith in something, anything, however wrong, to catch him by. There is nothing strong about him, except his passions when aroused. I am convinced that he adopts Christianity, when he adopts it at all, as he puts on American clothes, with what the politicians would call an ulterior motive, some sort of gain in the near prospect—washing, a Christian wife, perhaps, anything he happens to rate for the moment above his cherished pigtail. It may be that I judge him too harshly. Exceptions may be found. Indeed, for the credit of the race, I hope there are such. But I am bound to say my hope is not backed by lively faith.

Chinatown as a spectacle is disappointing. Next-door neighbor to the Bend, it has little of its outdoor stir and life, none of its gayly colored rags or picturesque filth and poverty. Mott Street is clean to distraction; the laundry stamp is on it, though the houses are chiefly of the conventional tenement-house type, with nothing to rescue them from the everyday dismal dreariness of their kind save here and there a splash of dull red or yellow, a sign, hung endways and with streamers of red flannel tacked on, that announces in Chinese characters that Dr. Chay Yen Chong sells Chinese herb medicines, or that Won Lung & Co.—queer contradiction—take in washing, or deal out tea and groceries.

Jacob Riis, *How the Other Half Lives*

Evaluate Riis's point of view by answering the following questions.

1. Characterize the writer. What do you learn about him from what you read?

2. From what point of view does he write about Chinatown? List some key words that help you identify his bias.

3. What is the main difference between the point of view of Baldwin writing about Harlem and that of Riis writing about Chinatown?

EXERCISE 5.4   Evaluating Other Kinds of Print Sources

Let's look at other kinds of sources besides books and articles. In this case, the subject for your research paper might be something about American slavery just before the Civil War (1861–1865). Examine this brief excerpt from an advertisement published in the 1850s by an angry slave owner whose valuable "property," a woman named Linda Brent (also known as Harriet Jacobs), had escaped.

Harriet Jacobs, *Incidents in the Life of a Slave Girl*

$300 REWARD! Ran away from the subscriber, an intelligent, bright, mulatto girl, named Linda, 21 years of age. Five feet four inches high. Dark eyes, and black hair inclined to curl; but it can be made straight. Has a decayed spot on a front tooth. She can read and write, and in all probability will try to get to the Free States. . . .

1. Is this a primary or a secondary source?

2. What information can be obtained about the skills of Harriet Jacobs from this source?

3. Does the writer of this ad, the slave owner, put a high value on his slave?

4. How does the owner identify his slave? What does this tell you about the bias or point of view of the owner?

Now read the following passage from a book published by Harriet Jacobs, *Incidents in the Life of a Slave Girl,* published in 1861. Jacobs's real name was Linda Brent, but she chose to write under a pseudonym to protect her identity, because she was writing when slavery was still legal in the southern states. Evaluate the source as you read. Ask the questions below the reading to help with your assessment.

Childhood

Such were the unusually fortunate circumstances of my early childhood. When I was six years old, my mother died; and then, for the first time, I learned, by the talk around me, that I was a slave. My mother's mistress was the daughter of my grandmother's mistress. She was the foster sister of my mother; they were both nourished at my grandmother's breast. In fact, my mother had been weaned at three months old, that the babe of the mistress might obtain sufficient food. They played together as children; and, when they became women, my mother was a most faithful servant to her whiter foster sister. On her death-bed her mistress promised that her children should never suffer for any thing; and during her lifetime she kept her word. They all spoke kindly of my dead mother, who had been a slave merely in name, but in nature was noble and womanly. I grieved for her, and my young mind was troubled with the thought who would now take care of me and my little brother. I was told that my home was now to be with her mistress; and I found it a happy one. No toilsome or disagreeable duties were imposed upon me. My mistress was so kind to me that I was always glad to do her bidding, and proud to labor for her as much as my young years would permit. I would sit by her side for hours, sewing diligently, with a heart as free from care as that of any freeborn white child. When she thought I was tired, she would send me out to run and jump; and away I bounded, to gather berries or flowers to decorate her room. Those were happy days—too happy to last. The slave child had no thought for the morrow; but there came the blight, which too surely waits on every human being born to be a chattel.

When I was nearly twelve years old, my kind mistress sickened and died. As I saw the cheek grow paler, and the eye more glassy, how earnestly I prayed in my heart that she might live! I loved her; for she had been almost like a mother to me. My prayers were not answered. She died, and they buried her in the little churchyard, where, day after day, my tears fell upon her grave.

I was sent to spend a week with my grandmother. I was now old enough to begin to think of the future; and again and again I asked myself what they would do with me. I felt sure I should never find another mistress so kind as the one who was gone. She had promised my dying mother that her children should never suffer from any thing; and when I remembered that, and recalled her many proofs of attachment to me, I could not help having some hopes that she had left me free. My friends were almost certain it would be so. They thought she would be sure to do it, on account of my mother's love and faithful service. But, alas! we all know that the memory of a faithful slave does not avail much to save her children from the auction block.

After a brief period of suspense, the will of my mistress was read, and we learned that she had bequeathed me to her sister's daughter, a child of five years old. So vanished our hopes. My mistress had taught me the precepts of God's Word: "Thou shalt love they neighbor as thyself." "Whatsoever ye would that men should do unto you, do ye even so unto them." But I was her slave, and I suppose she did not recognize me as her neighbor. I would give much to blot out from my memory that one great wrong. As a child, I loved my mistress; and, looking back on the happy days I spent with her, I try to think with less bitterness of this act of injustice. While I was with her, she taught me to read and spell; and for this privilege, which so rarely falls to the lot of a slave, I bless her memory.

She possessed but few slaves; and at her death those were all distributed among her relatives. Five of them were my grandmother's children, and had shared the same milk that nourished her mother's children. Notwithstanding my grandmother's long and faithful service to her owners, not one of her children escaped the auction block. These God-breathing machines are no more, in the sight of their masters, than the cotton they plant, or the horses they tend.

Harriet Jacobs, *Incidents in the Life of a Slave Girl*

1. What clue do the title and the year of publication give us to the writer's purpose, or bias, or point of view? Why would this help a modern reader evaluate her information?

2. Is she a reliable reporter about life during slavery? Why or why not?

3. Is the writer clear in identifying her point of view? Explain.

4. For what kind of topics would this passage be a useful source? Make a list of at least five topics.

5. Does your library own a copy of the book from which this passage is taken? If so, what is its call number?

EXERCISE 5.5 Evaluating Primary and Secondary Sources

Read this brief introduction to a modern paperback edition of Jacobs's book, and answer the questions that follow.

Introduction

Incidents in the Life of a Slave Girl represents a genre of writing as distinctive to American literature as blues is to American music: the experience that gave rise to slave songs also produced slave narratives.

Beginning in colonial times and continuing to the end of the Civil War, hundreds and possibly thousands of biographies and autobiographies of slaves and former slaves appeared in print, some brief, others book length. Many were incorporated in antislavery periodicals; a much smaller number were published on their own. They can be found in the Schomburg Collection of the New York Public Library, the Spingarn Collection at Howard University, the Boston Public Library, and in the libraries at Brown University, Cornell University, Hampton Institute, Harvard University, and

Oberlin College. Some have been reissued in recent years. *Incidents in the Life of a Slave Girl,* published in 1861, was one of the last and most remarkable of its genre and also one of the very few written by a woman. It is being reprinted here in its entirety for the first time, and with original spelling, capitalization, and punctuation retained.

1. Is this a primary or a secondary source?

2. What is the writer's point of view?

3. Does this appear to be a reliable, balanced source? Why or why not?

Evaluating Web Sites

Guidelines for Evaluating Electronic Sources

The same criteria that you used for print media can be applied to electronic sources, but with electronic sources, especially Web pages, the researcher has to be even more careful. Remember that *anyone* can post a Web page on the Internet. As you saw when you explored the various search engines and other tools for finding material (Chapter 4), the organization of the Web is arbitrary, even chaotic at times. Commercials for credit cards or computer software may influence what types of material are promoted. Many sites are still in progress, or under construction. URLs, the addresses used to find sites, can change. This does not mean you should avoid the Internet. On the contrary, working with the Web can make your research paper far more balanced and cosmopolitan, because it enables you to read sources that might never have been available otherwise. What is important is that, as you examine a site, you must *think critically.* Here are some questions to ask about each site:

THINKING CRITICALLY

- Dot what? Is the site an "edu" or an "org" or a "com" site? These abbreviations for U.S. sites will help you evaluate the reliability of the information. An "edu" is a site sponsored by an educational institution. An "org" is an organization, usually a not-for-profit. A "com" is the familiar commercial or business site, a for-profit sponsor. A commercial-free site is more likely to provide unbiased information and might be a better source than a heavily commercialized sponsor.

- What are the writer's credentials? Is he or she an authority?

- Does the site announce a particular policy, or advocate a position? If it does not, can you find clues to the sponsor's point of view?

- Avoid sites where the information is extremely brief. Look for substantial sites that include reliable links to other sites. (The quality of the links that a site provides offers insight into the reliability of the Webmaster's research.)

- The design, language, and general appearance of the site offer clues to its reliability. A violent or garish visual message can be a clue to poor quality or sensationalized point of view.

- Who is the intended audience?

EXERCISE 5.6   Evaluating a Web Site

Evaluate the Web page on writer Lorraine Hansberry (shown below). Use the points listed above to guide your evaluation. On a scale of 1 to 10, where would you rank this site in terms of its usefulness for a literature paper? (If possible, visit the site on the Web to get additional clues.)

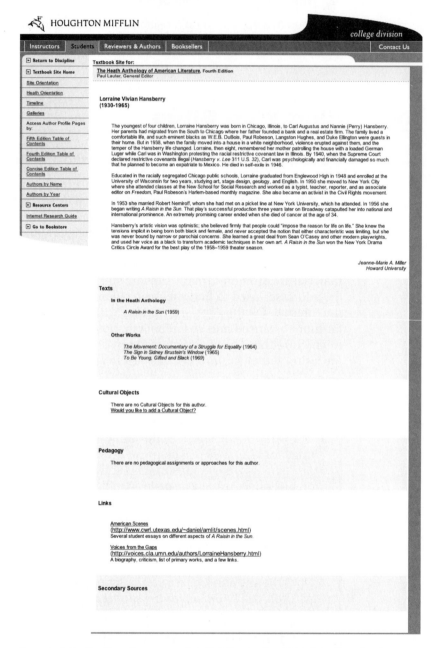

Source: http://college.hmco.com/english/lauter/heath/4e/students/author_pages/ contemporary/hansberry_lo.html. Copyright © Houghton Mifflin Company.

EXERCISE 5.7   Evaluating a Primary Source on a Web Site

Examine the page from the Web site "Slave Voices: The Problem of Freedom" (shown below), and answer the following questions.

The Problem of Freedom

The Destruction of American Slavery, Freedom's Strange Fruit

27. Remick, Clarke H. "Untitled Report in Quarterly Returns of Ordinance and Ordinance Stores in Company A, 35th United States Colored Troops, First Quarter 1864." 31 March 1864. Clarke H. Remick Papers. Special Collections Library, Duke University.

Description: Quarterly report of the 35th United States Colored Troops, designated the 1st North Carolina Colored Troops until March 1864.

28. Remick, Clarke H. "Abstract of Expenditures in Quarterly Returns of Ordinance and Ordinance Stores in Company A, 35th United States Colored Troops, First Quarter 1864." 1864. Clarke H. Remick Papers. Special Collections Library, Duke University.

Description: Quarterly report of the 35th United States Colored Troops, designated the 1st North Carolina Colored Troops until March 1864.

29. "Muster Roll of Captain Squire N. Osburn's Company A of the Forty-Sixth Regiment of U.S. Infantry (Colored)..." 30 April 1864. U.S. Army. Units. Regiments, 46th U.S. Infantry (Colored) Papers, 1863-1864. Special Collections Library, Duke University.

Description: The muster roll shows the soldiers are former Arkansas slaves, many in service longer than their commanders. Some of the remarks relating to specific soldiers are also of note: Hesikiah Booker is the chief musician. [Click on the image for a larger version.]

30. Liberian Exodus Association. October 1878. "The Liberian Exodus" [Pamphlet Circulars Nos. 3 and 4]. Special Collections Library, Duke University.

Description: Circular of the Liberian Exodus Association, an organization dedicated to helping blacks resettle in Liberia.

Full title page information reads:

> The Liberian Exodus; First Voyage of the Azor; Liberia A Delightful Country; Climate, Soil and Productions; Character of the People in Liberia and How They Live; Full Information on the Exodus Movement; The Steamship

31. Clay, Joseph. Letter to Louis Manigault. 9 September 1868. Louis Manigault Papers. (South Carolina) Special Collections Library, Duke University.

Description: Clay writes from Savannah, Georgia. It is unclear whether Bradley is a black man, or a radical white. The letter contains two interesting references concerning the social and political climate of the times--an allusion to blacks attacking white travelers and arming themselves with the guns of those waylaid, and a reference to the political aspirations of a certain Bradley. The relevant sections are briefly abstracted below:

> We have lately had a very brutal Murder to occur just outside our City. A young lad named Wilson went out...not returning in the afternoon his family became uneasy. He was missing for several days & then his body was found about 1 mile from the City. He was no doubt murdered by Negroes to get possession of his Gun which was a fine one. Several Negroes have been arrested upon suspicion. I never go outside the City without being armed with a Gun or Pistol for a rascally set of Negroes are prowling around the Country ready for any outrageous deed of infamy. You will see by the papers that we have got rid of the Negroes in our Legislature[.] I wish you could do the same in So. Ca., but they have the upper hand there. The 'Nigger Bradley' made a Speech to the darkeys yesterday & threatened [?] every horrible thing against the poor Whites. He said the time would come when a man would not be permitted to sit in the State Legislature because he was 'White.' Alas! What are we coming to?

32. Smith, Amanda. Amanda Smith' Own Story. Introduction. J. M. Thoburn. 1st ed. Chicago: Meyer & Brother Publishers, 1893. Special Collections Library, Duke University.

Description: Smith was born in slavery in Maryland in the 1830's. Her father purchased her freedom and moved her to Pennsylvania. She grew up there, helped runaway slaves, purchased a freeborn sister who had been sold into slavery, grew to be a missionary and taught in Africa.

Title page reads as follows:

> *An Autobiography*
> *The Story of the Lord's Dealings with*
> *Mrs. Amanda Smith*
> *The Colored Evangelist*
> *Containing an Account of Her Life Work of Faith, and Her Travels in America, England, Ireland, Scotland, India and Africa as an Independent Missionary*
> With an Introduction by
> Bishop Thoburn of India.

"The Problem of Freedom" section of the "Third Person, First Person; Slave Voices from the Special Collections Library" website. <http://scriptorium.lib.duke.edu/slavery/> Materials on the website are located in the Rare Book, Manuscript, and Special Collections Library, Duke University.

1. What is this site listing? What kinds of sources are these?

2. Who has prepared this list?

3. For what kind of subject might this source be useful?

4. Use your computer to access this site at http://scriptorium.lib.duke.edu/ slavery/freedom.html. Click on one of the documents, such as number 29. What would make using this source difficult for a student researcher? What would make it exciting?

EXERCISE 5.8   Selecting the Right Web Site for Your Research Subject

Using the list of Web sites you found on your subject, access three of the sites. Evaluate each site by answering the following questions.

1. Who sponsors it? (Dot what?) _____

2. How detailed is the information? _____

3. Who seems to be the intended audience? _____

4. How recently has the site been updated? _____

_____

Step 12   EVALUATING YOUR SOURCES

Select five electronic and print sources other than Web sites from those you have located so far for your research paper. Using the guidelines for print and electronic sources, carefully evaluate each. How many of the sources are worth keeping for your final paper?

Verifying URLs

It is important to remember that Web sites have a more limited usefulness. Since they don't tend to have dates of publication, like books and articles do, you may not be aware of when material was posted. In addition, some Web sites have not been renewed, or may move,. This means that the information on the URL will not be retrievable. Before you list a URL, be sure it is current.

Formulating a Working Bibliography

A working bibliography is a list of the sources you are collecting and evaluating for your research paper. When the paper is completed, you will be creating a list to appear at the back of your essay identifying all the sources from which you took information. For some research assignments you may be asked to include a bibliography, or a list of further references, to identify those works that provide additional material on the subject. The working bibliography, then, is an in-progress list of the sources you are locating. It is much easier to keep track of your sources as you find them than it is to go back and create the list after you have completed the essay. Save time and frustration by copying down *all* the necessary information about each source as you locate and retrieve it. Organizing this list in alphabetical order, using the author's last name as the starting point of each entry, will help you keep your research project on track.

EXERCISE 5.9   **Creating a Source Card on a Book for a Working Bibliography**

Look at page 111, where you will see the list of essential information that you copied down for your sources. This is the same information that will help you build the working bibliography. For example, a library online catalog screen for a book on Edith Wharton provides the following information:

Example   Title: Displaying women: spectacles of leisure in Edith Wharton's New York.

Publisher: New York: Routledge, 1998.

Subjects: Wharton, Edith, 1862–1937—Knowledge—New York (State)—New York.

Wharton, Edith, 1862–1937—Characters—Women.

Women and literature—New York (State)—New York.

Upper class—New York (State)—New York—History.

Upper class in literature.

Leisure in literature.

Women in literature.

Subjects: New York (N.Y.)—In literature.

LOCATION:	CALL NUMBER	STATUS:
Baruch Stacks	TEMPORARY CONTROL NUMBER: AX62114	On Order

By now you should be familiar with each of these items on the screen. Identify the following parts of the source information:

the author of the book: _____

the title of the book: _____

the publishing company: _____

the location of the publishing company: _____

the date of publication: _____

Each of these items is essential for the working bibliography.

———————————————

Here are three sample note cards with sources. The subject of this paper is American women writers. The student is creating a working bibliography by arranging these cards in alphabetical order. Use these note cards as a model for the ones you are making for your sources.

Example: Reference book

> Short article on Hansberry, Lorraine (1930–1965)
> In <u>The Bloomsbury Guide to Women's Literature</u>
> Edited by Claire Buck
> Pub. by Prentice Hall, New York
> Year of publication: 1992
> Article is on pages 617–618

Example: Book

> Morrison, Toni
> <u>Beloved</u>
> Vintage
> N.Y.
> 1987
> This is a novel.

Example: Web site

> "Red Cloud: Willa Cather State Historic Site"
> http://www.sightsmag.com/usa/ne/redc/sights/wica/wica.htm
> Topic: Cather's childhood home with Cather photograph

EXERCISE 5.10 Creating Your Working Bibliography

Create a working bibliography of all the book sources you have collected so far. Arrange them in alphabetical order by the authors' last names. Share it with your research group, either in class or on the discussion board.

EXERCISE 5.11   **Creating a Source Card on a Periodical for a Working Bibliography**

Using a periodical article or newspaper article that you have retrieved, make a card. Then place it alphabetically, by author's last name, among the books already in the working bibliography. Refer to the list about what to copy down for a periodical (page 118) to be sure you have all the information you need. Share it with your research group, either in class or on the discussion board.

EXERCISE 5.12   **Creating a Source Card on Internet Sources for a Working Bibliography**

Using an Internet site you located and retrieved, create a source card. Add it to the working bibliography. If there is no author listed on the Web site, use the title of the site, alphabetizing it among the other sources. Be sure to include the URL (address) and the date you retrieved it. Share it with your research group.

Documentation Basics

Documentation is the term used in research to mean showing where information comes from. A good researcher documents sources by using a system of documentation designed by one of several professional organizations. The *MLA Handbook for Writers of Research Papers,* published by the Modern Language Association, is one such tool used by those working in the areas of language and literature. Another, used by social scientists, is published by the American Psychological Association (APA). Other disciplines and professions may use other systems. A researcher must always find out which style guide is appropriate for the paper he or she is writing. In Chapters 8 and 9 you will learn how to document your essay correctly.

The basics of documentation are the following:

- in-text documentation with citations or footnotes in the body of the essay

- a Works Cited or References list giving details of the sources

Step 13   **PREPARING YOUR WORKING BIBLIOGRAPHY**

Make a source card of every source you found in the library or on the Internet for your research paper. Put the cards in alphabetical order.

Moving from Bibliography to Essay

Developing Your Research Topic

Having located and retrieved your sources, you are now nearly ready to begin writing your paper. That means looking more closely at your sources, using these sources to ask and answer questions on your topic, and taking notes on what you find. Your thesis must remain tentative until you have read and taken notes on your topic; good reading and diligent note taking are essential to forming and supporting your working thesis. What does "good reading" mean? It means reading carefully but selectively so that you understand what is in your source without having to read every word. It means taking down information that you can use later when you are doing the actual writing, and it means recording this information clearly, carefully, and in your own words so that you do not run the risk of plagiarizing (explained below). Using the famous *Titanic* disaster as a topic, the following section will take you through the steps of taking notes effectively.

NEW LINER *TITANIC* HITS AN ICEBERG; SINKING BY THE BOW AT MIDNIGHT; WOMEN PUT OFF IN LIFE BOATS; LAST WIRELESS AT 12:27 A.M. BLURRED

LATEST NEWS FROM THE SINKING SHIP.

1 CAPE RACE, N.F. Sunday night, April 14—At 10:25 o'clock to-night the White Star line steamship *Titanic* called "C. Q. D." to the Marconi wireless station here, and reported having struck an iceberg. The steamer said that immediate assistance was required.

2 Half an hour afterward another message came reporting that they were sinking by the head and that women were being put off in the lifeboats.

3 The weather was calm and clear, the *Titanic*'s wireless operator reported, and gave the position of the vessel as 41.46 north latitude and 50.14 west longitude.

4 The Marconi station at Cape Race notified the Allan liner *Virginian*, the captain of which immediately advised that he was proceeding for the scene of the disaster.

5 The *Virginian* at midnight was about 170 miles distant from the *Titanic* and expected to reach that vessel about 10 A.M. Monday.

6 2 A.M., Monday.—The *Olympic* at an early hour this, Monday, morning, was in latitude 40.32 north and longitude 61.18 west. She was in direct communication with the *Titanic* and is now making all haste toward her.

7 The steamship *Baltic* also reported herself as about 200 miles east of the *Titanic*, and was making all possible speed toward her.

8 The last signals from the *Titanic* were heard by the *Virginian* at 12:27 A.M.

9 The wireless operator on the *Virginian* says these signals were blurred and ended abruptly.

On April 14, 1912, the RMS *Titanic* struck an iceberg and within 2 hours and 40 minutes sank. More than half its passengers died. Since that day, the *Titanic* has inspired more romance, mystery, and legend than any other ship in modern times. Some of the richest people in the world were on the liner that was supposed to be "unsinkable." If you have seen the film *Titanic,* you may remember that it opens with a group of divers who want to salvage the wreck. Then it flashes back to the story of the ship's sinking. You can think of the modern characters as researchers. Like you, they want to find the "truth" about the famous disaster. Think about what they have done: They have read documents, perused maps, studied newspapers and journals, and performed scientific analyses. They know all the "facts" (dates, times, and so on). They even use a witness! The film was based on actual research. In 1985 a French American team of researchers using robotic submersibles set out to find the *Titanic*—and it did. Led by Robert Ballard, the team was able to answer some of the many questions surrounding the fate of the great ocean liner. Still the fable lives on, in film, in theater, in literature, and in the imaginations of the many people fascinated by stories of treasure buried deep beneath the sea.

EXERCISE 5.13 Asking and Answering Questions on Your Research Topic

After reading the short article from the *New York Times* (above), freewrite for ten minutes, writing down everything you think you know about the *Titanic* disaster, then answer the following questions.

1. List five questions you still have about the RMS *Titanic*.

   _____

   _____

   _____

   _____

   _____

2. Pick one of these questions for further exploration as a research question. _____

3. Using this question as your working thesis, generate ten questions prompted by this question.

   _____

   _____

   _____

   _____

   _____

   _____

   _____

   _____

   _____

   _____

Let's say the question you chose was "Why did the *Titanic* sink?" Here is an assortment of possible research questions on this topic:

1. Why was it called "unsinkable"?

2. Why or how does a boat sink?

3. How does a ship stay afloat?

4. What major theories have been advanced about the *Titanic*'s sinking?

5. Was it going too fast?

6. Was it built cheaply?

7. Did they test it first?

8. Did anything discovered in the wreckage change the prevailing viewpoint?

9. What was the ship made of?

10. How was it put together?

EXERCISE 5.14 **Answering Research Questions**

Read one or two selections on the *Titanic* from Part Two of this book (the Casebook). See whether these articles help you answer your sample working questions. In particular, consider the following issues:

1. How many of the questions in the foregoing list are answered in the articles?

2. Is there consensus on why the ship sank?

3. Are you confident about choosing one of these theories? (Do you have the technological knowledge needed?)

4. What kind of thesis can you form from what you have read so far?

5. Would you like to do more reading so that you will be better prepared to investigate and write about this topic? If so, what do you think you need to read?

Reading Sources Selectively

The previous activity should have helped you to see how you can focus your thesis by modeling the activities of reading, freewriting, and questioning. Try the above activities with your own research question and see whether you can come up with focused research questions to help you read more selectively. **Reading selectively** means reading with a purpose. When you read the preceding articles, you knew what questions you were researching. Therefore, you could skim through the articles, looking for these particular issues. If you draw up a list of questions you need to answer or prepare a focused list of smaller subtopics of your working thesis before you begin reading, you will find that the actual reading will be more productive and go more quickly.

But how did you make certain you would remember what you found? There are several techniques you can choose. *Underlining* words or phrases is useful as long as you own the source and it is something you can mark up. *Starring* (putting a star next to a word or phrase), *writing in the margin,* and *blocking off selected sections* are useful activities as well, and if you can photocopy the source, you can do all this without ruining a source you do not own. (Never mark up a library book.) *Highlighting* is very effective because the neon colors draw attention to lines and passages. If you don't have access to a photocopier so that you can mark up your sources, you can use self-stick removable notes next to lines or passages you wish to mark.

Taking Notes

When you go back over your marked-up sources, decide which of the many markings you want to record in your notes. If you select carefully at this stage, your paper will be much easier to write because you won't be overwhelmed by material. The process of note taking is an important step in actually preparing the draft of the essay. Note taking is a further step in focusing your essay; it helps you eliminate as well as collect information. Don't copy every sentence. Copy what helps you expand, clarify, or support your own working thesis—*and* any points that disagree with it, so that you can argue against them. It is important that you be specific in your notes to avoid confusion or errors. The following are some general guidelines on taking notes.

1. Include historical or biographical background information. For example, record who built the *Titanic* and when and why.

2. Include ideas that support or develop your thesis. For example, if your thesis is that the *Titanic* sank because of poor building materials, record anything that helps you explain your ideas. (Of course, if you find information that doesn't support your thesis, you must be open to doing more research and possibly changing your thesis.)

3. Include quotable words, phrases, or short passages that you want to use word for word. (*Copy carefully. Do not leave out or misspell any words, and include all punctuation.*) An example is Senator William Alden Smith's testimony from the Senate hearing on the disaster.

4. Include statistics that can be used to support or develop your ideas. For example, record the number of ships that sailed in the specific part of the Atlantic where the *Titanic* sank.

5. Include scientific or technical information. What you copy into notes should be related to *your* thesis. Keep track of facts, but select only those that will help you defend your own ideas. For example, you will find it useful to have taken notes on the way a ship is built (from a reputable source, of course) and on the technical safeguards against its sinking.

TAKING NOTES

The next section describes a number of ways to take notes. Whichever method you choose, be sure to record the following information (which is called **bibliographic information**) for each note:

- author's name

- title of book, article, etc.

- page number

- subject heading

- indication of whether the material you are copying is a quote (which should be in quotation marks), a paraphrase, or a summary. (This will help you guard against inadvertently plagiarizing. See the discussion on paraphrasing and plagiarism later in this chapter.)

Note Cards

While source cards contain bibliographic information about your sources, note cards or note sheets (sheets of paper instead of cardboard) contain the actual material you are using from a source. Note cards are often the most reliable and flexible system to use because you can carry notes with you, you can spread them around your writing table, and they are easy to organize. If you use pads or a computer or photocopies from articles and books, the notes can still be copied onto note cards, which will help you organize them. (When you are writing a long paper, judicious organization is particularly important.) Finally, a note card is generally larger than a source card: 5 × 7 instead of 3 × 5. This gives you extra room to write your notes. You will need a different note card for each note. Thus you may have ten cards for a single book. It is important to include the basic information (see above) about the source and to write neatly and legibly. A good practice is to consider whether someone else would be able to read your notes.

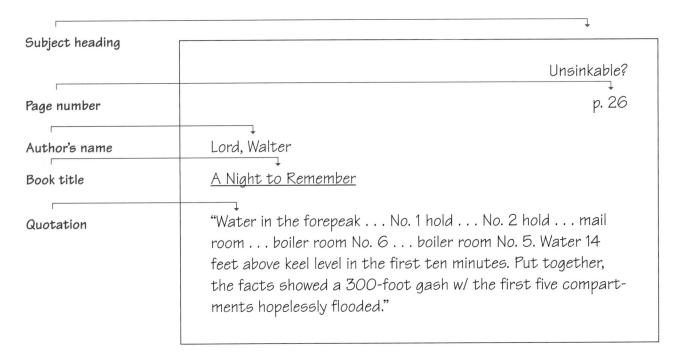

Subject heading — Unsinkable?

Page number — p. 26

Author's name — Lord, Walter

Book title — A Night to Remember

Quotation — "Water in the forepeak . . . No. 1 hold . . . No. 2 hold . . . mail room . . . boiler room No. 6 . . . boiler room No. 5. Water 14 feet above keel level in the first ten minutes. Put together, the facts showed a 300-foot gash w/ the first five compartments hopelessly flooded."

Research Journal or Notebook

Another popular note-taking system is the research journal. You have seen one Anna kept in her paper for "Forty Whacks" in Chapter 2. Many students prefer keeping their research in a book because they are afraid cards will be easily lost. A notebook or pad has the advantage of keeping all notes together. As with note cards, it is important to use a different page for each note, and to write on one side only, so that you can keep the ideas separate. That way, if you need to spread out your ideas to organize them, you will be able to cut your pages and separate the notes. The pages from your notebook or pad can be organized to look like note cards.

Electronic Notes

Even if you are still using a typewriter it is helpful to learn to touch type. There are many commercial software programs that make learning touch typing into a game. Check with your college library or computer center to see what is available.

Because many students now have access to computers, the use of electronic notes has become widespread. Students even carry laptop computers into the library and take their notes directly from books in the stacks. All computers enable students to record notes quickly from books they have taken out of the library or photocopies they have made there. Electronic notes solve the problems of poor handwriting and illegible note taking. Be sure to double-space so that you can read your notes more easily, and to record all URLs or databases you may have used. With electronic notes, you can create a template or chart so that you can fill in the bibliographic and other information more easily. You can save this information and access it whenever you are taking notes. A sample template follows.

Subject heading:

Author's name:

Title of source:

Date:

Page number, database, or URL of source:

Comments:

Photocopies

Probably the easiest way to do your note taking is by photocopying the sections of your sources that are pertinent to your thesis. Most libraries have a substantial number of photocopy machines, and if you remember to bring rolls of small change (or buy a photocopying card), you will be able to take your material home with you. Many libraries also have printers attached to their databases and CD-ROMs so that you can print directly from the computers. Photocopying removes any doubt about whether you have recorded from your source accurately. However, photocopying is not note taking. First you must carefully read the source. And because you didn't take notes on the source, you still need to perform another step: copying your note from the photocopy onto a card, journal page or sheet, or computer, so you can easily use it in your paper. To save time later, make certain that you copy all the relevant source information onto each photocopy and that you note under which topic heading it fits.

EXERCISE 5.15   Evaluating Note Cards

For a paper on why the *Titanic* sank, read the pieces in the Casebook on pages 291 to 308. Then examine the note cards below and answer the questions that follow.

the Captain
p. 287–8

Wade, Wyn Craig
The Titanic: End of a Dream

Capt. Smith, while brave, was "overconfident." This led to problems.

Note Card 1

rivets
p. F1

Broad, William J.
NY Times, 1/27/98

"Two wrought-iron rivets from the *Titanic*'s hull were recently hauled up from the depths for scientific analysis & were found to be riddled w/unusually high concentrations of slag, making them brittle & prone to fracture."

Note Card 2

1. Does the note give the necessary information so the student can find the source card? Note card 1 _____ Note card 2 _____

2. Is the note written clearly enough to be read easily?

   Note card 1 _____ Note card 2 _____

3. Does the note give enough information to be useful?

   Note card 1 _____ Note card 2 _____

4. Does the subject heading fit the information on the card?

   Note card 1 _____ Note card 2 _____

5. Does the material on the note card plagiarize?

   Note card 1 _____ Note card 2 _____

_____

| Step 14 | **TAKING NOTES ON YOUR RESEARCH QUESTION** |

Now it's time to work on your own research question.

A. On the basis of your reading so far, write down your working thesis.

   _____

   _____

B. Modeling the process we used at the beginning of the "Reading Sources" section, generate a list of research questions related to your working thesis.

   _____

   _____

For example, our thesis on why the *Titanic* sank might be stated as follows: *Although earliest analyses blamed the sinking of the* Titanic *on puncture by an iceberg, research based on modern technology implies that the ship need not have sunk if the materials and mode of construction had been supervised carefully.*

The questions we generated are repeated below. They serve as a guide to reading so that the notes we take will help support the thesis.

1. Why was it called "unsinkable"?

2. Why or how does a boat sink?

3. How does a ship stay afloat?

4. What major theories have been advanced about the *Titanic*'s sinking?

5. Was it going too fast?

6. Was it built cheaply?

7. Did they test it first?

8. Did anything discovered in the wreckage change the prevailing viewpoint?

9. What was the ship made of?

10. How was it put together?

Many of these questions will be related to the subject headings on our note cards and in our outlines. (See Chapter 6.)

C. Produce at least 15 note cards (five for each of three sources).

D. Use the evaluation criteria given earlier in this chapter to check your note taking.

Avoiding Plagiarism

Plagiarism! The word strikes terror in the hearts of students because it often means failure—on a paper or, in some cases, in a course. In professional life, people can be sued for what is extremely unethical behavior; reputations can be ruined. You would think with such penalties, people wouldn't do it; it's not worth getting caught. The fact is that although some people plagiarize on purpose, most do it accidentally because they don't understand what plagiarism is. **Plagiarism** is using someone's words, ideas, or concepts without giving that person credit. Nowhere in that definition does it say the act has to be intentional or how easy it is to break the rules.

With recent advances in technology, plagiarism has become easier to commit but, at the same time, much easier for instructors to spot. Online businesses have set up sites where both students and faculty can have a paper reviewed for plagiarism. One such site is www.turnitin.com.

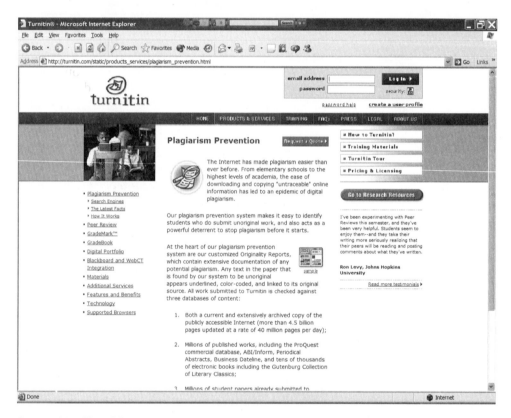

Source: http://turnitin.com. Reprinted by permission of iParadigms, LLC.

As you see from the claims on this site, faculty can identify almost instantly material that has been taken from electronic sources; if there are no citations or other attribution for this material, the professor will know the student stole the material, whether intentionally or not. (A number of faculty ask their students to do the preliminary checking since they realize that most students do not want to plagiarize.) Another way both faculty and students can check for plagiarism is by using a search engine like Google or Yahoo! to search a phrase or sentence. If the words have been plagiarized, the search engine often will be able to locate where the phrase was first used.

In order to know when to document a source, you need to know when *not* to document. (See Chapters 8 and 9 for more information on documentation.) It is not necessary to document facts that most people accept as true (the *Titanic* set sail on its maiden voyage on April 10, 1912) or opinions held by a large number of people (many people thought the *Titanic* was unsinkable). In both of these cases you have to make a judgment call. If a fact—that is, something that cannot be disputed—is not the result of original work (such as a survey or new historical research), you can use it. (If it can be or has been disputed, it is not a fact.) Most dates are common knowledge; for example, the time at which the *Titanic* sank (2:20 A.M.) is common knowledge. Even if you have just learned it, if this information is widely available—that is, if it appears in a number of books without attribution (without the source being identified)—you may use it without documenting it. What needs to be documented? In general, you must document the following information:

1. An opinion or fact that is not common knowledge

2. The specific words or expressions used or the organization imposed by someone else (the words need to be quoted as well)

3. Original research, including statistics, surveys, and other findings

Note that only the exact language of someone else needs to be quoted, but even when you put someone's ideas into your own words, you must provide documentation.

When you are just learning about your subject, you will find it more difficult to decide what needs to be documented. If you were writing about the *Titanic*, it would be acceptable to write, without documentation, that it probably sank because of puncture by an iceberg, because this is an opinion that many people shared until recently. However, if you wrote that faulty rivets were probably the cause of the disaster, you would have to give credit to the scientist who developed this theory, because *he* is the expert on rivets, not you. It would be appropriate to write that the *Titanic* was a ship steeped in romance and glamour without documenting these words, but if you called it a "monster ship," you would have to cite Wyn Craig Wade, who first called it that by giving the title "Monster Ship" to Chapter 1 of his book *The Titanic: End of a Dream.* His title refers to an article in *Engineering News* dated January 12, 1911, which called the ship one of many "marine monsters." Whenever you are uncertain about whether to cite, always ask your instructor. You can also add sources you consulted as background to your list of sources at the end of the essay to be sure you eliminate any possibility of plagiarism.

EXERCISE 5.16   Recognizing When Sources Need to Be Documented

Look at the following list. Place a checkmark next to the sentences that definitely need documentation, an M next to those that may need documentation, and an X next to those that do not need documentation. Briefly note your reasons beneath the sentence. (The first three have been completed as examples.)

1. The *Titanic* was part of the White Star Line.

     X   *This is a fact and does not need documentation.*

2. Captain E. J. Smith was an excellent captain.

     ✔   *This is an opinion, and if it is someone else's opinion, you need to tell us whose opinion it is and where you read it.*

3. Class hatred permeated the ship.

     ✔   *You weren't there, so you must rely on a source who was there or who analyzed the events on the* <u>*Titanic*</u> *in a written work.*

4. The ship was built in Belfast, Ireland.

_____ _____

5. The *Titanic* was the most luxurious ship of its time.

_____ _____

6. The *Titanic* was almost 900 feet long.

_____ _____

7. Many people knew that the ship was unsinkable.

_____ _____

8. The *Titanic* sank because it was going too fast.

_____ _____

9. The rivets had too much slag and thus could be cracked easily.

_____ _____

10. The *Titanic* struck an iceberg on April 14, 1912.

_____ _____

11. Most people did not drown; they froze to death.

_____ _____

12. There were not enough lifeboats.

_____ _____

13. Many gentlemen were valiant in their efforts to save others.

_____ _____

14. Modern technology made possible the rediscovery of the *Titanic.*

_____ _____

15. It would be wrong to scavenge the *Titanic* for memorabilia.

_____ _____

_____

Paraphrasing

Good note taking will help prevent plagiarism. It's easy to forget which words or ideas are yours and which are an author's, but clearly marked note cards will remind you where you got ideas that weren't your own. On your cards, you should try to quote rather than paraphrase whenever possible. (You can always translate quotations into paraphrases or summaries, but you cannot transform paraphrases and summaries into quotations.) You can't quote everything, however, so you need to learn the techniques of paraphrase and summary. Using these techniques correctly will ensure that you do not commit plagiarism.

A **paraphrase** is an expression in your own words of an idea or passage written by someone else. In a good paraphrase, you show that you understand what has been written by changing the language while remaining faithful to the original meaning. A paraphrase is always documented. **Although the words are yours, the ideas are those of the original author.**

Paraphrasing is difficult. Words, phrases, and syntax tend to stay in your head and intrude on your writing. The following are guidelines to help you put the ideas you read into your own words.

PARAPHRASING

- Begin by reading carefully and thinking about what you have read.
- Cover the material that you are paraphrasing with a piece of paper (or your hand) so that you can't see it.
- Paraphrase the material.
- Paraphrase your paraphrase.
- Check what you've written against the original, and make more changes where necessary.
- If you are really stuck, quote the original word or phrase, but only if you simply can't put it into your own words.

EXERCISE 5.17   Evaluating Paraphrases

Look at the following paraphrases and check them against the original text to evaluate their quality. Explain your thinking below each paraphrase. First, let's look at an example:

Original

Walter Lord wrote in the preface to *A Night to Remember,* "On April 10, 1912, the . . . ship left Southampton on her <u>maiden voyage</u> to New York. Her cargo included <u>a priceless copy of *The Rubáiyát of Omar Khayyám*</u> and a list of passengers collectively worth two hundred and fifty million dollars. <u>On her way over she . . . struck an iceberg</u> and went down <u>on a cold April night</u>" (xii).

Paraphrase 1

Walter Lord writes that the *Titanic* embarked from Southampton for her first and only voyage on April 10, 1912, carrying many extremely wealthy passengers and expensive cargo. She hit an iceberg and sank on her way to New York City.

Though short, it captures the author's meaning.

Paraphrase 2

According to Lord, the Titanic left port on April 10, 1912, for her <u>maiden voyage.</u> Among her cargo she had <u>a priceless copy of *The Rubáiyát of Omar Khayyám*</u> and many extremely wealthy passengers. <u>On her way she struck</u> an iceberg and sank <u>on a cold night in April.</u>

Although this is not an exact copy of the original, it uses too many noun phrases from Lord's writing and similar syntax.

Similar phrases in the original and in paraphrase 2 are underlined to illustrate the borrowing. Compare the phrases in paraphrase 2 to the wording of the original to see why they are close to plagiarism.

Original

> In *National Geographic,* December 1985, Robert Ballard writes, "The ship carried lifeboats for only 1,178, and many boats were launched only partly filled. Of the 2,227 on board, more than 1,500 perished, including Captain Edward J. Smith. . . . A veteran of 43 years at sea, Smith had planned to retire after *Titanic's* maiden voyage" (700).

Paraphrase 1

> The ship didn't have enough lifeboats for its many passengers, and they were only partly filled when launched. Many perished, including the captain, who was about to retire.

_____

_____

Paraphrase 2

> There were only 1,178 spaces in the *Titanic's* lifeboats, although there were 2,227 passengers and even those few spaces were not completely filled. Captain Edward J. Smith was among the more than 1,500 who died.

_____

_____

Paraphrase 3

> The ship had lifeboats for only 1,178 of its 2,227 passengers and many lifeboats were only partly filled when launched. Among the more than 1,500 who perished was Captain Edward J. Smith, whose plans were to retire after the voyage.

_____

_____

Original

> In *National Geographic,* December 1985, Robert Ballard writes, "The Woods Hole team did not find the 300-foot-long gash that has long been held to be *Titanic's* undoing. Rather, [they] observed a hole on the starboard side, along with several plates that had been bent inward, springing the rivets. Any additional damage suffered by the bow, whether caused by the iceberg or by impact with the bottom, lies hidden in the mud" (719).

_____

_____

Paraphrase 1

> Much of the *Titanic's* bow was buried in mud, and the "300-foot-long gash" thought to have been the cause of the disaster was not located. Instead Ballard found a starboard hole and plates that had popped their rivets.

_____

_____

Paraphrase 2

The excavation team did not find the gash they had thought to be the cause of the disaster. There was a hole on the side and plates bent in that had sprung their rivets. The rest of the ship was hidden in the mud.

_____

_____

Paraphrase 3

Although Ballard didn't find the famous 300-foot-long gash that was reputed to be the reason why the *Titanic* sank, he did find a hole on the starboard side and plates with sprung rivets. The rest of the bow was covered by mud.

_____

_____

Original

Robert Ballard writes in *National Geographic,* December 1985, "The relief of rescue was tempered by a grim statistic: while all children in first and second class were saved, two-thirds of the children in third class perished. Nor were the ship's owners disposed to generosity toward survivors. Against claims amounting to more than 16 million dollars, the White Star Line reportedly paid a total of $663,000" (718).

_____

_____

Paraphrase 1

The following statistic should be noted. Although all the children in first and second class were rescued, two-thirds of third-class children were not. Also, the ship's owners were not generous to survivors. Claims were more than 16 million dollars, but the White Star Line supposedly paid only $663,000.

_____

_____

Paraphrase 2

Rescue efforts managed to save all first- and second-class children, but third-class children were not apparently considered as valuable. Two-thirds died in the disaster. Also, compensation for the wreck was minimal. Although $16 million was claimed, only $663,000 was paid.

_____

_____

Paraphrase 3

Whereas all children of first- and second-class passengers were rescued, most third-class children perished, and little compensation was paid to survivors.

_____

_____

EXERCISE 5.18   Writing Paraphrases

Now you are ready to practice writing paraphrases. Paraphrase the following three passages in the spaces below.

1. On April 10, 1912, the *New York Times* reported, "Although essentially similar in design and construction to her sister ship, the *Olympic,* the *Titanic* is an improvement of the *Olympic* in many aspects. Cap't Smith has been promoted from the *Olympic* to take her across. There are two pursors, H. W. McElroy and R. L. Baker" (1).

_____

_____

_____

_____

_____

_____

2. "The world's greatest ocean liner lay rusting in solitude for more than 70 years, though it was not for lack of trying to find her. Then in 1985, in the last hours of a joint French–American mission, Robert Ballard's Woods Hole crew finally spotted one of the boilers on the video feed from the camera they were towing. Ballard returned the next year and explored the wreck with the submersible Alvin . . . dubbing the cascades of rust festooning the metal 'rusticles'" (Discovery Channel Online).

_____

_____

_____

_____

_____

_____

3. Wyn Craig Wade writes in *The Titanic: End of a Dream,* "Morning news snuffed all hopes of any survivors beyond those already reported. The captain of the *Olympic* had sent the White Star Line a message via the *Cedric.* 'Please allay rumors that the *Virginian* has any of the *Titanic*'s survivors,' wired Captain Haddock. 'I believe that the only survivors are on the *Carpathia.*' Shortly thereafter, the *Virginian* came back into wireless range and confirmed; she had simply arrived too late to be of any help. The *Parisian* forwarded the same message and added a note of grisly finality. The weather had been quite cold, the captain of the *Parisian* reported. 'Any persons who might have clung to wreckage undoubtedly would have died of exposure'" (43–44).

_____

_____

_____

_____

_____

_____

Summarizing

A **summary** is an outline of a document. It is shorter than a paraphrase, usually covering only the main points. A summary may be done in words, phrases, or sentences. When doing a summary, you should include

1. the article or chapter's main ideas

2. the major ideas supporting or explaining these main ideas

You do not need to include the details that expand these main ideas unless they are essential to the writer's main point. The advantage of a summary over a paraphrase is that it is shorter, written as it often is in outline form, and thus reduces the note-taking process. The disadvantages of summarizing are that you might leave out material important to the meaning of the whole piece and that what you leave out may distort your summary.

Read the passage below and compare it to the paraphrase and summary that follow.

Original

> Walter Lord wrote in *A Night to Remember*, "On April 10, 1912, the . . . ship left Southampton on her maiden voyage to New York. Her cargo included a priceless copy of *The Rubáiyát of Omar Khayyám* and a list of passengers collectively worth two hundred and fifty million dollars. On her way over, she . . . struck an iceberg and went down on a cold April night" (xii).

Paraphrase

> Walter Lord writes that the *Titanic* embarked from Southampton for her first and only voyage on April 10, 1912, carrying many extremely wealthy passengers and expensive cargo. She hit an iceberg and sank on her way to New York City.

Summary

> Ship left 4/10/12 for NY. "Maiden voyage." Valuable cargo.

EXERCISE 5.19   Writing Summaries

Below are the passages you have already paraphrased. Summarize them in the spaces that follow.

1. The *New York Times* reported on April 10, 1912, "Although essentially similar in design and construction to her sister ship, the *Olympic,* the *Titanic* is an improvement of the *Olympic* in many respects. Cap't Smith has been promoted from the *Olympic* to take her across. There are two pursors, H. W. McElroy and R. L. Baker" (1).

   _____

   _____

   _____

2. The Discovery Channel's online program reports: "The world's greatest ocean liner lay rusting in solitude for more than 70 years, though it was not for lack of trying to find her. Then in 1985, in the last hours of a joint French–American mission, Robert Ballard's Woods Hole crew finally spotted one of the boilers on the video feed from the camera they were towing. Ballard returned the next year

and explored the wreck with the submersible Alvin . . . dubbing the cascades of rust festooning the metal 'rusticles.'"

_____

_____

3. Wyn Craig Wade writes in *The Titanic: End of a Dream,* "Morning news snuffed all hopes of any survivors beyond those already reported. The captain of the *Olympic* had sent the White Star Line a message via the *Cedric.* 'Please allay rumors that the *Virginian* has any of the *Titanic*'s survivors,' wired Captain Haddock. 'I believe that the only survivors are on the *Carpathia.*' Shortly there-after, the *Virginian* came back into wireless range and confirmed; she had simply arrived too late to be of any help. The *Parisian* forwarded the same message and added a note of grisly finality. The weather had been quite cold, the captain of the *Parisian* reported. 'Any persons who might have clung to wreckage undoubtedly would have died of exposure'" (41).

_____

_____

_____

_____

Quoting

Quoting involves copying the exact words of a writer—word for word, punctuation mark for punctuation mark. Although you should quote frequently in your notes, in your final papers you should quote only when there is no other way to represent adequately the language or ideas of the original source.

It is, however, necessary to quote in certain cases:

- Authoritative and/or famous people. For example, an expert on marine engineering testifying on the cause of the *Titanic* disaster would warrant quoting rather than paraphrasing.

- Writers and poets. Quoting is often necessary to preserve their unique use of language.

- Special terminology: scientific, legal, or technical language. It is almost impossible to paraphrase this information, and it is too dense to summarize. For example, William E. Broad quotes Dr. Timothy Foecke, a metallurgist, in the *New York Times* on January 24, 1998: "The microstructure of the rivets is the most likely candidate for becoming a quantifiable metallurgical factor in the loss of the *Titanic*" (F5).

Ellipsis

Quoting too much can make the reader lose the sense of your argument. Your paper can become a mass of quotations rather than a means to convey your own ideas. That is why you should try to use ellipses to shorten your quotations when they contain more information than you really need to make your point. An **ellipsis** is three dots that indicate that words have been omitted from a quotation. If you can leave words out of a quotation to shorten it or because you don't need them, you can use this punctuation symbol to indicate an omission. You must not, however, alter the meaning of the whole. If you use an ellipsis at the end of a sentence, you still need to include a period.

For example, let's look at a quotation from the *National Geographic News:*

> The *Titanic* has significantly deteriorated since its discovery in 1986, explorer Robert D. Ballard announced yesterday during a telephone press conference from a research ship above the wreck in the North Atlantic. Ballard found the *Titanic* in 1986. He is currently leading an expedition to see how the wreck has changed since then and to ensure its future protection.

Here is a helpful use of the ellipsis in shortening the above quotation: "The *Titanic* has significantly deteriorated since its discovery in 1986, explorer Robert D. Ballard announced yesterday. . . . He is currently leading an expedition . . . to ensure its future protection."

Brackets

You can also insert explanatory material into a quote by enclosing it in **brackets,** [ ].

For example, in the *New York Times* article by William Broad referred to above, we need to add explanatory material to make the meaning of the quotation clear. "The new analysis [of the rivets] was done by Dr. Timothy Foecke, a metallurgist at the National Institute of Standards and Technology . . ." (F5).

Step 15	PARAPHRASING, SUMMARIZING, AND QUOTING YOUR SOURCES

Using your own sources from your research, create three note cards. One should be a paraphrase, one a summary, and one a quotation.

CHECKLIST   EVALUATING AND RECORDING INFORMATION FROM SOURCES

❑ Have you located and retrieved at least 10 possible sources on your topic in books, periodicals, newspapers, nonprint media (radio, television, film, video, and photographs), interviews, Internet sites, newsletters, pamphlets, and more?

❑ Have you used the evaluation guidelines and reviewed the sources carefully? Web sources in particular need to be checked carefully for reliability.

❑ Did you create a working bibliography card for each source and did you put all the cards in alphabetical order?

❑ Have you read your sources carefully and selectively, using techniques such as underlining and highlighting to enable you to retrieve what you found?

❑ Are your notes clearly written and understandable?

❑ Have you taken notes selectively, focusing on what you need to support your thesis and answer your research questions?

❑ Are you aware of what constitutes plagiarism?

❑ Do you know when sources need documentation?

CHECKLIST EVALUATING AND RECORDING INFORMATION FROM SOURCES (continued)

❏ Do you know when words need to be in quotation marks?

❏ Are your quotes accurate? Have you checked them against the original sources?

❏ Do you know how to paraphrase so that you don't inadvertently plagiarize (by copying the exact words or ideas of someone else)?

❏ Do you know how to summarize the major points of an article or chapter so that you can remember the main idea?

CHAPTER **6**

Organizing and Outlining Research Material

■ **Understanding Outlines**

■ **Organization: Formal Outlines**

■ **Types of Formal Outlines**

■ **Choosing an Outline Form**

In this chapter you will practice how to begin planning your own essay using source material you have collected to support your thesis. The best way to prepare for the difficult task of writing is to make an outline, an organized listing of the major topics and subtopics of your thesis. An outline provides you with a guide to follow when you are writing your paper. In addition, if you can make a plan to organize your notes, you will have an easier time visualizing the whole of your essay and figuring out whether you have enough material. In Chapter 3 you created a preliminary outline for the purposes of note taking by listing a working thesis and major topics, which were your research questions. You then took notes, using those topics to guide you in your search for material on your thesis. The purpose of this chapter is to help you revise, expand, and organize this outline so that you can organize your notes before you begin writing.

Using material from the life and writings of Frederick Douglass, we will practice making outlines. Because strategies change depending on the kind of essay you want to write and the type of research question you are trying to answer, we will look at a variety of outline formats. Your instructor may ask you to follow a specific kind of outline or let you choose your own. In either case, you need to be familiar with different kinds of outlines and how they act as the "skeleton" of the essay's body, giving it shape and definition. Once you understand the basic steps in outlining, you will be able to create your own outline and begin writing the paper.

Outlines normally evolve from lists of topics and/or research questions (known as running outlines) into one of several kinds of more formal working outlines. Whichever kind you choose, you must remember that an outline is there to be changed if, once you begin to write your paper, you find it doesn't reflect the paper you want to write. It is a guide, but it is not the law.

165

Understanding Outlines

Running Outlines

EXERCISE 6.1 **Identifying the Elements of a Running Outline**

Outlining what we read can help us understand how writers approach the outlining process. Read the following summary of Frederick Douglass's life.

Frederick Douglass was born in slavery as Frederick Augustus Washington Bailey near Easton in Talbot County, Maryland. He was not sure of the exact year of his birth, but he knew that it was 1817 or 1818. As a young boy he was sent to Baltimore, to be a house servant, where he learned to read and write, with the assistance of his master's wife. In 1838 he escaped from slavery and went to New York City, where he married Anna Murray, a free colored woman whom he had met in Baltimore. Soon thereafter he changed his name to Frederick Douglass. In 1841 he addressed a convention of the Massachusetts Anti-Slavery Society in Nantucket and so greatly impressed the group that they immediately employed him as an agent. He was such an impressive orator that numerous persons doubted if he had ever been a slave, so he wrote *Narrative of the Life of Frederick Douglass.* During the Civil War he assisted in the recruiting of colored men for the 54th and 55th Massachusetts Regiments and consistently argued for the emancipation of slaves. After the war he was active in securing and protecting the rights of the freemen. In his later years, at different times, he was secretary of the Santo Domingo Commission, marshall and recorder of deeds of the District of Columbia, and United States minister to Haiti. His other autobiographical works are *My Bondage and My Freedom* and *Life and Times of Frederick Douglass,* published in 1855 and 1881 respectively. He died in 1895.

Frederick Douglass,
*Narrative of the Life of
Frederick Douglass,*
Introduction

Below is an example of a running outline derived from this paragraph. Look it over and see whether you can identify the elements of a running outline.

Frederick Douglass born 1817 or 1818 and died 1895

Gained fame for his oratory skills

Addressed Anti-Slavery Society in 1841

Married Anna Murray 1838

Served as minister to Haiti

Assumed other diplomatic posts

Recruited African American slaves to fight with the North in Civil War

Wrote *Narrative of the Life of Frederick Douglass*

Wrote *Life and Times of Frederick Douglass*

What you probably noticed is that each of these separate phrases represents a topic or idea. It is, indeed, a summary of the main ideas in the essay. The purpose of a running outline is to list your ideas as they come to you. A running outline might precede your note taking, because you need a list of ideas in order to do your search. Conversely, if you took the major ideas from all your notes and put them in a list, you would have a running outline.

EXERCISE 6.2   Creating Your Own Running Outline

Now look back at the newspaper account of the murder of Lizzie Borden's mother and father in Chapter 1. Make a running outline by picking out the major topics.

Step 16   MAKING A RUNNING OUTLINE OF YOUR PAPER

Organization: Formal Outlines

Looking at the elements of your running outline should help you choose the right formal outline for your essay. In creating a formal outline you take the notes from your running outline and organize them.

Classification and Arrangement

Before you make a formal outline, you first need to **classify** your material—that is, separate it into like groupings, and then arrange it into an order that makes sense for your topic. Our running outline of Douglass's life might be divided into the following classes:

childhood

Civil War

life changes

later life

antislavery activities

EXERCISE 6.3   Classifying Topics

What has been done to classify the elements of Douglass's life? List the topics in the running outline that fit under each major grouping.

childhood _____

Civil War _____

life changes _____

later life _____

antislavery activities _____

Arrangement is the process of making order from your groupings. The arrangement of a biography is often **chronological** (arranged in terms of time). Other common arrangements are **spatial** (in terms of geography or space) and **logical** (in terms of abstract relationships).

EXERCISE 6.4   Arranging Topics

Note that the arrangement of the topics above is random—that is, the order in which they appear is not guided by any logical principle of organization. List the topics in a logical order.

_____

_____

_____

_____

EXERCISE 6.5   Identifying the Arrangement of an Outline

Read the following two outlines of Douglass's life. How would you identify the arrangement of the topics?

Outline A   **Arrangement**

  I. Childhood   _____

    A. Born in Maryland, 1817 or 1818

    B. Taken to Baltimore as a slave

    C. Learns to read and write

  II. Life changes   _____

    A. Escape

    B. Marriage

    C. Name change

  III. Antislavery activity   _____

    A. Employed by abolitionists

    B. Writes *Narrative*

  IV. Civil War   _____

    A. Recruits African Americans for Union army

    B. Advocates for rights of African Americans after the war

  V. Later life   _____

    A. Government positions

    B. Dies in 1895

Outline   **Arrangement**

  I. 1817–1818   _____

    A. Douglass's birth in Maryland

    B. Childhood in Baltimore

    C. Education

  II. 1838   _____

    A. Escape from slavery

    B. Marriage

    C. Name change

III. 1841–1845 _____
   A. Recognition and employment by antislavery movement
   B. Writing of *Narrative*

IV. 1860s _____
   A. Recruitment of African Americans for Union army
   B. Advocate of rights for African Americans

V. 1870s to 1890s _____
   A. Prestigious government positions
   B. Death in 1895

EXERCISE 6.6   Practicing Logical Arrangements

Read Chapter VII of Douglass's *Narrative of the Life of Frederick Douglass* (below), and try to assign the following abstract terms to sections of the chapter: *triumph, assistance, despair, rebellion, anger, betrayal.*

Narrative of the Life of Frederick Douglass

Frederick Douglass

Chapter VII

1   I lived in Master Hugh's family about seven years. During this time, I succeeded in learning to read and write. In accomplishing this, I was compelled to resort to various stratagems. I had no regular teacher. My mistress, who had kindly commenced to instruct me, had, in compliance with the advice and direction of her husband, not only ceased to instruct, but had set her face against my being instructed by any one else. It is due, however, to my mistress to say of her, that she did not adopt this course of treatment immediately. She at first lacked the depravity indispensable to shutting me up in mental darkness. It was at least necessary for her to have some training in the exercise of irresponsible power, to make her equal to the task of treating me as though I were a brute.

2   My mistress was, as I have said, a kind and tender-hearted woman; and in the simplicity of her soul she commenced, when I first went to live with her, to treat me as she supposed one human being ought to treat another. In entering upon the duties of a slaveholder, she did not seem to perceive that I sustained to her the relation of a mere chattel, and that for her to treat me as a human being was not only wrong, but dangerously so. Slavery proved as injurious to her as it did to me. When I went there, she was a pious, warm, and tender-hearted woman. There was no sorrow or suffering for which she had not a tear. She had bread for the hungry, clothes for the naked, and comfort for every mourner that came within her reach. Slavery soon proved its ability to divest her of these heavenly qualities. Under its influence, the tender heart became stone, and the lamblike disposition gave way to one of tiger-like fierceness. The first step in her downward course

was in her ceasing to instruct me. She now commenced to practise her husband's precepts. She finally became even more violent in her opposition than her husband himself. She was not satisfied with simply doing as well as he had commanded; she seemed anxious to do better. Nothing seemed to make her more angry than to see me with a newspaper. She seemed to think that here lay the danger. I have had her rush at me with a face made all up of fury, and snatch from me a newspaper, in a manner that fully revealed her apprehension. She was an apt woman; and a little experience soon demonstrated, to her satisfaction, that education and slavery were incompatible with each other.

3   From this time I was most narrowly watched. If I was in a separate room any considerable length of time, I was sure to be suspected of having a book, and was at once called to give an account of myself. All this, however, was too late. The first step had been taken. Mistress, in teaching me the alphabet, had given me the *inch*, and no precaution could prevent me from taking the *ell*.

4   The plan which I adopted, and the one by which I was most successful, was that of making friends of all the little white boys whom I met in the street. As many of these as I could, I converted into teachers. With their kindly aid, obtained at different times and in different places, I finally succeeded in learning to read. When I was sent on errands, I always took my book with me, and by doing one part of my errand quickly, I found time to get a lesson before my return. I used also to carry bread with me, enough of which was always in the house, and to which I was always welcome; for I was much better off in this regard than many of the poor white children in our neighborhood. This bread I used to bestow upon the hungry little urchins, who, in return, would give me that more valuable bread of knowledge. I am strongly tempted to give the names of two or three of those little boys, as a testimonial of the gratitude and affection I bear them; but prudence forbids;—not that it would injure me, but it might embarrass them; for it is almost an unpardonable offence to teach slaves to read in this Christian country. It is enough to say of the dear little fellows, that they lived on Philpot Street, very near Durgin and Bailey's ship-yard. I used to talk this matter of slavery over with them. I would sometimes say to them, I wished I could be as free as they would be when they got to be men. "You will be free as soon as you are twenty-one, *but I am a slave for life!* Have not I as good a right to be free as you have?" These words used to trouble them; they would express for me the liveliest sympathy, and console me with the hope that something would occur by which I might be free.

5   I was now about twelve years old, and the thought of being *a slave for life* began to bear heavily upon my heart. Just about this time, I got hold of a book entitled "The Columbian Orator." Every opportunity I got, I used to read this book. Among much of other interesting matter, I found in it a dialogue between a master and his slave. The slave was represented as having run away from his master three times. The dialogue represented the conversation which took place between them, when the slave was retaken the third time. In this dialogue, the whole argument in behalf of slavery was brought forward by the master, all of which was disposed of by the slave. The slave was made to say some very smart as well as impressive things in reply to his master—things which had the desired though unexpected effect; for the conversation resulted in the voluntary emancipation of the slave on the part of the master.

6   In the same book, I met with one of Sheridan's mighty speeches on and in behalf of Catholic emancipation. These were choice documents to me. I read them over and over again with unabated interest. They gave tongue to interesting thoughts of my own soul, which had frequently flashed through my mind, and died away for want of utterance. The moral which I gained from the dialogue was the power of truth over the conscience of even a slaveholder. What I got from Sheridan was a bold denunciation of slavery, and

a powerful vindication of human rights. The reading of these documents enabled me to utter my thoughts, and to meet the arguments brought forward to sustain slavery; but while they relieved me of one difficulty, they brought on another even more painful than the one of which I was relieved. The more I read, the more I was led to abhor and detest my enslavers. I could regard them in no other light than a band of successful robbers, who had left their homes, and gone to Africa, and stolen us from our homes, and in a strange land reduced us to slavery. I loathed them as being the meanest as well as the most wicked of men. As I read and contemplated the subject, behold! that very discontentment which Master Hugh had predicted would follow my learning to read had already come, to torment and sting my soul to unutterable anguish. As I writhed under it, I would at times feel that learning to read had been a curse rather than a blessing. It had given me a view of my wretched condition, without the remedy. It opened my eyes to the horrible pit, but to no ladder upon which to get out. In moments of agony, I envied my fellow-slaves for their stupidity. I have often wished myself a beast. I preferred the condition of the meanest reptile to my own. Any thing, no matter what, to get rid of thinking! It was this everlasting thinking of my condition that tormented me. There was no getting rid of it. It was pressed upon me by every object within sight or hearing, animate or inanimate. The silver trump of freedom had roused my soul to eternal wakefulness. Freedom now appeared, to disappear no more forever. It was heard in every sound, and seen in every thing. It was ever present to torment me with a sense of my wretched condition. I saw nothing without seeing it, I heard nothing without hearing it, and felt nothing without feeling it. It looked from every star, it smiled in every calm, breathed in every wind, and moved in every storm.

7   I often found myself regretting my own existence, and wishing myself dead; and but for the hope of being free, I have no doubt but that I should have killed myself, or done something for which I should have been killed. While in this state of mind, I was eager to hear any one speak of slavery. I was a ready listener. Every little while, I could hear something about the abolitionists. It was some time before I found what the word meant. It was always used in such connections as to make it an interesting word to me. If a slave ran away and succeeded in getting clear, or if a slave killed his master, set fire to a barn, or did any thing very wrong in the mind of a slaveholder, it was spoken of as the fruit of *abolition*. Hearing the word in this connection very often, I set about learning what it meant. The dictionary afforded me little or no help. I found it was "the act of abolishing;" but then I did not know what was to be abolished. Here I was perplexed. I did not dare to ask any one about its meaning, for I was satisfied that it was something they wanted me to know very little about. After a patient waiting, I got one of our city papers, containing an account of the number of petitions from the north, praying for the abolition of slavery in the District of Columbia, and of the slave trade between the States. From this time I understood the words *abolition* and *abolitionist*, and always drew near when that word was spoken, expecting to hear something of importance to myself and fellow-slaves. The light broke in upon me by degrees. I went one day down on the wharf of Mr. Waters; and seeing two Irishmen unloading a scow of stone, I went, unasked, and helped them. When we had finished, one of them came to me and asked me if I were a slave. I told him I was. He asked, "Are ye a slave for life?" I told him that I was. The good Irishman seemed to be deeply affected by the statement. He said to the other that it was a pity so fine a little fellow as myself should be a slave for life. He said it was a shame to hold me. They both advised me to run away to the north; that I should find friends there, and that I should be free. I pretended not to be interested in what they said, and treated them as if I did not understand them; for I feared they might be treacherous. White men have been known to encourage slaves to escape, and then, to

get the reward, catch them and return them to their masters. I was afraid that these seemingly good men might use me so; but I nevertheless remembered their advice, and from that time I resolved to run away. I looked forward to a time at which it would be safe for me to escape. I was too young to think of doing so immediately; besides, I wished to learn how to write, as I might have occasion to write my own pass. I consoled myself with the hope that I should one day find a good chance. Meanwhile, I would learn to write.

8   The idea as to how I might learn to write was suggested to me by being in Durgin and Bailey's ship-yard, and frequently seeing the ship carpenters, after hewing, and getting a piece of timber ready for use, write on the timber the name of that part of the ship for which it was intended. When a piece of timber was intended for the larboard side, it would be marked thus—"L." When a piece was for the starboard side, it would be marked thus—"S." A piece for the larboard side forward, would be marked thus—"L.F." When a piece was for starboard side forward, it would be marked thus—"S.F." For larboard aft, it would be marked thus—"L.A." For starboard aft, it would be marked thus—"S.A." I soon learned the names of these letters, and for what they were intended when placed upon a piece of timber in the ship-yard. I immediately commenced copying them, and in a short time was able to make the four letters named. After that, when I met with any boy who I knew could write, I would tell him I could write as well as he. The next word would be, "I don't believe you. Let me see you try it." I would then make the letters which I had been so fortunate as to learn, and ask him to beat that. In this way I got a good many lessons in writing, which it is quite possible I should never have gotten in any other way. During this time, my copy-book was the board fence, brick wall, and pavement; my pen and ink was a lump of chalk. With these, I learned mainly how to write. I then commenced and continued copying the Italics in Webster's Spelling Book, until I could make them all without looking on the book. By this time, my little Master Thomas had gone to school, and learned how to write, and had written over a number of copy-books. These had been brought home, and shown to some of our near neighbors, and then laid aside. My mistress used to go to class meeting at the Wilk Street meetinghouse every Monday afternoon, and leave me to take care of the house. When left thus, I used to spend the time in writing in the spaces left in Master Thomas's copy-book, copying what he had written. I continued to do this until I could write a hand very similar to that of Master Thomas. Thus, after a long, tedious effort for years, I finally succeeded in learning how to write.

EXERCISE 6.7   Practicing Spatial Arrangements

Look at Douglass's Chapter VII again. Would it make sense to use spatial arrangements in outlining this chapter? If so, how would you do it? If not, why not?

Development Models

Many writers depend on a variety of what are called **development** (or rhetorical) **models** (or strategies) to guide the overall organization of their work. These strategies include narration, comparison and contrast, argument, analysis, and others. Writers often combine strategies within an essay, depending on their thesis. You may have decided on one of these strategies when you wrote your preliminary outline, because the choice of a thesis often determines what kind of organizational model a writer will use.

- In **narratives**, chronological order is used to present a story such as a life history (biography, autobiography) or to recount an event. Douglass's *Narrative of the Life of Frederick Douglass* is an example of this rhetorical strategy.

- **Comparison and contrast** is a strategy that weighs and balances two (or more) ideas, usually for the purpose of selecting one over the other or to analyze common issues and appreciate differences. For example, Douglass's life as a slave could be compared to and contrasted with his life after slavery. The *Titanic* could be compared to other ships of the time.

- **Arguments** intend to persuade. Writers use many tactics (including reasons, statistics, moral and ethical values, and other persuasive devices) to convince readers to share their points of view. For example, one could argue that Lizzie Borden most definitely did not kill her mother and father, that Frederick Douglass lived an exceptionally heroic life, or that the *Titanic* was not a well-constructed ship.

- **Analysis** breaks down (analyzes) the topic so the reader can better understand and evaluate it. Analysis is often used in scientific studies (Do certain kinds of vitamins help people combat colds?), in sociological reports (Do male students do better on standardized tests than female students?), and in literary criticism (What effect is Frederick Douglass seeking to achieve in *Narrative*, and how does his language work to help him achieve this effect?).

EXERCISE 6.8   **Considering Development Models**

Read the following research topics. Next to each, fill in the name of the model that would be the best one to use in developing the topic. For each, choose one of the following models:

    analysis

    argument

    comparison and contrast

    narrative

_____ 1. an essay that examines the lives of female slaves as similar to or different from the lives of male slaves

_____ 2. an essay that presents new biographical information on Edith Wharton

_____ 3. an essay that explores the reasons why *Uncle Tom's Cabin* (the novel by Harriet Beecher Stowe that presents a fictional account of the horrors of slavery and sold over a million copies) was the first bestseller in American history, making Stowe an international celebrity in 1852

_____ 4. an essay that advocates that Douglass's house be maintained by the National Park Service as a historic landmark

---

It could be said that all of the foregoing development models fit under the umbrella of analysis, given that the purpose of research writing is to use the research process to explain a topic in some way (and that way might be comparison and contrast or it might be argument). Writers want to help their readers understand something by breaking it down into its component parts and explaining how those parts are related to their main idea. What they want the reader to understand is their thesis (see Chapter 3 for a discussion of the thesis). The purpose of their essay is to explain or develop this thesis.

EXERCISE 6.9   Focusing on Analysis

Read the following paragraph from Chapter VIII of Douglass's *Narrative*, and see whether you can determine the thesis Douglass wants the reader to understand. What argument does he make in support of this thesis? Fill in the model of an analysis outline below.

Very soon after my return to Baltimore, my mistress, Lucretia, died, leaving her husband and one child, Amanda; and in a very short time after her death, Master Andrew died. Now all the property of my old master, slaves included, was in the hands of strangers,—strangers who had had nothing to do with accumulating it. Not a slave was left free. All remained slaves, from the youngest to the oldest. If any one thing in my experience, more than another, served to deepen my conviction of the infernal character of slavery, and to fill me with unutterable loathing of slaveholders, it was their base ingratitude to my poor old grandmother. She had served my old master faithfully from youth to old age. She had been the source of all his wealth; she had peopled his plantation with slaves; she had become a great grandmother in his service. She had rocked him in infancy, attended him in childhood, served him through life, and at his death wiped from his icy brow the cold death-sweat, and closed his eyes forever. She was nevertheless left a slave—a slave for life—a slave in the hands of strangers; and in their hands she saw her children, her grandchildren, and her great-granchildren, divided, like so many sheep, without being gratified with the small privilege of a single word, as to their or her own destiny. And, to cap the climax of their base ingratitude and fiendish barbarity, my grandmother, who was now very old, having outlived my old master and all his children, having seen the beginning and end of all of them, and her present owners finding she was of but little value, her frame already racked with the pains of old age, and complete helplessness fast stealing over her once active limbs, they took her to the woods, built her a little hut, put up a little mud-chimney, and then made her welcome to the privilege of supporting herself there in perfect loneliness; thus virtually turning her out to die! If my poor old grandmother now lives, she lives to suffer in utter loneliness; she lives to remember and mourn over the loss of children, the loss of grandchildren, and the loss of great-grandchildren.

thesis: _____

_____

explanation 1: _____

_____

explanation 2: _____

_____

explanation 3: _____

_____

explanation 4: _____

_____

_____

As you will see in the discussion of formal outlines that follows, these supporting reasons become major topics, and the subtopics are the details that will develop each argument.

Types of Formal Outlines

Once you have classified and arranged the elements of your outline and selected a rhetorical model, you need to choose the general pattern you will follow when writing your paper. Three useful outline formats are the traditional outline, the topic sentence and phrase outline, and the sentence and quotation outline. These methods are very flexible, and many outlines represent a combination of the three—using sentences only or phrases only or even single words. Your teacher may have an outline model she or he wants you to use, and if so, that should guide you. What is important is that you are comfortable with your outline; if you are not, it won't be useful to you. Making a good outline, on the other hand, can save you a lot of time and energy.

Traditional Outline

The traditional outline uses Roman numerals, uppercase (capital) letters, Arabic numerals, and lowercase letters to organize the ideas in an essay. This type of outline provides the most information about your essay, because it reflects the many levels of topics and subtopics in the essay. For larger research projects with many levels of material it is extremely useful, but for a research project of any size, it is a helpful way of putting all the information on your note cards or sheets into an organized whole. Below is Outline A from the previous section, expanded into a traditional research outline. (We have broken down the first major topic into major and minor subtopics so you can see the logical arrangement of the elements of the outline.)

The Life of Frederick Douglass: Outline A

I. Childhood *(major topic)*

  A. Born in Maryland 1817 or 1818 *(major subtopic)*

  B. Childhood in Baltimore *(major subtopic)*

    1. House slave *(minor topic)*

      a. Duties *(minor subtopic)*

      b. Friendships *(minor subtopic)*

    2. Education *(minor topic)*

      a. Reading *(minor subtopic)*

      b. Writing *(minor subtopic)*

II. Life changes *(major topic)*

  A. Escape

    1. Attitude toward owners

    2. Preparation

    3. Escape

    4. Aftermath

  B. Marriage

  C. Name change

III. Antislavery activities

    A. Abolition

        1. Why recruited

        2. Specific activities

            a. Oration

            b. Administrative

    B. *Narrative of the Life of Frederick Douglass*

        1. Reasons for writing it

        2. Content

        3. Reception

IV. Civil War

    A. Recruiter for Union

    B. Postwar advocate

        1. Legal rights of freemen

        2. Human needs of freemen

            a. Jobs

            b. Homes

            c. Food

V. Later life

    A. Government positions

        1. Secretary of Santo Domingo Commission

        2. Recorder of deeds for the District of Columbia

        3. U.S. minister to Haiti

    B. Other writings

Note that not all levels have the same amount of material, because the outline depends on what material was uncovered initially. You should also use the traditional outline for discovering where you need to do more research.

EXERCISE 6.10   Using an Outline to Guide Your Research

Look at Outline A (above) and find at least five areas that seem to need more material.

1. _____

2. _____

3. _____

4. _____

5. _____

EXERCISE 6.11   Making a Traditional Outline

Using the traditional format we just discussed, read Chapter VIII of *Narrative of the Life of Frederick Douglass* (below) and outline it as if you were writing your whole paper on that chapter. (We have seen one section of this excerpt on page 174.)

_____

Narrative of the Life of Frederick Douglass

Frederick Douglass

Chapter VIII

1   In a very short time after I went to live at Baltimore, my old master's youngest son Richard died; and in about three years and six months after his death, my old master, Captain Anthony, died, leaving only his son, Andrew, and daughter, Lucretia, to share his estate. He died while on a visit to see his daughter at Hillsborough. Cut off thus unexpectedly, he left no will as to the disposal of his property. It was therefore necessary to have a valuation of the property, that it might be equally divided between Mrs. Lucretia and Master Andrew. I was immediately sent for, to be valued with the other property. Here again my feelings rose up in detestation of slavery. I had now a new conception of my degraded condition. Prior to this, I had become, if not insensible to my lot, at least partly so. I left Baltimore with a young heart overborne with sadness, and a soul full of apprehension. I took passage with Captain Rowe, in the schooner Wild Cat, and, after a sail of about twenty-four hours, I found myself near the place of my birth. I had now been absent from it almost, if not quite, five years. I, however, remembered the place very well. I was only about five years old when I left it, to go and live with my old master on Colonel Lloyd's plantation; so that I was now between ten and eleven years old.

2   We were all ranked together at the valuation. Men and women, old and young, married and single, were ranked with horses, sheep, and swine. There were horses and men, cattle and women, pigs and children, all holding the same rank in the scale of being, and were all subjected to the same narrow examination. Silvery-headed age and sprightly youth, maids and matrons, had to undergo the same indelicate inspection. At this moment, I saw more clearly than ever the brutalizing effects of slavery upon both slave and slaveholder.

3   After the valuation, then came the division. I have no language to express the high excitement and deep anxiety which were felt among us poor slaves during this time. Our fate for life was now to be decided. We had no more voice in that decision than the brutes among whom we were ranked. A single word from the white men was enough—against all our wishes, prayers, and entreaties—to sunder forever the dearest friends, dearest kindred, and strongest ties known to human beings. In addition to the pain of separation, there was the horrid dread of falling into the hands of Master Andrew. He was known to us all as being a most cruel wretch,—a common drunkard, who had, by his reckless mismanagement and profligate dissipation, already wasted a large portion of his father's property. We all felt that we might as well be sold at once to the Georgia traders, as to pass into his hands; for we knew that that would be our inevitable condition,—a condition held by us all in the utmost horror and dread.

4   I suffered more anxiety than most of my fellow-slaves. I had known what it was to be kindly treated; they had known nothing of the kind. They had seen little or nothing of the world. They were in very deed men and women of sorrow, and acquainted with grief. Their backs had been made familiar with the bloody lash, so that they had become callous; mine was yet tender; for while at Baltimore I got few whippings, and few slaves could boast of a kinder master and mistress than myself; and the thought of passing out of their hands into those of Master Andrew—a man who, but a few days before, to give me a sample of his bloody disposition, took my little brother by the throat, threw him on the ground, and with

the heel of his boot stamped upon his head till the blood gushed from his nose and ears— was well calculated to make me anxious as to my fate. After he had committed his savage outrage upon my brother, he turned to me, and said that was the way he meant to serve me one of these days,—meaning, I suppose, when I came into his possession.

5   Thanks to a kind Providence, I fell to the portion of Mrs. Lucretia, and was sent immediately back to Baltimore, to live again in the family of Master Hugh. Their joy at my return equalled their sorrow at my departure. It was a glad day to me. I had escaped a worse than lion's jaws. I was absent from Baltimore, for the purpose of valuation and division, just about one month, and it seemed to have been six.

6   Very soon after my return to Baltimore, my mistress, Lucretia, died, leaving her husband and one child, Amanda; and in a very short time after her death, Master Andrew died. Now all the property of my old master, slaves included, was in the hands of strangers,—strangers who had had nothing to do with accumulating it. Not a slave was left free. All remained slaves, from the youngest to the oldest. If any one thing in my experience, more than another, served to deepen my conviction of the infernal character of slavery, and to fill me with unutterable loathing of slaveholders, it was their base ingratitude to my poor old grandmother. She had served my old master faithfully from youth to old age. She had been the source of all his wealth; she had peopled his plantation with slaves; she had become a great grandmother in his service. She had rocked him in infancy, attended him in childhood, served him through life, and at his death wiped from his icy brow the cold death-sweat, and closed his eyes forever. She was nevertheless left a slave—a slave for life—a slave in the hands of strangers; and in their hands she saw her children, her grandchildren, and her great-grandchildren, divided, like so many sheep, without being gratified with the small privilege of a single word, as to their or her own destiny. And, to cap the climax of their base ingratitude and fiendish barbarity, my grandmother, who was now very old, having outlived my old master and all his children, having seen the beginning and end of all of them, and her present owners finding she was of but little value, her frame already racked with the pains of old age, and complete helplessness fast stealing over her once active limbs, they took her to the woods, built her a little hut, put up a little mud-chimney, and then made her welcome to the privilege of supporting herself there in perfect loneliness; thus virtually turning her out to die! If my poor old grandmother now lives, she lives to suffer in utter loneliness; she lives to remember and mourn over the loss of children, the loss of grandchildren, and the loss of great-grandchildren. They are, in the language of the slave's poet, Whittier,—

7
> *"Gone, gone, sold and gone*
>
> *To the rice swamp dank and lone,*
>
> *Where the slave-whip ceaseless swings,*
>
> *Where the noisome insect stings,*
>
> *Where the fever-demon strews*
>
> *Poison with the falling dews,*
>
> *Where the sickly sunbeams glare*
>
> *Through the hot and misty air:—*
>
> *Gone, gone, sold and gone*
>
> *To the rice swamp dank and lone,*
>
> *From Virginia hills and waters—*
>
> *Woe is me, my stolen daughters!"*

8 The hearth is desolate. The children, the unconscious children, who once sang and danced in her presence, are gone. She gropes her way, in the darkness of age, for a drink of water. Instead of the voices of her children, she hears by day the moans of the dove, and by night the screams of the hideous owl. All is gloom. The grave is at the door. And now, when weighed down by the pains and aches of old age, when the head inclines to the feet, when the beginning and ending of human existence meet, and helpless infancy and painful old age combine together—at this time, this most needful time, the time for the exercise of that tenderness and affection which children only can exercise towards a declining parent—my poor old grandmother, the devoted mother of twelve children, is left all alone, in yonder little hut, before a few dim embers. She stands—she sits—she staggers—she falls—she groans—she dies—and there are none of her children or grandchildren present, to wipe from her wrinkled brow the cold sweat of death, or to place beneath the sod her fallen remains. Will not a righteous God visit for these things?

9 In about two years after the death of Mrs. Lucretia, Master Thomas married his second wife. Her name was Rowena Hamilton. She was the eldest daughter of Mr. William Hamilton. Master now lived in St. Michael's. Not long after his marriage, a misunderstanding took place between himself and Master Hugh; and as a means of punishing his brother, he took me from him to live with himself at St. Michael's. Here I underwent another most painful separation. It, however, was not so severe as the one I dreaded at the division of property; for, during this interval, a great change had taken place in Master Hugh and his once kind and affectionate wife. The influence of brandy upon him, and of slavery upon her, had effected a disastrous change in the characters of both; so that, as far as they were concerned, I thought I had little to lose by the change. But it was not to them that I was attached. It was to those little Baltimore boys that I felt the strongest attachment. I had received many good lessons from them, and was still receiving them, and the thought of leaving them was painful indeed. I was leaving, too, without the hope of ever being allowed to return. Master Thomas had said he would never let me return again. The barrier betwixt himself and brother he considered impassable.

10 I then had to regret that I did not at least make the attempt to carry out my resolution to run away; for the chances of success are tenfold greater from the city than from the country.

11 I sailed from Baltimore for St. Michael's in the sloop Amanda, Captain Edward Dodson. On my passage, I paid particular attention to the direction which the steamboats took to go to Philadelphia. I found, instead of going down, on reaching North Point they went up the bay, in a north-easterly direction. I deemed this knowledge of the utmost importance. My determination to run away was again revived. I resolved to wait only so long as the offering of a favorable opportunity. When that came, I was determined to be off.

Topic Sentence Outline

A topic sentence outline is similar to the traditional outline but simpler because it contains only major topics (expressed in complete sentences) and major subtopics (expressed in phrases). It can be done more quickly and is less prescriptive than a traditional outline, which is a real advantage to students who need to get a quick feeling about how their research is shaping up and what kind of information they are missing. The disadvantage is that it doesn't offer as much information when the student is writing the paper and doesn't provide as much structure. To convert the sample of the traditional outline to a topic sentence outline, you would keep just the Roman numerals and the capital letters. The Roman numerals would be followed by complete sentences, the letters by phrases. Conversely, to convert a topic sentence outline to a traditional outline, you would have to fill in the numerous levels of major and minor topics.

For example, converting the traditional Outline A of the paper on Frederick Douglass's life yields the following topic sentence outline:

I. Frederick Douglass had an unusual childhood.
   A. Born in Maryland in 1817 or 1818
   B. Childhood in Baltimore

II. Many things in Douglass's life changed because of his extraordinary abilities.
   A. Escape
   B. Marriage
   C. Name change

III. Douglass worked very hard for the antislavery cause.
   A. Abolition
   B. *Narrative of the Life of Frederick Douglass*

IV. Douglass's Civil War activities were numerous.
   A. Recruiter for Union
   B. Postwar advocate

V. In his later life, Douglass had many outlets for his abilities.
   A. Government positions
   B. Other writings

Topic Sentence and Quotation Outline

As we have seen, outlines can be used to help you understand both what you have read and what you are going to write. By outlining you can get a summary of the material in each selection. So far, we have been outlining "back" from the text. That is, we are "pulling out" an outline that has been incorporated in the text. Before we move on to creating outlines as *preparation* for writing, let's look at one more type of outline that can be pulled out of the reading. This kind of outline uses topic sentences and quotations to support the topics. It is an extremely useful kind of outline because the process of creating it pinpoints useful quotations that you will need, when you are writing, to support your major topics. This method can be combined with the topic sentence outline above.

EXERCISE 6.12   **Creating a Topic Sentence and Quotation Outline**

Look at Chapter VII of *Narrative of the Life of Frederick Douglass* (page 169), and create a sentence and quotation outline by picking out two quotations for each major topic.

Example: Douglass decided to escape from slavery because his owners turned against his education.

"Under [slavery's] influence, the tender heart [of my mistress] became stone, and the lamblike disposition gave way to tiger-like fierceness. The first step in her downward course was in her ceasing to instruct me" (p. 163).

Choosing an Outline Form

Electronic Outlining

Depending on your platform, you probably have outlining capability included with your computer software. Ways to access this capability differ in small ways. In order to use the outlining capability, you may have to highlight the major and subordinate headings; in other words, you may have to tell the program what is more and less important. This can be a good way to think through your paper's organization.

PowerPoint

PowerPoint is an excellent tool to help you with organization, for in creating a PowerPoint presentation, you need to put your paper into outline form. This is a relatively easy program to learn and the templates that are available with this program will help guide your content, as the sample illustration of templates below shows.

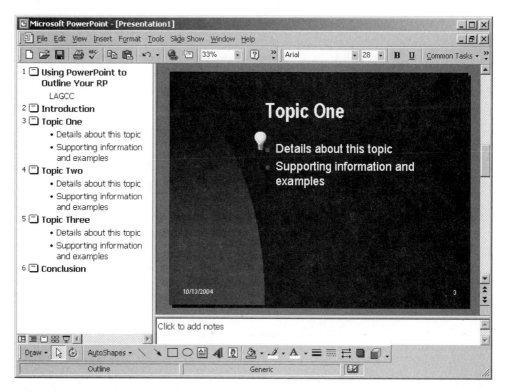

A Microsoft PowerPoint Page. Reprinted by permission from Microsoft Corporation.

Step 17	DEVELOPING YOUR OWN OUTLINE

Now it is time for you to choose the type of outline you want to use for your own essay and develop it in preparation for the next chapter, in which you will begin drafting your essay.

1. Write down your working thesis.

2. Take out your notes and list your major topics in a running outline.

3. With your running outline in front of you, consult your working thesis. Do your notes seem to support your thesis? If they do, you're on the right track; if they do not, you may have to adjust or change your thesis.

4. Think about selecting an appropriate development model.

5. Pick one of the three types of outlines we have discussed (or use one assigned by your teacher), and plot your outline by providing at least two major topics and at least two subtopics for each major topic. (If you choose the traditional outline, you will need to fill it in with more detail.)

CHECKLIST   ORGANIZING AND OUTLINING RESEARCH MATERIAL

❏ Have you made a running outline of the main ideas in your essay?

❏ Have you classified your main ideas into larger groupings?

❏ Are you aware of the variety of development models that can help you arrange your ideas meaningfully?

❏ Have you made a formal outline of your essay?

CHAPTER 7

Writing the Paper

- ■ Before You Write
- ■ Writing Out Your Paper

Now, finally, you have narrowed your topic, done your research, taken your notes, and made your outline, and you are ready to write your paper. This chapter will help you with the process of writing your paper by showing you how to work with the notes and outline you generated in the previous two chapters, as well as how to weave the research material into the design of your writing so it is smooth and serves its purpose of supporting your thesis. Because plagiarism is a major problem with beginning researchers, we will review and practice ways to avoid plagiarism in this chapter once again, drawing on examples from previous chapters.

Before You Write

Your Writing Space

When we discussed notes, we mentioned the optimal space for writing a research paper—a big, flat, empty desk with lots of room to shuffle papers or note cards around. But even if you do not have that much space, you should try to give your-self the luxury of quiet—to concentrate and to focus. You will need that. Up until now you have been doing largely mechanical tasks: running to the library, clicking onto the Internet, photocopying, and printing. Making your outline was somewhat more demanding, but writing it out so that it is clear, fluid, and logical takes real concentration. Distractions in the form of friends, family, phones, television, music, and the like will make it harder for you to write well, breaking up the flow of your ideas and affecting your sense of organization. The best place to write is an empty room or a room with a silence policy: a study hall or a library.

Your Writing Instruments

What you write on and what you write with are very personal decisions. Some people need to write the first version or draft of their papers on a pad and in pen or pencil. Then, after they have a first draft, they are willing to move to the computer or typewriter. Other people have only limited access to these instruments and are quite proficient at writing neatly. However, more and more people are writing their papers on computers, because computers offer such ease of writing and revision and they are becoming cheaper and more readily available. Typed papers are neater and easier to read. One can check mistakes on the spelling program. There are also computer programs for grammar, and a thesaurus is usually available. (Note, however, that these programs are not perfect, and none of them should replace intelligent proofreading.) When you use a computer, copies can be printed easily, corrections made neatly (a major advantage), and data saved readily.

You must decide which instrument suits you best. Your teacher may insist that your final draft be typed, but your first draft, when you are pounding ideas into shape, should be written on whatever you find convenient and comfortable.

The Writing Process

As should be clear from the preceding paragraph, you will not be writing your paper all in one draft. Writing is a way of learning, of discovering what you think and believe, and of thinking through *why* you believe what you believe. You must give yourself the opportunity to work out what you want to say by going through all the stages of the writing process, from prewriting to writing to revision. That is, you must get the ideas on paper, shape them into an essay, rewrite to make the essay better, and finally proofread for grammar and spelling. When your paper contains research, it is even more important to go through this entire process, because you also will be checking every step of the way for the quality and quantity of your research.

EXERCISE 7.1   **Freewriting for Your First Draft**

Freewriting is a way of getting your mind to work creatively. You did it before when you were beginning the research process. Now freewriting can help you to get an overview of what you have accomplished, to see what fits and what doesn't, and to ask questions and speculate about answers.

First look at the notes on your cards or sheets, in your journal, and on your printouts and pads. Then look at your outline. Finally, look at your working thesis. Now put these out of sight and write for 10 minutes. When you are finished, read your freewriting and see what ideas it gives you for rearranging and adding to your outline. Check the questions you asked in your freewriting. Do they point to gaps or confusion in your material? How close is what you have written to your original outline? Does any discrepancy between the two plans point to additional areas that need development or research? Revise your outline where necessary so it reflects what you actually want to do.

Arranging Your Notes

When you created your working outline you were guided by the subject headings on the upper-right-hand corner of your notes or sheets. Picking out major and minor topics and arranging them to support your working thesis enabled you to outline your paper so that you could look at its shape and scope. In order to write your paper, you need to work backward—to lay out your notes by subject heading so that you can see your material in front of you. Then you need to figure out how your subject headings are transformed into your topics and subtopics.

EXERCISE 7.2   **Arranging Notes**

Below is the outline for a short paper on the *Titanic* disaster, followed by the notes on which the outline was based.

Outline

Working thesis: There are many theories about why the *Titanic* sank.

   I. Human error
      A. Captain
      B. Crew
  II. Negligence
      A. Owners
      B. Builders
 III. Miscalculations in construction
      A. Steel
      B. Rivets
      C. Size

Notes

1. Mark the notes according to where they fit in the outline (IA, IB, etc.).

2. Are there any topics that have no supporting notes or are poorly supported by notes?

3. Are there any notes that don't fit in your outline?

4. Are any of these "extra" notes appropriate for an introduction or a conclusion?

---

unsinkable?

p. 26

1.   Lord, Walter
       A Night to Remember

       "Water in the forepeak . . . No. 1 hold . . . No. 2 hold . . . mail-room . . . boiler room No. 6 . . . boiler room No. 5. Water 14 feet above keel level in the first ten minutes. . . . Put together, the facts showed a 300-foot gash with the first five compartments hopelessly flooded."

captain
pp. 287–288

2. Wade, Wyn Craig
<u>The Titanic: End of a Dream</u>

Cap't Smith, while brave, was "over-confident." This led to problems.

rivets
p. F1

3. Broad, William J.
<u>New York Times</u> 1/27/98

"Two wrought-iron rivets from the <u>Titanic</u>'s hull were recently hauled up from the depths for scientific analyses and were found to be riddled with unusually high concentrations of slag, making them brittle and prone to fracture."

unsinkable?

4. <u>Encyclopaedia Britannica</u>
online—no author, no title

The ship was thought unsinkable because four compartments could be flooded without endangering the ship's ability to float.

builders
p. 287

5.

Smith, William Alden
Qtd from Wyn Craig Wade
<u>The Titanic</u>

"From the builders' hands, she was plunged straightaway to her fate. . . ." They were overconfident and didn't test adequately.

owners
p. 287

6.

Smith, William Alden
Qtd from Wyn Craig Wade
<u>The Titanic</u>

"Officers and crew were strangers to one another. . . . [N]either was familiar with the vessel or its implements or tools. . . ." The crew was not prepared when the crisis came.

captain
p. 287

7.

Smith, William Alden
Qtd from Wyn Craig Wade
<u>The Titanic</u>

"In the face of warning signals, speed was increased; and messages of danger seemed to stimulate her to action rather than persuade her to fear."

captain

. p. 287

8.

Smith, William Alden
Qtd from Wyn Craig Wade
<u>The Titanic</u>

Captain Smith was an experienced sailor, but his overconfidence made him "indifferent to danger." While others in his
place would have heeded warnings of danger, he ignored them.

lifeboats

p. 290

9.

Smith, William Alden
Qtd from Wyn Craig Wade
<u>The Titanic</u>

Steerage passengers did not get a warning of the danger
until it was too late for them to get into a lifeboat.

lifeboats

p. 290

10.

Smith, William Alden
Qtd from Wyn Craig Wade
<u>The Titanic</u>

Lifeboats "were only partially loaded and in all instances
unprovided with compasses and . . . lamps." Nearly 1,500 people
died because they could not get into a boat.

aftermath
p. 235

11.　Smith, William Alden
Qtd from Wyn Craig Wade
<u>The Titanic</u>

Smith requested a medal for Captain Arthur Restron, of
the <u>Carpathia</u>, and two bills on investigating and changing
maritime law.

unsinkable?
p. 174

12.　Lord, Walter
<u>A Night to Remember</u>

"At full speed [the <u>Titanic</u>] could make 24 to 25 knots. . . . She
had a double bottom and was divided into 16 watertight
compartments. . . . [S]he could float with any two compartments flooded, and since no one could imagine anything worse
than a collision at the juncture of two compartments, she was
labeled 'unsinkable.'"

unsinkable?

p. 26

13.

Lord, Walter

<u>A Night to Remember</u>

"What did this mean? . . . The <u>Titanic</u> could float with any two of her 16 watertight compartments flooded . . . [or] with any three of her first five compartments flooded . . . [or even] with all of her first four compartments gone. But no matter how they sliced it, she could not float with all of her first five compartments full. . . . If the first five . . . were flooded, the bow would sink so low that water in the fifth compartment must overflow into the sixth . . . and so on."

unsinkable?

p. 702

14.

Ballard, Rob't

<u>National Geographic</u>

"How We Found the <u>Titanic</u>"

"In response to the warning [of an iceberg] her officer-in-charge tried to reverse engines and turn hard to starboard. The reversal actually turned the ship slowly to port, and she suffered the fatal gash in her starboard side. Had she rammed the berg head-on, she would likely have flooded only two or three compartments and remained afloat."

rivets
p. 717

15.

Ballard, Rob't
"A Long Last Look at <u>Titanic</u>"
<u>National Geographic</u>

"The Woods Hole team did not find the 300-foot-long gash that has long been held to be <u>Titanic</u>'s undoing. Rather, they observed a hole on the starboard side, along with several plates that had been bent inward, springing the rivets. Any additional damage suffered by the bow, whether caused by the iceberg or by impact with the bottom, lies hidden from view in the mud."

unsinkable?
p. 7

16.

<u>The Congressional Record</u>

"Not even God himself could sink this ship." Employees of the White Star Line at the launch of the <u>Titanic</u>, May 31, 1911. They were so confident they had only 20 lifeboats to hold half the people.

17.

steel
Arnold, Gary

"Shattering Evidence"
arkania@ilap.com

Taken from an article in Feb. 1995 Popular Mechanics.
The hull was made from brittle, inferior steel and fractured
rather than bent.

18.

size

Encyclopaedia Britannica
online, no author, no title

Although scientists on the Ballard expedition theorized that
"seams in the adjacent hull plates" were loosened by the collision, there are some who believe "the ship was simply too large
for the technology available; vibrations from its massive engines
may have played some part in the buckling of the hull plates."

19.

commodification
pp. 226–227

Biel, Stephen
Down with the Old Canoe: A Cultural History of the Titanic
Disaster

"The Titanic remains a part of our cultural vocabulary through
sheer momentum. In the marketplace this translates into the
notion that with the right amount of modification and repack-
aging, what has sold before will continue to sell."

After looking over the notes, you probably found that the notes about the *Titanic*'s "unsinkability" and its "aftermath" do not fit, nor does the note about the lifeboats. However, they might be extremely suitable for your introduction and conclusion. We'll be discussing introductions and conclusions later in the chapter, so put these notes aside until we get to them. In the meantime, let's consider the questions from the previous exercise (page 185).

Reviewing Your Source Material for Quantity: Are there any topics that have no supporting notes or are poorly supported by notes?

An outline is there to help you arrange your material and determine whether you have sufficient material to develop your thesis. To decide whether you have enough material to construct a paper, you must balance the scope of the paper with other criteria: purpose and audience. Are you writing a memo, fact sheet, high school student paper, college paper, or scholarly article? Are you writing primarily for your teacher, fellow students, business colleagues, the general public, or specialists?

Looking at it another way, ask yourself, "Do I have enough sources to develop my thesis?" Let's think about this question carefully, using Frederick Douglass as our example. Douglass wrote his autobiography at a particular moment in history, 1845. He wrote it with a goal: to argue for the abolition of slavery. Because the anti-slavery side won the American Civil War in 1865, and because President Abraham Lincoln signed the Emancipation Proclamation in 1863, freeing all slaves, it is easy for us today to feel that Douglass is great. But a good researcher has to be sure to look beyond the "easy" cases to build a strong essay. Even if Douglass were undeniably "victorious," you need more evidence from other sources to build a convincing case and to understand further what makes Douglass a great man, which is your thesis. Otherwise, someone would only have to read Douglass's book and skip your essay. What are *you* contributing to a better understanding of these issues? What will your essay say that isn't in Douglass's book? A reader wants to see *your* mind at work in the research, to grasp *your* unique perspective in the discussion of events or issues. (That is why a good thesis is so important.)

To convince the reader that your view (or working thesis) is valid, your sources must provide information on several different points of view, even if you plan to disagree with some of them. This shows that you have fully and fairly examined all sides of the question. When writing on Douglass, for instance, you might want a source that quotes a slave owner so as to show the opposing viewpoint. You might also quote from a contemporary newspaper account of one of Douglass's speeches to see how the press was reporting his work. And you could read works *about* Douglass by modern scholars and critics to sample their perspectives of his life and work. In other words, as you reevaluate your sources before you write and when you begin your writing, keep in mind that it is not the number of sources that matters **but how these sources help you develop your thesis.**

Returning to the paper on the *Titanic*, let's assume that this is a short (600-word) college essay; the working thesis is "There are many reasons why the *Titanic* sank."

1. Look at the notes on "human error": notes 2, 7, and 8. These deal with the captain's potential negligence.

2. Look at the notes for "negligence," notes 5 and 6, which deal with the builder and the owners.

3. Look at the notes for "construction": notes 3 and 15, on rivets; note 17, on steel; and note 18, on the size of the ship.

Unless the sources on the owner and builder are extremely strong, you may need another note for the section on negligence. Of course, it is possible that there are no more sources and no appropriate quotes or paraphrases available. If that is the case, you can adjust your argument accordingly and not highlight corporate negligence as a main reason why the *Titanic* sank. But you need to reconsider. Look at the sources again; are there any other sections in which they might be useful? If not, you may need to conduct more research.

Reviewing Sources to See That They Are Appropriate: Are there any notes that don't fit in your outline?

Although you should have checked your sources for usefulness and reliability while you were collecting them, you still need to check your individual notes to make certain each quotation or paraphrase is appropriate where you plan to use it. Researchers often fall in love with a quotation and feel the need to use it whether or not it fits their topic. As a result, they may try to make it fit when and where it doesn't, and this always shows, even though it might not be apparent to the writer. Check again to be sure all of your sources actually support or explain what you are trying to say in the particular part of the paper where you plan to use them. If one doesn't fit, take it out; put it away for use in another section of this paper, or save it for another paper.

EXERCISE 7.3 **Examining Sources to See Whether They Are Appropriate**

Here are three notes. Consider whether they really fit the outline that appears in the first section of this chapter (page 185).

17.

steel
Arnold, Gary

"Shattering Evidence"
arkania@ilap.com

Taken from an article in Feb. 1995 Popular Mechanics.
The hull was made from brittle, inferior steel and fractured rather than bent.

rivets
p. 717

15.

Ballard, Rob't
"A Long Last Look at <u>Titanic</u>"
<u>National Geographic</u>

"The Woods Hole team did not find the 300-foot-long gash
that has long been held to be <u>Titanic</u>'s undoing. Rather, they
observed a hole on the starboard side, along with several
plates that had been bent inward, springing the rivets. Any
additional damage suffered by the bow, whether caused by
the iceberg or by impact with the bottom, lies hidden from
view in the mud."

commodification
pp. 226–227

19.

Biel, Stephen
<u>Down with the Old Canoe: A Cultural History of the Titanic
Disaster</u>

"The <u>Titanic</u> remains a part of our cultural vocabulary through
sheer momentum. In the marketplace this translates into the
notion that with the right amount of modification and repack-
aging, what has sold before will continue to sell."

EXERCISE 7.4   Examining Your Own Notes

Take out your outline. Now lay out your notes by subject area. See what fits under
each subject heading. Once you have done this, arrange each subject heading into
major and minor topics. Finally, ask yourself the questions on page 185, and examine your notes to see whether you have enough research material and whether your
research is appropriate to your topic.

Evaluating Quotations

You're ready to write! Your notes are in sorted piles in front of you, with your outline. Some of your notes are in your own words, but (because you heeded our advice) many are direct quotations. When you write, you will need to decide which of these should remain quotations and which should be paraphrased or summarized. Therefore, let's reexamine this topic before you begin to write. In Chapter 5 we discussed guidelines to use when deciding in what form to integrate source material into an essay. Keep these principles in mind. Quotations should be used only to support your ideas, not to fill space or reproduce facts. Use the source's exact words only when you cannot paraphrase effectively because the source uses language in a unique or technical way.

EXERCISE 7.5   Evaluating Quotations

Following are four quotations for topics we have discussed. Which of them should remain quotations and which should be paraphrased? Justify your decision in the space below each quotation.

1. "The best available estimate sets the year of Douglass's birth as 1818. His mother, Harriet Bailey, was a slave belonging to Captain Aaron Anthony. His father, says Douglass, 'was a white man. . . .' In accord with the slaveholding practices of his day, the young Douglass assumed both the surname and the enslaved condition of his mother." (Houston A. Baker, Jr., "Introduction to *Narrative of The Life of Frederick Douglass,*" p. 16)

   _____

   _____

   _____

2. "At 10:25 o'clock to-night [sic] the White Star line steamship Titanic called 'C.Q.D.' to the Marconi wireless station here, and reported having struck an iceberg." (*New York Times,* April 12, 1912, p. 1)

   _____

   _____

   _____

3. "He was surprised when his inquiries disclosed 9.3 percent slag in one rivet and similar levels in the other." (William J. Broad, "Faulty Rivets Emerge as Clues to Titanic Disaster," *NY Times,* January 27, 1998, p. 5)

   _____

   _____

   _____

4. "Why did she kill Abby too? Perhaps because her stepmother had known about the incest and had been unable to stop it, or worse, had blamed Lizzie for it." (Marcia R. Carlisle, "What Made Lizzie Borden Kill?")

_____

_____

_____

_____

You probably decided that the first quotation, about Frederick Douglass, did not have to be quoted. Indeed, it should *not* be quoted. Each piece of information it offers is a *fact,* not an opinion, and one that would not stir controversy anywhere. Facts are facts. No one owns them. They should not be quoted or cited. The second piece of information, about the *Titanic,* also offers facts, but we would probably want to quote it because it is from the original 1912 *New York Times* article about the disaster. Having an original source adds a sense of excitement and drama.

Statistics, on the other hand, such as figures on what percentage of slag is in a rivet from the *Titanic,* have to be gathered and analyzed. Whoever does that should get credit for it, so you should treat statistics as you would quotations. You must introduce and cite them. *General knowledge* is more difficult to analyze. It consists of opinions or statistics that have been familiar to so many people for so long that they don't need to be attributed to any particular person. Frederick Douglass was a great orator; the *Titanic* has become a symbol of extraordinary wealth; many people have been fascinated by the Lizzie Borden case. If you are at all unsure about whether something can be considered general knowledge, use a citation. It can't hurt; it can only protect you from plagiarizing.

Opinion, when it is the product of a specific person's analysis and thought, and *creativity* (such as that shown in the quotation from "What Made Lizzie Borden Kill?"), need to be credited. Anything someone has written that sheds light on a subject in a particular way needs to be credited, *whether or not you use the person's exact words.* If you do not, you will be guilty of plagiarism.

EXERCISE 7.6   Guarding against Plagiarism

In the following exercise, mark a ✔ next to those paraphrases that need a citation and an X next to those that are either facts or general knowledge and hence do not need citations.

_____ 1. Frederick Douglass speaks of being so depressed about his situation that he wanted to kill himself.

_____ 2. One theory about why Lizzie Borden might have murdered her parents comes from Marcia Carlisle, who thinks that Lizzie may have been abused by her father.

_____ 3. According to records, 60 percent of the *Titanic*'s first-class passengers were saved, while 44 percent of those in second class, 25 percent of those in steerage, and 24 percent of the crew members were saved.

_____ 4. Jacob Riis found Chinatown clean but dull.

_____ 5. Morocco is a country in North Africa lying 14 kilometers from Spain across the Strait of Gilbraltar.

_____ 6. Frederick Douglass wrote *Narrative of the Life of Frederick Douglass.*

_____ 7. Dr. Timothy Foecke posits that a low-grade iron rivet was the reason for the *Titanic* disaster.

_____

Incorporating Source Material into Paragraphs

Selection is only part of the process of using a quotation or paraphrase in your essay. It must be punctuated correctly (with quotation marks) and integrated into your writing via the proper introduction, transition, and citation (see Chapter 8) so it becomes a seamless part of your paper. Because the quotation or paraphrase is inserted between two distinct parts of the paragraph—an introduction to the source and a commentary on it, including a citation—this method can be referred to as the "sandwich" technique. The introduction to the source can be a few words or a few sentences, but its purpose is to serve as a transition, linking the source, what came before it in the paragraph, and the topic sentence of the paragraph. It should give you information on where the source came from and who wrote it. After the source, you must provide a citation for the source and some commentary showing how the source illuminates the topic sentence of the paragraph.

THE SANDWICH TECHNIQUE

- The **topic sentence** announces the main idea of the paragraph.

- The **introduction to the source** prepares the reader for the upcoming quotation. The first time you mention a writer you should give his or her full name and indicate where the writer gets his or her authority. For reference after that you can use the author's last name and omit other details.

  Here is a list of words that are commonly used to introduce quotations:

—According to [author's name]	—declares	—points out
—adds	—believes	—insists	—reports
—admits	—claims	—maintains	—says
—agrees	—comments	—notes	—suggests
—argues	—confirms	—observes	—writes
—asserts	—contends		

- The **direct quotation** or **paraphrase** consists of words taken exactly from a source or put into the writer's own words, respectively.

- The **commentary on the source** discusses the research paper writer's understanding of the source.

- The **citation** indicates where the quote or paraphrase was taken from.

Making a Sandwich

Below is an example of sandwiching. It is taken from a student's paper on Lorraine Hansberry's play about racism in postwar Chicago, *A Raisin in the Sun.*
    Here are two notes the student took from the screenplay version of the play:

A.

> "The camera roams at medium close over the surrounding houses. There is an imposed starkness in the shot, reflecting these surroundings as they seem to Ruth and Walter. These are American homes where rather ordinary types and varieties of Americans live; but at the moment something sinister clings to them. . . . The faces [behind the windows]—eyes of women and children, in the main—look hard with a curiosity that, for the most part, is clearly hostile."
> This quotation appears on page 155.

B.

> Lindner says, "But you've got to admit that a man, right or wrong in some of the things, has the right to have the neighborhood he lives in a certain kind of way. And at the moment the overwhelming majority of our people out there feel that people get along better and take more of a common interest in the life of a community, when they share a common background. I want you to believe me when I tell you that race prejudice simply doesn't enter into it. It is a matter of the people of Clybourne Park believing, rightly or wrongly, as I say, that for the happiness of all concerned that our Negro families are happier when they live in their *own* communities."
> This quotation appears on pages 164–165.

Here is another quotation from a reference source on African American studies called *Black Metropolis: A Study of Negro Life in a Northern City,* by St. Clair Drake and Horace B. Cayton.

C.

"This tremendous demand for houses resulted in an immediate skyrocketing of rents [in Chicago] for all available accommodations and in the opening of new residential areas to Negroes. . . . Artificial panics were sometimes created in white areas by enterprising realtors who raised the cry, 'The Negroes are coming,' and then proceeded to double the rents after the whites had fled."
This quotation appears on page 62.

Here is the student's "sandwich" using the material quoted above. The boldface type highlights the "sandwich" devices for you; you would not boldface this material in an actual paper.

White people in Chicago had been driven to a racist panic by the prospect of sharing their newly found security with African Americans. **In A Raisin in the Sun, when the African American Younger family goes to visit the house they have bought in the white neighborhood of Clybourne Park, they find** "the eyes of women and children . . . clearly hostile" (Hansberry 155). **While disavowing any "race prejudice," Lindner, a representative of the Clybourne Park Improvement Association, tells them,** "the people of Clybourne Park believing, rightly or wrongly, as I say, that for the happiness of all concerned, that our Negro families are happier when they live in their <u>own</u> communities" (Hansberry 164–165). **As St. Clair Drake and Horace R. Cayton propose in their book Black Metropolis, however, the hostility may have had an economic base. They write,** "Artificial panics were sometimes created in white areas by enterprising realtors who raised the cry, 'The Negroes are coming,' and then proceeded to double rents after the whites had fled" (62). **In other words, the white people were incited to fear African Americans by unscrupulous and greedy realtors.**

As you can see, the student used the play and a reference book to support the topic sentence—that is, the student's own findings.

EXERCISE 7.7   Evaluating Introductions to Quotations and Paraphrases

Beginning students often find it difficult to integrate quotations and paraphrases into their essays, so we are going to give you the opportunity to practice inserting quotations and paraphrases in three stages: (1) introductions to the source material; (2) commentary after the sources in this chapter; and (3) in citation form in Chapter 8. First we will consider introductions. Look at the five paragraphs below. (*Note:* We have left the citations out because we are examining only introductions.) Are the sandwiched quotations adequately introduced so that we can tell both why they are being used and where they came from? Rewrite those that are not satisfactory.

1. Harlem is located in the northern section of Manhattan. James Baldwin writes, "Rents are 10 to 58 per cent higher than anywhere else in the city; food, expensive everywhere, is more expensive here and of an inferior quality; and now that the war is over and money is dwindling, clothes are carefully shopped for and seldom bought."

   _____

   _____

   _____

   _____

   _____

2. Edith Wharton became extremely knowledgeable about the life of harem women by actually visiting a harem during her travels to Morocco in 1919. In her book *In Morocco,* she compares the harem to a "mouldering prison" and to a mine, as she describes "the descent through the steep tunnelled streets." The reader experiences her claustrophobia: "At each step the strip of sky grew narrower, and was more often obscured by the low vaulted passages into which we plunged."

   _____

   _____

   _____

   _____

   _____

3. Harriet Jacobs's childhood was not unhappy. Her grandmother was much admired in the household and was given much independence. Her mother was loved by her mistress and when her mother died, this love was transferred to Harriet, who was safe as long as her mistress remained alive. When she died, Harriet hoped that she would be freed, because her mistress had promised Harriet's dying mother to protect her children. Instead of freeing Harriet, however, she left her to her 5-year-old niece, which embittered Harriet greatly: "We all know that the memory of a faithful slave does not avail much to save her children from the auction block," she lamented.

   _____

   _____

   _____

   _____

   _____

4. The Senate charged the Commerce Committee with investigating the *Titanic* disaster. I read the report as written by William Alden Smith, its chairman, and he wrote that "Builders of renown had launched her on the billows with confident assurance of her strength. . . ."

_____

_____

_____

_____

_____

5. Marcia R. Carlisle asks the question "What Made Lizzie Borden Kill?" in her 1992 article in *American Heritage Magazine.* In the article she discusses the "battered-woman syndrome" and theorizes that Borden and her sister Emma might have been abused by their father. "Mr. Borden might have abused first Emma, then Lizzie."

_____

_____

_____

_____

_____

_____

All of the above paragraphs end with a quotation, something you should try to avoid. Quotations must never usurp the focus—your point of view must dominate. Most quotations should be enclosed, *sandwiched within your own material.* The quotation or paraphrase should be introduced and then commented on, *and your commentary should serve as a transition to the next point in your essay,* as in the paragraph that follows.

Although the Shakers are extinct, they left behind an important heritage. Their finely crafted furniture and their spiritual values can still help us live better lives today. **As the film by Ken Burns reveals,** the Shakers lived by the motto of "hands to work and hearts to God" *(The Shakers).* When visiting the Metropolitan Museum in New York, we saw that the **Shaker furniture is simple and without ornament. It demonstrates fine craftsmanship because each chair was a kind of prayer, according to their belief: Everything they did was for God, as Flo Morse explains in her study, for the Shakers' work was worship. She says** that the group advised members to "do all [their] own work as though [they] had a thousand years to live" but also to behave as though they knew they were going to die tomorrow. **In other words, believers should take time to produce the best work they could, whether in making a chair, baking a pie, spinning yarn, or singing a song, because each of these activities was dedicated to God** (Morse 38). As a result, the Shaker furniture we can see in museums is finely made, with precise technique and careful details. Their message to us is that all our work should be done in the best way we can do it.

EXERCISE 7.8   Finishing Your Sandwich

Take each of the five revised paragraphs in the previous exercise and create a sandwich by adding a sentence or two that comments on the quoted material and, if possible, acts as a transition in an essay you might be writing on the topic. (Be creative!)

Writing Out Your Paper

Writing the Introduction

The introduction to an essay, a chapter, or a book is very important. A reader sees it first, and may judge quickly whether the paper is interesting or worth reading. What makes a good introduction? First, it should present a brief and fair summary of the writer's main idea. But because it needs to engage the reader's interest, it should also use lively and appealing language and should pull the reader in with an interesting opening device. Here are some ideas for beginning your papers:

1. Begin with a very short story related to your topic. For example, if you are writing about the *Titanic,* begin by telling the story of the night it sank.

2. Begin with a question, the answer to which is your thesis. For example, "Did Lizzie Borden kill her parents? Many people believe she did."

3. Take a word from your working thesis and discuss it. For example, if your working thesis is that Frederick Douglass was an exceptional man, you can explore the meaning of the word *exceptional.*

4. Begin with a shocking or dramatic incident. For example, "Early one morning in 1892, people in Fall River, Massachusetts were shocked to hear a blood-curdling scream coming from the house of a quiet family named Borden."

5. You can start with a reference to a historical or biographical fact. For example: "In 1865, President Abraham Lincoln signed the Emancipation Proclamation and, with that signature, freed the African American slaves in the South from a life of hopeless bondage. Much of what we know about the life of slaves comes from the pens of freed or escaped slaves, and one of the most extraordinary of these was the great statesman and orator Frederick Douglass."

6. You can start with a quotation or paraphrase. For example, "'Lizzie Borden took an ax and gave her mother forty whacks. When she saw what she had done, she gave her father forty-one.' Children have sung this rhyme for over a hundred years, but do they know the real story of Lizzie and her crime?"

EXERCISE 7.9   Examining Introductions

Read the introductory paragraphs below. For each paragraph, do the following:

1. Underline once the sentence that gives the main idea of the work being introduced.

2. Underline twice the most interest-provoking sentence—the one that might "sell" the work.

3. Circle three special vocabulary words that attract your attention, either because they seem "right" or because you need a dictionary to look them up.

4. Identify any of the techniques described in this section that you notice the writer using.

A. Tracy Kidder

Mrs. Zajac wasn't born yesterday. She knows you didn't do your best work on this paper, Clarence. Don't you remember Mrs. Zajac saying that if you didn't do your best, she'd make you do it over? As for you, Claude, God forbid that you should ever need brain surgery. But Mrs. Zajac hopes that if you do, the doctor won't open up your head and walk off saying he's *almost* done, as you just said when Mrs. Zajac asked you for your penmanship, which, by the way, looks like you did it and ran. Felipe, the reason you have hiccups is, your mouth is always open and the wind rushes in. You're in fifth grade now. So, Felipe, put a lock on it. Zip it up. Then go get a drink of water. Mrs. Zajac means business, Robert. The sooner you realize she never said everybody in the room has to do the work except for *Robert,* the sooner you'll get along with her. And . . . Clarence. Mrs. Zajac knows you didn't try. You don't just hand in junk to Mrs. Zajac. She's been teaching an awful lot of years. She didn't fall off the turnip cart yesterday. She told you she was an old-lady teacher.

Tracy Kidder, *Among Schoolchildren*

B. Walter Teller

Incidents in the Life of a Slave Girl represents a genre of writing as distinctive to American literature as blues is to American music: the experience that gave rise to slave songs also produced slave narratives.

Beginning in colonial times and continuing to the end of the Civil War, hundreds and possibly thousands of biographies and autobiographies of slaves and former slaves appeared in print, some brief, others book length. Many were incorporated in anti-slavery periodicals; a much smaller number were published on their own. They can be found in the Schomburg Collection of the New York Public Library, the Spingarn Collection at Howard University, the Boston Public Library, and in the libraries at Brown University, Cornell University, Hampton Institute, Harvard University, and Oberlin College. Some have been reissued in recent years. *Incidents in the Life of a Slave Girl,* published in 1861, was one of the last and most remarkable of its genre and also one of the very few written by a woman. It is being reprinted here in its entirety for the first time, and with original spelling, capitalization, and punctuation retained.

Walter Teller, Introduction to *Incidents in the Life of a Slave Girl,* by Harriet Jacobs

C. Herbert Leibowitz

The man is only half himself, the other half is his expression.
—EMERSON, "The Poet"

A writer has more than one mind, V. S. Pritchett once said, and nowhere is the truth of this remark more evident than in autobiographies. Because the autobiographer often dresses up in fictions and disguises himself in slanted fact, the reader must pass like a secret agent across the borders of actuality and myth, following a winding trail of hallowed lies and profane truths. "Our deeper intentions are plans and evasions inseparably linked," Sartre warned in *Les Mots,* so the task of the literary sleuth is to sift and analyze the slippery clues that the autobiographer leaves behind about childhood, family, race, sex, work, class, the errors of commission and omission smudged on the page and hastily or carefully rubbed out. Autobiographers and their exegetes agree on one point, that the truth is a cunning snare, sometimes "a crystal residue, indissoluble in memory's stream," as Virgil Thomson puts it, and at other times a comedy of delusions that also bears witness to a historical epoch's contradictions.

Herbert Leibowitz, *Fabricating Lives: Explorations in American Autobiography*

D. Emily W. Sunstein

Mary Wollstonecraft was born in mid-eighteenth-century England into a society that believed women to be inferior morally and intellectually, and into a class whose ideal women were the sheltered, submissive, lifelong wards of fathers or husbands—decorative, domestically useful sex objects. The system, maintained by church and state law, normally protected and rewarded its dependents. However, it did not work for Mary Wollstonecraft. She could not depend on her family, which failed her in every way; she would not marry for security; she had intellectual ambitions; she rebelled against injustice and defied the presumption of inferiority. Educated as few women were, and solely on her own initiative, she made herself independent, became an educator, a pioneer career writer, a political radical, and, at thirty-two, produced what one historian has called perhaps the most original book of her century, *A Vindication of the Rights of Woman,* rights which she alone gave equal weight with Rights of Man proclaimed in the two revolutions through which she lived. She was so far ahead of her time as to be isolated and reviled, but posterity has paid her the tribute—given only to authentic revolutionaries—of taking for granted her substantive insights while continuing to debate their exact application.

Emily W. Sunstein, A Different Face: The Life of Mary Wollstonecraft

E.   Harvey Green and Mary E. Perry

Nearly every antique and curio shop in America has fragments of the everyday domestic life of the people who lived before us. If they are old enough, these trivets, mixing bowls, cups, saucers, and other household goods are endowed with the qualities of relics, to be purchased and lovingly displayed on mantels, shelves, or bookcases. What was once used to feed a family, nurse a child, clean and polish a teapot, or carry on the social graces and customs of another era has a different function in the present. These objects from the past suggest some sort of life that seems like ours but is foreign. Yet the common wares of the middle class in the late nineteenth century are more than decoration in the antique shops, museums, and homes of the 1980s; they are evidence of the customs and ideals of life in the domestic setting.

Harvey Green and Mary E. Perry, The Light of the Home: An Intimate View of the Lives of Women in Victorian America

The purpose of this book is to understand the domestic lives of women in the late nineteenth century and the first decade of the twentieth century. In order to do that, it is necessary to examine not only what the protagonists read and the little that they wrote about their daily lives, but also the things with which they lived.

EXERCISE 7.10   Preparing Your Introduction

Write three different introductory paragraphs for your research topic.

1. In one version, begin with a quotation and put the thesis in the last sentence in the paragraph. (See the excerpt from Herbert Leibowitz, *Fabricating Lives: Explorations in American Autobiography.*)

2. In the next version, begin with something dramatic. (See the excerpt from Tracy Kidder, *Among Schoolchildren.*)

3. In the third version, place your subject in a historical context. (See the excerpt from Walter Teller's Introduction to *Incidents in the Life of a Slave Girl,* by Harriet Jacobs.)

Writing the Body of Your Research Paper

The body of your essay—that is, everything but your introduction and conclusion (and documentation paraphernalia)—is where you will do the bulk of your writing.

Nevertheless, if you prepared for it, this part should not be overwhelming. Let's review what you have to guide you through the process:

1. your working thesis

2. your notes

3. your outline (and perhaps a development model)

4. your introduction

Reexamining Your Working Thesis

Your working thesis guided your note-taking and helped direct your outline. It also may have directed your development model. If, for example, your working thesis argued that the *Titanic* sank because of poor management, then your model would be an argument, because your purpose would be to argue a point. If, on the other hand, your working thesis were that the *Titanic* disaster is an interesting model of class conflicts at the beginning of the century, then your purpose would be to discuss and explain and your development would be more analytical. It is at this point, when you have read through your notes and thought about your development model, that you need to look at your working thesis once more. Does it reflect the research you have done and the conclusions you have drawn, or is it stuck at your beginning stage, before you started to explore your topic?

Suppose, for instance, that you begin with the working thesis "Lizzie Borden was a kindly, warm person incapable of murder." Then you find little research to support that working thesis. Obviously you have to change your working thesis. However, what if your research yields a mixed result? What if you discover that some critics agreed with your early findings and some had a totally opposite point of view? (They found Lizzie to be a cold, scheming killer.) Your thesis must reflect this ambiguity. It would be dishonest to throw out half your evidence in order to argue your original thesis, and you would have to do that if you wanted your essay to make sense. Your new thesis would be something like this: "Although many critics have portrayed Lizzie Borden as a cold-blooded killer, there have been some who found her to be a sweet, misunderstood woman, incapable of the crime of which she was accused." Now is the time to revise your hypothesis. Think about it carefully before you move on to writing.

Writing the First Draft

All your revision should be reflected in your outline, and if you follow your outline, you should be able to explore, argue, and explain your thesis because you set it up with topics, topic sentences, subtopics, and subtopic sentences. In that way, a research paper is like any other college essay. The complication is the use of sources to support or explain your ideas. If you follow the guidelines for quotations and paraphrases, using the sandwiching technique outlined in this chapter, and if you keep in mind that the main writing should be yours—that sources are used merely to help you discuss your ideas—you should not have too much difficulty. Remember, this is a first draft. You will be reviewing its form, content, and style when you prepare your finished version (see Chapter 10). But you need to get your first version down on paper, and if you can do this in one sitting (or in two that are close together), you will be better able to keep the disparate elements of your paper together.

Writing the Conclusion

The conclusion is the ending to your paper, and like all endings, it must leave the reader with a sense of completion. Thus it is a cardinal rule that no new information should be introduced in a conclusion, no new points raised, and no new ideas generated. The easiest way to finish your paper is to restate your thesis—that is, to say it in a different way—and to summarize your main point in different words. You could, perhaps, show how your topic has greater significance. (For example, what does the story of the *Titanic* teach us?) But *you must guard against starting a new subject!*

Putting in Graphs, Charts, Photos, and Links

Computer technology has made it simple to insert visual and print material from a variety of sources. Depending on your platform, you need only click on the part of your paper where you want to add something and click on your menu (in Microsoft Word it will be Insert). You will have a list of choices to insert, including symbol, reference, diagram, textbox, file hyperlinks, and pictures such as a choice of clip art, charts, drawings, and shapes.

Reviewing for Plagiarism

You first encountered the subject of plagiarism in Chapter 5, because that is where you were first at risk of plagiarizing—when you were gathering your research and putting it on cards and sheets. Now that you are using these notes as the basis for your essay, you are once again in danger of losing your way. Particularly where you have paraphrased, you must be careful to go back to your original source to check that (except for credited quotations) you have expressed your material entirely in your own words.

EXERCISE 7.11   Practicing Paraphrasing

Below are sections from three different sources. Paraphrase them, and then review them to make sure they are (1) accurate and (2) correctly and *legally* paraphrased.

1. Fatima Mernissi's essay "My Harem Frontiers":
   I was born in a harem in 1940 in Fez, a ninth-century Moroccan city some five thousand kilometers west of Mecca, and one thousand kilometers south of Madrid, one of the dangerous capitals of the Christians. The problems with the Christians start, said Father, as with women, when the *hudad,* or sacred frontier, is not respected.

   _____

   _____

   _____

   _____

   _____

2. Harriet Jacobs (from her autobiography):
   When I was nearly twelve years old, my kind mistress sickened and died. As I saw the cheek grow paler, and the eye more glassy, how earnestly I prayed in my heart that she might live! I loved her; for she had been almost like a mother

to me. My prayers were not answered. She died, and they buried her in the little church yard, where, day after day, my tears fell upon her grave.

_____

_____

_____

_____

_____

3. Stephen Biel, *Down with the Old Canoe:*
   One way to begin to think about the *Titanic* disaster is to look at other events that occurred at the same time. Synchronicity, of course, may or may not imply deeper connections, but for now let's simply juxtapose them, as if they were snapshots taken at the same time but from different vantage points.

   _____

   _____

   _____

   _____

   _____

EXERCISE 7.12   Reviewing for Plagiarism

Below are paraphrases of paragraphs from previous chapters. Analyze whether they adequately and correctly put the material into other words or whether they constitute plagiarism.

1. From the *New York Times:*
   Two wrought-iron rivets from the Titanic's hull were recently hauled up from the depths for scientific analysis and were found to be riddled with unusually high concentrations of slag, making them brittle and prone to fracture. "We think they popped and allowed the plates to separate and let in the water," said William H. Garzke, Jr., a naval architect.

   They found two rivets that had a lot of slag, which made the rivets easy to break into pieces. They probably popped and the plates separated.

   _____

   _____

   _____

2. From the online Folger Shakespeare Library home page:
   The Folger Shakespeare Library is an independent research library. . . . A major center for scholarly research, the Folger houses the world's largest collection of Shakespeare's printed works, in addition to a magnificent collection of other rare Renaissance books and manuscripts on all disciplines—history and politics, theology and exploration, law and the arts.

The largest collection of Shakespeare's works in print is found in the Folger Shakespeare Library, including magnificent rare Renaissance manuscripts and books.

_____

_____

_____

3. From "Lizzie Borden Took an Axe" by Mary Cantwell:
   On Aug. 4, 1892, the younger daughter of the Borden house discovered a body sprawled on a settee in the sitting room. A short time later the maid and a neighbor found a second body face down on the floor of the guest room. Death in both cases came at the hands of a person, still officially unknown, wielding a small, sharp hatchet.

   Lizzie Borden found someone murdered in the sitting room of her house on August 4, 1892. Sometime later that day, another murdered body was discovered in the guest room by Lizzie's neighbor and her maid. The murder weapon was a small hatchet.

_____

_____

_____

Step 18   WRITING YOUR OWN FIRST DRAFT

CHECKLIST   WRITING THE PAPER

❑ Have you picked out a clear, quiet space to write in?

❑ Have you decided what medium you are going to use to write your paper? If you are writing on a computer, do you have access to one that is in good repair and compatible with an available printer?

❑ Have you reviewed your material and jotted down (perhaps using freewriting) your sense of the whole?

❑ Have you laid out your notes according to your outline to evaluate whether you are prepared to write the paper or might need to find more appropriate source material?

❑ Have you reevaluated your source material for quantity?

CHAPTER 8

Documenting Your Sources Using MLA Style

- ■ MLA Documentation Style for Works Cited
- ■ Annotated Student Research Paper

Documenting means identifying and giving credit to the sources you used for information and ideas to explain and support your research. In-text documentation shows the reader where your information came from and thus enables anyone who reads your paper to evaluate the credibility of your sources. It also helps you avoid plagiarism; citations to sources give credit for materials written by others that you used in your essay. Finally, a Works Cited list is a chance to demonstrate your hard work, because you list all the sources you cited, and to allow others to learn more about your topic.

This chapter introduces one style or model for documentation, the MLA style. The MLA is the Modern Language Association of America, a large professional organization of teachers and scholars who study literature and modern languages. You can visit their Web site, www.mla.org, to learn more about this system. In Chapter 9 we will introduce alternative styles of documentation: APA, CBE, and the number systems. Which style you use for your research essay will depend on what your instructor requires or on the subject of your essay. Most college freshmen start off with the MLA style, which is among the most widely used in literature and many humanities fields. The APA style is preferred by social scientists, whereas biologists favor CBE. What is important now is that you understand what documentation is and how to apply the style models to your own sources. We will focus primarily on the MLA style. Once you become familiar with this style, you should be able to use any other style an instructor assigns.

Briefly put, documentation has two parts: the Works Cited list and the in-text citations. The **Works Cited** list appears at the end of the essay (or article or book). It lists, according to a precise system, all the sources referred to or cited in the paper. Books, magazines, journals, and online resources are combined into an alphabetical list. Generally, the last name of the author is the first item in each entry and thus is used for the alphabetical ordering of the entries. The in-text documentation occurs in the body of the essay. The writer puts a **citation** immediately after a source has been used. That citation identifies the exact place in the source where the information appeared.

A Works Cited entry for a basic book would look like this:

Holland, Ruth Robins. <u>Mill Child</u>. New York: Crowell, 1970.

The first item is the author's name, with the last name first. This is followed by a period and two spaces. Next is the title of the book, which is underlined. Two spaces are typed. Then comes the city where the book was published, followed by a colon. Next is the name of the publishing company, followed by a comma. Then comes the year of publication, followed by a period. The first line starts at the margin, and when there is no more room on the first line, the second line is indented five spaces and double-spaced.

The in-text citation in the body of the essay where this book has been quoted would look like this in most cases:

(Holland 78)

The reader is told here that information in the paragraph in which this citation appears comes from a work by the author Holland and appears on page 78. The reader would then be able to turn to the back of the paper and look at the Works Cited entry to learn full details of where the information came from. The reader who wants additional information on the topic can then go to the library, locate the book, and read further. A reader who doubts the writer's accuracy or who wants to verify controversial or unclear material can use the Works Cited list and the in-text citation to learn more. Here is an example of a research essay paragraph with the in-text citation and the Works Cited entry that would appear at the end of the essay:

Although America was celebrated as the land of opportunity and the place where streets were paved with gold in the early twentieth century, some immigrants found that entry to the New World was in reality difficult, cruel, and disappointing. While many new arrivals were able to pass through Ellis Island quickly and smoothly, some were subjected to dehumanizing medical examinations and other humiliating experiences. One eyewitness who provides evidence of the ways immigrants could be mistreated was Fiorello LaGuardia, who worked as a translator because he spoke at least six languages. Himself the son of immigrants who later became one of New York City's greatest mayors, he was sympathetic to the plight of newcomers and wrote an autobiography in which he described what he saw on Ellis Island around 1910. He writes of "a case that haunted" him of "a young girl in her teens, from the mountains of northern Italy." Young and innocent, the girl was subjected to a medical examination in which the doctor insensitively began to "rap at her knees, getting reflexes of her eyes, turning her on her back, tickling her spine. . . . " He calls this "the most cruel case" he ever saw (LaGuardia 38). Clearly, this case is dreadful, driving the girl to madness, as LaGuardia later asserts. For an innocent girl from an isolated rural area, the doctor's treatment would have seemed like a sexual attack. Unprepared for such intimate contact, the young woman fought back and was labeled as crazy. For this young woman, the American dream turned nightmare.

Work Cited

LaGuardia, Fiorello H. <u>The Making of an Insurgent: An Autobiography 1882–1919</u>. New York: J. P. Lippincott, 1948.

The writer has used the "sandwich" method (Chapter 7) to synthesize the quotation into her own paragraph, or blend the source with the paragraph. Because she has used phrases from the source but has not given the entire sentence, a reader might want to look at the original source to read more about the incident and see the entire sentence as LaGuardia wrote it. By using the Works Cited entry, the reader can easily locate the book using the library's OPAC. Once the book is located, the reader can turn to page 38 and read the entire sentence or sentences to which the writer referred. At the same time, the writer gives credit to LaGuardia, the source, because it was he, in 1910, who witnessed the scene, not the writer herself. To put it in legal terms, the scene is the intellectual property of LaGuardia.

What is important when using MLA, or any other style of documentation, is that the citation and the entries on the Works Cited list must be arranged *exactly* according to the models. If you examine the two entries we have used so far, you'll see that they are arranged in the same form:

Author's name, last name first. <u>Title of Book</u>. City of Publication: Publishing
      Company, year.

EXERCISE 8.1   Practicing the MLA Works Cited Form for Basic Books

Using the information given, create a Works Cited entry for the following books. Important words have been capitalized. Remove the capitals and use the MLA style of capitalization and punctuation. After you have the entry for each book, arrange the three in alphabetical order as they would appear at the end of a research paper:

1. The title of the book is W.E.B. DUBOIS. The book was published in BOSTON in 1986 by TWAYNE publishers. The author's name is MARABLE MANNING.

    _____

    _____

2. MARY LAWLER'S book called MARCUS GARVEY was published in NEW YORK by CHELSEA HOUSE publishers in the year 1988.

    _____

    _____

3. A book published by PRINCETON UNIVERSITY PRESS, which is located in PRINCETON, New Jersey, was written by MYRON WEINER. His book was called THE CHILD AND THE STATE IN INDIA: CHILD LABOR AND EDUCATION POLICY IN COMPARATIVE PERSPECTIVE. It appeared in 1991.

    _____

    _____

    _____

EXERCISE 8.2   Using an Online Catalog Entry to Create an MLA Entry

Read the following screen from a library online catalog. Create a correct MLA Works Cited entry for this book.

Title:	Understanding a raisin in the sun: a student casebook to issues, sources, and historical documents
Publisher:	Westport, Conn.: Greenwood Press, 1998.
Subjects:	Hansberry, Lorraine, 1930–1965. Raisin in the sun.
	Hansberry, Lorraine, 1930–1965. Raisin in the sun— Sources.
	Domestic drama, American—History and criticism.
	Afro-American families in literature.
	Afro-Americans in literature.
Title:	A raisin in the sun: the unfilmed original screenplay
Publisher:	New York, N.Y., U.S.A.: Plume Book, c1992.

LOCATION:	CALL NUMBER:	STATUS:
LaGuardia Reserves	PN 1997 .R2259 1992	Not checked out

Now let's look at two MLA-style entries for periodicals. The first is for a magazine that is published *monthly,* the second for a magazine that is published *weekly.* Note how these models differ from the one for a basic book and how each is different from the other magazine entry.

Article in a Monthly Magazine

Baker, Kenneth. "When the Nazis Took Aim at Modern Art." <u>Smithsonian</u> July 1991: 86–95.

Article in a Weekly Magazine

Gorman, Christine. "The Fight over Food Labels." <u>Time</u> 15 July 1991: 52–56.

EXERCISE 8.3   Understanding MLA Style for Magazines

1. What is the first item in each entry? What marks of punctuation are used?

_____

2. What is placed inside the quotation marks in each entry? How did you figure it out?

_____

3. What is underlined in each entry? Is there any punctuation after this item?

_____

4. What is different about the date in each entry? Where is the *day* placed in the second entry? Can you figure out why the second entry has the "15" and the first entry does not?

_____

5. What is the punctuation after the date? Is it the same in each entry?

_____

6. What do you think the numbers after the date represent?

_____

_____

As you saw, the two entries are similar, but closer examination reveals that the weekly magazine has a *day* as well as a month and a year, because a researcher would need to know which *Time* magazine the article appeared in. There are usually four magazines published each month. The date the magazine is issued lets the researcher know exactly which copy to examine for the article required. The *Smithsonian* is published only once a month, so no day is given. If you look on the cover of each of these magazines, you will see that the dates appear on the magazines the same way they are recorded in the MLA entry, except that MLA places the day (15) before the month. The first item is the author's name. This is followed by the title of the article in the magazine. Note that the article is identified by being placed in quotation marks. The title of the magazine (the longer work) is underlined, like a book title. After the date, we have the page numbers for the article. Finally, note that the punctuation is precise: both entries use the same system, and you will follow these models in punctuating your own Works Cited entries.

EXERCISE 8.4   Creating a Works Cited Entry for a Magazine Article

Using the following information about a source, create the entry as it would appear if this source were used in a paper. The important information is in capital letters. Change the form so that it is right for MLA style.

An article entitled SIX CENTS AN HOUR was written by SYDNEY H. SCHAN-BERG. This article was published in LIFE magazine. It appeared in the JUNE 1996 issue on pages 38 to 46.

_____

_____

_____

Now let's look at a newspaper article. Here is the basic form for an article that appeared in a daily newspaper.

Erlich, Reese. "India Battles Illegal Child Labor." Christian Science Monitor
    8 Nov. 1995: 9.

EXERCISE 8.5   Newspaper Articles in MLA Style

Look carefully at the newspaper entry and answer these questions:

1. What is the author's first name? _____

2. What punctuation is used to identify the article title? _____

3. What punctuation is used to identify the name of the newspaper? _____

_____

4. Why is there a period after "Nov."? _____

5. What clue do you have about the length of this article? _____

_____

This is only the beginning! For every different type of source, there is another form a researcher must follow. We will discuss many more of these models later in this chapter. As you are no doubt beginning to realize, using MLA style to create a Works Cited list is not intellectually difficult, but it *does* require patience and great attention to rather tiny (and seemingly boring) details. Why is this system—any documentation system—so detailed? Because researchers must be precise to be believed. The documentation is a code by which writers demonstrate that their work is founded on carefully collected information. It also makes the sources readily available for future researchers. In this way, knowledge and information are disseminated. Once you "crack" the code, you will be able to read other writers' Works Cited lists, evaluate their research, and use their hard work to advance your own writing.

EXERCISE 8.6   Interpreting an MLA-style Works Cited List

"Crack the code" of MLA by examining the following Works Cited list from a student essay on the subject of child labor. (You can read the complete paper at the end of this chapter.) Look carefully at each entry. To the left of each, label the ones you can recognize so far: book, weekly magazine, monthly magazine, newspaper. Take an educated guess at what some of the other sources are. (*Note:* Although the following entries are single-spaced to save room, Works Cited entries should be double-spaced.)

Koefman 11

Works Cited

Barr, Cameron. "India's Education Problems." Christian Science Monitor 11
    May 1992: 14.

Basu, Kaushik. Letter. "The Poor Need Child Labor." New York Times 29 Nov.
    1994: A24.

"Child Labor." The Encyclopedia Americana 1992 ed.

"Child Labor Around the World: It's Anything But a Pretty Picture." National
    Journal 25 June 1994. N. pag.

The Child Labor Coalition. Rugmark Consumer Campaign: Organizers Kit.
    Washington: National Consumers League, 1995. N. pag.

Daughters of Free Men. By Kate Pfordresher. Pro. Steve Brier. American Social
    History Productions Inc., 1987.

Davis, Rebecca Harding. Life in the Iron Mills and Other Stories. New York:
    The Feminist Press at The City University of New York, 1985.

Erlich, Reese. "India Battles Illegal Child Labor." <u>Christian Science Monitor</u>
 8 Nov. 1995: 9.

Harkin, Tom. "Put an End to the Exploitation of Child Labor." <u>USA Today</u> Jan.
 1996: 73–5.

Harvey, Pharis J. "Where Children Work: Child Servitude in the Global
 Economy." <u>The Christian Century</u> 5 Apr. 1995: 362–5.

Holland, Ruth Robins. <u>Mill Child</u>. New York: Crowell, 1970.

International Child Labor Study Office. <u>By the Sweat and Toil of Children: The
 Use of Child Labor in American Imports</u>. Vol. 1. Sept. 1994.

——. <u>By the Sweat and Toil of Children: The Use of Child Labor in U.S.
 Agricultural Imports & Forced and Bonded Child Labor.</u> Vol. 2. Sept. 1995.

Quindlen, Anna. "Out of the Hands of Babes." <u>New York Times</u> 23 Nov. 1994:
 A23. <u>New York Times on the Web</u> <http://www.nytimes.com/library/
 tech/94/06/biztech/articles/21voice.html> (19 Sept. 1999).

Schanberg, Sydney. "Six Cents an Hour." <u>Life</u> June 1996: 38+.

Senser, Robert A. "The Crime of Child Slavery: Child Labor in South Asia."
 <u>The Current</u> Mar.–Apr. 1994: 29–33.

Weiner, Myron. <u>The Child and the State in India: Child Labor and Education
 Policy in Comparative Perspective</u>. Princeton, N.J.: Princeton UP, 1991.

MLA Documentation Style for Works Cited

Your college library's home page or reference desk should have available a style sheet that provides samples of entries in the MLA style for print and online resources. You can see the icon for such a resource on the screen shown on page 113 from LaGuardia Community College. Be sure to locate your library's style sheet; it may have important information that is unique to the courses you are studying or the local resources you are using. Below you will find a list of many of the types of sources commonly used in college research papers. Keep in mind, however, that, especially with electronic sources, information changes quickly. Ask your instructor or librarian if you cannot find the model you want below. You can also use a number of online tools to help you. Several of these are listed in the appendix.

When you are preparing your Works Cited list, match the type of source you are using to one of the models below. Then arrange your information exactly according to the form of the example, including punctuation. Unless otherwise indicated, you must double-space after periods, but single-space after other punctuation. Double-space between lines of each entry and between entries, unless your instructor requires a different format.

Books

Book by a Single Author (Basic Book)

Dwight, Eleanor. <u>Edith Wharton: An Extraordinary Life</u>. New York:
 Abrams, 1994.

This is the basic format you have already examined: Author, last name first, separated by a comma, and followed by a period.

Dwight, Eleanor.

Next comes the book title, underlined. Two spaces after author. Capitals on key words. A colon (:) separates title from subtitle.

Edith Wharton: An Extraordinary Life.

The city where the *publishing company* is located, from the book's title page, follows. (Do not use the place where the book was *printed.*) Add a colon after the city.

New York:

Then comes the publishing company. Abbreviate common phrases (for example, change University Press to UP), and omit *Company* and *Inc.* The publishing company is followed by a comma.

Abrams,

Finally, give the date of publication. It can be found on the copyright page, which is usually on the back of the title page. Add a period.

1994.

Note that the second line needs to be double-spaced and indented five spaces. If the entry were very long, all lines after the first would be indented five spaces, just like the second line.

Book by Two or Three Authors

Burrows, Edwin G., and Mike Wallace. Gotham: A History of New York City to 1898. New York: Oxford UP, 1999.

The first author (the one whose name appears first on the title page of the book) is set up just as in the basic book. The second author goes in first name first. The word *and* links the two names. Note that there is a period after the initial G. The period remains, and the comma is added directly after the period. If there are three authors, the entry could appear as

Burrows, Edwin G., Richard Lieberman, and Mike Wallace.

or it could be arranged with the abbreviation "et al." This Latin abbreviation means "and others" and is used in the next entry.

Book by Three or More Authors

Burrows, Edwin G., et al. Gotham: A History of New York City to 1898. New York: Oxford UP, 1999.

Book by a Corporate Author

Edith Wharton Society. The Mount: Preserving Edith Wharton's Home. Lenox, MA: 2000.

In this book there is no individual author named. The Society replaces an author's name. Note that because Lenox is a small city and could be confused with other places with the same name, the state (Massachusetts) is added in abbreviated form (MA).

Book with No Author

<u>Brownstone Architecture.</u> New York: Appleton, 1893.

Omit the author. Begin with the title. Use the first letter of the title when alphabetizing the list.

Book by an Editor

Speyer, Catherine, ed. <u>The Illustrated Guide to Urban Living.</u> Philadelphia:
   Franklin Press, 1987.

The abbreviation "ed." follows the author's name. The two are separated by a comma. Otherwise, the entry is exactly like the one for a basic book.

Translation

Machiavelli, Niccolo. <u>The Prince.</u> Trans. Daniel Donno. New York: Bantam, 1981.

The year is the year the translation was published in the edition you are using, not the date the original book was published in Italian, which was 1513. The entry refers a reader to the exact edition the researcher used (which in this case is not the original edition), unless the writer is quoting in Italian from the actual 1513 rare edition.

Edition

Jansen, H. W. <u>History of Art.</u> 5th ed. New York: Abrams, 1997.

The edition is added if the book is a popular one that has appeared in revised versions, or editions. You need to indicate which one you are using because new editions might not have the same pages or the same information as older ones. Note that the term *edition* refers to the book; an editor is the person who prepares the edition.

Reprint

Taylor, Elizabeth. <u>Mrs. Palfrey's Closet.</u> 1943; rpt. New York: Penguin
   Virago, 1986.

A book identified as a reprint (rpt.) is a book that has been unavailable (out of print) and has been reissued, usually by a publishing company other than the original one. The first date indicates the original date of publication, and "rpt." is followed by the new publisher and date. This form is generally used if the writer wants to call attention to the date of the original. Otherwise, it is usually adequate to cite a reprint in the same manner as a basic book.

Book with Author and Editor

Shakespeare, William. <u>Hamlet.</u> Ed. Harold Jenkins. London: Methuen, 1982.

The person who wrote the original play is Shakespeare. Jenkins is the modern scholar who prepared the play for publication in a modern book and may have also added notes or comments on the original play.

Multivolume Work

Jordan, William Chester, ed. <u>The Middle Ages: An Encyclopedia for Students.</u>
     4 vols. New York: Scribners, 1996.

The only difference between this entry and the one for a basic book is the addition of the "4 vols." Use the arabic number and abbreviate as indicated in the example.

Book in a Series

Heisler, Martin O., and Barbara S. Heisler. <u>From Foreign Workers to Settlers?:</u>
     <u>Transnational Migration and the Emergence of New Minorities.</u> Annals
     of the American Academy of Political and Social Science. 485. Beverly
     Hills, CA: Sage, 1986.

In publishing a series, the organization or publisher has published several titles as part of a continuing project or as a group of related books. Here, the title of the book is underlined. The Annals indicates who published the series. The number is the locator in the series: This work is number 485, so we can presume there are 484 other items published before this one. Note that there are two authors with the same last name but that they are arranged just as in a book with two authors.

Work in an Anthology

Wharton, Edith. "The Other Two." <u>The Norton Anthology of Literature by</u>
     <u>Women: The Traditions in English.</u> 2nd ed. Comp. Sandra M. Gilbert and
     Susan Gubar. New York: Norton, 1996. 999–1012.

Here the writer refers to a short story, in quotation marks, by the author Edith Wharton. This story is collected in the larger anthology, title underlined. "Comp." means compilers, or collectors: Gilbert and Gubar selected the many works that are in this anthology. The story appears on pages 999–1012 in the book. This is a useful model if you are taking an English class and using an anthology of literary works that includes poetry, stories, and plays.

Introduction, Preface, Foreword, or Afterword in a Book

Macheski, Cecilia. Introduction. <u>The Believers.</u> By Janice Holt Giles.
     Lexington: University Press of Kentucky, 1989. vii–xiii.

The research paper cites the introduction, which is written by Macheski. Therefore, the entry begins with her name. Giles is the author of the novel for which the introduction was written. If the paper also quotes from the text of the novel, the novel might be listed again in the Works Cited under "Giles, Janice Holt." Use the same form for references to a preface, foreword, or afterword. These are all "extras" added to the original text of a work such as a novel, a play, or a famous or classic work to update it for modern readers or to add commentary to guide new readers. Because the state, Kentucky, appears in the name of the publisher, the abbreviation "KY" is not needed after Lexington, even though there are many cities of that name.

Encyclopedia: Signed Article

Auchincloss, Louis. "Edith Wharton." <u>The Encyclopedia Americana.</u> 1978 ed.

The title of the article in the encyclopedia is in quotation marks. The name of the encyclopedia is underlined. Note that the entry *does not* include a volume number or page numbers.

Encyclopedia: Unsigned Article

"Morocco." <u>Encyclopaedia Britannica.</u> 1995 ed.

This entry is the same as the previous one, minus the name of an author. (Look at the very end of the article to see whether an author is identified.)

Government Documents

United States. Department of Labor. Women's Bureau. <u>Sexual Harassment in Government Jobs.</u> Washington: GPO, 1987.

National Cancer Institute. Tobacco Research Implementation Group. <u>Tobacco Research Implementation Plan: Priorities for Tobacco Research Beyond the Year 2000.</u> Bethesda, MD: National Cancer Institute, National Institutes of Health, 1998.

Keep in mind that there are many kinds of government documents—local, state, federal, and international. The main goal is to provide enough information for readers to locate the same source you used. Identify the agency that produced the document, the title, where it was published, any "sponsor data" that would provide a source for obtaining the document, and the year of publication.

Pamphlet, Brochure, or Circular

Treat a pamphlet as you would a book. If in doubt about the exact form, give *as much information as possible.* Look for an author, a title, a sponsoring agency or affiliation, the city, and a date. Be cautious about using circulars or pamphlets of uncertain origin; these are difficult to evaluate.

Periodicals: Magazines and Journals

The basic entry for a magazine or journal article includes the author of the article, the title of the article (in quotation marks), the title of the magazine or journal, and the publication information, followed by the page. Check the periodical carefully to determine how frequently it is published, because some are issued weekly, others biweekly, and others monthly, quarterly, semiannually (twice a year), or annually.

Article in a Weekly Magazine

Gallagher, Richard. "Teaching Teachers in Venice." <u>Tourist</u> 27 January 1999: 49–52.

The entry begins with the author's name, last name first.

Gallagher, Richard.

If there is no author, begin with the title. Then comes the title of the article, in quotation marks.

"Teaching Teachers in Venice."

Next is the title of the magazine in which the article appears, underlined.

Tourist

The date appears with the day first, followed by the month and year, with no punctuation between the items:

27 January 1999

Note, below, that for monthly magazines the date may include only the month and year. The last item is the page or pages on which the article appears.

49–52.

In this case, the article is printed with continuous pagination. If the article is scattered through the magazine instead, and the pages are not continuous, use the first page followed by a plus sign: 49+.

Article in a Monthly Magazine

Spencer, Leonard. "Queering the Millennium: Gay Travel for the Next
    Century." Abroad December 1999: 13–14.

If it is a magazine issued twice a month, use the date and month.

Article in a Scholarly Journal with Continuous Pagination

Bulliet, Richard W. "Twenty Years of Islamic Politics." Middle East Journal 53
    (1999): 189–200.

Continuous pagination means that throughout the year, the issues of the journal are numbered as though they were all part of one book. The first issue starts with page 1, the second issue continues with the next page after the end of the first issue, and so on. There is no month or date; the number "53" in this example is the locator needed to find this article.

Article in a Scholarly Journal That Pages Issues Separately

Montgomery, Rodney, and Maureen Foster. "Dysfunction in University
    Management in New South Wales in 1947 and 1983." Journal of Higher
    Education Management 43.2 (1989): 6–17.

This article has two authors. Note that their names are arranged in the same way as for a book entry. In this type of journal, each issue is paginated starting with page 1. The issue number in this case is 43.2, which shows that each issue for this year will be identified with 43 plus a number indicating its place in the sequence for the year. Some journals start the year in the fall, following the academic calendar.

Book Review

Elliott, Arial. "Snow Falling on Murder." Rev. of The Desperate Season, by
    Michael Blaine. Metropolitan 10 October 1999: 8–11.

The book, its title underlined, is written by the author Blaine. What this entry is citing is not that novel but a review (a critical evaluation) of it that appeared in a magazine, in this case *Metropolitan*. The quotation marks are used to enclose the title of the review (as for an article), "Snow Falling on Murder." The title of the source (a magazine) where the review appeared is also underlined. The numbers 8–11 are the magazine pages on which the review was printed. If you were citing Blaine's book by quoting directly from the book, the entry would start with Blaine's name and would follow the format for basic book.

Periodicals: Newspaper Articles

Newspapers appear in different formats. Some have only one section; others have lettered or numbered sections. Sometimes there are special city editions, or editions for special audiences, such as an international edition. The entries for these differ, reflecting the specific type of source you are using and identifying the location of the article as precisely as possible.

Article in a Single-section Newspaper

Sellers, S. H. "Hat Museum Opens." <u>Wright County Clarion</u> 15 July 2000: 2.

The author is listed, last name first.

Sellers, S. H.

The article title is next, in quotation marks.

"Hat Museum Opens."

The name of the newspaper, underlined, follows. Omit any articles (*the, a, an*), so write <u>New York Times</u>, not <u>The New York Times</u>.

<u>Wright County Clarion</u>

The date comes next—day, month, and year—followed by a colon and the page number.

15 July 2000: 2.

Items are separated by periods, except for the name of the newspaper and the date. A final period concludes the entry.

Article in a Newspaper with Sections Identified by Letter

Rusconi, Patrick. "Opera House Sponsors Architectural Tour." <u>Ann Arbor Valley Record</u> 17 May 2001: C5.

The entry is the same as for the single-section newspaper, but the page is identified by section, C, followed by the page number, 5.

Article in a Newspaper with Sections Identified by Number

French, Alan. "Immigration Patterns Alter as EU Raises Import Quotas." <u>Phoenix Mercury</u> 14 July 1999, sec. 4:1.

The basic entry is the same as the two above, but the page is now identified by the abbreviation "sec." for section, the number of the section, 4, followed by a colon, and then the number of the page on which the article appears in that section.

Newspaper Editorial (No Author Listed)

"Cement Plant Will Ruin Local Tourism." Editorial. <u>Troy Record</u> 11 January
    2000: 3B.

Begin with the title or headline. Note that this newspaper identifies pages with
the number first, whereas in the earlier example, the section was listed first. Your
entry must record the page as it appears in the newspaper.

Other Sources

CD-ROM Issued in a Single Edition

Sheehy, Donald, ed. <u>Robert Frost: Poems, Life, Legacy.</u> CD-ROM. New York:
    Holt, 1997.

This type of entry is similar to that for a book. Only the addition of "CD-ROM"
makes it different.

CD-ROM Issued Periodically

Wattenberg, Ruth. "Helping Students in the Middle." <u>American Educator</u> 19.4
    (1996): 2–18. ERIC. CD-ROM. SilverPlatter. Sept. 1996.

In this example, the researcher refers to a database, ERIC, which is available on
a library CD-ROM file. The reference is to an article from the journal (title underlined), by the author Wattenberg. SilverPlatter produced the CD-ROM.

Video

<u>The Bostonians.</u> Dir. James Ivory. Perf. Vanessa Redgrave, Jessica Tandy, Eva
    Marie Saint, and Christopher Reeve. Merchant Ivory Productions, 1984.

The entry begins with the title of the video, underlined, followed by the abbreviation "Dir." for Director. Next is "Perf." for performers. The main actors and actresses
are listed, first name first. The production company is next, followed by the date.

If you need to check the information on a video or film, you can use the
Internet; http://us.imdb.com is the International Movie Database site. Search by
entering the title or a performer, and you should find the details you need. There is
a database for both the United States and the United Kingdom.

Television Program

"Ellis Island." <u>The American Experience.</u> Narr. David McCullough. PBS.
    WGBH, Boston. 7 Aug. 1990.

The name of the individual program in a series, "Ellis Island," comes first in
quotation marks, followed by the name of the series, which is underlined. The
"Narr." is the narrator. The network is PBS; it is followed by the local station, WGBH,
with the station's city. The date is the date on which the show was broadcast.

Personal Interview or Letter

Pacino, Al. Telephone interview. 12 October 1999.

The researcher interviewed the actor Al Pacino by telephone. If the interview
had been conducted in person, the citation would read "Personal interview"; if

electronically, "E-mail." The date appears with day first, then month and year, just as in the listing of periodicals.

King, Stephen. Letter to the author. 15 October 1999.

> The novelist King has written a letter to the author of the research paper.

Broadcast Interview

King, Stephen. Interview. <u>Charlie Rose.</u> Channel 17. WMHT, Albany, NY. 14 October 1998.

> King has been interviewed on the program (underlined) on public television.

Work of Art

Sargent, John Singer. <u>Madame X.</u> Museum of Fine Arts. Boston.

> The name of the work of art is underlined. The painter is listed as an author is, last name first.

Cartoon

MacNelly, Jeff. Untitled. Cartoon. <u>Chicago Tribune</u> 15 April 1999: B6.

> If the cartoon has a title, put it in quotation marks; use "Untitled" if there is no title. Include the name of the source where the cartoon appeared, followed by the date and the page.

Chart or Map

<u>San Francisco City Plan.</u> Map. New York: Frommer, 1998.

> Underline the title of the map. Then include the identification word "Map" or "Chart." This is followed by the same publishing information as for a book.

Electronic Sources

Guidelines for the most recent MLA electronic sources can be found at http://www.mla.org. As mentioned earlier, you should also consult your college library's style sheet. Here are models for some of the most commonly used sources.

Note: When an Internet address in a Works Cited entry must be divided at the end of a line, break it after a slash. Do not insert a hyphen.

Online Scholarly Project or Reference Database

"Gog and Magog." <u>The Encyclopedia Mythica.</u> Ed. Micha F. Lindemans. 2 Jan. 1998. 31 Jan. 1998 <http://www.pantheon.org/mythica/articles/gog and magog.html>.

> The first date is the publication date, the second the user's date of access.

Personal or Professional Web Site

<u>MLA.</u> Modern Language Association. 11 November 2005 <http://www.mla.org>.

> The date is the date the user accessed the site.

Spanoudis, Steve, Bob Blair, and Nelson Miller. <u>Poets' Corner.</u> 2 Feb. 1998.
    4 Feb. 1998 <http://www.geocities.com/spanoudi/poems>.

The first date, as in the example above, is the publication date, and the second is the user's date of access.

Online Book

Brontë, Charlotte. Jane Eyre. 1846. <u>Bartleby.com: Great Books Online</u>. 2000.
    5 May 2005 <http://www.bartleby.com/127/41.htm>.

The year 1846 is the original date of publication of the book. The second date is the user's date of access.

Article in an Online Periodical

Romano, Jay. "Computers That Tend the Home." <u>New York Times on the Web</u>
    14 Oct. 1999 <http://www.nytimes.com/library/Tech/99/10/biztech/
    articles/15home.html>.

E-mail

Ivory, James. "Re: Henry James." E-mail to the author. 22 Nov. 1999.

Other Online Sources

"City of New Orleans, LA." Map. <u>Yahoo! Maps.</u> Yahoo! 2000. 3 Jan. 2000.
    <http://maps.yahoo.com/yahoo>.

Work from a Licensed Subscription Service: Article in a Magazine

James, Al. "Community College Economics." <u>Harvard Business Review</u> Jan.
    2005: 78–79. Academic Search Premier EBSCOhost WEB. LaGuardia
    Community Coll. Lib. Long Island City, NY. 31 March 2005
    <http://search.epnet.com>.

The student has used the database EBSCOhost to locate the article by James. The article was originally printed in the *Harvard Business Review* and then put online by EBSCOhost. The student found the article at the college library, which has license to use the online service. The article was published in January 2005; the student accessed it in March.

Work from a Licensed Subscription Service: Article in a Newspaper

Jewett, Karen. "Many Children Left Behind: Enemies of Public Education."
    Herald News 21 April 2005, educ. General News. LexisNexis Academic.
    LaGuardia Community Coll. Lib., Long Island City, NY.18 July 2005
    <http://web.lexis-nexis.com/universe>.

Here the student has used an article that appeared in the newspaper Herald News and was available online from LexisNexis. The article was originally published in April; the student read it in July 2005.

EXERCISE 8.7	**Identifying Works Cited Entries from Print Sources**

Examine the following Works Cited list from an essay on literature about World War II. Then identify the type of source that is being cited by comparing each entry to those in the samples above. (Note: Although the following entries are single-spaced to save room, Works Cited entries should be double-spaced.)

Works Cited

Bainbridge, Beryl. <u>The Dressmaker</u>. London: Fontana, 1973.

Dwan, Allan, dir. <u>Around the World</u>. RKO, 1943. Reissued on VHS by RKO Collection, 1990.

Fussell, Paul. <u>Wartime</u>. New York: Oxford, 1989.

Gallagher, Joyce. "Before Private Ryan: <u>Film Noir</u> Effects in John Ford's Wartime Epics." <u>Journal of Film and History</u> 17.3 (1997): 13–35.

Lieberman, Roberta. "Steinway Goes to War: Piano Music of WWII Finds a New Audience." <u>Vanity Fair</u> January 2000: 47–53.

McClung, Nellie. "What Do Women Think of War? (Not That It Matters)." From <u>In Times Like These</u>, 1915; rpt. 1972; excerpted in <u>Longman Anthology of World Literature by Women 1875–1975</u>, ed. Marian Arkin and Barbara Shollar. New York: Longman, 1989: 156–59.

Muir, Edwin. "Telemachos Remembers." <u>One Foot in Eden</u>. London: Faber and Faber, 1956: 30–31.

Powell, Colin. Personal interview. 6 August 1995.

Southern, Alvina. "Military Millinery." Rev. of <u>Mrs. Miniver</u>, by Nevil Shute. <u>Iowa Monitor</u> 10 October 1997: 4–5.

"World War II." <u>Encyclopedia Americana.</u> 1946 ed.

Fill in the type of source for each entry.

Example:

Bainbridge: _____*Basic book*_____   McClung: _____

Dwan: _____   Muir: _____

Fussell: _____   Powell: _____

Gallagher: _____   Southern: _____

Lieberman: _____   "World": _____

EXERCISE 8.8	**Practicing MLA-style Works Cited Forms for Print Sources**

1. Select an article from your daily paper. Make a Works Cited entry following the model for a newspaper in the MLA examples.

2. Select an article from a weekly news magazine. Make a Works Cited entry following the correct MLA model.

3. Select one of your textbooks. Create a Works Cited entry for this book.

4. Locate an article in a scholarly journal in your library. Select one article from the issue and create a Works Cited entry for this article.

5. Find a photograph that is printed in a source. Create an MLA Works Cited entry for this image.

EXERCISE 8.9   **Creating a Works Cited List in Alphabetical Order**

Using the five items in the previous exercise, create an alphabetical Works Cited page just as it would appear at the end of a research paper in which these were the sources the writer used. Share the list with your research group or post it on your discussion board.

EXERCISE 8.10   **Creating MLA-style Works Cited Entries for Electronic Sources**

1. Using EBSCOhost, locate an article for which the full text is available online. Create an entry for this source in MLA format.

2. Using LexisNexis, find a newspaper article from a paper other than your local daily. Create a Works Cited entry in MLA format.

3. Using a search engine, find a Web page sponsored by a professional organization (.org). Create a Works Cited entry for this site.

EXERCISE 8.11   **Expanding a Works Cited List**

Take the list you alphabetized with print sources and add the electronic sources in alphabetical order. Post your expanded list on the DB or share it with your research group.

Step 19   **PREPARING YOUR WORKS CITED LIST IN MLA STYLE**

Using the source note cards you created for your own research subject, prepare a complete Works Cited list for your research paper. Refer to the sample essay at the end of this chapter to review the form.

In-Text Documentation in MLA Style

In-text documentation is how a writer indicates, in the body of the essay, which work is being quoted, paraphrased, or summarized in a particular sentence or paragraph. The basic model in MLA is that a parenthetical citation is placed directly after a source is used, pointing the reader to the Works Cited entry for further information on the source. This system replaces the use of footnotes or endnotes to identify sources. Here is an example from the sample paper that appears on page 233.

Rebecca Harding Davis asks the reader to reflect on the life course of one
    young man in the iron mills of nineteenth-century America with these
    lines, "I want you to look back, as he does every day, at his birth in
    vice, his starved infancy; to remember the . . . heavy years of constant,
    hot work. So long ago he began . . . " (25).

In this paragraph, the writer announced the name of the author he is quoting at the beginning of the sentence, Rebecca Harding Davis. He introduces the quotation, using the sandwich method, and then offers the direct quotation. In order to refer his reader to the exact source he puts, in parentheses after the quotation, the number of the page in Davis's book where he found the quotation: (25). The reader can now refer to the Works Cited entry, where the book is listed.

Davis, Rebecca Harding. <u>Life in the Iron Mills and Other Stories.</u> 1851; rpt.
New York: The Feminist Press at The City University of New York, 1985.

Now the reader knows that the quotation in this paragraph appears on page 25 of the book by Davis. If the essay did *not* contain the name of the author, Davis, the writer would have to include that name in the citation.

(Davis 25).

For instance, later in the same essay the writer quotes from an article in the *New York Times.* He is quoting Senator Harkin, who is being discussed in the article. The article is not written by Harkin; it was written by the reporter Anna Quindlen. In this case the in-text documentation looks like this:

Senator Harkin's bill met stiff opposition both from home and abroad. The
<u>New York Times</u> reports that "Mr. Harkin's bill . . . would probably be a
violation of the GATT, which provides only for those restrictions spelled
out in the trade pact" (Quindlen 23).

Now the reader refers to the Works Cited list to locate the article written by Quindlen and finds the quotation on page 23 of that source.

Models for In-Text Citations in MLA Style

Source with One Author

The first time you cite (quote, paraphrase, or summarize), give the full name of the author *in the essay.* Include a brief phrase to identify the credentials or authority of this writer. After that, when you cite from this source, use the last name and page number.

(Davis 25).

If you do not introduce the author, the citation looks the same: (Davis 25). Note that there is no comma between author and page. Note also that there is no use of "*p.*" or "*pp.*" to abbreviate *page* or *pages,* and there is no use of the word *page.* Using these is incorrect. The period belongs *after* the citation.

Source with More Than One Author

If the work has two or three authors, include all of the last names in your citation if these are not mentioned in the essay. Include the page number where the quote appears.

(Arkin and Macheski 189).

(Arkin, Gallagher, and Macheski 211–12).

If the work has four or more authors, use only the name of the first author, followed by the abbreviation "et al."

(Arkin et al. 178–79).

Note that if the number is over 100, the second page number is shortened to the last two digits: (178–79), *not* (178–179).

More than One Source by the Same Author

If you are referring to more than one work by the same author, include the title and author in the text of the essay to avoid confusion.

After she published <u>In Morocco</u>, Edith Wharton went on to record her war
experiences in <u>Fighting France</u>, where she observed "deserted villages,
with soldiers lounging in the doors where old women should have sat
with their distaffs, soldiers watering their horses in the village pond,
soldiers cooking over gypsy fires in the farm-yards" (67).

Otherwise, you have to include an abbreviated title, as well as the author's
name and the page, in the in-text citations:

(Wharton, <u>Fighting</u> 67).

Source in an Edited Anthology

Cite the author of the work you are quoting from, not the editor of the anthology.
Sometimes a Works Cited entry might cite a short story by Wharton in an
anthology, such as this:

Wharton, Edith. "The Other Two." <u>The Norton Anthology of Literature by
Women: The Traditions in English.</u> 2nd ed. Comp. Sandra M. Gilbert and
Susan Gubar. New York: Norton, 1996. 999–1012.

Then the in-text citation refers to the story, not the anthology.

(Wharton 1001).

Source Quoted in Another Source

If you are quoting words that are quoted in the source you are using, the in-text
citation uses the abbreviation "qtd. in" for "quoted in." The source in which you
found the quote is the indirect source. This indirect source is the one you put in
your Works Cited list. In this example, the information comes from a biography of
Isabella Stewart Gardner by Louise Hall Tharp called *Mrs. Jack.* The writer is relying
on Tharp for the information, and the in-text citation therefore is to her book. Here
is the reference in the essay, followed by the in-text citation:

Edith Wharton once described the quality of the society hostess Isabella
Stewart Gardner's hospitality as "about what you would get in a
railroad restaurant in provincial France" (qtd. in Tharp 245).

Reference to an Entire Work, Not a Specific Page

If you are referring to an entire work, use only the author's name, with no page
number in the citation.

Isabella Stewart Gardner was a woman ahead of her time, who shocked turn-
of-the-century Boston society by putting herself and her house on
public display (Tharp).

Source with No Author Named

If the source has no author identified, give the complete title in the essay. Use a shortened form of the title in the in-text citation.

> According to <u>The Columbia Book of Knitting Patterns</u>, published in 1911, a "fascinator" was a fashionable scarf that was worn both over the head and around the neck of women (<u>Columbia Book</u> 111).

Electronic and Nonprint Sources

Many sources that appear on the computer screen do not have page numbers. (Do not consider the pagination that appears on printouts as a page number; these usually indicate the pages being printed, not the permanent numbers of pages on the documents.) Therefore, in-text citations can refer only to the author or, when there is no author, to the title of the source. However, most sources in databases that originally appeared in print form, such as news articles from LexisNexis, will have page numbers. These need to be included in the Works Cited entry.

Because of the lack of pages, it is important that you identify precisely where the information was found. See whether there is a section or other heading that you can use instead of a page number to help a reader locate the exact place.

Provide as much information in the essay text as possible. Include the title, the authors, and credentials or Web site name.

> According to the biographical information on Edith Wharton available from www.edithwharton.org, Wharton never mentioned her divorce in her autobiography, *A Backward Glance.*

Here the writer has included both the name of the Web site and the section (biography) to identify the source, so no parenthetical citation is needed.

If the source is paginated, then cite it exactly as a print source.

Other Nonprint Sources

For television programs, interviews, films, recordings, works of art, and other nonprint sources, place the first word of the Works Cited entry in parentheses after the reference to the source. Because there are no pages in these sources, you cannot include a page number.

> According to a recent documentary on the Shakers, most of the members of this utopian community were vegetarians (Burns).

Source Produced by a Business or Corporation

Use the name of the business or corporation in the essay, and provide a shortened form of the name and a page in the in-text citation.

> The Proficiency Examination Board assures incoming freshman that testing at The City University will be "gender and race neutral" (PEDCUNY 2).

Multivolume Sources

Include the volume number and the page in your parenthetical citation. Separate the volume from the page with a colon and a space.

As William Chester Jordan argues, transnational migration has had more impact on women than on men (2: 244).

Several Sources in One Citation

If you are listing more than one source in the same parenthetical citation, separate entries with semicolons. To avoid confusion, do not include a very long list in one parenthetical entry.

Many Wharton biographers have been curious about the author's intense relationship with her father (Wolff 13; Benstock 223).

E-mail, Letter, Interview, or Other Personal Communication

Identify in the body of the essay the person with whom you communicated. In the Works Cited entry, indicate the type of communication and the date.

According to James Ivory, his film version of Henry James's novel The Golden Bowl was released in the fall of 2000.

Standard Works as Sources

Some classic or standard works of literature are cited so that readers can locate the quote in whichever edition they are using. For a *novel,* include chapter number and page in the edition you used: (133; ch. 4). For a *poem,* provide line numbers. The first reference uses "lines," but later references include only the line numbers, not the word "lines": (lines 14–19) and later (23–27). For a *classic poem* such as Homer's *Odyssey,* provide the book or part number, followed by line numbers: (2. 92–97). For a *play,* provide act, scene, and line numbers, using arabic numerals, not Roman numerals: (*Macbeth* 3.2.15–20).

The Bible as a Source

Provide the book, chapter, and verse or verses in the essay: Psalms 2.14–15. Or abbreviate the name of the book in a parenthetical citation if it is longer than one syllable: (Gen. 15.22) for Genesis, Chapter 15, Verse 22. *Do not* underline the title of a book from the Bible. If you use a translation other than the King James Bible, include it in your Works Cited list.

Annotated Student Research Paper

Read carefully through the research paper on the following pages. Note how the in-text citations are used and how each one is linked to an entry in the Works Cited list.

MLA

MLA-style title page
(optional)

Child Labor:
Crisis in the Global Village
by
Jonathan J. Koefman

Writing the Research Paper   English 103.03
Professor Cecilia Macheski
October 24, 2005

Koefman 1

Jonathan J. Koefman

Professor C. Macheski

English 103.03

24 October 2005

Child Labor: Crisis in the Global Village

Industrialization breeds many diseases, one of which is child labor. In the 1800s child labor was one of several issues causing controversy in the United States. From the beginning of this century major changes have been made because of new legislation won by activists opposed to child labor. Child labor has been almost eradicated in the United States, but it is a recurring nightmare for millions of pairs of hands throughout the globe. They work incessantly to fuel the industrialization of their country, obtaining nothing but physical and mental degradation. By looking back on ways America rid itself of child labor, developing countries can avoid making the same mistakes.

In-text citation— author cited in paragraph

American writer Rebecca Harding Davis asks the reader to reflect on the life course of one young man in the iron mills of nineteenth-century America with the lines, "I want you to look back, as he does every day, at this birth in vice, his starved infancy; to remember the heavy years he has groped through as boy and man—the slow heavy years of constant, hot work. So long ago he

Quote appears on p. 25 of the Davis work

began . . ." (25). The young man has spent his life a slave of an industrial society that has denied him the right to live his life with a minimum of decency. The monotony of his life has embedded itself deeply within him. He cannot distinguish between childhood and adulthood, for he has spent all his days, as far as he dares to remember, toiling in the mills. Although Davis describes one man, in one mill, at one moment in time, she manages to paint a picture that can be framed by a myriad of wasted lives worldwide.

MLA

Koefman 2

The exploitation of children abounded in the late nineteenth century in the textile mills of the United States. In her study on the subject, Mill Child, Ruth Holland describes the monotonous cycle of the children's lives, "twelve hours a day, six days a week, the children fed the endless, ravening hunger of the machines" (16). They worked constantly in the mills, having no control over the days or the hours they worked. The implacable pace of the machines dictated the speed at which they worked, and the overseers saw that they kept up. Kate Pfordresher's Daughters of Free Men shows how at the end of the day, the children would trudge back to the boarding houses too tired to eat. They slept in rooms with four to six beds in each. The boarding houses were owned by the mill owners, who inflated the price of board and lodging. The children would never be able to save the money that the factory owners had led them to believe they would get, and their dreams of sending a part of their wage to their families quickly vanished. Unable to save money for anything more than bare necessities, the children found themselves dependent on their own slavery. It was not until the passing of labor and compulsory-education laws that child labor began to disappear.

A similar situation to that in the United States can be found in India's carpet industry today. The locations have changed, but not the methods. An article in the Current describes "boys and girls working long hours—usually seven days a week and fifty-two weeks a year . . . " (Senser 31). The children are forced to work for up to twenty hours a day, during which they are not permitted to take breaks. The Child Labor Coalition reports that the employers deliberately provide inadequate food as the hunger helps to keep the children awake (Child Labor Coalition N. pag.). Children as young as five years old work at the looms. The report issued by the International Child Labor Study Office states that the conditions

Direct quotation

In-text citation

Book title underlined (or in italics)

In-text citation using author's last name and page on which quotation appears in Senser's book.

In-text citation for source without an author and unpaginated.

Koefman 3

In-text citation for multivolume source (full title given in paragraph)

they work in leave them with a variety of health problems: skeletal deformities caused by maintaining a crouched position, impaired vision as a result of working in poor light, and damaged lungs from the inhalation of woolen particles (ICLSO 2: 85–86). Employers maintain control by instilling fear into the children with the cruelest

Source introduced with author's name

of methods. Sidney Schanberg reports that one boy's "master branded his right cheek with a glowing iron rod, then inserted a toxin that blinded his left eye" (46).

Page citation to Schanberg article

The majority of the children are forced to work at the looms. The most predominant type of forced labor is debt bondage. The International Child Labor Study Office report describes debt bondage as "the status or condition arising from a pledge by a debtor of his personal services or of those of a person under his control as a security for a debt" (ICLSO 2: 80). Recruiters working for the loom owners entice the parents of poor families into taking out loans. Many parents have no alternative to their economic troubles, and the children are effectively sold into slavery.

The Indian Commerce Ministry says that child labor is essential for India's export industries to remain competitive. Myron

Phrase added to explain the authority of the source

Weiner, in an interview with a top Indian Labor Ministry official, writes, "They tell me that the carpet industry would collapse if children were not employed" (49). The extra cost of employing adults would subsequently reduce the competitiveness of the final product on world markets. India's carpet industry expanded in the 1970s when Iran outlawed the labor of children in its carpet

Title of journal in which article appears along with author's name to support use of paraphrased information.

industry. In an article in The Christian Century, Pharis J. Harvey writes that a large portion of Iran's market was lost to India. The Indian Commerce Ministry now fears that a ban would cause India to lose its market share to other countries that continue to use child labor (364).

Koefman 4

Same journal source
used again

Introduces a quote
within a source

Presents quote
followed by in-text
citation of page in
Weiner

Parents claim that they need their children to work in order to survive. Harvey states, "parents with no security except the hope that children will care for them in old age have large families" (363). The parents need the children to look after them. Their wages are valuable to their well-being. Weiner quotes Nasir Tyabji, an Indian economist, as saying, "the amount added by the child to household income seems to be small, but it is often stable" (50). Parents regard schooling as non-productive for their child's future adult life. They believe their children should be trained from an early age to perform tasks that increase the income and overall benefit of the family.

Individuals and organizations of both Indian and Western cultures have joined together to promote legislation of anti-child-labor laws. One of the main figures on the forefront to advocate such laws is United States Senator of Iowa, Tom Harkin. Senator Harkin has introduced a bill to Congress called "The Child Labor Deterrence Act." This bill proposes ways to deter the use of child labor in the production of goods destined for the United States. Any industry identified as using child labor, and the country from which they operated, would be blacklisted by the United States Secretary of Labor, and their products banned from entering the United States. Furthermore, the bill proposes that the President of the United States seek to implement anti-child-labor initiatives on an international level (Harkin 74).

In-text citation by
author and page for
newspaper article
by Harkin

Reference to news
article about Harkin
by Quindlen

In-text citation to
identify source of
paraphrased
information

Senator Harkin's bill has met stiff opposition both from home and abroad. The New York Times reports that "Mr. Harkin's bill . . . would probably be a violation of the GATT, which provides only for those restrictions spelled out in the trade pact" (Quindlen 23). This means that the bill would probably have little chance of being passed. Abroad the bill is seen by developing countries as protectionist (Basu 25). It is argued that it is designed to hinder the

Koefman 5

ability of industries in developing countries to compete. Although
the bill has had as yet no direct effect on child labor, it has
generated considerable political attention to the issue.

In India the South Asian Coalition on Child Servitude (SACCS),
a group of activists led by Kailash Satyarthi, has conducted raids
on loom factories in India. An article in <u>Life</u> states that 29,000
children have been freed by Kailash's team. The price of freeing
the children has been costly. Two of the activists have already lost
their lives (Schanberg 46). As it is estimated that 300,000 children
work in the carpet industry, many more lives might still have to be
lost (Senser 31).

The Child Labor Coalition, based in the United States, has set
up a campaign called "Rugmark." Companies that avoid the use of
child labor will be certified by anti-child-labor monitoring groups,
such as SACCS. On certification, the companies will receive labels
with a "Rugmark" logo to be sewn into the carpets. But a report in
the <u>Christian Science Monitor</u> states, "the Rugmark system is
corrupt, and the labels are available without workplace inspection"
(Erlich 9). The designing and passing of laws and initiatives is hard
enough, but their implementing is even harder.

All the efforts to combat child labor are of considerable value,
for they create considerable publicity and political awareness.
However, the export market of many industrial nations is only a
small percentage of their national output, and the effects of these
initiatives on a country's child labor force would be at most
marginal. Interviewed in an article on child labor, Gabriela Stoikov,
expert on child labor, states, "Abolition of child labor in one sector
alone, such as the export sector, cannot eliminate child labor in
that country" ("Child Labor Around . . . " n.p.). She fears that the
children will be forced into industries that are far more dangerous,
such as prostitution. Here lies the basis of an argument that

Source without an
author cited by title;
long title is shortened

Koefman 6

divides anti-child-labor activists into two camps. On the one side stand those who advocate an immediate ban on all forms of child labor, the strict application of compulsory education, paralleled with laws to enforce a minimum working age for children. They stress that an all-out ban would be the easiest to implement.

The other side maintains that any laws should be applied by taking an overall view of the impact they could have on the society in question. As Stoikov upholds, it is seen that the most abusive forms of child labor, such as bonded labor and prostitution, should be eradicated. And the less abusive industries should be strictly regulated but not totally abolished in consideration for the children who rely on the work to survive. Although differences in opinion exist, the two main trains of thought do agree on several key points: the implementation of compulsory primary education laws, and abolition of bonded labor and child prostitution (ICLSO 1: 4).

It is generally agreed among experts that education laws would be easier to enforce than child labor restrictions. In referring to aspects of American labor history, Weiner writes, "Reformers also noted that enforcing school laws, by no means simple, was easier than enforcing child-labor laws and factory acts" (121). Few Indian states have mandatory primary education. But where they do, as in Kerala, children are less likely to be employed (Harvey 364). Swani Agnivesh, a former state minister for education, comments, "The only way to end child labor is to sincerely implement . . . primary education" (Barr).

The United States had tried to force individual states to implement laws of their own. These laws had little effect, since competing industries in each state were preoccupied by the possible loss of competition to rival states. It was not until 1938 that the United States passed the Fair Labor Standards Act. The Act and its amendments are the basis of national, anti-child-labor

Koefman 7

legislation today. Each state could now adhere to a unified standard, and child labor could cease to be the mainstay of inter-state competition ("Child Labor" 462).

Anonymous source from encyclopedia; title used in citation requires same punctuation as in Works Cited

These fears are a mirror image of India's concerns on the international level. The transition from national standards to international standards in a global economy is the direction in which Western efforts should be aimed. As Senser writes, "The challenge is to adjust national and international rules on child labor to reach beyond the boundaries of individual nations" (33).

Only page is needed because author is identified in the paragraph

Education is a central part of democracy. Through education individuals embark on a passage of self-discovery and their minds evolve. If children were guaranteed an education, they would start a life in which they could learn to respect themselves and others. Their own children would no longer be valued as prospective income, but each for their priceless individuality. Educated parents would be able to provide for their children and reverse the income flow. Family size would decrease, and the perpetual cycle of child labor would be broken (Weiner 114).

By raising the bottom end of the social-economic scale, all societies, whether national or global, will benefit. Some forms of poverty are likely to remain, but a poverty in which parents rely on child labor for survival would disappear. Through national legislation the United States was able to make headway against child labor. International standards of education and employment would extend this progress further. This principle was, and still is, applicable to all developing nations. As Schanberg writes, "a child's pain is the same everywhere" (43). The remedy is also universal.

Koefman 8

Title of article in quotations   Title of newspaper, underlined

Works Cited

Author of article — Barr, Cameron. "India's Education Problems." Christian Science

NEWSPAPER — Monitor 11 May 1992: 14. Date of publication   Page

Basu, Kaushik. Letter. "The Poor Need Child Labor." New York

NEWSPAPER in sections — Times 29 Nov. 1994: A24+. Section and page   Date of publication

ENCYCLOPEDIA — "Child Labor." The Encyclopedia Americana. 1992 ed. (no volume or page needed)

JOURNAL ARTICLE, no author — "Child Labor around the World: It's Anything But a Pretty Picture."

National Journal 25 June 1994. N. pag.

The Child Labor Coalition. Rugmark Consumer Campaign:

GOV'T PUBLICATION — Organizers Kit. Washington: National Consumers League,

1995. N. pag.

VIDEO — Daughters of Free Men. By Kate Pfordresher. Pro. Steve Brier.

American Social History Productions Inc., 1987.

Title, underlined

Author — Davis, Rebecca Harding. 1851. Life in the Iron Mills and Other

BASIC BOOK (republished in 1985; original pub. date is 1851) — Stories. New York: The Feminist Press at The City Publisher University of New York, 1985. Date of publication

City of publication

Erlich, Reese. "India Battles Illegal Child Labor." Christian Science

NEWSPAPER ARTICLE — Monitor 8 Nov. 1995: 9.

Harkin, Tom. "Put an End to the Exploitation of Child Labor." USA

NEWSPAPER ARTICLE — Today Jan. 1996: 73–5.

Harvey, Pharis J. "Where Children Work: Child Servitude in the

MAGAZINE ARTICLE   BOOK — Global Economy." Christian Century 5 Apr. 1995: 362–5.

Holland, Ruth Robins. Mill Child. New York: Crowell, 1970.

MULTI-VOLUME BOOK — International Child Labor Study Office. By the Sweat and Toil of

Children: The Use of Child Labor in American Imports. Vol. 1.

Sept. 1994.

---. By the Sweat and Toil of Children: The Use of Child Labor in

U.S. Agricultural Imports and Forced and Bonded Child Labor.

Vol. 2. Sept. 1995.

INTERNET SITE on World Wide Web (home page) — "International Labor Rights Fund." Online. Internet. Available:

http://www.laborrights.org.

ONLINE NEWSPAPER
ARTICLE with
publication date first
and URL followed by
date of access in
parentheses

Koefman 9

Quindlen, Anna. "Out of the Hands of Babes." <u>New York Times</u> 23

Nov. 1994: A23. <u>New York Times on the Web</u> http://

www.nytimes.com/library/tech/94/06/biztech/articles/

21voice.html (19 Sept. 1999).

MAGAZINE

Schanberg, Sydney. "Six Cents an Hour." <u>Life</u> June 1996: 38+. ARTICLE

Senser, Robert A. "The Crime of Child Slavery: Child Labor in South

Asia." <u>Current</u> Mar.–Apr. 1994: 29–33.   JOURNAL ARTICLE

BOOK

Weiner, Myron. <u>The Child and the State in India: Child Labor and

Education Policy in Comparative Perspective.</u> Princeton, NJ:

Princeton UP, 1991.

✔ **CHECKLIST   DOCUMENTING YOUR SOURCES USING
MLA STYLE**

❑ Does your documentation follow all of the MLA guidelines exactly?

❑ Are the sources listed alphabetically?

❑ Are all titles correctly identified by underlining or italics or quotation
marks, as shown in the appropriate model?

❑ Do you have in-text citations for all references to sources?

❑ Are all of the sources in the in-text citations listed in the Works Cited list at
the end of the paper?

❑ Have you included the URL for Internet sources?

❑ Is everything spelled correctly?

CHAPTER 9

Documenting Your Paper in APA and Other Documentation Styles

■ APA Style

■ Other Styles of Documentation

■ Sample Pages from Research Papers in MLA and APA styles

The APA is the American Psychological Association. This professional organization has prepared a style manual for researchers working in the fields of social science, behavioral science, and the natural sciences. Unlike the humanities, these fields emphasize the date of source material, in both the in-text citations and the List of References (equivalent to Works Cited in the MLA models you examined in Chapter 8). You must decide which system to use on the basis of your instructor's requirements or the subject of your paper.

You can contact the APA at http://www.apa.org/journals/webref.html for the most recent information on citing Internet sources. Its site for frequently asked questions (faqs) is http://www.ap.org/journals/faq.html. Keep in mind that there are now a number of commercial softwa re packages to help you create your list of sources. At www.xumbrus.com, you can find Scholarword; at www.academicsuperstore.com you will find Citation; and at www.netsnippets.com you can view Net Snippets. These tools, however, can be fairly expensive, and while they may be helpful, you will never learn to understand the logic of documentation unless you practice doing at least some of the entries manually.

As you will see when you compare the following models to those in MLA, there are important differences to note:

1. MLA uses a Works Cited list, whereas APA requires a List of References at the end of the paper.

2. APA places the date after the author's name, not at the end of the entry, as in MLA.

3. MLA asks the writer to use the present tense when referring to sources within the essay: "As Bradley says of Shakespeare's tragedy *Macbeth* . . . (27)." Using APA, the writer more commonly cites the source in the present perfect or past tense.

Let's look at an example of this last point. An author adhering to APA style might write:

> The importance of the Steinway Piano Company to the history of Queens, in New York City, is undisputed. Richard Lieberman has presented the employment statistics as "unquestionably supporting Steinway's contribution to the maintenance of a middle-class community in the neighborhood of Astoria, Queens, from 1910 to the late 1970's" (p. 78).

In MLA form, the same reference in the essay would be in the present tense:

> The importance of the Steinway Piano Company to the history of Queens, in New York City, is undisputed. Richard Lieberman presents the employment statistics as "unquestionably supporting Steinway's contribution to the maintenance of a middle-class community in the neighborhood of Astoria, Queens, from 1910 to the late 1970's" (78).

Note that both styles use the same tense, usually the present, to make comments, and generally to discuss how source material is related to the thesis of the essay. However, there are also differences.

In the APA model, the present perfect is used to introduce quotations. Note that the verb is "has presented," whereas in MLA it is "presents." Note also the difference in the in-text citation: APA includes a "p." and MLA does not. As you can see, it is very important that you keep the model in front of you as you work and that you are careful to follow the model exactly. Don't guess! Here are several more pointers on APA style:

- List ONLY those works that you have referred to directly and those from which you have quoted, summarized, or paraphrased. Do not list everything you read as background.

- Begin your list on a clean page at the end of your essay. Head the page References, centered, without quotes or underlining or italics and without a period.

- Arrange the sources in alphabetical order by the authors' last names. Use last name followed by first initial. Separate these with a comma: Arkin, M.

- Do not number entries. If there is more than one work by the same author, arrange these so that the earliest by date comes first.

- Examine the models that follow for details on punctuation.

- Double-space throughout.

APA Style

Books

Book by a Single Author (Basic Book)

Lieberman, R. K. (1995). <u>Steinway & Sons</u>. New Haven: Yale University Press.

The author's last name is followed by the first initial, not the full first name. The year of publication follows in parentheses. The title of the book is underlined, and only the first word in the title is capitalized, unless there is a proper name. If there is a subtitle, capitalize only the first word of the subtitle. Next comes the place of publication (the city), a colon, and the publishing company. Do not abbreviate. Omit commonly used words such as *Publishing Company* and *Inc.*

If you are listing more than one book by the same author, list them by date, not alphabetically, as you would in MLA.

Lieberman, R. K. (2000). <u>Robert Wagner: A political life</u>. Boston: Houghton Mifflin.

Lieberman, R. K. (1995). <u>Steinway & Sons</u>. New Haven: Yale University Press.

Entries are double-spaced. Second and subsequent lines should be either indented three spaces or tabbed in once. Choose one and be consistent.

Book by More Than One Author

Taylor, I., Walton, P., & Young, J. (1973). <u>The new criminology: For a social theory of deviance</u>. New York: Harper & Row.

Last names are used first for all of the authors. Use only an initial for the first name. A period after the initial is followed by a comma. An ampersand—&—comes before the last author's name.

Book by a Corporate Author

National Immigration Service. (1997). <u>Uniform immigration reports for the United States: 1996</u>. Washington, DC: U.S. Government Printing Office.

Book with No Author Given

<u>Exploring transfer: Encouraging community college students</u>. (1998). Poughkeepsie: New York Empire College Publications.

Book by an Editor: Collection of Essays

Gonzalez, S., Eng, D., & Wzyck, S. (Eds). (2000). <u>Teaching new teachers: model curricula for adjunct training</u>. New York: Sunnyside Press.

Translation

Weber, M. (1964). <u>The theory of social and economic organization</u> (A. M. Henderson & T. Parsons, Trans). New York: Free Press. (Original work published 1947.)

Edition Other Than the First

Jansen, H. W. (1997). <u>History of art</u> (5th ed.). New York: Abrams.

Reprint

Wharton, E. & Codman, O. (1997). <u>The decoration of houses</u>. (H. H. Reed, Preface) New York: W. W. Norton. (Original work published 1897.)

Note that there is no comma after the first author's name.

Signed Encyclopedia Article

Auchincloss, L. (1987). Edith Wharton. In Collier's encyclopedia (Vol. 13, pp. 709–10). New York: Macmillan Educational.

Unsigned Encyclopedia Article

Titanic. (1998). In <u>Encyclopedia of disasters</u> (Vol. 2, pp. 14–19). Los Angeles: Hollywood Press.

Multivolume Work

Beveridge, A. J. (1916–1919). <u>The life of John Marshall</u> (Vols. 1–4). Boston: Ticknor Fields.

Chapter in an Anthology

Stern, C. & Speyer, M. (1999). Parenting in perspective: the evolving role of the modern mother. In E. Bowen (Ed.), Childrearing (pp. 265–286). Beverly Hills, CA: Sage.

Periodicals

Article in a Weekly Magazine

Rusconi, R. (1998, May 18). Eighteenth-century lighting. <u>Antiques Weekly</u>, pp. 46–55.

Article in a Monthly Magazine

De Wolfe, E. (1999, August). The psychology of decorating. <u>Shelter</u>, pp. 15–19.

Unsigned Article—Weekly Magazine

On the trail of Zora Neale Hurston. (1997, May 17). <u>Literary Travel</u>, p. 32.

Book Review

Costanza, C. (1987). Emily's Evergreens. [Review of the book <u>Emily Dickinson's horticultural wisdom</u>]. <u>Contemporary Botany, 27</u>, pp. 466–467.

Article in a Scholarly Journal, Continuously Paged

Dishonski, R. (2000). Local history for the social studies classroom. <u>Modern Pedagogy, 52</u>, pp. 361–367.

Begin with the author's last name, followed by the initial of the first name. Write the title of the article without quotation marks. Capitalize only the first letter. Underline the name of the journal, with only the first word and proper nouns in capital letters; a comma follows. Add the volume number and underline it. Finally, use "p." if it is a one-page article, "pp." for two or more pages.

Article in a Scholarly Journal Paged by Issue

Schofield, Agnes. (1996). Women's history in the General Studies curriculum. <u>The Pedagogical Quarterly, 24</u> (2), pp. 37–58.

Article in a Newspaper—Signed

Moser, T. B. (1986, Feb. 14). Edith Wharton's "motor flight" to New York. <u>Lenox News</u>, p. B12.

Article in a Newspaper—Unsigned

Antiques dealers revive downtown economy. (1987, July 3). <u>River Valley Daily</u>, pp. 3–4.

Report

Clayton, D. (1986). Computer regulations (HVCC No. 90–19). Troy, NY: Community Media Center.

Nonprint Sources

Videotape

Pantel, H. (Producer). (1998). <u>Dressmaking history</u>. [Videotape]. Austin, TX: Borderline Network.

Interview

Rice, A. (1990, October 31). "Cemeteries in Southern Culture." [Interview]. New Orleans, LA.

Electronic and Internet Sources

Internet sources are expanding, and as a result, new forms for references are being created. If you do not see the item you want in this list, use the APA Web site to locate the closest possible model. The main point is to provide your readers with the information they need to locate the material to which you are referring. Model your entry on the basic APA format: author; date of the work; title of the work; print publication information if the item was available as a print item first; and identification of the type of source, in square brackets (for example, [Online serial]). Also give the name of the service that provided the information and a document number if one is available. If there is no such number, use the phrase "Retrieved (date) . . . from the World Wide Web" followed by a colon and the exact electronic address (the URL). The URL is underlined, but the period at the end is not. If there are any special log-in instructions, include them. The screen image from the APA's online guide on pages 247 and 248 offers illustrations of how to cite electronic sources even if you cannot find the exact model in your style sheet.

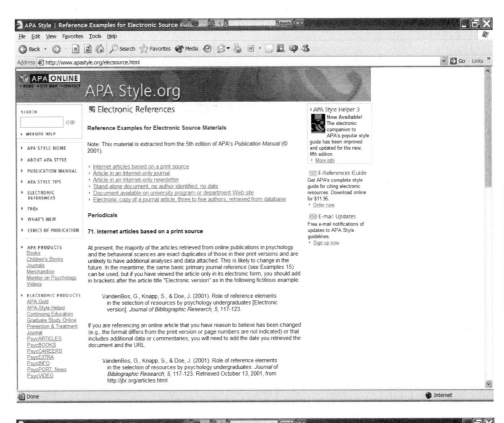

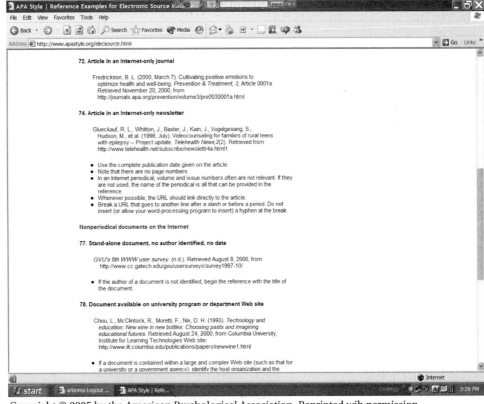

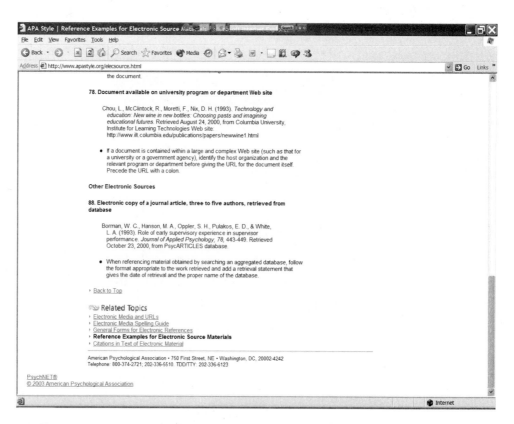

Online Article with a Print Source

Lieberman, K. (1998). Lonely or lovely day? Deciphering penmanship in the
Steinway family manuscripts. La Guardia Review 28, 118–125. Retrieved
October 20, 2000, from the World Wide Web: http://www.lagcc.cuny.
edu/archives/steinway/default.htm.

Article in an Online Journal with No Print Source

Dagner, Ron. (1998, June 26). Uncovering local history in Ohio. [16
paragraphs]. Regional History Forum [Online serial], 1 (Article 004a).
Retrieved January 11, 2000, from the World Wide Web:
http://journals.apa.org/regional/volume1/pre00010002a.html.

E-mail, Contributions to Discussion Lists, and Usenet Groups

Do not include e-mail correspondence as an entry in your references list. Instead,
provide all of the information in the body of the essay as personal communication.
Identify the sender, the subject, and the date of the communication.

Film, Recording, or Videotape

Ivory, J. (Director). (1984). The Bostonians [Video]. New York: Merchant Ivory
Productions.

Television or Radio Program

McCullough, D. (Narrator). (1989). Coney Island. New York: WNET.

Computer Software

Citation [Computer software]. (1996). New York: MLA.

EXERCISE 9.1   **Practicing the Form for APA List of References Entries**

Using your source cards, create an APA references list for five items you are using for your research paper.

EXERCISE 9.2   **Using APA List of References Style**

Look again at the student's Works Cited list in MLA style from Chapter 8. Using the APA models, rewrite each entry in this list in APA form.

Example:

The entry for a certain book in MLA form is:

Holland, Ruth Robins. Mill Child. New York: Crowell, 1970.

Revised into APA, the same entry would appear as follows:

Holland, R. (1970). Mill child. New York: Crowell.

Now convert each of the remaining entries using the APA models in this section as guides.

Works Cited

Barr, Cameron. "India's Education Problems." Christian Science Monitor 11
    May 1992: 14.
Basu, Kaushik. Letter. "The Poor Need Child Labor." New York Times 29 Nov.
    1994: A24.
"Child Labor." The Encyclopedia Americana. 1992 ed.
"Child Labor Around the World: It's Anything But a Pretty Picture." National
    Journal 25 June 1994. N. pag.
The Child Labor Coalition. Rugmark Consumer Campaign: Organizers Kit.
    Washington: National Consumers League, 1995. N. pag.
Daughters of Free Men. By Kate Pfordresher. Pro. Steve Brier. American Social
    History Productions Inc., 1987.
Davis, Rebecca Harding. 1851. Life in the Iron Mills and Other Stories. New
    York: The Feminist Press at The City University of New York, 1985.
Erlich, Reese. "India Battles Illegal Child Labor." Christian Science Monitor 8
    Nov. 1995: 9.
Harkin, Tom. "Put an End to the Exploitation of Child Labor." USA Today Jan.
    1996: 73–5.
Harvey, Pharis J. "Where Children Work: Child Servitude in the Global
    Economy." The Christian Century 5 Apr. 1995: 362–5.
Holland, Ruth Robins. Mill Child. New York: Crowell, 1970.

International Child Labor Study Office. <u>By the Sweat and Toil of Children: The Use of Child Labor in American Imports</u>. Vol. 1. Sept. 1994.

---. <u>By the Sweat and Toil of Children: The Use of Child Labor in U.S. Agricultural Imports & Forced and Bonded Child Labor</u>. Vol. 2. Sept. 1995.

Using APA Style for In-Text Citations

APA style requires that the user include the last name of the author or authors and the year of publication of the source. As noted at the beginning of this chapter, APA style prefers the writer to use the present perfect or the past tense when referring to sources.

The following examples will provide general guidelines for citing sources in the body of the research paper:

A Work with One Author

Lieberman (1986) has described in detail the social importance of the Steinway family to the life of their community.

Because this is a general reference, no specific page citation is required, though it is strongly recommended that the page be added. If the author is not mentioned in the sentence, include both the name and the year in parentheses, separated by a comma.

The social importance of the Steinway family to their community has been well-documented (Lieberman, 1986).

A Work with More than One Author

Pulitzer prize-winning historians Wallace and Burrows (1999) argue that the history of New York City is, in reality, the story of America because of New York's crucial role in immigration and commerce.

If you include a direct quotation, follow this model:

New York remains "a model of rough-hewn cosmopolitanism and multicultural tolerance, with an astonishing mix of peoples living side by side in reasonable harmony" (Wallace & Burrows, 1999, p. xviii).

If there are three to five authors, use all the names in the first reference in the essay, but in later references use only the name of the first author followed by "et al."

Susser, Lucino, Langerud, McMurphy, and Kowalski (1998) have examined the collaborative learning model in the community college classroom.

Increasingly, classroom teachers are using learning communities to incorporate students with nontraditional backgrounds into college-level courses (Susser et al., 1998).

An Author with More Than One Work in One Year

If an author has published two or more works in the same year, use a small letter "a," then "b," then "c," and so forth to put the works in sequence.

(Lieberman, 1997a, 1997b).

The List of References must then contain the same small letters after the year of each corresponding work.

A Work in an Edited Anthology

Use the original date of the work and the name of the author of the work itself, not the editor of the anthology. Use the date the anthology was published. Here, James Baldwin is the author of a short story in an anthology published in 1998:

Baldwin's view of Harlem is evident in the description he wrote of the streets in his story "Sonny's Blues" (1998).

A Work Cited in a Secondary or Indirect Source

If you are referring to a quotation from a source that you read in another source, use the following model:

Lieberman argues that Fiorello La Guardia's three terms as mayor of New York "set a pattern for what all future mayors would become" (as cited in Kressner, 1989, p. 17).

A Work in Which the Author Is Not Named

Include enough information in the essay body to guide your reader to the source. Note that in the in-text citation, capital letters are used on the main words in the title, though they are not used in the List of References.

According to Exploring Transfer: Encouraging Community College Students (1998), financial support is essential to facilitate transfer from two-year to four-year institutions by underrepresented populations.

Electronic or Internet Sources

Include the year of electronic publication in the body of the essay when you refer to the source. If there is a recent update, use that date. If no year of publication is given, include the year in which you retrieved the source.

If you are referring to a film, television, or other nonprint source, identify the main contributor or the originator of the information (director, subject of interview, performer, letter writer), along with the year of production or publication; for example (Ivory, 1984).

A Work by a Corporation or Organization

Use the full title of the institution the first time you refer to the source. After that, employ an abbreviation if one is in common use.

The City University of London (CUL) advocates for admission of "women and minorities into such underrepresented disciplines as biological science and engineering" (CUL, 1997, p. 5).

More Than One Source in the Citation

If you are citing more than one source in the same citation, list the sources in alphabetical order, separated by semicolons (;). If you are listing more than one work by the same author, list these chronologically with the earliest first or, if the works are published in the same year, identified with a, b, c, and so on.

> The struggles of immigrants to become part of the mainstream of American society are fully documented by historians (Lieberman, 1987a, 1987b; Wallace & Burrows, 1999; Zhang, 1987).

E-mail or Personal Communication

> According to actor Al Pacino, Shakespeare's play Richard III is among the most frequently acted of any in the canon of the Bard's works (personal communication, January 11, 2000).

Do not include the source in the List of References at the end of the paper.

Classic Works

You do not need a List of References entry for the Bible or ancient classical works such as Homer's epics. Just include the book and verse number in the text of your essay after the quotation. For other works, use "n.d." for "no date" if none is available. If you use a translation, provide the year of the translation, not the date of the original work, with the abbreviation "trans." before the year.

Other Styles of Documentation

Most beginning researchers will find that understanding MLA documentation is adequate. Some may find that instructors will ask for APA in courses in the social sciences. However, it is important for you to know that as you advance into upper-level courses that require more specialized research papers, you may have to use other styles. Below are brief explanations of several of these. Always ask your instructor which style is preferred if you are in doubt.

CBE Style of Documentation in the Sciences and Mathematics

This style is recommended by the Council of Biology Editors (CBE) for papers in scientific disciplines. For detailed models, consult *Scientific Style and Format: The CBE Manual for Authors, Editors, and Publishers,* 6th ed. (New York: Cambridge UP, 1994).

In the text of the essay, each reference to a source is followed by a superscript number. This is a small number raised slightly above the line.

Here is a sample essay sentence with the superscript:

> One experiment on deer ticks[1] revealed that they carried Lyme disease in 69% of the cases . . .

If you wish to refer to two sources, use the numbers separated by a comma ([1,2]); use a hyphen if there are more than two ([1-4]).

The list of references goes on a separate page at the end of the paper. It is labeled References or Cited References. Entries are numbered in order of their use in the essay. Thus the first source you cite is 1, the second is 2, and so on. The list is not alphabetized as it is in MLA. Each entry begins with an arabic number, followed by a period and a space. Do not indent the first line. Second and subsequent lines are aligned under the first letter of the first line (not under the number). Do not underline or use quotation marks for titles. Journal titles and organization titles are abbreviated. Periods are used between the main parts of the entry. Use a semicolon to separate the name of the publisher and the date of publication of a book. Use a semicolon (without a space) between the date and volume of a journal. If you are citing a book, provide the total number of pages, followed by a space and "p." If you are citing a journal, give the page span, including the first and last pages: 135–6; 215–45; 300–2. Use only as many numbers as are necessary to indicate the pages.

Sample CBE Entries

Book with One Author (Basic Book)

3. Koefman, P. Engineering modern bridges. Los Angeles: UCLA Pr; 1990.
543 p.

This is the third book cited in the essay. Note that there is no period between the initials. The title is not underlined, and only the first letter of the first word of the title is capitalized. 543 is the total number of pages in the book.

Article in a Scholarly Journal

1. James, H. Variations in awareness in genetic transplants. Science 1994;
260: 1445–7.

This journal is paginated by issue. The citation includes the issue number.

Documenting Your Sources Using the Number System

This style is preferred in mathematics, chemistry, computer science, medicine, and physics. In brief, this system requires an in-text number. You can consult *A Manual for Authors of Mathematical Papers*, rev. ed. (Providence, RI: American Mathematical Society, 1990), for additional models. References at the end correspond to the in-text numbers. In other words, the writer puts a number after each reference to a source in the body of the essay. Then, when the essay is finished, a references list is prepared. The references are arranged in the order in which the sources are used in the essay. The in-text citation can be done in two ways if the author is mentioned in the text:

1. The number in the essay may be placed in parentheses (2) or brackets [2] with or without the name of the source.

A recent study by Rodriquez, Greenwich, and Franelli (2) argues that . . .

2. Alternatively, the number may be placed in a superscript.

A recent study by Rodriquez, Greenwich, and Franelli[2] . . .

If the author is not named in the text, there are two ways to handle the in-text citation.

1. Insert both the name and the number in parentheses following the reference.

Further research by astronomers (Rodriquez, 78) has placed the galaxy beyond the black hole . . .

2. Place the number of the source either in a superscript or in parentheses.

Astronomers argue[3]

Astronomers argue (3) . . .

Or provide both the name of the author and the source number in parentheses.

Fruit flies show significant genetic alteration (Rodriquez and Greenwich, 47) . . .

Or, if a specific reference is necessary, include both the superscript and the page number to refer to the source and the exact page on which the information appears.

"Green plants use inhalation of gas to induce enzyme production" (Lynch,[4] p. 678).

The references list is arranged in the order in which the sources are cited in the essay.

Book

4. Lynch, C. In <u>College Physics</u>. 3rd ed.; Sung, C. Ed.: Gyrfalcon Press: New York, 1987; Vol. II, Ch. 6.

Journal

1. Greenwich, G., et al. J. Biol. Chem. **(1995)**, <u>321</u>, 2745–2767.

The year of the journal must be in boldface, as above, or marked for boldface (with a squiggle underline) (1995). Note that dates of books are not put in boldface.

Using the Footnote or Endnote System for Documenting Your Paper

In fields in the humanities other than literature, such as fine arts or music, instructors may ask students to use the system of footnotes or endnotes. In this system of documentation, which derives from *The Chicago Manual of Style,* 14th ed., 1993, you use superscript numbers that correspond to footnotes at the bottom of the page. These footnotes contain full information about the sources. Thus a list of references is not usually needed, although some instructors may ask for one. Alternatively, the footnotes may be presented as endnotes, grouped together on a page or pages at the end of the paper (or chapter). Many word processing programs include software to make the placement of footnotes or endnotes much easier than it was with a typewriter. In most software the computer will insert the superscript and then automatically scroll to the correct place in the text. You must then write out the information for the note in the correct form.

Here is an example of the footnote system and the corresponding notes as they would appear at the bottom of the page or in the endnotes:

Jeremiah Rusconi introduced the use of authentic period sets to Merchant Ivory Productions. Writing about the history of the early years of the stylish company, the location scout and artistic director wrote, "Hollywood was accustomed to building sets. We decided to use real historic sites instead. Not only did these sets provide a vibrant and accurate background for the scripts, but we were able to promote the preservation of several sites as a result of the films' success."[3] *After the Europeans* was nominated for a BAFTA award, the appeal of the historic sets was confirmed.

    3. Jeremiah Rusconi. *Late for Dinner: A Memoir* (Claverack: New York Press, 1993), 27.

    The rules for using footnotes are as follows:

1. Each note must be single-spaced, but use double spacing between notes.

2. Use the Tab key to indent five spaces at the beginning of each note.

3. Start the first note with 1. and continue to number consecutively until the end of the essay.

4. All notes that appear on a given page must have the corresponding footnote placed at the bottom of the same page.

5. Place a line (———) or leave extra space by triple-spacing between the end of the essay page and the footnotes.

    Here are some of the most commonly used formats for footnotes:

Basic Book

1. Miranda Stern, <u>Elizabeth Bowen: Houses and Novels</u> (Lincoln: University of Nebraska Press, 1989), 89.

Article in a Journal

2. David Whitbeck, "Hudson River Villas: Postmodern Design in a Pastoral Setting," <u>River Valley Review of Architecture</u> 46 (1989), 43–51.

Article in a Magazine

3. Fishbeiner, Randolph, "Ravenna Mosaics," <u>Art News</u>, 15 January 1999, 41–47.

Article in a Newspaper

4. Speyer, Anne, "Nature's Classroom: Teaching Ecology in the Woods," <u>The Chronicle of Higher Education</u>, 9 October 2001, sec. B, pp. B34–35.

Government Document (Online)

5. United States Congress, Senate, Sexual Harassment Statutes of 1997 [database online] (107th Cong. Senate Bill 13, 11 January 1999 [cited 4 March 2000]); available on the World Wide Web at <u>http://Thomas.loc.gov/cgi-bin/query/3?C107:S.13/</u>.

CD-ROM

6. "Immigration," in <u>Compton's Interactive Encyclopedia</u> [CD-ROM] (Softkey Multimedia, 1998 [cited 11 April 1999]).

Online Journal

7. Phyllis Harris, "Exhibiting Post-colonial History," in <u>Museum News</u>, par. 7 [online journal] (vol. 34.3, March 1997 [cited 9 March 1998]); available from World Wide Web at <u>http://museum.news.cuny.edu/scripts/VanSlyck.html.</u>

Online Magazine

8. Catherine Leung, "Wharton: Portraits of a Gilded Age Celebrity," in <u>Women's Biography</u>, par. 35 [online magazine] (1997 [cited 14 April 1998]); available from World Wide Web at <u>http://www.biography.cc.emory.edu/articles/1997/0978-text.htm.</u>

Listserv (E-mail Discussion Group)

9. Rosemarie Capone, "Cosmetic Appeal" [electronic bulletin board] (10 May 1998 [cited 11 March 1999]); available from <u>listserv@CUNYTALK.cuny.edu</u>.

Encyclopedia

10. <u>The World Book Encyclopedia</u>, 1979 ed., s.v. "Wharton, Edith."

Film

11. <u>The Golden Bowl</u>. Merchant Ivory Productions, 2000.

Work of Music

12. Wolfgang A. Mozart, <u>Sonata #4</u>.

Preparing a Source List for a Paper Using Footnotes or Endnotes

Some instructors may ask you to include a list of the references you used for general background or for material that informed your paper but was not directly referred to in the essay. This list may be labeled "Selected Bibliography," "Works Cited," or "Sources Consulted." If you have prepared complete footnotes or endnotes, such a source list is probably repetitive. Ask your teacher whether it is needed and, if so, which heading is preferred.

This list is presented in alphabetical order, by last name of the author. The basic forms are as follows:

Basic Book

Brodie, Fawn. <u>Thomas Jefferson: An Intimate Biography</u>. New York: Avon, 1987.

Journal Article

French, Isabella. "Slave Quarters at Monticello." <u>Virginia Quarterly</u> 115
    (1987): 456–478.

Newspaper

Friehopher, Frederick, Jr. "Is There Truth in Sally Hemmings Rumors?" <u>Times</u>
    <u>Union</u>, 16 June 1989, sec. 5, p. 9.

Sample Pages from Research Papers in MLA and APA Styles

MLA Style First Page from Student Essay (without a title page)

Koefman 1

Jonathan J. Koefman
Professor C. Macheski
English 103.03
24 October 2005

Child Labor: Crisis in the Global Village

Industrialization breeds many diseases, one of which is child labor. In
the 1800s child labor was one of several issues causing controversy in

APA Style with Title Page and First Page of the Same Student Paper (title page with running head and page number)

Crisis 1

Child Labor:
Crisis in the Global Village

Jonathan J. Koefman

La Guardia Community College

First Page of the Same Paper in APA Style

Crisis 2

Child Labor: Crisis in the Global Village
Industrialization breeds many diseases, one of which is child labor. In the 1800s child labor was one of several issues causing controversy in

---

Sample In-text Citation Using MLA (from Koefman 3)

The Indian Commerce Ministry says that child labor is essential for India's export industries to remain competitive. Myron Weiner, in an interview with a top Indian Labor Ministry official, writes, "They tell me that the carpet industry would collapse if children were not employed" (49). The extra cost of employing adults would subsequently reduce the competitiveness of the final product on world markets. India's carpet industry expanded in the 1970s when Iran outlawed the labor of children in its carpet industry. In an article in The Christian Century, Pharis J. Harvey writes that a large portion of Iran's market was lost to India. The Indian Commerce Ministry now fears that a ban would cause India to lose its market share to other countries that continue to use child labor (364).

Same Paragraph in APA Style

The Indian Commerce Ministry says that child labor is essential for India's export industries to remain competitive. Myron Weiner (1995) wrote in an interview with a top Indian Labor Ministry official, "They tell me that the carpet industry would collapse if children were not employed" (p. 49). The extra cost of employing adults would subsequently reduce the competitiveness of the final product on world markets. India's carpet industry expanded in the 1970s when Iran outlawed the labor of children in its carpet industry. In an article in The Christian Century, Pharis J. Harvey (1995) has written that a large portion of Iran's market was lost to India. The Indian Commerce Ministry now fears that a ban would cause India to lose its market share to other countries that continue to use child labor (p. 364).

CHECKLIST   DOCUMENTING YOUR PAPER IN APA AND OTHER DOCUMENTATION STYLES

❑ Have you chosen the appropriate style of documentation for your essay, on the basis of your teacher's instructions or the discipline in which you are working?

❑ Have you carefully checked the punctuation for each entry?

❑ Do the in-text references match the list of references at the end of the paper?

❑ If you are using footnotes, are they typed in superscripts (smaller raised numbers)?

❑ Have you carefully proofread your work?

APA

CHAPTER **10**

Preparing and Proofreading the Final Draft

■ **Formatting the Final Manuscript**

■ **Research Mechanics**

■ **Reviewing for Style**

■ **Revising the Paper**

In Chapter 7 you completed a first draft, integrating your research with your own work. In the past two chapters you have been learning to document your research according to the very specific style of the field for which your paper was written. Now it is time to revise your paper—to put it into final shape so it expresses what you want to say clearly and forcefully and so it follows the many rules of research writing that determine the finished form of your paper.

Formatting the Final Manuscript

Before you begin your final draft, you need to know the required format. Your teacher may give you a format to follow; however, if she or he doesn't, there are customary formats you need to know:

1. **Paper**   Use 8 1/2 × 11 plain white bond (or plain white lined if you are handwriting the paper). Write or type on one side of the page only.

2. **Print**   Print neatly and legibly in black ink. If you type your paper on a computer, use 12 point standard black type. Do not use fancy types or all capital letters.

3. **Title page**   If your instructor asks for MLA style, your title page and first page are 1. In the upper-right-hand corner of the paper one-half inch from the top, and in the left-hand corner of the page, one inch from the top, put the information shown below (an example follows the general layout).

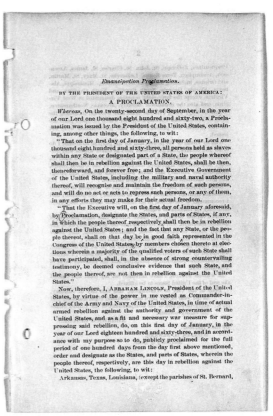

Handwritten version, edited draft, and published version of Abraham Lincoln's Emancipation Proclamation, issued January 1, 1863

Your last name 1 (for first page)

Your name
Your professor's name
Course and section number
Date, military style

The title is centered below this information.

Griffith 1

Helen Griffith
Professor Erber
French Literature 30, Section 3
5 October 2005

Marguerite Duras and the Theme of Loneliness

If your instructor requires APA format you will have to do a separate title page, with the information below, centered about one-third of the way down the page. (An example follows.)

Title is capitalized and centered
(see Chapter 9 for the use of capital letters in titles).
Your name
Either college name or course name and section
Professor's name (if course name is required)
Date

The Quality of Mercy
Randolph Hart
Biology 220, Section 4
23 January 2005

4. **Page numbers**   Pages should be numbered. Put numbers in the upper-right-hand corner of the paper, after your last name. (Your instructor may not want you to number the first page.) Numbering on a computer can be done electronically, through the use of a header or insert.

5. **Margins**   Leave one inch all around. Leave the right margin ragged, although set for one inch (do not block). Indent five spaces for paragraphs.

6. **Spacing**   Double-space everything, including long quotations, Works Cited, and Endnotes, unless your instructor tells you otherwise. Do not put extra spaces between paragraphs.

7. **Binding**   If your teacher does not state a preference, clip your pages together with a clip. Do not staple, and do not use a plastic folder.

8. **Copy**   Make a copy of everything you hand in. Do not throw away your notes or your copies of research articles. You may need them for revision or authentication.

Research Mechanics

Underlining

The underline is a message to the typesetter to use italic type when setting the type for the word. Both underlines and italics are acceptable, but whichever type you use, you must be consistent.

- Underlines or italics are used for books or complete works, such as the names of journals, magazines, newspapers, films, TV programs, and works of art.

- Underlines or italics are used for foreign words or expressions.

- Do *not* underline sacred texts, editions, shorter works published in texts (such as poems, short stories, and essays), chapter titles, TV or radio episodes, or unpublished works.

Quotation Marks

1. The most common use of the quotation mark is to signal when you are using someone's exact words. These marks signal the beginning and end of such words.

2. Quotation marks are also used around the title of a shorter work or a work within a larger text, such as a short story, poem, essay, or article.

   Here are some things to remember about quotation marks:

   - Check your source carefully. Only the writer's exact words should be quoted.

   - Quotation marks come in pairs. When you begin a quotation, you must end it: "_____."

   - Do not confuse double quotation marks "_____" with single marks '_____.' Single quotation marks are used inside double quotation marks when the quoted source is referring to something *else* that is in quotation marks—for example, a short story. John Wight once wrote, "There is no short story more poignant than 'Home Poem.'"

3. Use proper punctuation before quotation marks. Use a colon after a complete sentence followed by a quotation, which should begin with a capital letter.

   Ginny Forster loved to travel: "I find it invigorating," she said.

   - After introductory phrases like *he said* and *she explained,* use a comma and begin the quotation with a capital letter.

She said, "Dinner is served at 8:00."

- Quotations that are not set off with introductions need no introductory punctuation and should be woven into the sentence.

Ian Kershaw describes Ron Rosenbaum's biography of Hitler as "intriguing," as well as "thought-provoking" and "intelligent."

- End punctuation marks, except the colon and semicolon, go inside the quotation marks. You might have to add a comma or period if your sentence requires it, as in the previous example, even if the section of the quotation you are using did not have it. The exception is question marks and exclamation points, which go outside the quotation marks when they refer to the whole sentence, not just to the words in quotation marks.

What could Polonius have meant when he said, "To thine own self be true"?

4. When you place a quotation in the middle of a sentence, change the capital letter to a lowercase letter so it fits in with the sentence.

I think "the quality of mercy" is the question here.

5. In writing dialogue, indent five spaces and use a different pair of quotation marks each time the speaker changes:

"I need to travel more often," Rowena cried.

"You don't need to travel. You need to settle down."

6. Ellipses (see Chapter 5) are used to show that you have removed material from a quotation. Use a line of spaced dots to show when you have omitted a paragraph from a long quotation.

7. Quotations of more than four lines do not use quotation marks. They are block quoted.

8. Do not use quotation marks with indirect quotations.

My father told my mother that she must marry him or he would sing outside her door every night.

Capitalization

In research, as in other kinds of writing, you must capitalize proper nouns (and adjectives). Specifically pertinent for research papers: capitalize the first letter of most words in titles, including the first and last word but excluding coordinating conjunctions, articles, and prepositions.

Bill Bryson wrote *Notes from a Small Island*.

Abbreviations

Spell out all words in the text of the essay except commonly used abbreviations and acronyms, and then, on first use, give the full term with the abbreviation in parentheses.

City University of New York (CUNY).

Abbreviations should be used in the documentation (Works Cited, Bibliography, etc.). Be certain you know the correct abbreviation or acronym by looking it up in the dictionary. Never use the ampersand (&) to abbreviate the word *and* (unless it is an official part of a name, such as Steinway & Sons).

Accent Marks

Include all foreign accent marks (as in, for example, résumé). If your computer or typewriter doesn't have them, insert them by hand.

Statistics, Graphics, Photographs, and Artwork

If you use a graph, photograph, chart, work of art, cartoon, or statistics that you took from a source such as a Web site, a newspaper, a journal, or a book, you must give credit to the source, just as though it were a sentence or a paragraph you were quoting. One way to cite is to put a caption directly under the picture or graph and identify the source. You should then include the source in which you found the picture in your Works Cited list if it is a print or electronic source, just as you would if you had quoted from it. For example, if you wanted to include a portrait of Edith Wharton in your essay, you would caption the painting as follows: Source: The American Academy of Arts and Letters, New York City. You must tell where it came from unless you painted the portrait of Wharton yourself, and even then you need to give yourself credit! Some sources, both print and illustration, are available in what is called *public domain*. This means that the copyright or legal ownership has expired, and anyone may use the image without paying a permission fee. However, the user must still cite and give credit to the source from which the text or image was taken. If you are not sure where the source originally came from, and you got the photo or graph from a secondary source, it is safer to caption it to avoid plagiarism.

EXERCISE 10.1   Reviewing for Research Mechanics

Correct the following sentences, where necessary.

1. I read in PEOPLE MAGAZINE that the film "The House of Sand and Fog" is finally out on tape.

2. My daughter was assigned *The Nick Adams Stories* for her summer reading.

3. My biology professor often said, "If you really like biology read *The Lives of the Cell* and you'll be able to understand the philosophy of biology.

4. Carol Abell wrote in the high school paper, the *Argus,* "When I read Hemingway's short story, 'Hills like white elephants' I wanted to cry.

5. Did he say, "I think your photographs are wonderfully moving?"

6. I have often told him that "he is the strongest man I know."

7. I can never remember who wrote: *The Scarlet Letter.*

8. She joined the Army ten years ago and is now a Colonel.

9. When I first heard the Beatles sing about "Love, love, love" I immediately sang along.

10. Polonius instructed his son Laertes, "To Thine Own Self Be True."

Reviewing for Style

Audience and Purpose, Voice and Tone

In earlier chapters we discussed the question of audience and purpose and how the identity of the people who will read your essay—that is, your potential audience—helps determine which sources to use in your essay. You would use different kinds of sources in a memorandum read by your boss at work than you would in an academic paper for your professor. The language you use in your essay, your "voice," is another facet of your paper that is determined by your audience and purpose. That memorandum needs to have a professional tone; it should be serious and brief, perhaps with individual points bulleted in the margin. Your research paper also needs to be serious in tone and concise about what it is trying to say, but it should make its point with more care. Though equally objective, it also needs to be reflective.

The following are some things to remember when revising your essay for voice and tone:

1. To make your writing more lively, do not use the passive voice, where something is done *to* the subject. Rather, use the active voice, where the subject does something.

   Two books were read this term. (passive)

   The class read two books this term. (active)

2. So that the tone of your writing will be more objective, do not use the personal pronoun *I* or preface your remarks with *in my opinion* or *I think*. Just state what you want to say directly.

3. Do not use slang, jargon, or inflated, overly formal language. For every slang word, there is a perfectly good alternative in standard use (*mad = very; chill = relax*). Jargon tends to obscure meaning for all but the initiated. Inflated language, like the use of long, Latinate words, tends to make the tone of the writing stiff. Also, too often these words are used incorrectly because the writer is unfamiliar with them and is using them to impress rather than to communicate. Remember that research writing must impress by its ideas and how well they are presented, not by its use of fancy words that will only serve to draw attention to themselves and distract the reader from the ideas.

   Her friend approached her with a profession of conciliation, but she negated his efforts.

   Much better: Her friend tried to apologize, but she would not let him.

4. Sometimes specific terminology or subject-specific references must be used—particularly in the sciences, but also in culture-specific writing. Define or explain these references, where necessary. Knowing your audience will help you determine how much you need to define. For example, one of the authors has written essays on Australian literature. When she writes for an American audience, she must tell her readers that the Miles Franklin Award is one of the most prestigious literary awards in Australia. When her audience consists of Australians or scholars of Australian literature, she would be insulting them if she explained the award. Scientific or mathematical terminology is often used to explain certain occurrences or equations to others in the field. If it is used in a popular journal or news report, it must be accompanied by an explanation; otherwise, most readers won't understand it.

5. Write with authority. You are the author. Do not hesitate or overly qualify your ideas with words like *might, perhaps, somewhat, maybe, in my opinion,* or *I think.* Of course, if you are truly unsure you must say so, but in general, you should have come to a conclusion about your topic and should be prepared to write with assurance about it.

6. Be careful to avoid using sexist or other discriminatory language. The language you use must not offend anyone or make anyone feel uncomfortable. Make sure your language is gender neutral and inoffensive to people of different cultures. Words such as *chairman, postman, fireman, master teacher, actress,* and *girl* (for a grown woman) should be replaced by synonyms that are more appropriate.

EXERCISE 10.2   Reviewing for Voice and Tone

Look at the following sentences and evaluate whether the voice and/or tone is appropriate for a research paper. Rewrite those you feel are not appropriate.

1. When Howard Adams published his first novel, he was just a kid.

2. When Adams received the Pulitzer Prize, no one was surprised.

3. The proliferation of his tomes was veritably prodigious.

4. It is, perhaps, somewhat difficult to understand how he managed to write so much and so well.

5. Many critics praised his extraordinary control of language.

6. In my opinion, his parents exerted a great influence on him.

7. He wrote so well that Brian Gallagher called him a "prodigy exemplified."

8. It is assumed that his early works were quite impressive.

9. I believe his best work, *The Veil of Winter,* was also a popular success.

_____

_____

10. It is unfortunate that he died so young and did not have a chance to fulfill his potential.

_____

_____

Revising the Paper

One of the best ways to learn to recognize good writing is to critique model papers or parts of papers to evaluate how a particular aspect of writing was handled in context. The following examples from research papers are not perfect: they use and at times misuse research methodology to give you a chance to practice before you try your hand at critiquing your own writing.

Introductions

We'll start with introductions, because they set the tone for your paper. Here are some things to look for in a good introduction and thesis (see Chapter 7). The introduction should

1. provide a good summary of what the paper will be about

2. arouse the reader's interest

3. use a lively writing style

4. end with a clearly focused thesis

EXERCISE 10.3   Analyzing Introductions

Below are three model research paper introductions. Look at each and answer the following questions:

1. What is the thesis of this paper?

2. How does the introduction prepare the reader for the thesis? Is it effective? appropriate? sufficient?

3. How can it be improved?

To help you with this exercise, paragraph 2 is evaluated below.

Paragraph 1

Many women immigrants suffer while and after immigrating, but no one suffered more than the immigrants who came to the United States during the 1900s. These immigrants suffered for many reasons, but the main reason most of the immigrant women suffered in the 1900s was the physical examinations. These examinations were being held at Ellis Island, which was the principal federal immigration station in the United States from 1892 to 1954. In the following essay, I, Luis Menendez, will write about the history of Ellis Island before and after it became the principal Federal immigration site.

I will also write about the examinations conducted at Ellis Island for the admission of immigrants to the United States. I will also write about the suffering of women at Ellis Island and why this examination was a big price to pay for some women.

_____

_____

_____

Paragraph 2

Industrialization breeds many diseases, one of which is child labor. In the 1800s child labor was one of several issues causing controversy in the United States. From the beginning of this century major changes have been made from the result of new legislation won by anti-child-labor activists. Child labor has been almost eradicated in the United States, but it is a recurring nightmare for millions of pairs of hands throughout the globe. They work incessantly to fuel the industrialization of their country, obtaining nothing but physical and mental degradation. By looking back on ways America rid itself of child labor, developing countries can avoid making the same mistakes.

_____

_____

_____

Paragraph 3

Statistics show that in this century some fifty million immigrants have come to the U.S. seeking freedom and economic opportunity (Briggs & Moore 77). Nevertheless, callous immigrants' opponents have called these hard-working people "burdens." They do not realize that the so-called "burdens" contribute prominently to the economy of this country. Immigrants are highly entrepreneurial; they contribute to the labor market of the country. Moreover, many children of immigrants become professionals, contributing in high-technology industries and adding to tax revenues.

_____

_____

_____

Evaluation of Paragraph 2

The thesis of this introduction is clear. By looking back on ways America rid itself of child labor, developing countries can avoid making the same mistakes. The writer gives a brief history of child labor in this country and effectively links it to today's global problems of child labor, which culminates in the thesis. My one problem with this introduction is that it should be more interesting. The writer should enliven his or her style with specific examples, details, and descriptive adjectives.

_____

Sources

In Chapters 5 and 7 we discussed when and when not to use quotations and practiced integrating quotations into a research paper. Locating the material is only part of the process; knowing when and how to use this material in your paper so that it supports your hypothesis and accurately identifies your sources is an art that becomes more refined with practice.

EXERCISE 10.4   Analyzing Sources

Read the excerpts from student papers below and evaluate them. Ask yourself the following questions, as appropriate:

1. Is there a topic sentence in the paragraph?

2. Does the writer introduce the quotation and blend it into the paragraph?

3. Is the direct quotation put in quotation marks and punctuated correctly?

4. Is there a clear paraphrase of the quotation?

5. Has the writer analyzed the quoted passage and connected it to the topic sentence?

6. Does the source have authority?

As in the previous exercise, we will evaluate a paragraph, this time paragraph 3, to help you understand this assignment.

Paragraph 1

The Steinway family was a particularly patriarchal and misogynous one. According to their 1861 partnership agreement, ". . . the family modified the co-partnership agreement to restrict the rights of Steinway women: they could inherit the value of their husband's share in the business but could not become partners of Steinway & Sons (Lieberman 35). In other words, the nineteenth-century Steinway men were afraid that Steinway women would take over the family business. However, approximately a hundred and sixty years later, Julia D. Steinway would step forward as the most influential and powerful of all Steinway women. So great was her unofficial position that she was called "duchess of Steinway Hall" during her prosperous reign during the 1920s (Lieberman 165). Still, although Julia was very influential within the family and business, she still couldn't have fully recognized power because she was a woman.

_____

_____

_____

_____

_____

Paragraph 2

All parties involved in a sexual harassment lawsuit can be affected, from the victim and the business that is being used to the accused perpetrator. We already know how it affects the victim; economically it affects the business, and it can have devastating effects for the perpetrator if he (or she) is falsely accused. Businesses being sued are paying out large amounts of money to victims of sexual harassment to make up for the mistakes made by a particular employee who didn't know where to draw the line. As Michael Losey confirms in his article "Sexual Harassment: A Growing Workplace Dilemma" "Jurors awarded [in 1993] 1,546 employees $25,200,000 in monetary benefits from their employers to cover back pay, remedial relief, damages, promotions lost, and reinstatements (38). As for how it can affect the accused perpetrator depends on whether or not he (or she) actually sexually harassed a female (or male) employee or co-worker. In his article "The Joke that Killed" Christopher Byron speaks about a man by the name of Holt Euliss who killed himself as a result of being falsely accused of sexual harassment. According to Byron, many people who knew Euliss claimed he was not the type of man who would sexually harass a woman. During the investigation the woman who came forward with the allegations "... tried to retract her complaint but the company wouldn't let her" (89).

_____

_____

_____

_____

_____

Paragraph 3

On the other hand, marriages increased after the war because victims sought to avoid loneliness and replace people they lost because of the Holocaust. When they had kids, they often named their children after relatives and friends that had died in the Holocaust. Even sights, smells, or certain noises brought back memories of the horrible treatment they had received under Nazi rule. People expressed their pain in different ways. Some refused to talk about the Holocaust. Some talked incessantly about their trials and tribulations to their children or family members "to impress on them the importance of memory" (7).

_____

_____

_____

_____

_____

Evaluation of Paragraph 3

Paragraph 3 needs much revision. It does not have a clear topic sentence. The quotation is not clearly introduced, and the paraphrased material is not documented. It reads like a summary of one person's ideas, and if it is, it needs to be introduced and documented as such—and integrated into a paragraph that includes more of the writer's own ideas.

_____

The Conclusion

The main thing to remember when reviewing your conclusion is that you must not add any new information or introduce a new subject. Use your conclusion as a way of summing up, restating, and putting your ideas in a larger context.

EXERCISE 10.5 **Reviewing Conclusions**

Look at the three conclusions below and answer the following questions for each:

1. Can you identify the thesis of the paper from this conclusion?

2. What technique is the writer using to conclude the paper?

3. Is there a sense of completion in the conclusion? Why or why not?

4. What would you do to improve the conclusion?

See the evaluation of paragraph 2 below.

Paragraph 1

If both parent and adolescent do it harmoniously, growing up will be less confusing and there will be fewer conflicts between an adolescent and her parents. Annie and her mother started out their relationship right, but along the way, during that period called adolescence, things went wrong. This left Annie feeling that she didn't love her mother anymore. It doesn't have to be that way forever. Annie left her parents' home to go to college in a place far away from her home, but the relationship is still capable of being saved. If only one of them started to communicate with the other about what happened and both were willing to admit mistakes, they would be able to save their wonderful relationship with one another. It might not be as wonderful as the one they had before, but it would surely be better than the one they had at the end of the novel.

_____

_____

_____

_____

Paragraph 2

Most Americans find it hard to believe that their own government could be involved in a crime as devious as this one. Based upon my findings, it is certain the actions of the CIA, Secret Service, and FBI were treasonous. In my opinion they were all involved in President Kennedy's death, some more than others.

_____

_____

_____

_____

Paragraph 3

By raising the bottom end of the socio-economic scale, all societies, whether national or global, will benefit. Some forms of poverty are likely to remain, but a poverty in which parents rely on child labor for survival would disappear. Through national legislation the United States was able to make headway against child labor. International standards of education and employment would extend this progress further. This principle was, and still is, applicable to all developing nations. As Sydney Schanberg writes, "a child's pain is the same everywhere" (43). The remedy is also universal.

_____

_____

_____

_____

Evaluation of Paragraph 2

Paragraph 2 ends rather abruptly. You can guess at the thesis of the paper but not be completely certain. The author is trying to do a short, terse summary but needs to add more material, more depth. The conclusion appears to be introducing new information ("some more than others"), which will only leave the reader confused.

In-Text Citations

As we have discussed throughout this book (particularly in Chapters 8 and 9), when you use a source in your paper that has been written or expressed or compiled by someone else, you must give the author credit. When you give credit in the text, it is called an in-text citation. It can be a rather frustrating task, for you must recognize when you need a citation, determine what particular kind of citation you need, and then painstakingly copy the correct form for that citation.

EXERCISE 10.6   Revising In-Text Citations

Using the models we supplied in Chapters 8 and 9 for the major kinds of citations, read the following three excerpts from student research papers and correct them as much as possible according to either MLA or APA format, as noted. Then answer these questions:

1. What would you have to know that isn't already there in order to document these citations correctly?

2. Which model would you follow? (for example, the form for a book with one author)

When you have completed this exercise, go over it with your instructor.

Paragraph 1 (MLA)

An article in the New York Times states, "When World War II began in September 1939 with Hitler's invasion of Poland, Warsaw was home to nearly 400,000 Jews, second only to New York City. Early the next year, the Nazis forced the Jews to wear white armbands marked with the Star of David. By October of 1940, the Nazis had created a ghetto and pushed the Jews into the area, which was sealed with a 10-foot wall (Perlez p2).

Paragraph 2 (APA)

Some people knew about Henry Lee Lucas's childhood. Joel Norris states, "A neighbor's report confirmed Lucas' story about his early years" (110). There was also a teacher that gave him food and dressed him in pants [to replace the dresses his father made him dress in]. She felt sorry for him because the kids would make fun of him. I believe Lucas's life of crime could have been prevented. I think a neighbor could have reported what was going on. Maybe the teacher could have said something to somebody. As Joel Norris states, "Had Lucas's schoolteacher, Annie Hall, been able to help Henry without fear of reprisal, he might have become a different person."

Paragraph 3 (Other)

According to the Equal Employment Opportunity Commission, the definition of sexual harassment is "unwelcome advances, requests for sexual favors and other verbal or physical contacts that 1) become a condition of employment, 2) become the basis employment decisions, 3) interfere with the employee's work performance or create an intimidating, hostile or offensive work environment" (1991). Sexual harassment is now a household word. This is an issue of such magnitude that it strongly affects all parties involved. Michael Losey points out in his article "Sexual Harassment: A Growing Workplace Dilemma" that "In 1993, ten thousand sexual harassment complaints were resolved by the Equal Employment Opportunity Commission" (39). In "The Nature of the Beast" an article written by Anita Hill, she states that "42 to 90 percent of women will experience some form of harassment during their employed lives" (424). Sexual harassment can have devastating emotional effects on the victim and can be avoided if the perpetrator just decides to "keep his (or her) hands to himself (or herself)."

The Works Cited List

As we saw in Chapters 8 and 9, like adding in-text citations, compiling the list of works that you have cited in your paper (Works Cited) involves learning to identify and copy the correct form. There is no mystery to it.

EXERCISE 10.7   Analyzing Works Cited Lists

Following are three Works Cited lists. Check the Works Cited models in Chapter 8 and decide which items on this list are correct and, if not, say what is wrong with them. (Evaluate list 1 for MLA style, list 2 for APA style, and list 3 for another style of your choosing.) When you have completed this exercise, look it over with your instructor.

Works Cited List 1

Catron, Linda S. "Childhood Stress and Adaptation to Divorce: A Shaping Condition." Divorce 1991: 25–29

Kantzler, Mel. "Seeing the Person in the Child." Creative Divorce 1973, 1974: 192–193

Everett, Craig A. "Custodial Patterns and Influences." The Consequences of Divorce 1991: 297

Macoby and Mnookin. Dividing the Children 1992

Alexander Plateris. Divorces and Divorce rates, United States 1978

_____

_____

Works Cited List 2

"Unwed Moms: It's Not Just a Teen Thing," U.S. News and World Report
    19 June 1995, p. 17.

_____

_____

Benson, Peter L. "Family Patterns Today." "Education Digest" Feb. 1995: 47.

_____

_____

McLanahan, Sara, and Garry Sandefur. "Growing Up With A Single Parent: What
    hurts, what helps." New England Journal of Medicine, Leon Eisenberg,
    M.D. Cambridge, MA. Harvard University Press. 6 April 1995: 196.

_____

_____

Works Cited List 3

Aiken, Lewis R. Later Life. Philadelphia: Saunders, 1978.

_____

_____

Fannie, Flagg. Fried Green Tomatoes At The Whistle Stop Café. New York:
    Random House, 1988.

_____

_____

Yurick, Gera Ann., et al. The Aged Person And The Nursing Process. Norwalk:
    Connecticut, 1984.

_____

_____

EXERCISE 10.8 Using a Checklist to Revise Your Paper

Now is the time to revise your own paper. Peer critiquing is done in groups of three or four, and if you have others available, it is a good way of gaining insight into your writing. However, you may also do a critique of your own paper. The point is to examine your paper in terms of how well it meets your assignment. If you review your paper carefully and systematically, you should be able to find trouble spots and clear them up. Use the Research Paper Checklist below to evaluate each element of your paper.

RESEARCH PAPER CHECKLIST

AREAS TO LOOK AT	WHAT TO LOOK FOR
I. Structure and content	
A. Introduction	Is it effective? (See Chapter 7.) _____
B. Hypothesis	Does it answer the research question? Is it strong and clear? (See Chapter 3.) _____
C. Organization	Is it logical? appropriate? (See Chapter 6.) _____
D. Development	Does the text develop the thesis? (See Chapter 7.) _____
E. Integration of quotations	Are they done smoothly and clearly? (See Chapter 7.) _____
F. Conclusion	Is it effective? (See Chapter 7.) _____
II. Documentation	
A. Quality of research	Is it appropriate? (See Chapter 4.) _____
B. Quantity of research	Is there enough? (See Chapter 4.) _____
C. Quotation form	Is it correct? (See Chapter 10.) _____
D. In-text documentation	Is the form correct? (See Chapters 8 and 9.) _____
E. Works Cited list	Is the form correct? (See Chapters 8 and 9.) _____
III. Style	Has the writer looked for audience, purpose, voice, and tone? _____
IV. Format	Has the writer followed guidelines for format? (See Chapter 10.) _____

A Warning about Spelling Checkers, Grammar Checkers, and Style Checkers

Depending on your computer's platform, you will have available to you spelling, grammar, and/or style checkers that will highlight a word, phrase, or sentence; give you suggestions for alternatives; and, in the case of grammar and style, tell you why the checker marked something as incorrect. That sounds helpful, and many students use these tools despite their professors' warnings. Like your professors, we are warning you to handle these programs with care. They do not always give accurate information. In the case of spelling, the checker may tell you a word is spelled correctly because a word exists that is spelled that way, although it is not the word you had meant to use. (For example, you may write, "They're home was made of wood." "They're" would not be highlighted as incorrect, although it is spelled incorrectly in the context of your sentence.) In addition, the grammar program is often inaccurate. It may tell you something is wrong that isn't, or won't highlight something that is wrong. Remember: the computer does not have a brain You have the brain and must let the computer help you use it. Be careful!

Step 20   **PROOFREADING YOUR OWN PAPER**

CHECKLIST PROOFREADING

Here are some ways to proofread. Pick one or more when you read over your paper.

1. Take a blank piece of paper and move it slowly down the paper, from beginning to end.

2. Take a blank piece of paper and move it slowly up the paper, from the end to the beginning.

3. Read your paper aloud, *slowly.*

4. Read through your paper again, focusing on those areas that you know you have trouble with.

5. Read your paper to a friend.

6. Do all the above, put your paper aside, and proofread it again a day later.

Casebook

Part Two contains readings on a variety of topics from a number of disciplines. Along with more material about **Lizzie Borden** and **The _Titanic_ Disaster,** introduced in Chapters 1 and 5, this casebook includes readings from three different subject areas: **Issues in War and Peace, Global Health,** and **Food Controversies**. The essays, news articles, poems, play, abstracts from memoirs, and fiction provided in this casebook can suggest a direction for your own research. We do not mean for these works to replace your own investigation. Instead, these readings can be the beginning of your list of sources for a general subject or specific topic that you want to pursue. Your teacher may even want to use the casebook to guide you through a short research project before you begin your work on a long essay. We've chosen readings that are timely, controversial, and interesting so they will invite excitement, discussion, and further research—our real goals.

CASEBOOK

Lizzie Borden

In Chapter 1 you read about Lizzie Borden of Fall River, Massachusetts, who was acquitted of killing her father and stepmother on August 4, 1892, despite overwhelming evidence of her guilt. In this section of the casebook we have included four newspaper articles published in the *New York Times* during the time that the case was being investigated and argued. This will give you a feeling for how Lizzie's contemporaries responded to her.

STORY OF A GREAT CRIME

DOUBLE MURDER WHICH LED TO LIZZIE BORDEN'S ARREST.

How Her Father and His Wife Were Found Hacked to Death with an Axe—Clues Which Led to Nothing—Family Disputes Believed to Have Led to the Killing.

1 FALL RIVER, MASS., Aug. 13.—The double murder of Andrew J. Borden and his wife, culminating as it has in the arrest of his younger daughter, Lizzie Borden, is one of the most extraordinary and mysterious criminal episodes of the century. Who was there among those who read the first story of that tragedy who did not feel his imagination thrill with the recollection of Poe's strange and morbidly-fascinating tale of the murders in the Rue Morgue? In the nature of things murder is committed for but one, or at most two, of four motives—jealousy, revenge, self-gain, and that other reason suggested by De Quincey in his essay on "Murder as a Fine Art." The person who kills is either a maniac or a murderer.

2 The circumstances surrounding the assassination of Borden and his wife, who was Lizzie's stepmother, were such as to astound those who would pounce, offhand, upon a motive. Borden was a rich and pious skinflint, aged seventy-six years, whose probity was equal to his thrift. He had not led a public life, he had no known enemy who, it could be conjectured, would go to the extent of killing him, much less his wife, and when the mutilated bodies of the couple were discovered, in their own house, shortly before noon on Aug. 4, the police and the public were utterly at a loss for a motive, and in the intense excitement that overwhelmed the community they turned to one another in helpless astonishment and horror.

3 The body of Borden was found on a velvet sofa in the parlor of the house. His head had been literally hacked to pieces. There were seven long gashes on his face and skull, some of them an inch and a half deep through the flesh and bone. In the "spare" bedchamber on the second floor was discovered the body of Mrs. Borden, who was sixty-seven years old. There was at first no sight of blood, and the momentary supposition was that heart failure had occurred.

4 Mrs. Borden was lying prone on the floor on her face with her arms outstretched and the toes of her shoes resting on the carpet. On raising the body there was seen a pool of blood, and an examination disclosed the fact that death had been caused, as in the case of the husband, by repeated blows of some heavy sharp instrument on the face, neck, and head. In the case of both there was found a deep cut into the brain.

5 A circumstance which was not at once observed, but which was afterward noticed and put down as a clue, was the remarkable absence of blood from the numerous wounds on both bodies. It was as if the life current had been retarded and partly congealed from other causes before the murderous blows were struck. There was, it is true, a considerable pool of blood under Mrs. Borden, but the quantity was not equal to that which would have been expected in the case of a person in full vigor wounded as she was. There was very little blood on the sofa in the room where Mr. Borden's body was found.

6 Half of the police force of Fall River were off on a picnic when the murders occurred, and for that reason a strong guard of the premises was not furnished immediately, but several officers were quickly in the house after the alarm was given, and they learned enough to make it plain that

robbery had not been the purpose of the killing. No plate or money or any of the valuables of the mansion were missing, nor had a single thing been removed from the bodies. Borden's watch and money and Mrs. Borden's money and jewels were undisturbed.

7 A slight survey served to make it equally plain that the murders were both committed unexpectedly so far as the victims were concerned. Borden's body was reclining on the lounge, the legs were resting easily on the floor, the left arm lay on the hip, the right was folded across the breast, the eyes were closed, and the features were unmarked by any expression of surprise or apprehension. The attitude was one of repose. The features of Mrs. Borden were not drawn, and there was absolutely no evidence of a struggle.

8 A vigilant search failed to reveal a trace of blood, with the exception of one small spot on the wall, plainly due to a slight spattering of the blood when the first blow was dealt. The furniture of the room was in perfect order, and the position of the body was proof that it had fallen straight forward. The head was not even turned. The bed in the room had apparently just been made up for the day.

9 There were, so far as yet known, but two persons other than Borden and his wife on the premises when the murders were committed. These were Bridget Sullivan, a domestic, and Lizzie Borden, the younger of the two daughters. The older daughter was visiting in another town. To Lizzie Borden and Bridget Sullivan the police naturally turned for a description of the circumstances surrounding the murders.

10 The first alarm was given by Lizzie Borden, who ran out into the yard and called for help. A neighbor responded, and the police were telephoned for. When they arrived they were told the following story:

11 The elder daughter had been visiting for some time in Fair Haven. At 8 o'clock that morning Mrs. Borden received a note asking her to call on a friend who was ill. She left the house, and shortly after, her husband followed, and went to the bank, of which he was a Director. He returned about 10:30 o'clock and reclined on the sofa in the parlor for a doze. Bridget Sullivan, who had been working in the kitchen, passed through the parlor shortly after his return, and asked him how he felt.

12 The reason for this question was explained to the police. The whole family had been slightly ill for a day or two, and Dr. Bowen, the attending physician, had given it as his suggestion that they had been poisoned. Mr. Borden told Bridget that he was feeling all right, and she went up to the third floor and washed the windows.

13 According to Lizzie Borden she slept late that morning and did not get up until Mrs. Borden had gone out, as she thought, in response to the note from the neighbor. On going down stairs Lizzie passed through the parlor and saw and spoke to her father. Supposing her mother was out, she went into the yard and entered the barn in search of a piece of lead, from which to cut "sinkers" for a fishing excursion she expected soon to make to Marion to join some Sunday school friends who were already sojourning there. While in the barn she heard a cry of distress coming apparently from the house. Rushing in, she found her father dead on the sofa. She called Bridget, and they gave an alarm. Then they searched up stairs for Mrs. Borden, and found her as described. The door of the spare room, the police were told, was closed.

Such was the story as related to the police by Lizzie Borden and the servant, and it furnished no clues on which to work.

The first theory of the police was that a murderer familiar with the place had concealed himself in the house and had taken desperate chances for the plunder that might be at hand. This view was relinquished when it was found that nothing had been taken. The police next turned their attention to the theory that the murders were a family matter, and had grown out of the effort of one of the girls to secure a half interest in the estate, valued at $500,000. This was a bold theory to embrace in the absence of any positive evidence, but the police were so utterly at a loss for any other that they clutched at it desperately. They have since bent their whole endeavors to follow it up, with the result of the arrest of Miss Borden and the building up against her of what the police say they believe to be a strong case. Miss Borden denies her guilt, and has borne herself with wonderful composure.

16 At the outset there were several false clues on which the police worked. The first person to be suspected was a Swede employed on one of the Borden farms across the river from Fall River, who was known as

"the Swede." He was alleged to have had a difficulty with Mr. Borden, but investigation showed that he was not in Fall River the day of the murder, and he was not arrested.

17   A small boy reported that he had seen a man jump over the fence back of the Borden house about the time of the murder. This man was proved to be a myth by the testimony of a little girl who was in the adjoining yard at the time and saw no man scale the fence.

18   Suspicion was attracted to a rough-looking Frenchman who had been seen near the house. He was traced up and was found to be the leader of a gang of half-gypsy horse traders, who were operating among the farmers a few miles from Fall River. He proved an alibi to the satisfaction of the police, and was not molested.

19   There were other clues of that kind, chief among them being that furnished by a prominent physician of Fall River, who told the police that, while driving past the Borden house about 10 o'clock on the morning of the murders, he saw a strange-looking man lingering in front of the house. The man had a ghastly face and acted queerly. When this clue was followed to the end it was found that the ghastly stranger was a drunken mill hand, on the border of delirium tremens. He was fully identified as the man whom the doctor had seen, and thus ended that clue.

20   A careful examination of the bodies of Mr. and Mrs. Borden the day after the killing served to convince the physicians that Mrs. Borden had been dispatched some time—probably an hour and a half—before her husband. It was after this discovery, coupled with the failure to locate any suspicious character on or near the premises before or after the tragedy, and with the seeming improbability that a stranger could have lurked in the Borden house without detection by Lizzie Borden or the servant that the police fell back on the theory that the assassin was some member of the household who knew the premises thoroughly.

21   So much having been settled to their satisfaction, the police proceeded to look for their victim. Their attention was first drawn to John V. Morse, a cousin of Borden, living in a neighboring town. Morse was a sort of horse trader, had recently come from the West, and was known to have been at the Borden home several times, and especially on the morning of the murders. He was shadowed and questioned by the police, and several of the Borden relatives came out and aired their suspicions in relation to him, but he convinced the police of his innocence, and when the official inquest began he is said to have furnished evidence tending to the conviction of Lizzie Borden. Morse was undoubtedly in and about the Borden house shortly before the tragedy, but there was no evidence of any sort discovered against him, and he was not arrested, although he was under surveillance for several days.

22   There was one other clue which the police attempted to investigate before fixing on Lizzie Borden as the guilty one. Mrs. Joseph Durfee, a neighbor of the Bordens, said that some months before the killing she was going past the Borden house one night and saw a young man standing on the steps talking excitedly with Mr. and Mrs. Borden. Mrs. Durfee heard the young man say, "You've cheated me and I'll fix you." Mrs. Durfee could not see the young man's features, but he was well dressed and apparently very angry. The police were not able to find any clue to this young man.

23   Lizzie Borden was suspected chiefly by reason of certain discrepancies between her statements to the police as to the circumstances under which the bodies of Mr. and Mrs. Borden were found. Bridget Sullivan was involved in several of the earlier of these discrepancies, but the police decided that she was a victim of a bad memory and abandoned all suspicion of her.

24   The suspicion against Lizzie Borden was rendered stronger by a statement made to the police by Eli Bence, a clerk at D. R. Smith's drug store, to the effect that Miss Borden had been in his store two days before the murders inquiring for prussic acid or hydrocyanic acid. She failed to secure either. The drug clerk made a partial identification of Miss Borden, but later the accuracy of his identification was denied. Miss Borden denied that she had bought or tried to buy either poison. Hydrocyanic acid leaves no outward trace on the body, and it was the conjecture of the physicians for the prosecution that this was the drug that had been used. It was alleged that after her refusal at D. R. Smith's Miss Borden secured hydrocyanic acid at the drug store of W. J. Brow. The latter denied this to the police. He was personally acquainted with Miss Borden, he said.

25   Miss Borden was put under police surveillance two days after the murders, but was not arrested until last Thursday. Meanwhile, the inquest had been in progress several days, and she and others had made statements to the police which were considered to be radically at variance. In addition to the police, there was a Pinkerton detective early on the scene. The detective worked in the interest of the Borden family, and ridiculed the police theory. His idea was that the murders were the work of a lunatic.

26   The movements of Mr. Borden on the day of his death were investigated, with the result that the police were able to trace him up to within a half hour of his death. Thirty minutes after he was seen to enter the house his body was found on the sofa. It was between 10:50 and 10:52 A.M. when Borden entered the house; at 11:13 the news of the murder was on the street.

27   In the case of Mrs. Borden the police were utterly unable to locate her outside the house on that fateful morning, notwithstanding the statement of Lizzie Borden that Mrs. Borden had been summoned to a sick neighbor. According to Miss Borden the note was delivered to Mrs. Borden by a messenger boy, but she could not describe the boy. She did not know the neighbor, and diligent search has failed to reveal the slightest trace of either. These circumstances would not be singular in a large city, but in Fall River they are regarded by the police as significant. The note which Mrs. Borden is said to have received could not be found, and Miss Borden explained that by suggesting that it had probably been torn up. In a basket in the house were found fragments of several notes, but when they were pieced together the note to Mrs. Borden was found to be not among them.

28   It was regarded as singular by the police that neither Miss Borden nor Bridget Sullivan had heard the noise of the fall of Mrs. Borden's body. Mrs. Borden weighed 200 pounds, and it was clear that she had tumbled headlong and at full length to the floor.

29   Dr. Bowen, the family physician, who was called to the Borden house a few minutes after the discovery of the bodies, told the police that Mr. Borden was, in his judgment, asleep when attacked. He thought that an axe had been used, as there were several cuts on the head four and a half inches long.

30   Miss Borden told the police that she was in the barn when the murders occurred. A policeman visited the barn on the day of the tragedy and examined the floor, which was covered with a thick layer of dust. There were no footprints in this dust except those made by the officer in his investigation.

31   On the other hand, Benjamin Buffington, Deputy Sheriff of the county and a friend of the Bordens, went to the barn, according to his testimony, a day or two after the killing, and found not enough dust on the floor to show footprints.

32   Hiram Harrington, a brother-in-law of Borden, had an interview with Miss Borden the evening of the day of the murders. She told him, he says, that she was in the kitchen when the father came home at 10:30 o'clock. Mr. Borden sat down on the lounge in the next room and she went in there and helped him remove his coat, inquired solicitously as to his condition, put on his dressing gown, assisted him to a reclining position, and withdrew on finding him comfortable. She left the house and went to the barn about 10:45 o'clock, and staid there twenty to thirty minutes. On returning she found Mr. Borden's body. Miss Borden told Harrington that she thought the murders had been committed by strangers.

33   "Last Spring," she said, "the house was robbed while mother and father were at Swansea, and a large amount of money was stolen, together with diamonds. You never heard of it, because father did not want it mentioned, so as to give the detectives a chance to recover the property. That may have had some connection with the murder. Then, I have seen strange men around the house. A few months ago I was coming through the back yard, and as I approached the side door, I saw a man there examining the door and premises. I did not mention it to any one. The other day I saw the same man hanging around the house, evidently watching us. I became frightened and told my parents about it. I also wrote to my sister at Fair Haven about it."

34   Harrington said that for ten years there had been almost constant disputes between the daughters and Mr. and Mrs. Borden. They had been allowed $200 a year each and had been given property worth in the aggregate about $6,000. They were dissatisfied with this, Harrington said, and

thought they ought to have more. Miss Borden moved in the best society, and wanted money to "hold her end up," as Harrington expressed it.

35   The stomachs of Mr. and Mrs. Borden have been sent to Boston for chemical analysis, which will show not only whether poison was administered, but also is relied on to settle the question as to which of the couple died first. On this depends the disposition of a large part of the estate. If Mrs. Borden died first her relatives would not inherit her dower rights.

36   One of the most singular things in connection with the tragedy is that the weapon with which the murders were committed has not yet been found, beyond peradventure, although the house and its chimneys, the yard, cellar, barn, and every part of the premises were searched and dug over industriously. Several axes and hatchets were found, but none of them bore bona fide blood stains. Last Monday night a bloody hatchet was discovered on a farm in South Somerset, near Fall River, but it was found to belong to an old man named Sylvia, and had been used, according to his testimony, in killing chickens. A hatchet was found in the Borden cellar with what looked like blood-stains on it; but they were very old stains, apparently, and Miss Borden said that the hatchet had been used several weeks previous in killing pigeons.

37   On her second examination by the police Bridget Sullivan changed her former story in some details. She said that she began to wash the windows at 9:30 o'clock and did not get through until 10:30. During this hour she commanded a full view of all the entrances to the house, and was positive no one entered or departed. Just as she finished she saw Mr. Borden approaching and let him in. Then she attended to some matters in the kitchen and went up stairs to lie down because of a pain in her back. On her way up stairs she passed through the room where Mr. Borden was lying on the lounge and found him sleeping. She left Lizzie Borden ironing in the kitchen, and knew nothing of the murders until called down by Lizzie.

38   The axe found in the cellar has also been sent to Boston for microscopical examination. A piece of sheet lead was found in the barn by the authorities, but they did not disclose whether it bore marks of a knife. Indeed, the entire investigation by the police has been conducted secretly, and the public is not in possession of their information except in an inferential and more or less indirect way. Most of the evidence has "leaked," though.

39   The reward of $5,000, offered by Lizzie and Emma Borden, has filled the town with amateur detectives, but has resulted in no clues other than those discovered by the police and the newspaper correspondents.

40   The police are clear on the question of motive. They allege that it was the purpose of Lizzie Borden, by killing Borden and his wife, to inherit one-half of his estate. Bearing on this point, information was furnished the police only two days ago to the effect that Mr. Borden was about to make a will. The police consider the information reliable. No will has been found since his death, and he is believed to have died intestate. It is said that Lizzie Borden knew he was about to make a will.

41   Before the tragedy Lizzie Borden lived the humdrum life of a small place. She once taught a Sunday school class and was bright, but sedate. She made an extended tour of Europe a year or two ago, since which she has devoted herself largely to novels and has resumed her Sunday school teaching. Throughout her surveillance and arrest she has borne herself with wonderful calmness.

42   The reaction in the Borden case has set in. Three days ago it was the popular cry that Lizzie Borden was a criminal and should be placed behind prison bars. To-day, although the District Attorney and Judges have passed their opinions on the evidence, there are many thoughtful and influential men who believe a trial will substantiate Miss Borden's protestations of innocence.

43   The City Marshal said to-day that he was confident that the evidence to be submitted at the hearing on Aug. 22 would be strong enough to warrant the holding of Miss Borden for the Grand Jury. That body will not convene until November, and the time of the special session of the Superior Court that must be held will be decided on afterward.

44   While direct police surveillance has been removed from Mr. Morse and Miss Sullivan, yet their whole connection with the case will be gone over by the police again within the next few days, and they will not be far away should the police need them.

45   There will not be a great many witnesses summoned for the preliminary hearing

unless the present plans are changed. The Marshal again denies the statements made editorially and otherwise in some newspapers to the effect that no search was made until after the funeral. A search was made three times during the afternoon of the day of the murders, and Miss Lizzie's room was searched as thoroughly as other portions of the building.

46 Police inquiry is being made again into the details of a mysterious robbery which took place at the Borden homestead about a year ago. A lady's watch and several articles of jewelry were taking from a dressing case in one of the upper rooms, and to this day the police have been unable to trace the thief.

47 It is known here that the District Attorney is indifferent as to the opinions of people regarding the justice of the arrest of Miss Borden. It is reported that the prosecution will present but little of its case at the preliminary hearing, keeping back, if possible, the most important evidence.

48 To-night's *News* says: "So many conflicting stories have been told concerning the relations between the members of the Borden family that the testimony of Mrs. Charles J. Holmes will be of much interest. Mrs. Holmes has been one of the most intimate friends of the family. She admits that the family relations have not been as pleasant as they are in many families, that in years past they were decidedly unpleasant at times, but she pronounces foolish all talk of an open rupture between Lizzie and her father and stepmother.

49 "She says that, as a matter of fact, Lizzie had been on much more friendly terms with her father and Mrs. Borden during the past year or two than she had been for a long time previously—probably since her father's second marriage. Mrs. Holmes was with Lizzie every day from the murder to the arrest, and during all of that terrible week Lizzie maintained the same wonderful composure and self-control. People have exclaimed at her falling asleep Wednesday after the ordeal at the inquest, but until that time she had hardly closed her eyes since the murders, and exhausted nature could hold out no longer."

Bridget Sullivan, during an interview this afternoon, said: "Well, I don't wonder that they arrested Lizzie Borden." As Miss Sullivan is the most important State witness, her statement has startled the friends of the imprisoned girl. The remark undoubtedly simply represents the servant's view of the case.

AGAINST LIZZIE BORDEN.

EVIDENCE THAT A DRESS WAS BURNED AFTER THE MURDERS.

1 PROVIDENCE, R.I., Dec. 3.— The *Journal* says that one of the baffling points in the investigation by the Government in the Borden murder case was the method used by the murderer to destroy the garments which he or she had worn during the committal of the deed, and which, according to the medical experts, must have been covered with blood from the upward-spurting arteries of the murdered couple. The mind naturally suggested the destroying of the telltale garments by fire, for that element more than any other could effectually remove every trace which might lead to the apprehension of the assassin by a discovery of the clothing worn when the deed was committed.

2 In the evidence submitted at the preliminary trial it was developed that upon the arrival of the police officers at the scene of the murder they lifted the covers from the stove and discovered the dying embers of a fire, with the presence of ashes, the latter giving an indication that an attempt had been made to burn something.

3 It was disclosed before the Grand Jury by one of Lizzie Borden's most intimate friends that there was a bright fire in that stove but a short time before the curious officer lifted the cover; a fire strong enough to have destroyed evidences of crime even, were those evidences blood-stained clothing, and into that stove upon the morning when Andrew Borden and his wife were murdered there was thrust a women's dress and rapidly the blazing flames destroyed the garment until within a few moments after the introduction into the fire box nothing remained of it but a few ashes. Then the fire died away.

4 The prisoner's friends can say truthfully that there is no evidence to show that the dress which was destroyed by fire on the morning of Aug. 4 belonged to her. They

may add that the one who gave the above information to the Grand Jury did not describe the texture of this garment, did not say that it was in any way disfigured by bloodstains or any other kind of stains, and failed to say that, though familiar with Lizzie Borden's wardrobe, the witness had ever seen anything like this dress in the wearing apparel of the young woman. All this is equally true, but, nevertheless, the Grand Jury was told that a dress was burned.

5   The testimony presented yesterday morning in relation to the McHenry-Trickey episode was that during the negotiations between the two, the Fall River officers were kept acquainted with all particulars, and that every transaction between the two

was witnessed by officers connected with the case. The indictment against Trickey was found on the strength of stories to the effect that he attempted through Mrs. McHenry to secure the departure of Bridget Sullivan from the State by the payment of a sum of money.

6   The *Journal* further asserts that the ten days' adjournment of the Grand Jury was due solely to the desire of Attorney General Pillsbury and District Attorney Knowlton to secure a unanimous vote for an indictment by furnishing corroborative testimony to some already adduced, yet the vote was not unanimous, although it was practically so, as the dissenters refrained altogether from voting.

BORDEN MURDER TRIAL BEGUN

JURORS IMPANELED TO TRY THE CELEBRATED CASE.

THEY ARE TO DECIDE THE FATE OF A YOUNG WOMAN ACCUSED OF MURDERING HER FATHER AND STEPMOTHER—CROWDS SURROUND THE COURT HOUSE—NO SPECTATORS ADMITTED TO THE TRIAL CHAMBER—THE JURY TO VIEW THE PREMISES AT FALL RIVER WHERE THE CRIME WAS COMMITTED.

1   NEW-BEDFORD, MASS., June 5.—The trial of Lizzie Andrew Borden for the murder of her father and stepmother began here to-day. At an early hour crowds gathered about the Court House on County Street, and many remained there all day in the hope of securing a sight of the accused young woman. Hundreds attempted to gain entrance to the building, but the rule that there should be no spectators in the courtroom was rigidly enforced.

2   The selection of the jury was all that was done to-day. This work was completed before 5 o'clock. The ease with which the jury was secured was a surprise to everybody, particularly as almost every man examined had formed an opinion about the case, and many of the candidates were opposed to capital punishment. The majority of the jury are farmers. All are advanced at least to middle age, both sides having objected to the presence of young men in the box.

3   The prosecution is represented by District Attorneys H. M. Knowlton and H.

W. Moody. The attorneys for the defense are Andrew J. Jennings of Fall River, Col. Melvin O. Adams of Boston, and ex-Gov. George D. Robinson.

4   Each side had twenty-two challenges. When the jury was finally selected the prosecution had exhausted fourteen and the defense twenty-two. The jury is made up as follows:
Augustus Swift, New-Bedford.
John C. Finn, Taunton.
Louis D. Hodges, Taunton.
William F. Dean, Taunton.
George Potter, Westport.
Frederick C. Wilber, Raynham.
John Wilber, Somerset.
Frank G. Cole, Attleborough.
Charles I. Richards, North Attleborough.
Lemuel K. Wilber, Easton.
William Westcott, Seekouk.
Allen H. Wordell, Dartmouth.

5   The prisoner reached the courtroom at 11 o'clock. She entered the chamber from the jury room. She paused for a moment in the doorway and glanced over the room, apparently as self-possessed as ever. She looked unusually well. She wore a black brocade dress and a black lace hat.

6   Presently, as she stood there, the pink flush, which those who have watched her have learned to know denotes excitement, came to her cheeks.

7   She stepped forward as her attorneys, Mr. Jennings and Col. Adams, advanced to meet her. She gave her hand to each and smiled as she greeted them.

8 The three Judges who are to preside at the trial came in soon after. Those in the chamber rose as the Judges entered. Proceedings began with prayer by the Rev. M. C. Julien of the New-Bedford Congregational Church. He prayed that the innocent might be protected and the guilty exposed.

9 Then District Attorney Knowlton opened the trial. After announcing that, on account of the illness of the Attorney General, William H. Moody of Haverhill, State's Attorney of the Eastern District, had been assigned to assist him, he moved that the jury be selected.

10 After a few words relating to qualifications of jurors from Chief Justice Mason, the clerk, Simeon Borden, who by the way is not a relative of the accused, called the prisoner and informed her of her right of challenge, adding that all challenges must be made before the jury was sworn. Edward G. Baker was called. Mr. Baker is an elderly man with a gray beard and pleasant features. He stood before the court and the following interrogations were propounded by the Chief Justice, this being the form in each instance:

11 "Are you related to the prisoner, or to Andrew J. or Abby D. Borden?"

12 "Have you formed or expressed an opinion in relation to this case?"

13 "Are you sensible of any bias or prejudice in it?"

14 "Have you formed any opinion that would preclude you from finding the defendant guilty of an offense punishable by death?"

15 Mr. Baker had an opinion, he said, that could not be changed, and he was interrogated no further.

16 George Winslow was the next name called, and against him the first peremptory challenge of the defense was made. He is a man with a fierce black mustache. He had expressed no opinion, and appeared perfectly willing to serve.

17 "Juror, look on the prisoner," commanded the Chief Justice."

18 Winslow rolled his eyes toward the dock.

19 "Prisoner, look upon the juror."

20 As this sentence was spoken, Attorney Jennings hurried from his seat to that of his client and whispered to her.

21 She arose and, addressing the court, uttered the word, "Challenge."

22 Mr. Winslow retired.

The next man called, George Potter, was accepted as a juror. William F. Dean was accepted as the second juror. After this the proceedings took on a routine nature and the afternoon was a dull one.

The day was warm, the atmosphere inside the courtroom was oppressive, and it was an absolute relief to all concerned when the last man took his position in the jury box. To-morrow morning the indictment will be read and the prisoner will be arraigned. Then the jury will probably go to Fall River to view the scene of the tragedy.

BRIDGET SULLIVAN A WITNESS
THE BORDENS' SERVANT TELLS HER STORY OF THE MURDERS.

Her Testimony Establishes the Presence of Lizzie in the House at the Time the Crime Was Committed—She Weakens the State's Case, However, by Declaring That Lizzie and Her Stepmother Lived Together Peaceably—The Prisoner's Uncle Also Testifies

1 New-Bedford, Mass., June 7. Properly speaking, this was the first day of the Borden trial, for, while the two previous days had been occupied in the preparation of preliminaries, this day was marked by the rapid presentation of testimony. The progress made was marked, and was entirely in keeping with the course presaged by the prompt selection of the jury.

2 Judges and attorneys are alike interested in securing celerity, and the trial will now proceed as rapidly as possible to its conclusion.

3 The witnesses of the day comprised a number of persons who testified in relation to Andrew Borden's presence in the business portion of the city half an hour before his murder. John V. Morse, uncle of the prisoner, and Bridget Sullivan also testified.

4 Bridget Sullivan was the strongest witness of the day, but while her testimony placed Lizzie Borden, the accused, in the home at the hour of the murders, the effect of it was weakened by the statement, reiterated with emphasis, that between the

accused and her stepmother there had never been, to witness's knowledge, an unkind word.

5   The Government needs a motive and must have one in its presentation of its side of the case. Bridget Sullivan helped the District Attorney out a bit on that point.

6   When she told of the food served at the Borden homestead she laughed, and there was a smile on the lips of the prisoner. Others have been amused at the parsimony of the man whose possessions were more than a quarter of a million, and who fed his family on a diet of mutton and cold mutton and mutton broth.

7   Again the prisoner laughed when John V. Morse, her uncle, went through some mathematical calculations, the deduction of which was that the prisoner was thirty-three years of age. The latter shook her head vigorously at the assertion, and there spoke the woman.

8   The weakness of yesterday had vanished, and to-day her strong will was again in evidence. She appeared highly interested in the proceedings, and watched the developments closely. To-morrow it is expected that Medical Examiner Bowen will be a witness and the skulls will be produced.

9   Proceedings opened with the recall of Mr. Kiernan, the civil engineer, whose examination stopped yesterday when the jury started for Fall River to view the scene of the murder. Mr. Kiernan's testimony was devoted to locating various points upon the Borden place, describing the fences, barns, and outbuildings, explaining the arrangement of the rooms, stairs, and closets. He also gave the results of certain experiments that he had made to determine from what points of view the bodies of Mr. and Mrs. Borden could have been seen.

10   After Mr. Kiernan came a photographer, who exhibited pictures which he had made of the premises and of the bodies of the murdered man and his wife.

11   John V. Morse, uncle of the prisoner and brother of Mr. Borden's first wife, was the next witness. Mr. Morse is sixty years old. He lives at South Dartmouth. He said Mr. Borden was first married about forty-seven years ago and had three children by his first wife, one of whom was dead. He said Lizzie was thirty-three years old and Emma forty-one.

12   On Wednesday, Aug. 3, last, he went to the Borden house. He had been a visitor there several weeks before. The last time he saw Lizzie before that visit he could not place. He arrived at the Borden house at 1:30 o'clock. He did not see anybody that day except Mr. and Mrs. Borden and Bridget. He ate dinner there that day, but ate it alone. He left the house between 3 and 4 P.M. and got back about 8:30. He entered the front door, having been let in by Mrs. Borden. The door was shut after he went in.

13   He saw nobody there but the family. He went first into the sitting room and went to bed about 10:30. Mrs. Borden went to bed first, going out of the rear door to the back stairs.

14   "While we were sitting there," said Mr. Morse, "somebody entered the front door and went up stairs to Lizzie's room. Mr. Borden and I went to bed at the same time, I going into the guest room. The prisoner's room door was closed when I went into my room, but I do not know whether it was locked or not."

15   The next morning witness was up at 6 o'clock and breakfasted at 7 o'clock with Mr. and Mrs. Borden on mutton, bread, coffee, sugar cakes, and bananas. He didn't recall that there was fried johnny cake on the table. At 8:40 he left the house and did not return until after the murder. Reaching the back yard he ate part of a pear before going into the house. It was not until after he had seen the bodies of Mr. and Mrs. Borden that he caught sight of Lizzie Borden.

16   On cross-examination witness said that on reaching the Borden house after the murder he saw no officers in the yard, that the barn door was closed, and he heard no one inside. This contradicted the Government's allegation that officers, by immediate examination of the barn, ascertained that the prisoner could not have been there at the time of the murder.

17   Witness said that at the first meal Mrs. Borden brought in the food, and he saw nothing of Bridget Sullivan. On the evening previous to the murder both Mr. and Mrs. Borden were sick. Of his own knowledge he did not know whether Bridget was in the house that day or not. He first saw her at breakfast the day of the murder.

18   Abraham G. Hart, Treasurer of the Union Savings Bank of Fall River, of which Mr. Borden was President, and others were called to show at what time Mr. Borden was about town the morning of the murders. Their testimony established that he went toward his home soon after 10:30 o'clock.

19   Counsel Robinson stated that it was agreed, to save time, that Mr. Borden died intestate, and that his property was estimated at between $200,000 and $300,000.

20   A buzz of excitement went around the room at 12:30, when Mr. Moody called "Bridget Sullivan." She was dressed in a maroon colored, fashionably-made dress, and wore a large hat, with large feather, and black kid gloves. She leaned on the left side against the rail, looked straight at Mr. Moody, and spoke so low that he had to tell her to speak louder. The prisoner remained leaning back in the seat, but changed posture so as to see witness plainly, and watched her steadily with her large eyes wide open.

21   Bridget said that she had worked for the Bordens for two years and ten months doing general housework, but having no care of any sleeping room except her own. She remembered Mr. Morse's visit the night before the murder. She remembered, too, that Mr. and Mrs. Borden were ill Wednesday night. She herself felt well until Thursday morning, when she waked up with a headache. She was out Wednesday night until 10:30 o'clock. She entered the house by the back door, and hooked and bolted it.

22   Thursday, the day of the murder, she was up at 6:15 o'clock. She found all doors down stairs just as she had left them the night before. Witness then went on to detail minutely what happened in the house from the time of her getting up until the discovery of the murders.

23   At 1 o'clock the court took a recess until 2:15.

24   In the afternoon Miss Borden took her seat for the first time within the bar inclosure and near her counsel. She appeared to be in good spirits and fondled a small cluster of pansies, which seem to be her favorite flowers.

25   While Bridget Sullivan was taking a rest, Mrs. Caroline Kelley, who lives next door to the Borden house, was put on the stand to fix the time when Mr. Borden entered his house. According to her clock it was 10:32 o'clock when she saw him at his front door.

26   Resuming her testimony, Bridget Sullivan said that after Mr. and Mrs. Borden and Mr. Morse had finished their breakfast Lizzie Borden came to the kitchen and said that she would have coffee and cookies for her breakfast. Bridget left Lizzie in the kitchen and went outdoors feeling ill. When she came back there was nobody in the kitchen. She fastened the screen door on the inside as she came in.

27   About 9 o'clock Mrs. Borden told her to wash the windows, and she went at work at once obeying the order. Her work took her first to the front of the house, where she spent some time washing the outside of the parlor windows. She passed from the front of the house to the barn several times, and also entered the kitchen. At no time did she see any stranger about the premises.

28   She opened the door for Mr. Borden when he came in from down town. There were several locks on the door.

29   "I was so bothered with these locks," said Bridget, "that I said: 'Oh, pshaw!' and Lizzie, who was either at the head of the stairs or in her room, laughed as me."

    "When I let Mr. Borden in," continued the witness, "he did speak to me. He had a parcel in his hand. When he went into the dining room he sat in a chair at the head of the lounge and I went on washing my windows. Miss Lizzie came down stairs about five minutes after, and went into the dining room. I heard her ask her father if he had any mail, and she told him Mrs. Borden had received a note and had gone out. Then Mr. Borden took the key of his bedroom door and went up the back stairs. When he came down soon after he took a rocking chair in the sitting room, and I went on washing my windows, this time in the dining room.

31   "While I was doing this Lizzie came into the room, took an ironing board from the kitchen, and placed it in position. She asked me if I was going out that afternoon and I said I did not think I was. She says, 'Well, if you do, be sure and lock the doors, for Mrs. Borden has gone out on a sick call, and I may go out myself.'

32   "Then I went up to my room and lay down. The first notice I took of any time was when I heard the City Hall clock strike 11. I think I had been there three or four minutes. Don't think I went to sleep. Heard no noise. Am able to hear the opening and closing of the screen door if it is done by a careless person.

33   "The next thing I heard was when Lizzie called me to come down, as her father was dead: that was at least fifteen minutes after."

34   Counsel asked witness to describe the dress Lizzie had on that morning, but

objections stopped an answer. She remembered a light-blue dress with a sprig on it of darker blue, bought the previous Spring.

35   Continuing her narrative, witness said:

36   "When I heard the outcry from Lizzie I went down stairs and first saw Lizzie; I cannot tell what dress she had on that morning. When I came down the back way the wooden door was open, and she was leaning against the door. The screen door was shut, but I could not tell whether it was hooked or not. I went to go into the sitting room, and she said:

37   "'Oh, Maggie'—I was sometimes called by that name—'I've got to have a doctor right away. I was out in the back yard, and when I came in the screen door was open and I found father dead. Do you know where Miss Russell lives?'

38   "I did not, and she told me. I didn't find Dr. Bowen. Then I went to the corner of Second and Borden Streets for Miss Russell and she was not there. Then I found where she did live and told her what Lizzie wanted. I guess I ran to Dr. Bowen's, but I don't know. When I came back I found Mrs. Churchill. I said, when I came back, that if I knew where Mrs. Whitehead lived I would go and tell Mrs. Borden, if she was there, that Mr. Borden was very sick, and Lizzie said:

39   "'Oh, Maggie! I am almost sure I heard her come in; go up stairs and see if she is there.'

40   "I said, 'I will not go up stairs alone,' and Mrs. Churchill went up with me.

41   "When I got far enough on the stairs to see into the room I saw the body on the floor and ran in and stood by the foot of the bed. The door was wide open.

42   "When I came down stairs Lizzie was on the lounge with Miss Russell. Then I went for the second time to Dr. Bowen's house. The first I heard of the note was when Lizzie spoke to me of it. No one, to my knowledge, came to the house on that day with a message for Mrs. Borden."

43   On cross-examination Bridget said:

44   "I never saw or heard anything out of the way in the family relations, and during my nearly three years of service everything was pleasant. There were times when the girls did not eat at the same table with their parents—most of the time. They rarely arose when the old people got up. There were times when they ate alone, or

separately. Lizzie and her mother always spoke to each other.

45   "I heard them all talking in the sitting room that morning, and Mrs. Borden asked Lizzie some questions and she answered them civilly and properly. So far as I could see, they lived congenially and pleasantly. I waited on the table when all were there, and they conversed usually in a pleasant manner.

46   "I don't remember anything about any conversation about Christmas time."

47   Here ex-Gov. Robinson asked Bridget if she had not stated at the preliminary hearing that there was talk about Christmas time, and she replied that she did not remember saying "if Mrs. Borden was sick Lizzie did all she could for her."

48   Cross-examined about the screen door, Bridget admitted that she was not absolutely sure that on coming into the house after washing the windows she fastened it with the hasp. All the time she was washing windows that door was unhooked. She had told Lizzie that she needn't hook it, because she would look after it, but as a matter of fact she never went near it again until she went in. Any person could walk into that door at any time, she said, without her seeing him.

49   There was also a chance, she said, while she was at the back of the house talking to another servant girl over the fence for anybody to enter the front of the house without her knowledge.

50   Speaking of the intercourse between Mr. Borden and his daughter just before the murder witness said that they got along pleasantly and that she noticed nothing unusual in Lizzie's behavior.

51   She said that when Lizzie called for her to come down stairs she called in such a voice that witness asked her what was the matter, and Lizzie said, "Come down quickly, Maggie; father is killed."

52   Asked if she had stated this the same way before, if she had not used the word "dead," the witness replied she could not remember; it was all the same, anyhow; he was dead.

53   "When I got back," witness said, "from going after the people, I found Mrs. Churchill there and Dr. Bowen. Lizzie was on the lounge. Her dress was free from spots of blood and her hair was not disarranged."

54   At the close of Bridget Sullivan's examination, at 4:55, the court adjourned.

The Titanic *Disaster*

On April 14, 1912, the ocean liner *Titanic* struck an iceberg and within a short time sank. This great ship, deemed unsinkable by its builders, counted among her passengers a number of the wealthiest people in the United States. Perhaps because of the glamour that surrounded the ship, her sinking has taken on mythic proportions, provoking many essays, books, memoirs, poems, films, and Web sites. With the discovery and exploration of the wreck of the *Titanic* about 10 years ago, even more work on the disaster was produced. Although we have been able to include only a few of these works in this casebook, we are certain that those of you who are interested in the *Titanic* will find this a worthwhile research subject.

Faulty Rivets Emerge as Clues to *Titanic* Disaster

William J. Broad

1   Ever since the *Titanic* was discovered in the depths of the North Atlantic a dozen years ago, her steel plates melting into rivers of rust, expeditions have repeatedly probed the hulk. And investigators armed with a growing body of evidence have been working to solve riddles posed by the opulent liner's sinking.

2   The ship, of course, was moving too fast through a sea of towering ice when it struck a large floe on its inaugural voyage in 1912. But much uncertainty has surrounded the exact nature of the damage and whether it might have been avoided in whole or part if the ship's design or construction had been different, perhaps preventing the loss of more than 1,500 lives.

3   Now, after years of analysis and any number of false leads, experts say they have preliminary evidence suggesting that the *Titanic*, the biggest ship of her day, a dream of luxury come to life, may have been done in by structural weaknesses in some of her smallest and least glamorous parts: the rivets.

4   Two wrought-iron rivets from the *Titanic*'s hull were recently hauled up from the depths for scientific analysis and were found to be riddled with unusually high concentrations of slag, making them brittle and prone to fracture.

5   "We think they popped and allowed the plates to separate and let in the water," said William H. Garzke Jr., a naval architect who heads a team of marine forensic experts investigating the disaster.

6   The rivet analysis, which Mr. Garzke and other experts said must be considered tentative because of the small number of rivets sampled, sheds light on findings made public last year. Experts, diving down nearly two and a half miles to peer through thick mud with sound waves, discovered that the *Titanic*'s bow had been pierced by six thin wounds, the damage apparently done as hull seams were forced open. The finding laid to rest the myth that the iceberg had sliced open a 300-foot gash in the ship's side and strengthened interest in the possibility of rivet failure.

7   The new analysis was done by Dr. Timothy Foecke, a metallurgist at the National Institute of Standards and Technology, a Federal agency in Gaithersburg, Md. It helps set industry standards and employs some of the Government's top metallurgists.

8   Working with Mr. Garzke, who is chairman of the marine forensics panel of the Society of Naval Architects and Marine Engineers, a professional group based in Jersey City, Dr. Foecke analyzed the two *Titanic* hull rivets, cutting them in half and probing their composition with tools like microscopes and image analyzers. His work revealed an overabundance of slag, the glassy residue left over from the smelting of metallic ores.

9   "The microstructure of the rivets is the most likely candidate for becoming a quantifiable metallurgical factor in the loss of *Titanic*," Dr. Foecke concludes in a report, "Metallurgy of the R.M.S. *Titanic*," to be formally released early next month.

10   In the report and interviews, Dr. Foecke said the slag content of the rivets was more than three times as high as is normally found in modern wrought iron, making it less ductile and more brittle. While it is not clear whether a better grade of rivets would have saved the ship, he said, the developing evidence points in that direction.

11   It is also unclear whether such high concentrations of slag were typical for the era of the *Titanic*'s construction, from 1909 to 1912. But some historical evidence suggests that the excessive levels might have been abnormal, raising the issue of culpability.

12   The *Titanic*'s builder, Harland & Wolff, would make no comment on the findings, saying the topic was too old. "We don't have an archivist or anything like that," said Peter Harbinson, a spokesman for the company, in Belfast, Northern Ireland. "We don't have anybody in a position to comment."

13   The luxury liner was built for the White Star Line, a company that no longer exists because it merged with Cunard in the Depression.

14   Even if shoddy workmanship became a major issue, which would require the analysis of more *Titanic* rivets and more comparisons with the practices of the day, historians say that all issues of liability were settled long ago.

15   Addressing a more recent issue, experts say the rivet finding has no link to *Titanic*, the $200 million epic now playing in movie theaters. But both the finding and the movie demonstrate independently how advanced technology is opening up the sea's depths.

16   The Hollywood director James Cameron went down in a Russian submersible in 1995 to film the wreck. A year later, a different expedition used a French submersible to retrieve a number of artifacts, including the hull rivets.

17   That work is now opening a new chapter in the long investigation of why the ship, proclaimed unsinkable, went down so fast.

18   The 46,000-ton *Titanic* was made of steel held together with some three million rivets. They secured both beams and plates. Each rivet was formed at a factory into a mushroom shape; it was heated at the work site to incandescent temperatures and then inserted into the aligned holes of plates and beams. The glowing-hot end, or tail, was then hammered down to lock the parts firmly together.

19   The rivets were made of wrought iron, which contains some slag. This contaminant is useful because pure iron is very ductile, bending easily without breaking. Slag gives it added strength. Slag is fused dross that tends to separate from a metal during smelting. It is made largely of silicon, the main ingredient of rock, sand and glass. In wrought iron of high quality, slag is distributed finely and evenly in long microscopic threads. But too much of it can make the iron brittle, like glass.

20   Suspicions of rivet failure have long haunted the famous disaster, along with other possible culprits. The first hard evidence emerged only after the wreck was discovered in 1985, a ghost ship seemingly frozen in time. In 1986, the explorer Robert D. Ballard visited the grave site in a submersible and saw "plates knocked apart at their riveted seams."

21   But mysteries remained because the area in the lower bow damaged by the iceberg remained hidden under thick layers of mud.

22   The detective work turned away from rivets after expeditions in the late 1980's and early 1990's picked up *Titanic* parts and artifacts. Analysis showed that the hull plates were made of mediocre steel that was apt to fracture in cold water, suggesting that the iceberg caused wide cracking.

23   But the French expedition of 1996 found two tantalizing clues that undercut that theory.

24   The first was discovered by David Livingstone, an official from Harland & Wolff who dove down to the wreck. He found a bend of about 90 degrees where the port side had crumpled as the ship slammed into the bottom. That suggested that the hull steel had a substantial degree of flexibility.

25   The second finding was made by sonar experts who probed the starboard side of the lower hull where the iceberg struck, an area buried in mud up to 55 feet deep. Their readings disclosed six narrow slits.

26   "They appear to follow the hull plate," Paul K. Matthias, president of Polaris Imaging Inc. in Narragansett, R.I., who did the sonar work, said afterward. In early 1997, he speculated that the gaps had probably been created when rivets along plate seams had popped open, creating slits no wider than a person's hand.

27   Both findings were made under the auspices of the marine society forensics panel. Dr. Foecke, of the National Institute of Standards and Technology, a panel expert investigating the makeup of *Titanic*'s hull steel, became intrigued by the new findings and obtained two hull rivets, cutting them apart with a diamond saw.

28   He was surprised when his inquiries disclosed 9.3 percent slag in one rivet and similar levels in the other. By contrast, modern wrought iron has a slag content of 2 percent or 3 percent.

29   What was acceptable in the *Titanic*'s day? Rummaging through old books, Dr. Foecke found a 1906 entry for "medium quality" wrought iron. He analyzed a picture of the material and found that its slag content was from 2 percent to 2.5 percent, much lower than the *Titanic* rivets.

30   But he said in an interview that "as far as I can tell, there was no standard of the time" for the amount of slag in wrought iron.

31   Complicating the picture, Dr. Foecke found that the slag of the *Titanic* rivets was very coarsely distributed, creating lines of weakness. Most surprising, its grain changed abruptly just before the area where the ends popped off, turning perpendicular to the axis grain and suggesting an area of major weakness.

32   The grain might have been turned to the side, he said, when rivet ends were hammered too hard.

33   Dr. Foecke said that the examined rivets, though flawed by today's standards and suspicious by virtue of old evidence, had conceivably been "state of the art back then."

34   And both he and Mr. Garzke, the forensics panel's chairman, cautioned that a dozen or more *Titanic* rivets must eventually be analyzed to firm up the conclusions. An expedition this summer is to retrieve more rivets, they noted.

35   More historical evidence from other ships and documents is also needed, the experts stressed. Dr. Foecke said he now often found himself in the "rusty, musty" part of the library at the National Institute of Standards and Technology.

36   Both experts added, however, that some corroborative evidence existed. For instance, a *Titanic* crew member who survived testified about seeing water rushing through a riveted seam, between plates that had sprung open.

37   More evidence comes from the *Titanic*'s sister ship, the *Olympic,* which collided in 1911 with a small warship, receiving relatively minor but revealing damage. "You can count 37 missing rivets," Mr. Garzke said, referring to an old photograph of the *Olympic*'s wound.

CASEBOOK

38   George Tulloch, president of R.M.S. *Titanic* of New York City, the company that organized the 1996 French expedition and is raising parts of the ship, expressed doubt about the metallurgic analysis, saying rivets in the damaged area might, by design, have been made differently from the analyzed ones.

39   But Dr. Foecke said wrought iron used for the *Titanic*'s rivets was undoubtedly meant to be chemically uniform. The outstanding question, he added, was whether the two analyzed rivets were accidental oddballs or "representative of the class."

40   Paul Louden-Brown, a British maritime historian and author of "The White Star Line" (Ship Pictorial Publications, 1991), said in an interview that rivet failure was much more likely than hull-plate fracture. But he contended that Harland & Wolff, the ship's maker, had no incentive to scrimp on rivets because the *Titanic* was built on a cost-plus contract. All the liner's materials, he said, were "absolutely top-notch."

41   Dr. Foecke speculated that the rivet shortcomings, if confirmed to be widespread, had perhaps grown out of the hectic circumstances of the day rather than any kind of conscious decision to cut corners. From 1908 to 1914, the shipyard, he noted, was struggling to build three behemoths; the *Titanic, Olympic* and *Britannic.* Construction of the *Titanic* was even stopped at one point while emergency repairs were made to the *Olympic* after her collision.

42   In this frenzy of building and repair, he said, rivet-making plans might have slowly and almost unknowingly been compromised. "We have no way of knowing," he stressed. "That's conjecture."

43   He also said there was currently no way of knowing whether a better grade of rivets would have withstood the iceberg's blow and prevented or limited the great loss of life.

44   But Dr. Foecke said the current state of the evidence, while ambiguous, suggested such a possibility.

45   "It might have turned out differently," he said.

The *Titanic*: End of a Dream Senator William Alden Smith's Report on the *Titanic* Disaster

Wyn Craig Wade

1   At 11:00 A.M., after restricting debate to pending bills of a pedestrian nature, the Vice-President had just announced morning business closed when William Alden Smith bounded through the chamber doors, an enormous sheaf of papers under his arm. The senator had come directly from home where he had been up all night putting the finishing touches on the Commerce Committee's formal report on the *Titanic* investigation. Running out of time in which to write his scheduled speech, he had come prepared with only an outline, a few prose passages, and quotations jotted down from the testimony. Dropping the formal report into the hands of Commerce Chairman Knute Nelson, to whom he muttered something inaudible, William Alden dashed to his own desk, clamped his pince-nez on his nose, and addressed the Senate.

2   *Mr. President, I had expected to send to the Clerk's desk this morning the unanimous report of the Committee on Commerce. For the purpose of verifying some figures it*

will be delayed a few moments. I shall not detain the Senate, but will proceed with my address.

3   *Mr. President, my associates and myself return the commission handed to us on the eighteenth day of April last, directing an immediate inquiry into "the causes leading up to the destruction of the steamship* Titanic. . . ." *Mindful of the responsibility of our office, we desire the Senate to know that in the execution of its command we have been guided solely by the public interest and a desire to meet the expectations of our associates without bias, prejudice, sensationalism, or slander of the living or dead. That duty, we believed, would be best performed by an exact ascertainment of the true state of affairs.*

4   Expecting one of William Alden's famous "stampedes," news reporters were surprised to hear him speaking with such "deliberation and moderation of phraseology." Smith had correctly deduced that the facts of the disaster were sufficiently eloquent. After recounting the dramatic arrival of the *Carpathia* with the survivors of the disaster, Smith jumped backward in time to the building of the "practically unsinkable" *Titanic.*

5   *From the builders' hands, she was plunged straightaway to her fate—and christening salvos acclaimed at once her birth and death. Builders of renown had launched her on the billows with confident assurance of her strength, while every port rang with praise for their achievement. Shipbuilding to them was both a science and a religion; parent ships and sister ships had easily withstood the waves, while the mark of their hammer was all that was needed to give assurance of the high quality of the work. In the construction of the* Titanic, *no limit of cost circumscribed their endeavor, and when this vessel took its place at the head of the line every modern improvement in shipbuilding was supposed to have been realized. So confident were they that both owner and builder were eager to go upon the trial trip.*

6   *No sufficient tests were made of boilers or bulkheads or gearing or equipment, and no lifesaving or signal devices were reviewed. Officers and crew were strangers to one another (and passengers to both); neither was familiar with the vessel or its implements or tools. No drill or station practice or helpful discipline disturbed the tranquility of that voyage; and when the crisis came, a state of* absolute unpreparedness *stupefied both passengers and crew. And in their despair, the ship went down carrying as needless a sacrifice of noble women and brave men as ever clustered about the Judgment Seat in any single moment of passing time.*

7   *We shall leave to the honest judgment of England its painstaking chastisement of the British Board of Trade, to whose laxity of regulation and hasty inspection the world is largely indebted for this awful fatality. Of contributing causes there were very many. In the face of warning signals, speed was increased; and messages of danger seemed to stimulate her to action rather than persuade her to fear.*

8   The senator reviewed the ice warnings sent to the *Titanic* by the *Baltic, Amerika,* and *Californian,* and documented a fact the surviving senior officers of the *Titanic* had adroitly downplayed—that ice is a well-known hazard to navigation. He then moved toward the culpability of the *Titanic*'s late commander. The "heroism" of Captain E.J. had been praised from nearly every American and British pulpit, and introducing the inescapable fact of the captain's negligence was going to be a matter of the utmost delicacy. William Alden approached the task by adopting the sepulchral rhetoric of the clergy.

9   *Captain Smith knew the sea, and his clear eye and steady hand had often guided his ship through dangerous paths. For forty years storms sought in vain to vex him or menace his craft. But once before in all his honorable career was his pride humbled*

or his vessel maimed [the Olympic's *collision with the S.S.* Hawke]. *Each new advancing type of ship built by his company was handed over to him as a reward for faithful services and as an evidence of confidence in his skill. Strong of limb, intent of purpose, pure in character, dauntless as a sailor should be, he walked the deck of this majestic structure as master of her keel.*

10   *Titanic though she was, his* indifference to danger *was one of the* direct and contributing causes *of this unnecessary tragedy—while his own willingness to die was the expiating evidence of his fitness to live. Those of us who knew him well, not in anger but in sorrow, file one specific charge against him:* overconfidence *and neglect to heed the oft-repeated warnings of his friends.*

11   Many in the audience recalled the well-publicized words of E.J.'s last interview: "I have never been in any accident of any sort worth speaking about. . . . I never saw a wreck and never have been wrecked, nor was I ever in any predicament that threatened to end in disaster of any sort."

12   *The mystery of his indifference to danger, when other and less pretentious vessels doubled their lookout or stopped their engines, finds no reasonable hypothesis in conjecture or speculation. Science in shipbuilding was supposed to have attained perfection and to have spoken her last word. Mastery of the ocean had at last been achieved. And overconfidence seems to have dulled the faculties usually so alert. With the atmosphere literally charged with warning signals and wireless messages registering their last appeal, the stokers in the engine room fed their fires with fresh fuel, registering in that dangerous place her* fastest speed.

13   Since Ismay [the ship's owner] had refuted this last point, the senator recounted his recent trip to the engine room of the *Olympic,* where Fireman Fred Barrett had affirmed that at no other time on the *Titanic*'s maiden voyage had so many boilers been lit. Continuing, William Alden drew a comparison between the captain's disregard of wire-lessed warnings and the officers' blasé response to the warnings of nature. The sudden plunge in temperature as the liner approached the region of ice had been dismissed by senior officers, even though, as William Alden noted, sailors of the Grand Banks con-sider the thermometer "almost as necessary to their safety as the compass." The impor-tance of this precaution had quite recently been sustained by Rear Admiral Robert E. Peary in an article in the *Army and Navy Journal.*

14   The senator then discussed the collision and Officer Murdoch's error at the helm.

15   *At that moment the ice, resistless as steel, stole upon her and struck her in a vital spot, while the last command of the officer of the watch in his effort to avert disas-ter, distracted by the sudden appearance of extreme danger, sharply turned aside the prow—the part best prepared to resist collision—exposing the temple to the blow. At the turn of the bilge, the steel encasement yielded to a glancing blow so slight that the impact was not felt in many parts of the ship. . . . [Many] of the passengers and crew did not even know of the collision until tardily advised of the danger by anx-ious friends, and even then official statements were clothed in such confident assur-ances of safety as to arouse no fear. The awful force of the impact was well known to the master and builder, Mr. Andrews, who from the first must have known the ship was doomed and never uttered an encouraging sign to one another. Neither ever adjusted a life belt to himself. The builder, whose heart must have broken when he realized he had not prepared that ship to resist a blow so dangerous, seemed to have been quite willing to go down with the ship.*

16   *There is evidence to show that no final warning was given by any officer. . . . No general alarm was given, no ship's officers formally assembled, no orderly routine*

was attempted or organized system of safety begun. Haphazard, they rushed by one another on staircase and in hallway, while men of self-control gathered here and there about the decks, helplessly staring at one another or giving encouragement to those less courageous than themselves.

17   Avoiding technicalities, Senator Smith briefly explained that although the ship had been constructed to withstand flooding in any two adjacent compartments, the damage from the iceberg was such that, in the forward section, "five compartments filled almost instantly." The ship was thereby pulled down by the bow, the water in these compartments spilling over into those aft and culminating in the *Titanic*'s nosedive.

18   *I then reached a conclusion which in my opinion accounts for the small proportion of steerage passengers who were saved. The occupants of the forward steerage were the first of the passengers to realize the danger—one or two witnesses said they stepped out of their berths into water probably an inch or two inches deep. Those in the forward steerage knew directly of the impact and of the presence of water which came up from the lower part of the ship into the mail room and the forward steerage. Those steerage passengers went on deck and, as fast as they were able, took places in the lifeboats. While the after steerage, more than an eighth of a mile away, was by the operation of the added weight [the flooding forward] raised out of the water . . . so that these steerage passengers got their first warning of real danger as the angle of the deck became very great. I feel that the small number of steerage survivors was thus due to the fact that they got no definite warning before the ship was really doomed—when most of the lifeboats had departed.*

19   The senator strongly condemned the manner in which the lifeboats were loaded and manned.

20   *The* Titanic*'s boats were only partially loaded and in all instances unprovided with compasses and only three of them had lamps. They were manned so badly that, in the absence of prompt relief, they would have fallen easy victims to the advancing ice floe, nearly thirty miles in width and rising sixteen feet above the surface of the water. Their danger would have been as great as if they had remained on the deck of the broken hull. And if the sea had risen, these toy targets with over seven hundred exhausted people would have been helplessly tossed about upon the waves without food or water. . . . The lifeboats were filled so* indifferently *and lowered so quickly* that, according to the uncontradicted evidence, nearly five hundred people were needlessly sacrificed to want of orderly discipline in loading the few that were provided. . . . And yet it is said by some well-meaning persons that the best discipline prevailed. If this is discipline, what would have been disorder?*

21   The crowd in the Senate chamber murmured in agreement.

22   *Some of the [crew] men, to whom had been intrusted the care of passengers, never reported to their official stations, and quickly deserted the ship with a recklessness and indifference to the responsibilities of their positions as culpable and amazing as it is impossible to believe. And some of these men say that they "laid by" in their partially filled lifeboats and listened to the cries of distress "until the noise quieted down" and surveyed from a safe distance the unselfish men and women and faithful fellow officers and seamen, whose heroism lightens up this tragedy and recalls the noblest traditions of the sea.*

23   At this juncture, Smith turned to an issue with which he was now virtually obsessed—the wireless. After lavishing praise on the two "ill-paid" operators, Phillips and Bride, he launched an exhaustive criticism of the policies of the Marconi Company.

CASEBOOK

He condemned the laissez-faire status of the wireless and concluded with an emotional appeal for the international regulation of radio.

24   *When the world weeps together over a common loss, when nature moves in the same direction in all spheres, why should not the nations clear the sea of its conflicting idioms and wisely regulate this new servant of humanity? To that end, wages must be increased in proportion to the responsibility assumed, and service to be useful must be made continuous* night and day. *While this new profession must rid itself of the spirit of venality to which, in my opinion, the world is indebted for a systematic reign of silence concerning the details of this disaster.*

25   After reviewing the evidence for this last charge, Smith introduced a subject of striking interest, since, outside Boston, the matter had received scant attention in the press.

26   *It is not a pleasant duty to criticize the conduct or comment upon the shortcomings of others, but the plain truth should be told. Captain Lord of the steamship* Californian, *sailing from London to Boston, who stopped his ship in the same vicinity where the* Titanic *is supposed to have met with the accident, passed two large icebergs at 6:30 P.M. Sunday evening, April 14. At 7:15 he "passed one large iceberg and two more in sight to the southward." Because of ice, he stopped his ship for the night in latitude 42°5' North, longitude 50°7' West. And at 10:50 ship's time (and 9:10 New York time), he sent a wireless message to the* Titanic, *telling them he was "stopped and surrounded by ice." The* Titanic *operator brusquely replied to "shut up," that he was "busy." Captain Lord stated that "from the position we stopped in to the position in which the* Titanic *is supposed to have hit the iceberg was nineteen and a half miles . . ." I am of the opinion it was much nearer than the captain is willing to admit. . . .*

27   Had [Captain Lord] been vigilant . . . there is a strong possibility that every human life that was sacrificed through this disaster could have been saved.

From *Down with the Old Canoe: A Cultural History of the* Titanic *Disaster*

Steven Biel

1   The *Titanic's* commercial possibilities lay dormant from this initial outpouring of entrepreneurial energies until after World War II, when the disaster again reached mass audiences. In 1936 David O. Selznick launched a well-publicized movie project about the *Titanic*, intending to make the film Alfred Hitchcock's Hollywood debut, but immediately ran into a multitude of obstacles. Howard Hughes and a French company owned *Titanic* scripts and threatened lawsuits. British censors refused to permit a film that might criticize British shipping and so deprived Selznick of lucrative overseas markets. Then the war came, closing off still more markets and raising serious doubts about the appropriateness of a movie about a horrific ship disaster.[1] Hollywood didn't sink the liner on-screen until 1953, when Twentieth Century-Fox released *Titanic,* directed by Jean Negulesco and starring Clifton Webb and Barbara Stanwyck.

2   British obstructionism had the ironic result of ceding the *Titanic* to German filmmakers. Herbert Selpin's *Titanic* transformed the disaster into Nazi propaganda in 1943;

the hero of the film is the fictitious German first officer, who must combat the selfishness and stupidity of the British shipowner and passengers. Film historian Harry Geduld notes that as a result of Nazi propaganda minister Joseph Goebbels's artistic differences with Selpin, the director was "garrotted with his own suspenders." Two earlier German films about the disaster, E. A. Dupont's *Atlantic* (1929) and Arnold Fanck and Leni Riefenstahl's *S.O.S. Eisberg* (1933), "introduced the now familiar disaster-movie formula" of melodramatic plots and impressive special effects. (Germany also produced a novel about the disaster, Robert Prechtl's ponderous *Titanensturz: Roman eines Zeitalters,* published in 1937 and translated into English as *Titanic* in 1940. John Jacob Astor, the hero of Prechtl's book, speaks more like a German philosopher than an American tycoon. "Would this conception of a state of ecstasy lifting the mystic out of this world also explain divination?" he asks in a discussion of the Beyond among the first-cabin passengers.)[2]

3   The fate of Selznick's project suggests that the *Titanic*'s forty-year absence from American commercial culture was simply a result of mundane circumstance. But if we look at the particular ways in which the *Titanic* story was told in the 1950s, we can understand its rediscovery in more significant cultural and historical terms. Nobody deserves more credit for this rediscovery than Walter Lord, whose 1955 best seller *A Night to Remember* gave the disaster its fullest retelling since 1912 and made it speak to a modern mass audience and a new set of postwar concerns. In the creation of the *Titanic* myth there were two defining moments: 1912, of course, and 1955.

4   Lord's interest in the *Titanic* reached back to childhood. In 1926, when he was nine, he traveled to Europe on the *Titanic*'s sister ship, the *Olympic,* where he spent his time "prowling around" and trying to imagine "such a huge thing" going down in the middle of the Atlantic. At ten or eleven he was drawing pictures of the ship—"masses" of them, he recalls—and when he started collecting *Titanic* memorabilia, "people began to take notice of this oddity." After majoring in history at Princeton, serving with the Office of Strategic Services during World War II, and getting a degree from Yale Law School, Lord went to work as an editor of legal and business newsletters and then as a copywriter at the J. Walter Thompson advertising agency. He wrote *A Night to Remember* in his spare time.[3]

5   Published by Henry Holt in November 1955, the book was an immediate success. By January 1956 it had sold sixty thousand copies and climbed onto the best seller list, where it stayed for more than six months and briefly edged out Anne Morrow Lindbergh's *Gift from the Sea* (which had been at the top of the list for forty-four consecutive weeks) to take the number one spot. Without a doubt *A Night to Remember* owed much of its popularity to Holt's aggressive marketing campaign and—though Lord rightly observes that "there was virtually nothing on the subject between 1913 and 1955"—to the 1953 Webb-Stanwyck film and some recent *Titanic* articles in *Coronet, Cosmopolitan, Life,* and *Holiday.* Holt announced the book with a full-page ad on the cover of *Publishers Weekly* that showed the dust jacket illustration of the *Titanic* steaming toward the iceberg; the next page boasted that with ten thousand dollars' initial advertising and a fifty-thousand-copy first printing, it was a "sure best seller!" Lord published an account of the leadup to the crash in the December *American Heritage;* condensed versions of the book appeared in the November *Ladies' Home Journal* and the January *Reader's Digest,* and the Book-of-the-Month Club offered its own edition in June 1956. Kraft sponsored a live NBC-TV version on March 28, directed by George Roy Hill and narrated by Claude Rains, which attracted twenty-eight million viewers and helped boost hardcover sales over the hundred thousand mark. (Lord later remarked that "[m]ore people probably learned about the *Titanic* that night than at any time since 1912." The broadcast was "the biggest, most lavish, most expensive thing of its kind" yet

attempted, involving thirty-one sets, 107 actors, seventy-two speaking parts, and three thousand gallons of water and costing ninety-five thousand dollars.) Bantam issued a paperback edition in October 1956 and celebrated its fiftieth printing in 1988; the book has never been out of print.[4]

6   It would, however, be a mistake to say that marketing entirely—or even primarily— explains the resonance of *A Night to Remember*. Lord sees much of its appeal in its "breezy" style and "freshness" of form: short paragraphs, reconstructed conversation, anecdotes, and what he calls "the minute-by-minute idea." One reviewer perceptively described Lord's technique as "a kind of literary pointillism, the arrangement of contrasting bits of fact and emotion in such a fashion that a vividly real impression of an event is conveyed to the reader." The fact that the book so readily translated to television is important. The narrative is highly visual—it begins with *Titanic* lookout Frederick Fleet peering "into a dazzling night" and ends with the sun catching "the bright red-and-white stripes of the pole from the *Titanic*'s barber shop, as it bobbed in the empty sea"—and aural—full of dialogue, music, crashing, screaming, and silence.[5] Lord plunges his readers into the moment with the immediacy of a live broadcast or a television documentary. *A Night to Remember*'s appearance was bracketed by the four-year run (1953–1957) of the CBS show *You Are There*, in which actors re-created historical events (including the *Titanic* disaster, broadcast in May 1955) and Walter Cronkite interviewed the participants.[6] Though Lord claims that he hadn't seen the approach used before, Jim Bishop beat him to the best seller list in 1955 with *The Day Lincoln Was Shot*. Both authors successfully repeated the formula in 1957, Lord with *Day of Infamy*, Bishop with *The Day Christ Died*. Blurring history into news and drama, these books all collapse historical duration into intense moments of lived experience.

7   I mentioned earlier how the *Titanic* disaster confirmed a distinctly modern sense of time and space—the ability, through wireless communication, to experience events simultaneously across long distances. While this insight belongs to Stephen Kern rather than Walter Lord, *A Night to Remember* implicitly conveys much the same idea. Simple and chronological only on the most superficial level, Lord's narrative takes an imaginative approach to time and space in which hours and minutes prove extremely malleable, the ship itself seems almost infinitely complex, and the disaster assumes order and unity only from far away.

8   Fleet gazes from the crow's nest just before 11:40 P.M. on April 14, but before we can see the iceberg, Lord has shifted to the rich passengers' dogs and then back to Fleet at 10 o'clock. By the time the berg has passed from view, we have experienced the collision from the after bridge, the first class dining saloon, the galley, eleven passenger cabins, and the first class smoking room. After stopping time (or, more accurately, expanding it) for this tour through the ship, Lord moves to the bridge, repeats the collision, inspects the damage in the boiler rooms, repeats the collision again (this time from the aft boiler rooms), jumps ten miles away and half an hour back to the bridge of the *Californian*, and ends the scene with the *Californian*'s second officer watching a "big ship suddenly stop and put out most of her lights" at 11:40.[7]

9   Lord, in short, constructs a modernist narrative around a modernist event. While the subsequent chapters move the story ahead in discrete chunks of clock time, *A Night to Remember* routinely manipulates and violates this simple chronology. Moments are extended outward through space—to the *Californian*, to the survivors watching and listening from the boats, to the "wildly excited" New York City—and drawn out within the ship's expanse through the recurrent narration of simultaneous events. The narrative manages in this way to juggle an enormous cast of characters and convey a sense of the *Titanic*'s magnitude. "This book is really about the last night of a small town," Lord writes. "The *Titanic* was that big and carried that many people." As news of the collision

spreads, as passengers put on their life belts, as the boats are uncovered and the loading begins, Lord shifts the action from port to starboard, from the upper to the lower decks. The Strauses stop to reminisce about their lives together: "the ashes of the Confederacy . . . the small china business in Philadelphia . . . building Macy's into a national institution . . . and now the happy twilight that crowned successful life." But time moves differently for Second Officer Lightoller on another part of the boat deck: "His gauge showed time was flying. The pace grew faster—and sloppier." For a group of steerage women and children, the pace is agonizingly slow; their "long trip" to safety takes them "up the broad stairs to the Third Class lounge on C Deck . . . across the open well deck . . . by the Second Class library and into First Class quarters. Then down the long corridor by the surgeon's office, the private saloon for the maids and valets of First Class passengers, finally up the grand stairway to the Boat Deck." Every moment—the last boat departing, the rising of the water toward the stern, the final plunge, the boats adrift, the *Carpathia* steaming to the rescue, the rescue—Lord splits into multiple perspectives. For the women in the boats, there is an "agonizing stateliness" when the band plays "Autumn" (the hymn, not the popular song) at 2:15; for the men on deck, there is too much happening to pay attention.[8]

10   The book's main character is the *Titanic* itself, which Lord portrays in all its vastness and intricacy. While the story has an obvious beginning and end, he resists easy closure by suggesting that the multiple perspectives could be multiplied several times more; despite his painstaking research, including interviews with sixty-three survivors, to "tell everything that happened is impossible." Here again, *A Night to Remember* embeds a modernist event in a modernist form: fragmented, uncertain, open-ended. At the end of the book Lord pauses in his account of the *Carpathia*'s arrival in New York to present a list of ifs about the weather, the wireless ice warnings, the direction and timing of the collision, the construction of the ship, the number of lifeboats, the failure of the *Californian* to respond. The whole event hinges on these ifs—on alternatives and contingencies, any one of which could have radically changed the outcome.[9]

11   But there are limits to Lord's modernism. He doesn't actually call the ifs contingencies; they are "fate," and the disaster is "a classic Greek tragedy." More significantly, he interrupts the narrative at 2:20, just when the stern has disappeared into the ocean, for an extended piece of historical analysis. In addition to the book's style Lord attributes its appeal to "a new point" that *A Night to Remember* makes at this break in the story: that the sinking of the *Titanic* represented the end of an era. Admitting the class and ethnic "prejudices" of the "old days"—Lord's politics in these pages is a kind of genteel liberalism—he celebrates what he takes to be their disappearance after 1912. But he also expresses regret for "this lost world." Whether causally or symbolically, the disaster "marked the end of a general feeling of confidence." Uncertainty replaced the belief in "a steady, orderly, civilized life." The *Titanic* was "the first jar" in an "unending sequence of disillusionment. Before the *Titanic,* all was quiet. Afterward, all was tumult."[10] Not only has Lord stopped time here, but he has imposed an entirely different temporal scheme. The end-of-an-era theme grafts world-historical significance onto the minute-by-minute drama. The disaster becomes an epochal dividing line. The modernist narrative dissolves into nostalgia.

12   There is, of course, no inherent opposition between nostalgia and modernism (Henry Adams, the *Titanic* ticket holder, was a nostalgic modernist), and their compatibility in *A Night to Remember* goes a long way toward explaining the book's resonance in 1950s America. By then modernism as a literary form had become part of the mainstream, even if it was (and remains) rare in history books. Lord's narrative, moreover, offered a modernist style without a crucial element of modernist substance: irony. The disaster lends itself to irony—to a depiction of characters caught up in a frustrating and absurd situation—but Lord preferred to call it a tragedy. Faced with fate rather than

absurdity, the characters finally gain full knowledge of their predicament and act accordingly. In the end they do things rather than have things done to them. Established usages do not elude or fail them; they are not, like Hemingway's Frederic Henry, blown up while eating cheese.[11] There was nothing in Lord's book to jar its readers' sensibilities. He placed them in rather than above the action, at eye level rather than at ironic distance. Irony would have precluded Lord's kind of nostalgia.

13   What was *A Night to Remember* nostalgic *for?* Certainly not class or ethnic prejudice. But Lord also mentioned the disappearance of "some nobler instincts"—chivalry and noblesse oblige—and recognized, in retrospect, that "the women and children first idea was still very stirring" at the time he wrote the book. Tales of old-fashioned chivalry possessed obvious appeal in a postwar culture that celebrated the "traditional" family and sacralized the roles of male breadwinner and female homemaker. These roles, as Elaine Tyler May has shown, "represented a source of meaning and security in a world run amok."[12] Lord sounded a common Cold War theme when he waxed nostalgic about confidence and certainty, and though he debunked the most egregious myths about Butt and Astor, *A Night to Remember* told a new generation about how men protected women in times of danger. (Five years later, in *The Good Years,* he refined the end-of-an-era idea to give it more of a reformist bent and made the Great War rather than the *Titanic* the watershed event. "These years were good," he wrote, "because, whatever the trouble, people were sure they could fix it," an attitude no longer possible after the experience of world war. As alternatives to "Good," he suggested "Confident," "Buoyant," "Spirited," and "Golden.")[13]

14   Above and beyond its stated objects of nostalgia, Lord's narrative yearned for time itself. Review after review linked the book's excitement to its profusion of characters and, more specifically, to the ways in which Lord depicted "[w]hat they saw and felt and did at a particular moment"—"the human side of the Titanic story." Unlike the 1912 accounts, which described heroism and cowardice in terms of gender, class, and ethnicity, *A Night to Remember* revealed a spectrum of behavior among "men and women, rich and poor, officers and crew." How people "acted," said the *New York Times*, "is the core of Mr. Lord's account, and explains its fascination, a pull as powerful in its way as the last downward plunge of the ship itself." If what another reviewer called "legendary acts of gallantry" stood out most dramatically, what really mattered was the ability—the time—to think and feel and act in any way. "What would it be like to be aboard a sinking ocean liner?" began a *Newsweek* piece titled "The Fabric of Disaster." The night was "a mixture of overconfidence, heroism and stupidity," or, in a slightly different trinity, "devotion, gallantry, and stupidity." While noting Lord's "restraint," the *Christian Century* observed that "the terrible drama of this existential situation par excellence"— the fashionable Jean-Paul Sartre had even made his way into book reviews—"comes smashing through all the author's reticence."[14] In place of irony Lord posed a mimetic challenge to his readers: How would I have acted in the same situation?

15   Time to act: This is what links *A Night to Remember*'s modernism and nostalgia. Lord's method of stretching time to leap from point to point in space postponed the inevitable so that readers could see, over and over again, that the *Titanic* disaster happened slowly. Lord maintained "suspense . . . against a known conclusion"—suspense in the most literal sense, interruption and delay.[15] The *Titanic* took two hours and forty minutes to sink, and Lord's narrative, with its combination of quick jumps and recurrence, managed to move at a fast pace while dramatizing the disaster's full duration. The minute-by-minute, multiple-perspective technique and the end-of-an-era theme fused to create a double sense of lost time. Simultaneously wistful and anxious, *A Night to Remember* spoke of a bygone age in which disasters gave people time to die.

Notes

1. For a full discussion of the Selznick episode, see Eric Schaefer, "The Sinking of David O. Selznick's 'Titanic,'" *Library Chronicle of the University of Texas at Austin* 36 (1986), 57–73. At one point Selznick bought the rights to Hanson W. Baldwin's "R.M.S. Titanic," which appeared in *Harper's* in January 1934—one of the very few narrative treatments of the disaster to appear between 1913 and 1955. For a brief survey of the *Titanic*'s film career, see Harry M. Geduld, "Nearer My Wreck to Thee," *Humanist,* July–August 1987, 45.

2. Geduld, "Nearer My Wreck," 45; Robert Prechtl, *Titanic,* trans. Erna McArthur (New York: E. P. Dutton, 1940), 56, 333, 331.

Prechtl's *Titanic* sounded a Germanic version of the redemption theme. At the end of the novel Astor gives up his place in a lifeboat to a "miserable Polish woman" and her "dropsical" child, "two human mites among a million other swarming human mites." Prechtl's Astor is a kind of Nietzschean Superman, misdirecting his extraordinary will toward purely material ends until, at last, he achieves his full spiritual stature.

3. Lord, interview with author, October 17, 1992; "Walter Lord: Man behind the Book," *Titanic Commutator* 3, 28 (Winter 1980), 8.

4. *Publishers Weekly,* August 27, 1955, 1–2; Lord, interview with author; Gene Fowler, "The Unsinkable Mrs. Brown," *Coronet,* October 1949, 116–21; Lady Duff Gordon, "I Was Saved from the Titanic," *Coronet,* June 1951, 94–97; Robert Schwartz, "The Sea Tragedy That Shocked the World," *Cosmopolitan,* March 1953, 102; "Survivors Watch the 'Titanic' Go Down Again," *Life,* May 18, 1953, 91–96; Bud Greenspan, "Deaf to Disaster," *Coronet,* May 1953, 31; Jack Weeks, "Titanic," *Holiday,* June 1953, 91–94; Walter Lord, "A Night to Remember," *Ladies' Home Journal,* November 1955, 62–63, 125–62; Walter Lord, "Maiden Voyage," *American Heritage,* December 1955, 46–53, 103–05; Walter Lord, "A Night to Remember," *Reader's Digest,* January 1956, 43–48, 156–72; *Book-of-the-Month Club News,* June 1956, 12; Walter Lord, "Twenty-five Years Ago," and Edward S. Kamuda, *"A Night to Remember* in Retrospect," *Titanic Commutator* 3, 28 (Winter 1980), 9, 13, 6; "That 'Titanic' TV Triumph," *Variety,* April 4, 1956, 23; "Kraft Theatre Show Will Always Be a Night to Remember for Walter Lord," *Variety,* April 25, 1956, 27.

The sales figures are from *Publishers Weekly,* January 7–June 11, 1956.

5. Quoted in Kamuda, *"A Night to Remember* in Retrospect," 3; Lord, *Night to Remember,* 13, 167; Lord, interview with author.

6. Alex McNeil, Total Television: A Comprehensive Guide to Programming from 1948 to the Present, 3d ed. (New York: Penguin, 1991), 848.

7. Lord, *Night to Remember,* 21.

8. Ibid., 158, 177, 65, 68, 71–72, 96.

9. Ibid., 177, 166.

10. Ibid., 166, 112, 109, 114–15; Lord, interview with author.

11. See Paul Fussell, *The Great War and Modern Memory* (New York: Oxford University Press, 1975), esp. 312–13, and David M. Kennedy, *Over Here: The First World War and American Society* (New York: Oxford University Press, 1980), 214.

For two contemporary complaints about literary modernism's attainment of middle-class respectability, see Dwight Macdonald, "Masscult and Midcult" (1960), in *Against the American Grain* (New York: Random House, 1962), 3–75, and Lionel Trilling, "On the Teaching of Modern Literature" (1961), in *Beyond Culture: Essays on Literature and Learning* (New York: Viking, 1965), 3–30.

12. Lord, *Night to Remember*, 113; Lord, interview with author; Elaine Tyler May, *Homeward Bound: American Families in the Cold War Era* (New York: Basic Books, 1988), 24 and passim. Michael Kammen uses the phrase "nostalgic modernism" in a different context in *Mystic Chords of Memory: The Transformation of Tradition in American Culture* (New York: Knopf, 1991), 300.

13. Walter Lord, *The Good Years: From 1900 to the First World War* (New York: Bantam, 1962 [1960]), viii.

14. Orville Prescott, "Books of the Times," *NYT*, November 22, 1955, 33; William Hogan, "A Reconstruction of the Titanic Story," *SFC*, November 25, 1955, 19; Burke Wilkinson, "The Nightmare of April 14, 1912," *New York Times Book Review*, November 20, 1955, 3; John M. Connole, "A Night to Remember," *America*, December 10, 1955, 310; "The Fabric of Disaster," *Newsweek*, December 12, 1955, 126; Richard Blakesley, "A Night of Gallantry, Devotion, Death," *Chicago Tribune Book Review*, November 20, 1955, 1; "Down to the Sea," *Christian Century*, January 4, 1956, 19.

15. John K. Hutchens, "Book Review," *NYHT*, November 23, 1955, 17.

From *A Night to Remember*
Walter Lord

1 High in the crow's-nest of the New White Star Liner *Titanic*, Lookout Frederick Fleet peered into a dazzling night. It was calm, clear and bitterly cold. There was no moon, but the cloudless sky blazed with stars. The Atlantic was like polished plate glass; people later said they had never seen it so smooth.

2 This was the fifth night of the *Titanic*'s maiden voyage to New York, and it was already clear that she was not only the largest but also the most glamorous ship in the world. Even the passengers' dogs were glamorous. John Jacob Astor had along his Airedale Kitty. Henry Sleeper Harper, of the publishing family, had his prize Pekingese Sun Yat-sen. Robert W. Daniel, the Philadelphia banker, was bringing back a champion French-bulldog just purchased in Britain. Clarence Moore of Washington also had been dog-shopping, but the 50 pairs of English foxhounds he bought for the Loudoun Hunt weren't making the trip.

3 That was all another world to Frederick Fleet. He was one of six lookouts carried by the *Titanic*, and the lookouts didn't worry about passenger problems. They were the "eyes of the ship," and on this particular night Fleet had been warned to watch especially for icebergs.

4 So far, so good. On duty at 10 o'clock . . . a few words about the ice problem with Lookout Reginald Lee, who shared the same watch . . . a few more words about the cold . . . but mostly just silence, as the two men stared into the darkness.

5 Now the watch was almost over, and still there was nothing unusual. Just the night, the stars, the biting cold, the wind that whistled through the rigging as the *Titanic* raced across the calm, black sea at $22\frac{1}{2}$ knots. It was almost 11:40 P.M. on Sunday, the 14th of April, 1912.

6 Suddenly Fleet saw something directly ahead, even darker than the darkness. At first it was small (about the size, he thought, of two tables put together), but every second it grew larger and closer. Quickly Fleet banged the crow's-nest bell three

times, the warning of danger ahead. At the same time he lifted the phone and rang the bridge.

7   "What did you see?" asked a calm voice at the other end.

8   "Iceberg right ahead," replied Fleet.

9   "Thank you," acknowledged the voice with curiously detached courtesy. Nothing more was said.

10   For the next 37 seconds, Fleet and Lee stood quietly side by side, watching the ice draw nearer. Now they were almost on top of it, and still the ship didn't turn. The berg towered wet and glistening far above the forecastle deck, and both men braced themselves for a crash. Then, miraculously, the bow began to swing to port. At the last second the stem shot into the clear, and the ice glided swiftly by along the starboard side. It looked to Fleet like a very close shave.

11   At this moment Quartermaster George Thomas Rowe was standing watch on the after bridge. For him too, it had been an uneventful night—just the sea, the stars, the biting cold. As he paced the deck, he noticed what he and his mates called "Whiskers 'round the Light"—tiny splinters of ice in the air, fine as dust, that gave off myriads of bright colors whenever caught in the glow of the deck lights.

12   Then suddenly he felt a curious motion break the steady rhythm of the engines. It was a little like coming alongside a dock wall rather heavily. He glanced forward—and stared again. A windjammer, sails set, seemed to be passing along the starboard side. Then he realized it was an iceberg, towering perhaps 100 feet above the water. The next instant it was gone, drifting astern into the dark.

13   Meanwhile, down below in the First Class dining saloon on D Deck, four other members of the *Titanic*'s crew were sitting around one of the tables. The last diner had long since departed, and now the big white Jacobean room was empty except for this single group. They were dining-saloon stewards, indulging that the time-honored pastime of all stewards off duty—they were gossiping about their passengers.

14   Then, as they sat there talking, a faint grinding jar seemed to come from somewhere deep inside the ship. It was not much, but enough to break the conversation and rattle the silver that was set for breakfast next morning.

15   Steward James Johnson felt he knew just what it was. He recognized the kind of shudder a ship gives when she drops a propeller blade, and he knew this sort of mishap meant a trip back to the Harland & Wolff Shipyard at Belfast—with plenty of free time to enjoy the hospitality of the port. Somebody near him agreed and sang out cheerfully, "Another Belfast trip!"

16   In the galley just to the stern, Chief Night Baker Walter Belford was making rolls for the following day. (The honor of baking fancy pastry was reserved for the day shift.) When the jolt came, it impressed Belford more strongly than Steward Johnson—perhaps because a pan of new rolls clattered off the top of the oven and scattered about the floor.

17   The passengers in their cabins felt the jar too, and tried to connect it with something familiar. Marguerite Frolicher, a young Swiss girl accompanying her father on a business trip, woke up with a start. Half-asleep, she could think only of the little white lake ferries at Zurich making a sloppy landing. Softly she said to herself, "Isn't it funny . . . we're landing!"

18   Major Arthur Godfrey Peuchen, starting to undress for the night, thought it was like a heavy wave striking the ship. Mrs. J. Stuart White was sitting on the edge of her bed, just reaching to turn out the light, when the ship seemed to roll over "a thousand marbles." To Lady Cosmo Duff Gordon, waking up from the jolt, it seemed "as though somebody had drawn giant finger along the side of the ship." Mrs. John Jacob Astor thought it was some mishap in the kitchen.

CASEBOOK

19   It seemed stronger to some than to others. Mrs. Albert Caldwell pictured a large dog that had a baby kitten in its mouth and was shaking it. Mrs. Walter B. Stephenson recalled the first ominous jolt when she was in the San Francisco earthquake—then decided this wasn't that bad. Mrs. E. D. Appleton felt hardly any shock at all, but she noticed an unpleasant ripping sound . . . like someone tearing a long, long strip of calico.

20   The jar meant more to J. Bruce Ismay, Managing Director of the White Star Line, who in a festive mood was going along for the ride on the *Titanic*'s first trip. Ismay woke up with a start in his deluxe suite on B Deck—he felt sure the ship had struck something, but he didn't know what.

21   Some of the passengers already knew the answer. Mr. and Mrs. George A. Harder, a young honeymoon couple down in cabin E-50, were still awake when they heard a dull thump. Then they felt the ship quiver, and there was "a sort of rumbling, scraping noise" along the ship's side. Mr. Harder hopped out of bed and ran to the porthole. As he looked through the glass, he saw a wall of ice glide by.

22   The same thing happened to James B. McGough, a Gimbels buyer from Philadelphia, except his experience was somewhat more disturbing. His porthole was open, and as the berg brushed by, chunks of ice fell into the cabin.

23   Like Mr. McGough, most of the *Titanic*'s passengers were in bed when the jar came. On this quiet, cold Sunday night a snug bunk seemed about the best place to be. But a few shipboard die-hards were still up. As usual, most were in the First Class smoking room on A Deck.

24   And as usual, it was a very mixed group. Around one table sat Archie Butt, President Taft's military aide; Clarence Moore, the traveling Master of Hounds; Harry Widener, son of the Philadelphia streetcar magnate; and William Carter, another Main Liner. They were winding up a small dinner given by Widener's father in honor of Captain Edward J. Smith, the ship's commander. The Captain had left early, the ladies had been packed off to bed, and now the men were enjoying a final cigar before turning in too. The conversation wandered from politics to Clarence Moore's adventures in West Virginia, the time he helped interview the old feuding mountaineer Anse Hatfield.

25   Buried in a nearby leather armchair, Spencer V. Silverthorne, a young buyer for Nugent's department store in St. Louis, browsed through a new best-seller, *The Virginian*. Not far off, Lucien P. Smith (still another Philadelphian) struggled gamely through the linguistic problems of a bridge game with three Frenchmen.

26   At another table the ship's young set was enjoying a somewhat noisier game of bridge. Normally the young set preferred the livelier Café Parisien, just below on B Deck, and at first tonight was no exception. But it grew so cold that around 11:30 the girls went off to bed, and the men strolled up to the smoking room for a nightcap. Most of the group stuck to highballs; Hugh Woolner, son of the English sculptor, took a hot whisky and water; Lieutenant Hokan Bjornstrom Steffanson, a young Swedish military attaché on his way to Washington, chose a hot lemonade.

27   Somebody produced a deck of cards, and as they sat playing and laughing, suddenly there came that grinding jar. Not much of a shock, but enough to give a man a start—Mr. Silverthorne still sits up with a jolt when he tells it. In an instant the smoking-room steward and Mr. Silverthorne were on their feet . . . through the aft door . . . past the Palm Court . . . and out onto the deck. They were just in time to see the iceberg scraping along the starboard side, a little higher than the Boat Deck. As it slid by, they watched chunks of ice breaking and tumbling off into the water. In another moment it faded into the darkness astern.

28   Others in the smoking room were pouring out now. As Hugh Woolner reached the deck, he heard a man call out, "We hit an iceberg—there it is!"

29   Woolner squinted into the night. About 150 yards astern he made out a mountain of ice standing black against the starlit sky. Then it vanished into the dark.

30   The excitement, too, soon disappeared. The *Titanic* seemed as solid as ever, and it was too bitterly cold to stay outside any longer. Slowly the group filed back, Woolner picked up his hand, and the bridge game went on. The last man inside thought, as he slammed the deck door, that the engines were stopping.

31   He was right. Up on the bridge First Officer William M. Murdoch had just pulled the engine-room telegraph handle all the way to "Stop." Murdoch was in charge of the bridge this watch, and it was his problem, once Fleet phoned the warning. A tense minute had passed since then—orders to Quartermaster Hitchens to turn the wheel hard a-starboard . . . a yank on the engine-room telegraph for "Full-Speed Astern" . . . a hard push on the button closing the watertight doors . . . and finally those 37 seconds of breathless waiting.

32   Now the waiting was over, and it was all so clearly too late. As the grinding noise died away, Captain Smith rushed onto the bridge from his cabin next to the wheel-house. There were a few quick words:

33   "Mr. Murdoch, what was that?"

34   "An iceberg, sir. I hard-a-starboarded and reversed the engines, and I was going to hard-a-port around it, but she was too close. I couldn't do any more."

35   "Close the emergency doors."

36   "The doors are already closed."

37   They were closed, all right. Down in boiler room No. 6, Fireman Fred Barrett had been talking to Assistant Second Engineer James Hesketh when the warning bell sounded and the light flashed red above the watertight door leading to the stern. A quick shout of warning—an ear-splitting crash—and the whole starboard side of the ship seemed to give way. The sea cascaded in, swirling about the pipes and valves, and the two men leaped through the door as it slammed down behind them.

38   Barrett found things almost as bad where he was now, in boiler room No. 5. The gash ran into No. 5 about two feet beyond the closed compartment door, and a fat jet of sea water was spouting through the hole. Nearby, Trimmer George Cavell was digging himself out of an avalanche of coal that had poured out of a bunker with the impact. Another stoker mournfully studied an overturned bowl of soup that had been warming on a piece of machinery.

39   It was dry in the other boiler rooms farther aft, but the scene was pretty much the same—men picking themselves up, calling back and forth, asking what had happened. It was hard to figure out. Until now the *Titanic* had been a picnic. Being a new ship on her maiden voyage, everything was clean. She was, as Fireman George Kemish still recalls, "a good job . . . not what we were accustomed to in old ships, slogging our guts out and nearly roasted by the heat."

40   All the firemen had to do was keep the furnaces full. No need to work the fires with slice bars, pricker bars, and rakes. So on this Sunday night the men were taking it easy— sitting around on buckets and the trimmers' iron wheelbarrows, shooting the breeze, waiting for the 12-to-4 watch to come on.

41   Then came that thud . . . the grinding, tearing sound . . . the telegraphs ringing wildly . . . the watertight doors crashing down. Most of the men couldn't imagine what it was—the story spread that the *Titanic* had gone aground just off the Banks of Newfoundland. Many of them still thought so, even after a trimmer came running down from above shouting, "Blimey! We've struck an iceberg!"

42   About ten miles away Third Officer Charles Victor Groves stood on the bridge of the Leyland Liner *Californian,* bound from London to Boston. A plodding 6000-tonner, she

CASEBOOK

had room for 47 passengers, but none were being carried just now. On this Sunday night she had been stopped since 10:30 P.M., completely blocked by drifting ice.

43   At about 11:10 Groves noticed the lights of another ship racing up from the east on the starboard side. As the newcomer rapidly overhauled the motionless *Californian*, a blaze of deck lights showed she was a large passenger liner. Around 11:30 he knocked on the Venetian door of the chart room and told Captain Stanley Lord about it. Lord suggested contacting the new arrival by Morse lamp, and Groves prepared to do this.

44   Then, at about 11:40, he saw the big ship suddenly stop and put out most of her lights. This didn't surprise Groves very much. He had spent some time in the Far East trade, where they usually put deck lights out at midnight to encourage the passengers to turn in. It never occurred to him that perhaps the lights were still on . . . that they only seemed to go out because she was no longer broadside but had veered sharply to port.

Issues in War and Peace

This section of the Casebook gives you articles, press releases, poetry, memoir, graphic work, and even a song about people's rush to war and longing for peace. We begin with the Iraqi conflict and go back to early history. We hope that these selections will give you a sense of creative artists' responses to this important topic.

President Bush Addresses the Nation

George W. Bush

1   My fellow citizens, at this hour, American and coalition forces are in the early stages of military operations to disarm Iraq, to free its people and to defend the world from grave danger.

2   On my orders, coalition forces have begun striking selected targets of military importance to undermine Saddam Hussein's ability to wage war. These are opening stages of what will be a broad and concerted campaign. More than 35 countries are giving crucial support—from the use of naval and air bases, to help with intelligence and logistics, to the deployment of combat units. Every nation in this coalition has chosen to bear the duty and share the honor of serving in our common defense.

3   To all the men and women of the United States Armed Forces now in the Middle East, the peace of a troubled world and the hopes of an oppressed people now depend on you. That trust is well placed.

4   The enemies you confront will come to know your skill and bravery. The people you liberate will witness the honorable and decent spirit of the American military. In this conflict, America faces an enemy who has no regard for conventions of war or rules of morality. Saddam Hussein has placed Iraqi troops and equipment in civilian areas, attempting to use innocent men, women and children as shields for his own military— a final atrocity against his people.

5   I want Americans and all the world to know that coalition forces will make every effort to spare innocent civilians from harm. A campaign on the harsh terrain of a nation as large as California could be longer and more difficult than some predict. And helping Iraqis achieve a united, stable and free country will require our sustained commitment.

6   We come to Iraq with respect for its citizens, for their great civilization and for the religious faiths they practice. We have no ambition in Iraq, except to remove a threat and restore control of that country to its own people.

7   I know that the families of our military are praying that all those who serve will return safely and soon. Millions of Americans are praying with you for the safety of your loved ones and for the protection of the innocent. For your sacrifice, you have the gratitude and respect of the American people. And you can know that our forces will be coming home as soon as their work is done.

8   Our nation enters this conflict reluctantly—yet, our purpose is sure. The people of the United States and our friends and allies will not live at the mercy of an outlaw

regime that threatens the peace with weapons of mass murder. We will meet that threat now, with our Army, Air Force, Navy, Coast Guard and Marines, so that we do not have to meet it later with armies of fire fighters and police and doctors on the streets of our cities.

9   Now that conflict has come, the only way to limit its duration is to apply decisive force. And I assure you, this will not be a campaign of half measures, and we will accept no outcome but victory.

10   My fellow citizens, the dangers to our country and the world will be overcome. We will pass through this time of peril and carry on the work of peace. We will defend our freedom. We will bring freedom to others and we will prevail.

11   May God bless our country and all who defend her.

President's Message to the Iraqi People
George W. Bush

1   This is George W. Bush, the President of the United States. At this moment, the regime of Saddam Hussein is being removed from power, and a long era of fear and cruelty is ending. American and coalition forces are now operating inside Baghdad—and we will not stop until Saddam's corrupt gang is gone. The government of Iraq, and the future of your country, will soon belong to you.

2   The goals of our coalition are clear and limited. We will end a brutal regime, whose aggression and weapons of mass destruction make it a unique threat to the world. Coalition forces will help maintain law and order, so that Iraqis can live in security. We will respect your great religious traditions, whose principles of equality and compassion are essential to Iraq's future. We will help you build a peaceful and representative government that protects the rights of all citizens. And then our military forces will leave. Iraq will go forward as a unified, independent and sovereign nation that has regained a respected place in the world.

3   The United States and its coalition partners respect the people of Iraq. We are taking unprecedented measures to spare the lives of innocent Iraqi citizens, and are beginning to deliver food, water and medicine to those in need. Our only enemy is Saddam's brutal regime—and that regime is your enemy as well.

4   In the new era that is coming to Iraq, your country will no longer be held captive to the will of a cruel dictator. You will be free to build a better life, instead of building more palaces for Saddam and his sons, free to pursue economic prosperity without the hardship of economic sanctions, free to travel and speak your mind, free to join in the political affairs of Iraq. And all the people who make up your country—Kurds, Shi'a, Turkomans, Sunnis, and others—will be free of the terrible persecution that so many have endured.

5   The nightmare that Saddam Hussein has brought to your nation will soon be over. You are a good and gifted people—the heirs of a great civilisation that contributes to all humanity. You deserve better than tyranny and corruption and torture chambers. You deserve to live as free people. And I assure every citizen of Iraq: your nation will soon be free.

6   Thank you.

The Empire Backfires

Jonathan Schell

1   The first anniversary of the American invasion of Iraq has arrived. By now, we were told by the Bush Administration before the war, the flower-throwing celebrations of our troops' arrival would have long ended; their numbers would have been reduced to the low tens of thousands, if not to zero; Iraq's large stores of weapons of mass destruction would have been found and dismantled; the institutions of democracy would be flourishing; Kurd and Shiite and Sunni would be working happily together in a federal system; the economy, now privatized, would be taking off; other peoples of the Middle East, thrilled and awed, so to speak, by the beautiful scenes in Iraq, would be dismantling their own tyrannical regimes. Instead, 549 American soldiers and uncounted thousands of Iraqis, military and civilian, have died; some $125 billion has been expended; no weapons of mass destruction have been found; the economy is a disaster; electricity and water are sometime things; America's former well-wishers, the Shiites, are impatient with the occupation; terrorist bombs are taking a heavy toll; and Iraq as a whole, far from being a model for anything, is a cautionary lesson in the folly of imperial rule in the twenty-first century. And yet all this is only part of the cost of the decision to invade and occupy Iraq. To weigh the full cost, one must look not just at the war itself but away from it, at the progress of the larger policy it served, at things that have been done elsewhere—some far from Iraq or deep in the past—and, perhaps above all, at things that have been left undone.

Nuclear Fingerprints

2   While American troops were dying in Baghdad and Falluja and Samarra, Buhary Syed Abu Tahir, a Sri Lankan businessman, was busy making centrifuge parts in Malaysia and selling them to Libya and Iran and possibly other countries. The centrifuges are used for producing bomb-grade uranium. Tahir's project was part of a network set up by Abdul Qadeer Khan, the "father" of the Pakistani atomic bomb. This particular father stole most of the makings of his nuclear offspring from companies in Europe, where he worked during the 1980s. In the 1990s, the thief became a middleman—a fence—immensely enriching himself in the process. In fairness to Khan, we should add that almost everyone who has been involved in developing atomic bombs since 1945 has been either a thief or a borrower. Stalin purloined a bomb design from the United States, courtesy of the German scientist Klaus Fuchs, who worked on the Manhattan Project. China got help from Russia until the Sino-Soviet split put an end to it. Pakistan got secret help from China in the early 1970s. And now it turns out that Khan, among many, many other Pakistanis, almost certainly including the highest members of the government, has been helping Libya, Iran, North Korea and probably others obtain the bomb. That's apparently how Chinese designs—some still in Chinese—were found in Libya when its quixotic leader, Muammar Qaddafi, recently agreed to surrender his country's nuclear program to the International Atomic Energy Agency (IAEA). The rest of the designs were in English.

3   Were Klaus Fuchs's fingerprints on them? Only figuratively, because they were "copies of copies of copies," an official said. But such is the nature of proliferation. It is mainly a transfer of information from one mind to another. Copying is all there is to it. Sometimes, a bit of hardware needs to be transferred, which is where Tahir came in.

Indeed, at least seven countries are already known to have been involved in the Pakistani effort, which Mohamed ElBaradei, the head of the IAEA, called a "Wal-Mart" of nuclear technology and an American official called "one-stop shopping" for nuclear weapons. Khan even printed a brochure with his picture on it listing all the components of nuclear weapons that bomb-hungry customers could buy from him. "What Pakistan has done," the expert on nuclear proliferation George Perkovich, of the Carnegie Endowment for International Peace, has rightly said, "is the most threatening activity of proliferation in history. It's impossible to overstate how damaging this is."

4   Another word for this process of copying would be globalization. Proliferation is merely globalization of weapons of mass destruction. The kinship of the two is illustrated by other details of Tahir's story. The Sri Lankan first wanted to build his centrifuges in Turkey, but then decided that Malaysia had certain advantages. It had recently been seeking to make itself into a convenient place for Muslims from all over the world to do high-tech business. Controls were lax, as befits an export platform. "It's easy, quick, efficient. Do your business and disappear fast, in and out," Karim Raslan, a Malaysian columnist and social commentator, recently told Alan Sipress of the *Washington Post.* Probably that was why extreme Islamist organizations, including Al Qaeda operatives, had often chosen to meet there. Global terrorism is a kind of globalization, too. The linkup of such terrorism and the world market for nuclear weapons is a specter that haunts the world of the twenty-first century.

The War and Its Aims

5   But aren't we supposed to be talking about the Iraq war on this anniversary of its launch? We are, but wars have aims, and the declared aim of this one was to stop the proliferation of weapons of mass destruction. In his State of the Union address in January 2002, the President articulated the threat he would soon carry out in Iraq: "The United States of America will not permit the world's most dangerous regimes to threaten us with the world's most destructive weapons." Later, he said we didn't want the next warning to be "a mushroom cloud." Indeed, in testimony before the Senate Foreign Relations Committee, Secretary of State Colin Powell explicitly ruled out every other justification for the war. Asked about the other reasons, he said, "The President has not linked authority to go to war to any of those elements." When Senator John Kerry explained his vote for the resolution authorizing the war, he cited the Powell testimony. Thus not only Bush but also the man likely to be his Democratic challenger in this year's election justified war solely in the name of nonproliferation.

6   Proliferation, however, is not, as the President seemed to think, just a rogue state or two seeking weapons of mass destruction; it is the entire half-century-long process of globalization that stretches from Klaus Fuch's espionage to Tahir's nuclear arms bazaar and beyond. The war was a failure in its own terms because weapons of mass destruction were absent in Iraq; the war policy failed because they were present and spreading in Pakistan. For Bush's warning of a mushroom cloud over an American city, though false with respect to Iraq, was indisputably well-founded in regard to Pakistan's nuclear one-stop-shopping: The next warning stemming from this kind of failure could indeed be a mushroom cloud.

7   The questions that now cry out to be answered are, Why did the United States, standing in the midst of the Pakistani nuclear Wal-Mart, its shelves groaning with, among other things, centrifuge parts, uranium hexafluoride (supplied, we now know, to Libya) and helpful bomb-assembly manuals in a variety of languages, rush out of the premises to vainly ransack the empty warehouse of Iraq? What sort of nonproliferation

policy could lead to actions like these? How did the Bush Administration, in the name of protecting the country from nuclear danger, wind up leaving it wide open to nuclear danger?

8   In answering these questions, it would be reassuring, in a way, to report that the basic facts were discovered only after the war, but the truth is otherwise. In the case of Iraq, it's now abundantly clear that some combination of deception, self-deception and outright fraud (the exact proportions of each are still under investigation) led to the manufacture of a gross and avoidable falsehood. In the months before the war, most of the governments of the world strenuously urged the United States not to go to war on the basis of the flimsy and unconvincing evidence it was offering. In the case of Pakistan, the question of how much the Administration knew before the war has scarcely been asked, yet we know that the most serious breach—the proliferation to North Korea—was reported and publicized before the war.

9   It's important to recall the chronology of the Korean aspect of Pakistan's proliferation. In January 2003 Seymour Hersh reported in *The New Yorker* that Pakistan had given North Korea extensive help with its nuclear program, including its launch of a uranium enrichment process. In return, North Korea was sending guided missiles to Pakistan. In June 2002, Hersh revealed, the CIA had sent the White House a report on these developments. On October 4, 2002, Assistant Secretary of State for East Asia and Pacific Affairs James Kelly confronted the North Koreans with the CIA information, and, according to Kelly, North Korea's First Vice Foreign Minister, Kang Suk Ju, startled him by responding, "Of course we have a nuclear program." (Since then, the North Koreans have unconvincingly denied the existence of the uranium enrichment program.)

10   Bush of course had already named the Pyongyang government as a member of the "axis of evil." It had long been the policy of the United States that nuclearization of North Korea was intolerable. However, the Administration said nothing of the North Korean events to the Congress or the public. North Korea, which now had openly embarked on nuclear armament, and was even threatening to use nuclear weapons, was more dangerous than Saddam's Iraq. Why tackle the lesser problem in Iraq, the members of Congress would have had to ask themselves, while ignoring the greater in North Korea? On October 10, a week after the Kelly visit, the House of Representatives passed the Iraq resolution, and the next day the Senate followed suit. Only five days later, on October 16, did Bush's National Security Adviser, Condoleeza Rice, reveal what was happening in North Korea.

11   In short, from June 2002, when the CIA delivered its report to the White House, until October 16—the period in which the nation's decision to go to war in Iraq was made—the Administration knowingly withheld the news about North Korea and its Pakistan connection from the public. Even after the vote, Secretary of State Colin Powell strangely insisted that the North Korean situation was "not a crisis" but only "a difficulty." Nevertheless, he extracted a pledge from Pakistan's president, Pervez Musharraf, that the nuclear technology shipments to North Korea would stop. (They did not.) In March, information was circulating that both Pakistan and North Korea were helping Iran to develop atomic weapons. (The North Korean and Iranian crises are of course still brewing.)

12   In sum, the glaring contradiction between the policy of "regime change" for already disarmed Iraq and regime-support for proliferating Pakistan was not a postwar discovery; it was fully visible before the war. *The Nation* enjoys no access to intelligence files, yet in an article arguing the case against the war, this author was able to comment that an "objective ranking of nuclear proliferators in order of menace" would put "Pakistan first," North Korea second, Iran third and Iraq only fourth—and to note the curiosity that "the Bush Administration ranks them, of course, in exactly the reverse order, placing

Iraq, which it plans to attack, first, and Pakistan, which it befriends and coddles, nowhere on the list." Was nonproliferation, then, as irrelevant to the Administration's aims in Iraq as catching terrorists? Or was protecting the nation and the world against weapons of mass destruction merely deployed as a smokescreen to conceal other purposes? And if so, what were they?

A New Leviathan

13   The answers seem to lie in the larger architecture of the Bush foreign policy, or Bush Doctrine. Its aim, which many have properly called imperial, is to establish lasting American hegemony over the entire globe, and its ultimate means is to overthrow regimes of which the United States disapproves, pre-emptively if necessary. The Bush Doctrine indeed represents more than a revolution in American policy; if successful, it would amount to an overturn of the existing international order. In the new, imperial order, the United States would be first among nations, and force would be first among its means of domination. Other, weaker nations would be invited to take their place in shifting coalitions to support goals of America's choosing. The United States would be so strong, the President has suggested, that other countries would simply drop out of the business of military competition, "thereby making the destabilizing arms races of other eras pointless, and limiting rivalries to trade and other pursuits of peace." Much as, in the early modern period, when nation-states were being born, absolutist kings, the masters of overwhelming military force within their countries, in effect said, "There is now a new thing called a nation; a nation must be orderly; we kings, we sovereigns, will assert a monopoly over the use of force, and thus supply that order," so now the United States seemed to be saying, "There now is a thing called globalization; the global sphere must be orderly; we, the sole superpower, will monopolize force throughout the globe, and thus supply international order."

14   And so, even as the Bush Administration proclaimed US military superiority, it pulled the country out of the world's major peaceful initiatives to deal with global problems—withdrawing from the Kyoto Protocol to check global warming and from the International Criminal Court, and sabotaging a protocol that would have given teeth to the biological weapons convention. When the UN Security Council would not agree to American decisions on war and peace, it became "irrelevant"; when NATO allies balked, they became "old Europe." Admittedly, these existing international treaties and institutions were not a full-fledged cooperative system; rather, they were promising foundations for such a system. In any case, the Administration wanted none of it.

15   Richard Perle, who until recently served on the Pentagon's Defense Policy Board, seemed to speak for the Administration in an article he wrote for the *Guardian* the day after the Iraq war was launched. He wrote, "The chatterbox on the Hudson [*sic*] will continue to bleat. What will die is the fantasy of the UN as the foundation of a new world order. As we sift the debris, it will be important to preserve, the better to understand, the intellectual wreckage of the liberal conceit of safety through international law administered by international institutions."

16   In this larger plan to establish American hegemony, the Iraq war had an indispensable role. If the world was to be orderly, then proliferation must be stopped; if force was the solution to proliferation, then pre-emption was necessary (to avoid that mushroom cloud); if pre-emption was necessary, then regime change was necessary (so the offending government could never build the banned weapons again); and if all this was necessary, then Iraq was the one country in the world where it all could be demonstrated. Neither North Korea nor Iran offered an opportunity to teach these lessons—the first

because it was capable of responding with a major war, even nuclear war, and the second because even the Administration could see that US invasion would be met with fierce popular resistance. It's thus no accident that the peril of weapons of mass destruction was the sole justification in the two legal documents by which the Administration sought to legitimize the war—HJ Resolution 114 and Security Council Resolution 1441. Nor is it an accident that the proliferation threat played the same role in the domestic political campaign for the war—by forging the supposed link between the "war on terror" and nuclear danger. In short, absent the new idea that proliferation was best stopped by pre-emptive use of force, the new American empire would have been unsalable, to the American people or to Congress. Iraq was the foundation stone of the bid for global empire.

17   The reliance on force over cooperation that was writ large in the imperial plan was also writ small in the occupation of Iraq. How else to understand the astonishing failure to make any preparation for the political, military, policing and even technical challenges that would face American forces? If a problem, large or small, had no military solution, this Administration seemed incapable of even seeing it. The United States was as blind to the politics of Iraq as it was to the politics of the world.

18   Thus we don't have to suppose that Bush officials were indifferent to the spectacular dangers that Khan's network posed to the safety of the United States and the world or that the Iraqi resistance would pose to American forces. We only have to suppose that they were simply unable to recognize facts they had failed to acknowledge in their overarching vision of a new imperial order. In both cases, ideology trumped reality.

19   The same pattern is manifest on an even larger scale. Just now, the peoples of the world have embarked, some willingly and some not, on an arduous, wrenching, perilous, mind-exhaustingly complicated process of learning how to live as one indivisibly connected species on our one small, endangered planet. Seen in a certain light, the Administration's imperial bid, if successful, would amount to a kind of planetary coup d'état, in which the world's dominant power takes charge of this process by virtue of its almost freakishly superior military strength. Seen in another, less dramatic light, the American imperial solution has interposed a huge, unnecessary roadblock between the world and the Himalayan mountain range of urgent tasks that it must accomplish no matter who is in charge: saving the planet from overheating; inventing a humane, just, orderly, democratic, accountable global economy; redressing mounting global inequality and poverty; responding to human rights emergencies, including genocide; and, of course, stopping proliferation as well as rolling back the existing arsenals of nuclear arms. None of these exigencies can be met as long as the world and its greatest power are engaged in a wrestling match over how to proceed.

20   Does the world want to indict and prosecute crimes against humanity? First, it must decide whether the International Criminal Court will do the job or entrust it to unprosecutable American forces. Do we want to reverse global warming and head off the extinction of the one-third of the world's species that, according to a report published in *Nature* magazine, are at risk in the next fifty years? First, the world's largest polluter has to be drawn into the global talks. Do we want to save the world from weapons of mass destruction? First, we have to decide whether we want to do it together peacefully or permit the world's only superpower to attempt it by force of arms.

21   No wonder, then, that the Administration, as reported by Robert F. Kennedy Jr. in these pages, has mounted an assault on the scientific findings that confirm these dangers to the world. The United States' destructive hyperactivity in Iraq cannot be disentangled from its neglect of global warming. Here, too, ideology is the enemy of fact, and empire is the nemesis of progress.

CASEBOOK

22   If the engine of a train suddenly goes off the rails, a wreck ensues. Such is the war in Iraq, now one year old. At the same time, the train's journey forward is canceled. Such is the current paralysis of the international community. Only when the engine is back on the tracks and starts in the right direction can either disaster be overcome. Only then will everyone be able to even begin the return to the world's unfinished business.

Alice's Restaurant
A song by Arlo Guthrie

1   This song is called Alice's Restaurant, and it's about Alice, and the restaurant, but Alice's Restaurant is not the name of the restaurant, that's just the name of the song, and that's why I called the song Alice's Restaurant.

2   You can get anything you want at Alice's Restaurant
You can get anything you want at Alice's Restaurant
Walk right in it's around the back
Just a half a mile from the railroad track
You can get anything you want at Alice's Restaurant

3   Now it all started two Thanksgivings ago, was on—two years ago on Thanksgiving, when my friend and I went up to visit Alice at the restaurant, but Alice doesn't live in the restaurant, she lives in the church nearby the restaurant, in the bell tower, with her husband Ray and Fasha the dog. And livin' in the bell tower like that, they got a lot of room downstairs where the pews used to be in. Havin' all that room, seein' as how they took out all the pews, they decided that they didn't have to take out their garbage for a long time.

4   We got up there, we found all the garbage in there, and we decided it'd be a friendly gesture for us to take the garbage down to the city dump. So we took the half a ton of garbage, put it in the back of a red VW microbus, took shovels and rakes and implements of destruction and headed on toward the city dump.

5   Well we got there and there was a big sign and a chain across across the dump saying, "Closed on Thanksgiving." And we had never heard of a dump closed on Thanksgiving before, and with tears in our eyes we drove off into the sunset looking for another place to put the garbage.

6   We didn't find one. Until we came to a side road, and off the side of the side road there was another fifteen foot cliff and at the bottom of the cliff there was another pile of garbage. And we decided that one big pile is better than two little piles, and rather than bring that one up we decided to throw ours down.

7   That's what we did, and drove back to the church, had a Thanksgiving dinner that couldn't be beat, went to sleep and didn't get up until the next morning, when we got a phone call from Officer Obie. He said, "Kid, we found your name on an envelope at the bottom of a half a ton of garbage, and just wanted to know if you had any information about it." And I said, "Yes, sir, Officer Obie, I cannot tell a lie, I put that envelope under that garbage."

8   After speaking to Obie for about forty-five minutes on the telephone we finally arrived at the truth of the matter and said that we had to go down and pick up the

garbage, and also had to go down and speak to him at the police officer's station. So we got in the red VW microbus with the shovels and rakes and implements of destruction and headed on toward the police officer's station.

9   Now friends, there was only one or two things that Obie coulda done at the police station, and the first was he could have given us a medal for being so brave and honest on the telephone, which wasn't very likely, and we didn't expect it, and the other thing was he could have bawled us out and told us never to be seen driving garbage around the vicinity again, which is what we expected, but when we got to the police officer's station there was a third possibility that we hadn't even counted upon, and we was both immediately arrested. Handcuffed. And I said "Obie, I don't think I can pick up the garbage with these handcuffs on." He said, "Shut up, kid. Get in the back of the patrol car."

10   And that's what we did, sat in the back of the patrol car and drove to the quote Scene of the Crime unquote. I want tell you about the town of Stockbridge, Massachusets, where this happened here, they got three stop signs, two police officers, and one police car, but when we got to the Scene of the Crime there was five police officers and three police cars, being the biggest crime of the last fifty years, and everybody wanted to get in the newspaper story about it. And they was using up all kinds of cop equipment that they had hanging around the police officer's station. They was taking plaster tire tracks, foot prints, dog smelling prints, and they took twenty seven eight-by-ten colour glossy photographs with circles and arrows and a paragraph on the back of each one explaining what each one was to be used as evidence against us. Took pictures of the approach, the getaway, the northwest corner the southwest corner and that's not to mention the aerial photography.

11   After the ordeal, we went back to the jail. Obie said he was going to put us in the cell. Said, "Kid, I'm going to put you in the cell, I want your wallet and your belt." And I said, "Obie, I can understand you wanting my wallet so I don't have any money to spend in the cell, but what do you want my belt for?" And he said, "Kid, we don't want any hangings." I said, "Obie, did you think I was going to hang myself for littering?" Obie said he was making sure, and friends Obie was, 'cause he took out the toilet seat so I couldn't hit myself over the head and drown, and he took out the toilet paper so I couldn't bend the bars roll out the—roll the toilet paper out the window, slide down the roll and have an escape. Obie was making sure, and it was about four or five hours later that Alice (remember Alice? It's a song about Alice), Alice came by and with a few nasty words to Obie on the side, bailed us out of jail, and we went back to the church, had a another Thanksgiving dinner that couldn't be beat, and didn't get up until the next morning, when we all had to go to court.

12   We walked in, sat down, Obie came in with the twenty seven eight-by-ten colour glossy pictures with circles and arrows and a paragraph on the back of each one, sat down. Man came in said, "All rise." We all stood up, and Obie stood up with the twenty seven eight-by-ten colour glossy pictures, and the judge walked in sat down with a seeing eye dog, and he sat down, we sat down. Obie looked at the seeing eye dog, and then at the twenty seven eight-by-ten colour glossy pictures with circles and arrows and a paragraph on the back of each one, and looked at the seeing eye dog. And then at twenty seven eight-by-ten colour glossy pictures with circles and arrows and a paragraph on the back of each one and began to cry, 'cause Obie came to the realization that it was a typical case of American blind justice, and there wasn't nothing he could do about it, and the judge wasn't going to look at the twenty seven eight-by-ten colour glossy pictures with the circles and arrows and a paragraph on the back of each one explaining what each one was to be used as evidence against us. And we was fined $50 and had to pick up the garbage in the snow, but that's not what I came to tell you about.

CASEBOOK

13   Came to talk about the draft.

14   They got a building down New York City, it's called Whitehall Street, where you walk in, you get injected, inspected, detected, infected, neglected and selected. I went down to get my physical examination one day, and I walked in, I sat down, got good and drunk the night before, so I looked and felt my best when I went in that morning. 'Cause I wanted to look like the all-American kid from New York City, man I wanted, I wanted to feel like the all-, I wanted to be the all-American kid from New York, and I walked in, sat down, I was hung down, brung down, hung up, and all kinds o' mean nasty ugly things. And I walked in and sat down and they gave me a piece of paper, said, "Kid, see the psychiatrist, room 604."

15   And I went up there, I said, "Shrink, I want to kill. I mean, I wanna, I wanna kill. Kill. I wanna, I wanna see, I wanna see blood and gore and guts and veins in my teeth. Eat dead burnt bodies. I mean kill, Kill, KILL, KILL." And I started jumpin up and down yelling, "KILL, KILL," and he started jumpin up and down with me and we was both jumping up and down yelling, "KILL, KILL." And the sargeant came over, pinned a medal on me, sent me down the hall, said, "You're our boy."

16   Didn't feel too good about it.

17   Proceeded on down the hall gettin more injections, inspections, detections, neglections and all kinds of stuff that they was doin' to me at the thing there, and I was there for two hours, three hours, four hours, I was there for a long time going through all kinds of mean nasty ugly things and I was just having a tough time there, and they was inspecting, injecting every single part of me, and they was leaving no part untouched. Proceeded through, and when I finally came to see the last man, I walked in, walked in sat down after a whole big thing there, and I walked up and said, "What do you want?" He said, "Kid, we only got one question. Have you ever been arrested?"

18   And I proceeded to tell him the story of the Alice's Restaurant Massacre, with full orchestration and five part harmony and stuff like that and all the phenome . . . —and he stopped me right there and said, "Kid, did you ever go to court?"

19   And I proceeded to tell him the story of the twenty seven eight-by-ten colour glossy pictures with the circles and arrows and the paragraph on the back of each one, and he stopped me right there and said, "Kid, I want you to go and sit down on that bench that says Group W. . . . NOW kid!!"

20   And I, I walked over to the, to the bench there, and there is, Group W's where they put you if you may not be moral enough to join the army after committing your special crime, and there was all kinds of mean nasty ugly looking people on the bench there. Mother rapers. Father stabbers. Father rapers! Father rapers sitting right there on the bench next to me! And they was mean and nasty and ugly and horrible crime-type guys sitting on the bench next to me. And the meanest, ugliest, nastiest one, the meanest father raper of them all, was coming over to me and he was mean 'n' ugly 'n' nasty 'n' horrible and all kind of things and he sat down next to me and said, "Kid, whad'ya get?" I said, "I didn't get nothing, I had to pay $50 and pick up the garbage." He said, "What were you arrested for, kid?" And I said, "Littering." And they all moved away from me on the bench there, and the hairy eyeball and all kinds of mean nasty things, till I said, "And creating a nuisance." And they all came back, shook my hand, and we had a great time on the bench, talkin about crime, mother stabbing, father raping, all kinds of groovy things that we was talking about on the bench. And everything was fine, we was smoking cigarettes and all kinds of things, until the Sargeant came over, had some paper in his hand, held it up and said.

21   "Kids, this-piece-of-paper's-got-47-words-37-sentences-58-words-we-wanna-know-details-of-the-crime-time-of-the-crime-and-any-other-kind-of-thing-you-gotta-say-pertaining-to-and-about-the-crime-I-want-to-know-arresting-officer's-name-and-any-

other-kind-of-thing-you-gotta-say", and talked for forty-five minutes and nobody understood a word that he said, but we had fun filling out the forms and playing with the pencils on the bench there, and I filled out the massacre with the four part harmony, and wrote it down there, just like it was, and everything was fine and I put down the pencil, and I turned over the piece of paper, and there, there on the other side, in the middle of the other side, away from everything else on the other side, in parentheses, capital letters, quoted, read the following words:

22   ("KID, HAVE YOU REHABILITATED YOURSELF?")

23   I went over to the sargeant, said, "Sargeant, you got a lot a damn gall to ask me if I've rehabilitated myself, I mean, I mean, I mean that just, I'm sittin' here on the bench, I mean I'm sittin here on the Group W bench 'cause you want to know if I'm moral enough join the army, burn women, kids, houses and villages after bein' a litterbug." He looked at me and said, "Kid, we don't like your kind, and we're gonna send your finger-prints off to Washington."

24   And friends, somewhere in Washington enshrined in some little folder, is a study in black and white of my fingerprints. And the only reason I'm singing you this song now is cause you may know somebody in a similar situation, or you may be in a similar sit-uation, and if you're in a situation like that there's only one thing you can do and that's walk into the shrink wherever you are, just walk in say "Shrink, You can get anything you want, at Alice's restaurant." And walk out. You know, if one person, just one person does it they may think he's really sick and they won't take him. And if two people, two people do it, in harmony, they may think they're both faggots and they won't take either of them. And three people do it, three, can you imagine, three people walking in singin a bar of Alice's Restaurant and walking out. They may think it's an organization. And can you, can you imagine fifty people a day, I said fifty people a day walking in singin a bar of Alice's Restaurant and walking out. And friends they may thinks it's a movement.

25   And that's what it is, the Alice's Restaurant Anti-Massacre Movement, and all you got to do to join is sing it the next time it come's around on the guitar.

26   With feeling. So we'll wait for it to come around on the guitar, here and sing it when it does. Here it comes.

27   You can get anything you want, at Alice's Restaurant
You can get anything you want, at Alice's Restaurant
Walk right in it's around the back
Just a half a mile from the railroad track
You can get anything you want, at Alice's Restaurant

28   That was horrible. If you want to end war and stuff you got to sing loud. I've been singing this song now for twenty five minutes. I could sing it for another twenty five minutes. I'm not proud . . . or tired.

29   So we'll wait till it comes around again, and this time with four part harmony and feeling.

30   We're just waitin' for it to come around is what we're doing.

31   All right now.

32   You can get anything you want, at Alice's Restaurant
Excepting Alice
You can get anything you want, at Alice's Restaurant
Walk right in it's around the back
Just a half a mile from the railroad track
You can get anything you want, at Alice's Restaurant

33   Da da da da da da da dum
At Alice's Restaurant

From *Maus*

Art Spiegelman

The Family Is Sent to Auschwitz

WE WERE SO HAPPY WE CAME THROUGH. BUT WE WORRIED NOW—WERE OUR FAMILIES SAFE?

LOOK! THERE'S POPPA, WITH LOLEK AND LONIA!

WE SAW WOLFE AND TOSHA. OUR FAMILY SEEMS TO BE OKAY.

DID YOU SEE MY FATHER?

I COULDN'T SEE ANYWHERE MY FATHER.

BUT LATER SOMEONE WHO SAW HIM TOLD ME... HE CAME THROUGH THIS SAME COUSIN OVER TO THE GOOD SIDE.

HER, THEY SENT TO THE LEFT. FOUR CHILDREN WAS TOO MANY.

SPIEGELMAN... TO THE RIGHT.

THEN CAME FELA TO REGISTER...

FELA!

MY DAUGHTER! HOW CAN SHE MANAGE ALONE—WITH FOUR CHILDREN TO TAKE CARE OF?

AND, WHAT DO YOU THINK? HE SNEAKED ON TO THE BAD SIDE!

AND THOSE ON THE BAD SIDE NEVER CAME ANYMORE HOME.

THOSE WITH A STAMP *WERE* LET TO GO HOME. BUT THERE WERE VERY FEW JEWS NOW LEFT IN SOSNOWIEC...

ONE FROM THREE THEY KEPT AT THE STADIUM.... MAYBE 10,000 PEOPLE—AND WITH THEM, MY FATHER.

WELL.... IT'S ENOUGH FOR TODAY. YES, ARTIE?...

CASEBOOK

The Lost Pilot

James Tate

for my father, 1922–1944

Your face did not rot
like the others—the co-pilot,
for example, I saw him

yesterday. His face is corn-
5   mush: his wife and daughter,
the poor ignorant people, stare

as if he will compose soon.
He was more wronged than Job.
But your face did not rot

10   like the others—it grew dark,
and hard like ebony;
the features progressed in their

distinction. If I could cajole
you to come back for an evening,
15   down from your compulsive

orbiting, I would touch you,
read your face as Dallas,
your hoodlum gunner, now,

with the blistered eyes, reads
20   his braille editions. I would
touch your face as a disinterested

scholar touches an original page.
However frightening, I would
discover you, and I would not

25   turn you in; I would not make
you face your wife, or Dallas,
or the co-pilot, Jim. You

could return to your crazy
orbiting, and I would not try
30   to fully understand what

it means to you. All I know
is this: when I see you,
as I have seen you at least

once every year of my life,
35   spin across the wilds of the sky
like a tiny, African god,

I feel dead. I feel as if I were
the residue of a stranger's life,
that I should pursue you.

40   My head cocked toward the sky,
I cannot get off the ground,
and, you, passing over again,

fast, perfect, and unwilling
to tell me that you are doing
45   well, or that it was mistake

that placed you in that world,
and me in this; or that misfortune
placed these worlds in us.

The Death of the Ball Turret Gunner

Randall Jarrell

From my mother's sleep I fell into the State,
And I hunched in its belly till my wet fur froze.
Six miles from earth, loosed from its dream of life,
I woke to black flak and the nightmare fighters.
5   When I died they washed me out of the turret with a hose.

A ball turret was a Plexiglas sphere set into the belly of a B-17 or B-24, and inhabited by two .50 caliber machine-guns and one man, a short small man. When this gunner tracked with his machine guns a fighter attacking his bomber from below, he revolved with the turret; hunched upside-down in his little sphere, he looked like the foetus in the womb. The fighters which attacked him were armed with cannon firing explosive shells. The hose was a steam hose. [Jarrell's note]

Dulce et Decorum Est

Wilfred Owen

Bent double, like old beggars under sacks,
Knock-kneed, coughing like hags, we cursed through sludge,
Till on the haunting flares we turned out backs,
And towards our distant rest began to trudge.
5   Men marched asleep. Many had lost their boots,
But limped on, blood-shod. All went lame, all blind;
Drunk with fatigue; deaf even to the hoots
Of gas-shells dropping softly behind.

Gas! GAS! Quick, boys!—An ecstasy of fumbling
10 Fitting the clumsy helmets just in time,
But someone still was yelling out and stumbling
And flound'ring like a man in fire or lime.—
Dim through the misty panes and thick green light,
As under a green sea, I saw him drowning.

15 In all my dreams before my helpless sight
He plunges at me, guttering, choking, drowning.

If in some smothering dreams, you too could pace
Behind the wagon that we flung him in,
And watch the white eyes writhing in his face,
20 His hanging face, like a devil's sick of sin,
If you could hear, at every jolt, the blood
Come gargling from the froth-corrupted lungs
Bitter as the cud
Of vile, incurable sores on innocent tongues,—
25 My friend, you would not tell with such high zest
To children ardent for some desperate glory,
The old Lie: Dulce et decorum est
Pro patria mori.[1]

Grass

Carl Sandburg

Pile the bodies high at Austerlitz and Waterloo.
Shovel them under and let me work—
I am the grass; I cover all.

And pile them high at Gettysburg
5 And pile them high at Ypres and Verdun.
Shovel them under and let me work.
Two years, ten years, and passengers ask the conductor:
What place is this?
Where are we now?

10 I am the grass.
Let me work.

[1]It is sweet and proper to die for one's country.

From *Henry V*

William Shakespeare

ACT 3
Scene 1: France. Before the gates at Harfleur
Alarum. Enter the King, Exeter, Bedford, and Gloucester, followed by soldiers with scaling ladders.

KING HENRY: Once more unto the breach, dear friends, once more;
Or close the wall up with our English dead . . .
In peace, there's nothing so becomes a man,
As modest stillness, and humility:
5   But when the blast of war blows in our ears,
Then imitate the action of the tiger:
Stiffen the sinews, conjure up the blood,
Disguise fair nature with hard-favoured rage:
Then lend the eye a terrible aspect:
10   Let it pry through the portage of the head,
Like the brass cannon: let the brow o'erwhelm it
As fearfully as doth a galléd rock
O'erhang and jutty his confounded base,
Swilled with the wild and wasteful ocean.
15   Now set the teeth, and stretch the nostril wide,
Hold hard the breath, and bend up every spirit
To his full height! On, on, you noblest English,
Whose blood is fet from fathers of war-proof:
Fathers, that like so many Alexanders,
20   Have in these parts from morn till even fought,
And sheathed their swords for lack of argument.
Dishonour not your mothers: now attest
That those whom you called fathers did beget you!
Be copy now to men of grosser blood,
25   And teach them how to war! And you, good yeomen,
Whose limbs were made in England; show us here
The mettle of your pasture: let us swear,
That you are worth your breeding—which I doubt not:
For there is none of you so mean and base,
30   That hath not noble lustre in your eyes.
I see you stand like greyhounds in the slips,
Straining upon the start. The game's afoot:
Follow your spirit; and upon this charge,
Cry, 'God for Harry, England, and Saint George!'

They go.
Alarum, and chambers go off.

Address at Gettysburg
Abraham Lincoln

Address delivered at the dedication of the Cemetery at Gettysburg, November 19, 1863

1 Four score and seven years ago our fathers brought forth on this continent, a new nation, conceived in Liberty, and dedicated to the proposition that all men are created equal.

2 Now we are engaged in a great civil war, testing whether that nation, or any nation so conceived and so dedicated, can long endure. We are met on a great battle-field of that war. We have come to dedicate a portion of that field, as a final resting place for those who here gave their lives that that nation might live. It is altogether fitting and proper that we should do this.

3 But, in a larger sense, we can not dedicate—we can not consecrate—we can not hallow—this ground. The brave men, living and dead, who struggled here, have consecrated it, far above our poor power to add or detract. The world will little note, nor long remember what we say here, but it can never forget what they did here. It is for us the living, rather, to be dedicated here to the unfinished work which they who fought here have thus far so nobly advanced. It is rather for us to be here dedicated to the great task remaining before us—that from these honored dead we take increased devotion to that cause for which they gave the last full measure of devotion—that we here highly resolve that these dead shall not have died in vain—that this nation, under God, shall have a new birth of freedom—and that government of the people, by the people, for the people, shall not perish from the earth.

Waiting for the Barbarians
Constantine Cavafy

Translated by Edmund Keeley and Philip Sherrard

What are we waiting for: packed in the forum?

The barbarians are due here today.

Why isn't anything going on in the senate?
Why have the senators given up legislating?

5   Because the barbarians are coming today.
       What's the point of senators and their laws now?
       When the barbarians get here, they'll do the legislating.

Why did our emperor set out so early
to sit on his throne at the city's main gate,
10   in state, wearing the crown?

Because the barbarians are coming today
and the emperor's waiting to receive their leader.
He's even got a citation to give him,
loaded with titles and imposing names.

15   Why have our two consuls and praetors shown up today
wearing their embroidered, their scarlet togas?
Why have they put on bracelets with so many amethysts,
rings sparkling with all those emeralds?
20   Why are they carrying elegant canes
so beautifully worked in silver and gold?

Because the barbarians are coming today
and things like that dazzle barbarians.

And why don't our distinguished orators push forward as usual
to make their speeches, say what they have to say?

25   Because the barbarians are coming today
and they're bored by rhetoric and public speaking.

Why this sudden bewilderment, this confusion?
(How serious everyone looks.)
Why are the streets and squares rapidly emptying,
30   everyone going home so lost in thought?

Because it's night and the barbarians haven't come.
And some people just in from the border say
there are no barbarians any longer.

Now what's going to happen to us without them?
35   The barbarians were a kind of solution.

Hiroshima

Agyeya (Sachchidananda Vatsyaya)

Translated by Agyeya and Leonard Nathan

On this day, the sun
Appeared—no, not slowly over the horizon—
But right in the city square.
5   A blast of dazzle poured over,
Not from the middle sky,
But from the earth torn raggedly open.

Human shadows, dazed and lost, pitched
In every direction: this blaze,
Not risen from the east,
10   Smashed in the city's heart—
An immense wheel
Of Death's swart suncar, spinning down and apart
In every direction.

Instant of a sun's rise and set.
15   Vision-annihilating flare one compressed noon.

And then?
It was not human shadows that lengthened, paled, and died;
It was men suddenly become as mist, then gone.
The shadows stay:
20   Burned on rocks, stones of these vacant streets.

A sun conjured by men converted men to air, to nothing;
White shadows singed on the black rock give back
Man's witness to himself.

The Great War Dance

from *The Book of Songs* (Chinese, c. 800–500 B.C.)

Translated by Constance A. Cook

I. Lighting Up

Oh Lustrous! the king's army
      when reared
      at times, was dim
5   at times, was all aglow!
Thus with his Great Aid,
      we, the favored ones, received it.
Striding high, the king's creation
      initiated the succession
10   Culminating in this Your Lord's true army.

II. Martial Wu

Oh Brilliant! the Martial King Wu
      fearless, blazing
Truly accomplished, what the Accomplished King Wen
15   began for his descendents.
Wu, the successor, received it.
      Conquering the Yin nation, he
      exterminated
      slaughtered
20   So securing Your merit.

III. Return

Oh Brilliant! the Zhou peoples
Climbing those high mountains
    Narrow ridges
25   towering peaks
Gathered at the river.
"All under Vast Heaven"
    is the response of the assembly
    is the Mandate of the Zhou.

30 ### IV. Rewards

King's men's toil came to an end,
We in turn received it,
    the spreading bounty.
We then sought to secure
35   the Mandate of the Zhou.
Oh, it is bountiful!

V. [Silent Dance]

VI. Staunch

Pacifying the ten thousand nations,
40 Multiplying the full harvest years,
The Mandate of Heaven is not undone.
Staunch and Martial is King Wu,
    protective of his sons
    in the four regions of the world,
45   securing his house.
Oh, shining in Heaven
    Brilliant, he looks over it.

The Inaugural Poem
Nikki Giovanni

1 it's like sugar in a porcelain bowl or maybe a piece of crystal or just some fragile beautiful thing holding something sweet or maybe even just a handful of salt which is not normally thought of as sweet but if you've ever had fried chicken or fried fish or even very thin sliced fried green tomatoes though we are not limited to fried things we can consider even good Irish oatmeal not to mention a side order of grits which you can hardly find any place and when you do it is that stuff they call "instant" which isn't all that quick but it is pretty terrible and can you believe some people don't even know the difference which brings us to why we are here today

2   it isn't often that the so-called leader of the so-called free world asked a self-called poet to celebrate the various callings that people call us to and no matter what some folks say about wasting time there just are some things you need to be ready for because

if you get called all you can really do is bring yourself to the calling so I offer this poem for the president of the united states in the hopes that he is already ready since he will not have much time to learn on the job while even yet recognizing as JFK pointed out there is no school for presidents as there is no school for parenting though people keep doing things that make them parents just as voters keep doing things that make presidents so though we frequently do not know what we are doing and the people who vote for us know even less we hope the president will try to be a decent person while he is president and we hope there will be no more star-chambers because McCarthyism kills people not just hopes and dreams and Starrism has killed our spirit and if our spirit cannot live we the people cannot justify ourselves

3   glacial waters have dirt on top but are blue as they melt and even bluer as they break off and some people say this is an optical illusion because blue is the only color not absorbed but I think blue is there because the earth and sky are one and the same and if they are we all have a bit of heaven and a bit of earth and one of the things we definitely know is that the exact same proportion of salt to water in the sea is as salt to water in the human blood so all we really know is that we are connected with everything and each other and sometimes you just have to hand it to God when you see a baby hummingbird drinking at the petunias or you see your okra plant being consumed by little black bugs and you say to yourself I ought to spray those things because they are attacking one of my favorite vegetables but then you say to yourself as a better part of yourself maybe it's not the best idea to strike at something which is only trying to do what I am trying to do which is live out the full measure of its life

4   and somehow through the laughter and the tears we all will live so let's put the weapons down and let's put the guns away and let's not strike back at people whom we have initially violated and let's see if for just a brief moment we can talk it over and let's think about the new world we are borning and while we recognize we cannot repay the Indians nor the Blacks nor make whole again the Browns nor the Yellows we do not still think we should allow the Whites to run roughshod over the rest of us and we have to say that affirmative action is good and right that equal pay is good and right that paying our taxes is good and right that women have a right to our bodies and that life decisions cannot always reside with those who can enforce their desires with physical strength so this is an Inaugural poem wishing this country and this president well with the hopes that this country and this president do equal good to this earth so that this world and that sun will bring a brighter possibility to us all

Global Health

During the past few decades, numerous health crises have reached global proportions. Diseases that we had never heard of became household names when their spread could not be contained and the resulting epidemics and pandemics terrorized whole populations. The diseases we have highlighted in this casebook do not reflect the full spectrum of global diseases plaguing us today. As we imply—by including Giovanni Boccaccio and the article on bubonic plague—epidemics have long been with us. Technology has made the world smaller by allowing us to travel more easily and more frequently. But travel helps us to spread disease more easily, as well—and will continue to do so unless we are vigilant.

From *The Normal Heart*

Larry Kramer

ACT ONE
Scene 1

The office of DR. EMMA BROOKNER. *Three men are in the waiting area:* CRAIG DON-NER, MICKEY MARCUS, *and* NED WEEKS.

CRAIG: (*After a long moment of silence.*) I know something's wrong.

MICKEY: There's nothing wrong. When you're finished we'll go buy you something nice. What would you like?

CRAIG: We'll go somewhere nice to eat, okay? Did you see that guy in there's spots?

5 MICKEY: You don't have those. Do you?

CRAIG: No.

MICKEY: Then you don't have anything to worry about.

CRAIG: She said they can be inside you, too.

MICKEY: They're not inside you.

10 CRAIG: They're inside me.

MICKEY: Will you stop! Why are you convinced you're sick?

CRAIG: Where's Bruce? He's supposed to be here. I'm so lucky to have such a wonderful lover. I love Bruce so much, Mickey. I know something's wrong.

MICKEY: Craig, all you've come for is some test results. Now stop being such a
15 hypochondriac.

CRAIG: I'm tired all the time. I wake up in swimming pools of sweat. Last time she felt me and said I was swollen. I'm all swollen, like something ready to explode. Thank you for coming with me, you're a good friend. Excuse me for being such a mess, Ned. I get freaked out when I don't feel well.

20 MICKEY: Everybody does.

(DAVID *comes out of* EMMA's *office. There are highly visible purple lesions on his face. He wears a long-sleeved shirt. He goes to get his jacket, which he's left on one of the chairs.*)

DAVID: Whoever's next can go in.

25 CRAIG: Wish me luck.

MICKEY: (*Hugging* CRAIG.) Good luck.

(CRAIG *hugs him, then* NED, *and goes into* EMMA's *office.*)

DAVID: They keep getting bigger and bigger and they don't go away. (*To* NED.) I sold you a ceramic pig once at Maison France on Bleecker Street. My name is David.

30 NED: Yes, I remember. Somebody I was friends with then collects pigs and you had the biggest pig I'd ever seen outside of a real pig.

DAVID: I'm her twenty-eighth case and sixteen of them are dead. (*He leaves.*)

NED: Mickey, what the fuck is going on?

MICKEY: I don't know. Are you here to write about this?

35 NED: I don't know. What's wrong with that?

MICKEY: Nothing, I guess.

NED: What about you? What are you going to say? You're the one with the health column.

MICKEY: Well, I'll certainly write about it in the *Native,* but I'm afraid to put it in the stuff I write at work.

40 *NED:*   What are you afraid of?

MICKEY: The city doesn't exactly show a burning interest in gay health. But at least I've still got my job: the Health Department has had a lot of cutbacks.

NED: How's John?

MICKEY: John? John who?

45 *NED:*   You've had so many I never remember their last names.

MICKEY: Oh, you mean John. I'm with Gregory now. Gregory O'Connor.

NED: The old gay activist?

MICKEY: Old? He's younger than you are. I've been with Gregory for ten months now.

NED: Mickey, that's very nice.

50 *MICKEY:*   He's not even Jewish. But don't tell my rabbi.

CRAIG: *(Coming out of* EMMA's *office.)* I'm going to die. That's the bottom line of what she's telling me. I'm so scared. I have to go home and get my things and come right back and check in. Mickey, please come with me. I hate hospitals. I'm going to die. Where's Bruce? I want Bruce.

55 (MICKEY *and* CRAIG *leave.* DR. EMMA BROOKNER *comes in from her office. She is in a motorized wheelchair. She is in her mid-to-late thirties.)*

EMMA: Who are you?

NED: I'm Ned Weeks. I spoke with you on the 'phone after the *Times* article.

EMMA: You're the writer fellow who's scared. I'm scared, too. I hear you've got a big

60 mouth.

NED: Is big mouth a symptom?

EMMA: No, a cure. Come on in and take your clothes off.

(Lights up on an examining table, center stage. NED *starts to undress.)*

NED: Dr. Brookner, what's happening?

65 *EMMA:*   I don't know.

NED: In just a couple of minutes you told two people I know something. The article said there isn't any cure.

EMMA: Not even any good clues yet. And even if they found out tomorrow what's happening, it takes years to find out how to cure and prevent anything. All I know is

70 this disease is the most insidious killer I've ever seen or studied or heard about. And I think we're seeing only the tip of the iceberg. And I'm afraid it's on the rampage. I'm frightened nobody important is going to give a damn because it seems to be happening mostly to gay men. Who cares if a faggot dies? Does it occur to you to do anything about it. Personally?

75 *NED:*   Me?

EMMA: Somebody's got to do something.

NED: Wouldn't it be better coming from you?

EMMA: Doctors are extremely conservative; they try to stay out of anything that smells political, and this smells. Bad. As soon as you start screaming you get treated like a

80 nut case. Maybe you know that. And then you're ostracized and rendered worthless, just when you need cooperation most. Take off your socks.

(NED, *in his undershorts, is now sitting on the examining table.* EMMA *will now examine him, his skin particularly, starting with the bottom of his feet, feeling his lymph glands, looking at his scalp, into his mouth . . .)*

85 *NED:*   Nobody listens for very long anyway. There's a new disease of the month every day.

EMMA: This hospital sent its report of our first cases to the medical journals over a year ago. *The New England Journal of Medicine* has finally published it, and last week, which brought you running, the *Times* ran something on some inside page. Very inside: page twenty. If you remember, Legionnaires' Disease, toxic-shock, they

90 both hit the front page of the *Times* the minute they happened. And stayed there

until somebody did something. The front page of the *Times* has a way of inspiring action. Lie down.

NED: They won't even use the word "gay" unless it's in a direct quote. To them we're still homosexuals. That's like still calling blacks Negroes. The *Times* has always had trouble writing about anything gay.

EMMA: Then how is anyone going to know what's happening? And what precautions to take? Someone's going to have to tell the gay population fast.

NED: You've been living with this for over a year? Where's the Mayor? Where's the Health Department?

EMMA: They know about it. You have a Commissioner of Health who got burned with the Swine Flu epidemic, declaring an emergency when there wasn't one. The government appropriated $150 million for that mistake. You have a Mayor who's a bachelor and I assume afraid of being perceived as too friendly to anyone gay. And who is also out to protect a billion-dollar-a-year tourist industry. He's not about to tell the world there's an epidemic menacing his city. And don't ask me about the President. Is the Mayor gay?

NED: If he is, like J. Edgar Hoover, who would want him?

EMMA: Have you had any of the symptoms?

NED: I've had most of the sexually transmitted diseases the article said come first. A lot of us have. You don't know what it's been like since the sexual revolution hit this country. It's been crazy, gay or straight.

EMMA: What makes you think I don't know? Any fever, weight loss, night sweats, diarrhea, swollen glands, white patches in your mouth, loss of energy, shortness of breath, chronic cough?

NED: No. But those could happen with a lot of things, couldn't they?

EMMA: And purple lesions. Sometimes. Which is what I'm looking for. It's a cancer. There seems to be a strange reaction in the immune system. It's collapsed. Won't work. Won't fight. Which is what it's supposed to do. So most of the diseases my guys are coming down with—and there are some very strange ones—are caused by germs that wouldn't hurt a baby, not a baby in New York City anyway. Unfortunately, the immune system is the system we know least about. So where is this big mouth I hear you've got?

NED: I have more of a bad temper than a big mouth.

EMMA: Nothing wrong with that. Plenty to get angry about. Health is a political issue. Everyone's entitled to good medical care. If you're not getting it, you've got to fight for it. Do you know this is the only country in the industrialized world besides South Africa that doesn't guarantee health care for everyone? Open your mouth. Turn over. One of my staff told me you were well-known in the gay world and not afraid to say what you think. Is that true? I can't find any gay leaders. I tried calling several gay organizations. No one ever calls me back. Is anyone out there?

NED: There aren't any organizations strong enough to be useful, no. Dr. Brookner, nobody with a brain gets involved in gay politics. It's filled with the great unwashed radicals of any counterculture. That's why there aren't any leaders the majority will follow. Anyway, you're talking to the wrong person. What I think is politically incorrect.

EMMA: Why?

NED: Gay is good to that crowd, no matter what. There's no room for criticism, looking at ourselves critically.

EMMA: What's your main criticism?

NED: I hate how we play victim, when many of us, most of us, don't have to.

EMMA: Then you're exactly what's needed now.

NED: Nobody ever listens. We're not exactly a bunch that knows how to play follow the leader.

EMMA: Maybe they're just waiting for somebody to lead them.

NED: We are. What group isn't?

145 EMMA: You can get dressed. I can't find what I'm looking for.

NED: *(Jumping down and starting to dress.)* Needed? Needed for what? What is it exactly you're trying to get me to do?

EMMA: Tell gay men to stop having sex.

NED: What?

150 EMMA: Someone has to. Why not you?

NED: It is a preposterous request.

EMMA: It only sounds harsh. Wait a few more years, it won't sound so harsh.

NED: Do you realize that you are talking about millions of men who have singled out promiscuity to be their principal political agenda, the one they'd die before aban-

155 doning. How do you deal with that?

EMMA: Tell them they may die.

NED: You tell them!

EMMA: Are you saying you guys can't relate to each other in a nonsexual way?

NED: It's more complicated than that. For a lot of guys it's not easy to meet each other

160 in any other way. It's a way of connecting—which becomes an addiction. And then they're caught in the web of peer pressure to perform and perform. Are you sure this is spread by having sex?

EMMA: Long before we isolated the hepatitis viruses we knew about the diseases they caused and had a good idea of how they got around. I think I'm right about this. I

165 am seeing more cases each week than the week before. I figure that by the end of the year the number will be doubling every six months. That's something over a thousand cases by next June. Half of them will be dead. Your two friends I've just diagnosed? One of them will be dead. Maybe both of them.

NED: And you want me to tell every gay man in New York to stop having sex?

170 EMMA: Who said anything about just New York?

NED: You want me to tell every gay man across the country—

EMMA: Across the world! That's the only way this disease will stop spreading.

NED: Dr. Brookner, isn't that just a tiny bit unrealistic?

EMMA: Mr. Weeks, if having sex can kill you, doesn't anybody with half a brain stop

175 fucking? But perhaps you've never lost anything. Good-bye.

    (BRUCE NILES, *an exceptionally handsome man in his late thirties, rushes in carrying* CRAIG, *helped by* MICKEY.)

BRUCE: *(Calling from off.)* Where do I go? Where do I go?

EMMA: Quickly—put him on the table. What happened?

180 BRUCE: He was coming out of the building and he started running to me and then he . . . then he collapsed to the ground.

EMMA: What is going on inside your bodies!

    (CRAIG *starts to convulse.* BRUCE, MICKEY, *and* NED *restrain him.*)

EMMA: Gently. Hold on to his chin.

185 *(She takes a tongue depressor and holds* CRAIG's *tongue flat; she checks the pulse in his neck; she looks into his eyes for vital signs that he is coming around;* CRAIG's *convulsions stop.)*

    You the lover?

BRUCE: Yes.

190 EMMA: What's your name?

CASEBOOK

BRUCE: Bruce Niles, ma'am.

EMMA: How's your health?

BRUCE: Fine. Why—is it contagious?

EMMA: I think so.

195 MICKEY: Then why haven't you come down with it?

EMMA: *(Moving toward a telephone.)* Because it seems to have a very long incubation period and require close intimacy. Niles? You were Reinhard Holz's lover?

BRUCE: How did you know that? I haven't seen him in a couple of years.

EMMA: *(Dialing the hospital emergency number.)* He died three weeks ago. Brookner.

200   Emergency. Set up a room immediately.

(Hangs up.)

BRUCE: We were only boyfriends for a couple months.

MICKEY: It's like some sort of plague.

EMMA: There's always a plague. Of one kind or another. I've had it since I was a kid.

205   Mr. Weeks, I don't think your friend is going to live for very long.

Bush Administration Weighs Condom Warning

Lara Lakes Jordan   March 12, 2004

1   Following recent studies indicating that condoms do not safeguard against HPV, a widespread STD that can cause genital warts or cervical cancer, the Bush administration is considering requiring warning labels on condom packages stating that the condoms do not protect users from all STDs. Currently, packages say that condoms, if used properly, reduce the risk of AIDS and other STDs—but do not mention HPV.

2   The Food and Drug Administration "has developed a regulatory plan to provide condom users with a consistent labeling message and the protection they should expect from condom use," Dr. Daniel G. Schultz, director of the agency's Office of Device Evaluation, said Thursday. Schultz told members of a House Government Reform subcommittee the FDA "is preparing new guidance on condom labeling to address these issues."

3   The question is whether to provide any additional information regarding protection against HPV—without discouraging people from using condoms for HIV/AIDS protection. The FDA has considered warning labels since President Clinton directed the agency in 2000 to look into whether information included in packages accurately reflected condom effectiveness in preventing all STDs, including HPV.

4   "Are condoms perfect? Of course not. But reality requires us not to make a public health strategy against protection, but rather to ask a key question: compared to what?" responded Rep. Henry Waxman (D-Calif.). Waxman added that lawmakers who offer abstinence-only programs as the solution to STDs and teen pregnancy overlook evidence indicating "abstinence-only education works rarely, if at all."

5   But according to Rep. Jo Ann Davis (R-Va.), "This is not about social ideology, or religious ideology. It's about informing women. . . . And truly, the only way to be protected is abstinence. That's not ideology—it's fact."

6   More than 2 million American women are infected with HPV each year, said Dr. Ed Thompson, deputy director for public health services at CDC. Ten thousand women are diagnosed each year with cervical cancer, claiming 4,000 lives, Thompson said.

Washington: Safe Sex the "Norm" among Seattle Gays

Julie Davidow

1   Results of a study presented at the National STD Prevention Conference in Philadelphia showed that most gay and bisexual men in Seattle are taking steps to protect themselves and their partners from STDs. The telephone survey of 400 men around the city found that one in five gay men said they had unprotected anal sex with partners whose HIV status they did not know or who had a different status than theirs. The majority said they use condoms during anal intercourse, avoid sex with partners whose HIV status they do not know, and disclose their own HIV status before having sex.

2   "That means [safe sex] is the community norm," said Dr. Hunter Handsfield, director of King County STD Control Program and co-author of the study. "Most gay men are in fact sexually responsible."

3   Handsfield said a smaller group who practice unsafe sex likely drives a recent surge in HIV and other STDs among gay and bisexual men. Another study at the conference found that only about one-third of 149 gay and bisexual men interviewed after being tested for HIV at King County health clinics last year knew their most recent anal sex partner's HIV status. Handsfield said the telephone survey allowed health officials to gauge practices of a wider gay/bisexual male community than those populations that seek out county services and thus may be at higher risk for contracting STDs.

From the *Seattle Post-Intelligencer*, March 12, 2001. Reprinted by permission.

CASEBOOK

Fact Sheet 104: Tuberculosis

World Health Organization

1   Tuberculosis (TB) kills approximately 2 million people each year. The global epidemic is growing and becoming more dangerous. The breakdown in health services, the spread of HIV/AIDS and the emergence of multidrug-resistant TB are contributing to the worsening impact of this disease.

2   In 1993, the World Health Organization (WHO) took an unprecedented step and declared tuberculosis a global emergency, so great was the concern about the modern TB epidemic.

3   It is estimated that between 2002 and 2020, approximately 1000 million people will be newly infected, over 150 million people will get sick, and 36 million will die of TB—if control is not further strengthened.

Infection and Transmission

4   TB is a contagious disease. Like the common cold, it spreads through the air. Only people who are sick with pulmonary TB are infectious. When infectious people cough, sneeze, talk or spit, they propel TB germs, known as bacilli, into the air. A person needs only to inhale a small number of these to be infected.

5   Left untreated, each person with active TB will infect on average between 10 and 15 people every year. But people infected with TB will not necessarily get sick with the

disease. The immune system 'walls off' the TB bacilli which, protected by a thick waxy coat, can lie dormant for years. When someone's immune system is weakened, the chances of getting sick are greater.

- Someone in the world is newly infected with TB every second.
- Nearly 1 percent of the world's population is newly infected with TB each year.
- Overall, one third of the world's population is currently infected with the TB bacillus.
- 5–10 percent of people who are infected with TB (but who are not infected with HIV) become sick or infectious at some time during their life.

Global and Regional Incidence

6   Each year, more people are dying of TB. In Eastern Europe and Africa, TB deaths are increasing after almost 40 years of decline. In terms of numbers of cases, the biggest burden of TB is in southeast Asia.

Factors Contributing to the Rise in TB

7   • TB kills about 2 million people each year (including persons infected with HIV).

- More than 8 million people become sick with TB each year.
- About 2 million TB cases per year occur in sub-Saharan Africa. This number is rising rapidly as a result of the HIV/AIDS epidemic.
- Around 3 million TB cases per year occur in southeast Asia.
- Over a quarter of a million TB cases per year occur in Eastern Europe.

HIV Is Accelerating the Spread of TB

8   HIV and TB form a lethal combination, each speeding the other's progress. HIV weakens the immune system. Someone who is HIV-positive and infected with TB is many times more likely to become sick with TB than someone infected with TB who is HIV-negative. TB is a leading cause of death among people who are HIV-positive. It accounts for about 11 percent of AIDS deaths worldwide. In Africa, HIV is the single most important factor determining the increased incidence of TB in the past 10 years.

Poorly Managed TB Programs Are Threatening to Make TB Incurable

9   Until 50 years ago, there were no drugs to cure TB. Now, strains that are resistant to a single drug have been documented in every country surveyed and, what is more, strains of TB resistant to all major anti-TB drugs have emerged. Drug-resistant TB is caused by inconsistent or partial treatment, when patients do not take all their drugs regularly for the required period because they start to feel better, doctors and health workers prescribe the wrong treatment regimens or the drug supply is unreliable. A particularly dangerous form of drug-resistant TB is multidrug-resistant TB (MDR-TB), which is defined as the disease due to TB bacilli resistant to at least isoniazid and rifampicin, the two most powerful anti-TB drugs. Rates of MDR-TB are high in some countries, especially in the former Soviet Union, and threaten TB control efforts.

10   From a public health perspective, poorly supervised or incomplete treatment of TB is worse than no treatment at all. When people fail to complete standard treatment regimens, or are given the wrong treatment regimen, they may remain infectious. The bacilli in their lungs may develop resistance to anti-TB drugs. People they infect will

have the same drug-resistant strain. While drug-resistant TB is treatable, it requires extensive chemotherapy (up to two years of treatment) that is often prohibitively expensive (often more than 100 times more expensive than treatment of drug-susceptible TB), and is also more toxic to patients.

11   WHO and its international partners have formed the DOTS-Plus Working Group, which is attempting to determine the best possible strategy to manage MDR-TB. One of the goals of DOTS-Plus is to increase access to expensive second-line anti-TB drugs for WHO-approved TB control programmes in low- and middle-income countries.

Movement of People Is Helping the Spread of TB

12   Global trade and the number of people traveling in aeroplanes have increased dramatically over the past 40 years. In many industrialized countries, at least one-half of TB cases are among foreign-born people. In the United States, nearly 40 percent of TB cases are among foreign-born people.

13   The number of refugees and displaced people in the world is also increasing. Untreated TB spreads quickly in crowded refugee camps and shelters. It is difficult to treat mobile populations, as treatment takes at least six months and should ideally be supervised. As many as 50 percent of the world's refugees could be infected with TB. As they move, they may spread TB.

Effective TB Control

14   The WHO-recommended treatment strategy for detection and cure of TB is DOTS. DOTS combines five elements: political commitment, microscopy services, drug supplies, surveillance and monitoring systems and use of highly efficacious regimes with direct observation of treatment.

15   Once patients with infectious TB (bacilli visible in a sputum smear) have been identified using microscopy services, health and community workers and trained volunteers observe patients swallowing the full course of the correct dosage of anti-TB medicines (treatment lasts six to eight months). The most common anti-TB drugs are isoniazid, rifampicin, pyrazinamide, streptomycin and ethambutol.

16   Sputum smear testing is repeated after two months, to check progress, and again at the end of treatment. A recording and reporting system documents patients' progress throughout, and the final outcome of treatment.

17   Since DOTS was introduced on a global scale in 1991, about 10 million patients have received DOTS treatment. In half of China, cure rates among new cases are 96 percent. In Peru, widespread use of DOTS for more than five years has led to the successful treatment of 91 percent of cases and a decline in incidence.

18   By the end of 2000, all 22 of the highest burden countries which bear 80 percent of the world's estimated incident cases had adopted DOTS. Fifty-five percent of the global population had access to DOTS, double the fraction reported in 1995. In the same year, 27 percent of estimated TB patients received treatment under DOTS, two and a half times the fraction reported in 1995.

- DOTS produces cure rates of up to 95 percent even in the poorest countries.

- DOTS prevents new infections by curing infectious patients.

- DOTS prevents the development of MDR-TB by ensuring the full course of treatment is followed.

- A six-month supply of drugs for DOTS costs as little as US $10 per patient in some parts of the world.

CASEBOOK

- The World Bank has ranked the DOTS strategy as one of the "most cost-effective of all health interventions."

19   WHO targets are to detect 70 percent of new infectious TB cases and to cure 85 percent of those detected. Ten countries had achieved these targets in 2000. Governments, nongovernmental organizations and civil society must continue to act to improve TB control if we are to reach these targets worldwide.

Medieval Black Death Was Probably Not Bubonic Plague
Pennsylvania State University and *Science Daily*

1   The Black Death of the 1300s was probably not the modern disease known as bubonic plague, according to a team of anthropologists studying these fourteenth-century epidemics.

2   "Although on the surface, they seem to have been similar, we are not convinced that the epidemic in the fourteenth century and the present day bubonic plague are the same," says Dr. James Wood, professor of anthropology and demography at Penn State. "Old descriptions of disease symptoms are usually too non-specific to be a reliable basis for diagnosis."

3   The researchers note that it was the symptom of lymphatic swelling that led nineteenth-century bacteriologists to identify the fourteenth-century epidemic as bubonic plague.

4   "The symptoms of the Black Death included high fevers, fetid breath, coughing, vomiting of blood and foul body odor," says Rebecca Ferrell, graduate student in anthropology. "Other symptoms were red bruising or hemorrhaging of skin and swollen lymph nodes. Many of these symptoms do appear in bubonic plague, but they can appear in many other diseases as well."

5   The researchers, who also include Sharon DeWitt-Avina, Penn State graduate student in anthropology, Stephen Matthews and Mark Shriver, both professors in the Population Research Institute at Penn State, and Darryl Holman, assistant professor of anthropology, University of Washington, Seattle, are investigating church records and other documents from England to reconstruct the virulence, spacial diffusion and temporal dynamics of the Black Death.

6   They are looking especially closely at bishops' records of the replacement of priests in several English dioceses. Although these records are often incomplete and difficult to interpret, they clearly show that many priests died during the epidemic period of 1349 to 1350.

7   "These records indicate that the spread of the Black Death was more rapid than we formerly believed," Wood told attendees today (April 12, 2000) at the annual meeting of the American Association of Physical Anthropologists in Buffalo, N.Y. "This disease appears to spread too rapidly among humans to be something that must first be established in wild rodent populations, like bubonic plague. An analysis of the priests' monthly mortality rates during the epidemic shows a 45-fold greater risk of death than during normal times, a level of mortality far higher than usually associated with bubonic plague."

8   Modern bubonic plague typically needs to reach a high frequency in the rat population before it spills over into the human community via the flea vector. Historically, epidemics of bubonic plague have been associated with enormous die-offs of rats.

9   "There are no reports of dead rats in the streets in the 1300s of the sort common in more recent epidemics when we know bubonic plague was the causative agent," says Wood.

10   Instead of being spread by animals and insect vectors, the researchers believe that the Black Death was transmitted through person-to-person contact, as are measles and smallpox. The geographic pattern of the disease seems to bear this out, since the disease spread rapidly along roadways and navigable rivers and was not slowed down by the kinds of geographical barrier that would restrict the movement of rodents.

11   "It is possible that the Black Death was caused by any of a number of infectious organisms, but we are not ready to pinpoint the causative agent," says Wood. "The Black Death was too quickly identified with bubonic plague in the past. Indeed, historians took what was known about the bubonic plague and used it erroneously to fill in the many gaps in our picture of the Black Death. We do not want to make the same mistake by identifying some other possible cause prematurely."

12   The researchers do not rule out the possibility that the Black Death might have been caused by an ancestor of the modern plague bacillus, which might later have mutated into the insect-borne disease of rodents that we now call bubonic plague. The fact is that we can only trace modern bubonic plague reliably back to the late eighteenth century or early nineteenth century, according to Wood. Who knows when it first emerged?

13   "We too often make the assumption that while a lot of things change in the interaction of infectious diseases and human hosts, the microbe itself stays more or less the same," says Wood. "This is wrong. If anything is likely to change, it is a microbe that goes through millions of generations and an equal number of chances to mutate over a few centuries. We see no reason to think that the Black Death pathogen still exists in anything like its original form."

CASEBOOK

From *The Decameron*
Giovanni Boccaccio (1313–1375)

Translated by M. Rigg

1   I say, then, that the years of the beatific incarnation of the Son of God had reached the toll of one thousand three hundred and forty eight, when in the illustrious city of Florence, the fairest of all the cities of Italy, there made its appearance that deadly pestilence, which, whether disseminated by the influence of the celestial bodies, or sent upon us mortals by God in His just wrath by way of retribution for our iniquities, had had its origin some years before in the East, whence, after destroying an innumerable multitude of living beings, it had propagated itself without respite from place to place, and so calamitously, had spread into the West.

2   In Florence, despite all that human wisdom and forethought could devise to avert it, as the cleansing of the city from many impurities by officials appointed for the purpose, the refusal of entrance to all sick folk, and the adoption of many precautions for the preservation of health; despite also humble supplications addressed to God, and often repeated both in public procession and otherwise by the devout; towards the beginning of the spring of the said year the doleful effects of the pestilence began to be horribly apparent by symptoms that shewed as if miraculous.

3   Not such were they as in the East, where an issue of blood from the nose was a manifest sign of inevitable death; but in men and women alike it first betrayed itself by the emergence of certain tumors in the groin or the armpits, some of which grew as large as a common apple, others as an egg, some more, some less, which the common folk called *gavoccioli*. From the two said parts of the body this deadly gavocciolo soon began to propagate and spread itself in all directions indifferently; after which the form of the malady began to change, black spots or livid making their appearance in many cases on the arm or the thigh or elsewhere, now few and large, then minute and numerous. And as the gavocciolo had been and still were an infallible token of approaching death, such also were these spots on whomsoever they shewed themselves. Which maladies seemed set entirely at naught both the art of the physician and the virtue of physic; indeed, whether it was that the disorder was of a nature to defy such treatment, or that the physicians were at fault—besides the qualified there was now a multitude both of men and of women who practiced without having received the slightest tincture of medical science—and, being in ignorance of its source, failed to apply the proper remedies; in either case, not merely were those that covered few, but almost all within three days from the appearance of the said symptoms, sooner or later, died, and in most cases without any fever or other attendant malady.

4   Moreover, the virulence of the pest was the greater by reason the intercourse was apt to convey it from the sick to the whole, just as fire devours things dry or greasy when they are brought close to it, the evil went yet further, for not merely by speech or association with the sick was the malady communicated to the healthy with consequent peril of common death; but any that touched the clothes the sick or aught else that had been touched, or used by these seemed thereby to contract the disease.

5   So marvelous sounds that which I have now to relate, that, had not many, and I among them, observed it with their own eyes, I had hardly dared to credit it, much less to set it down in writing, though I had had it from the lips of a credible witness.

6   I say, then, that such was the energy of the contagion of the said pestilence, that it was not merely propagated from man to woman, but, what is much more startling, it was frequently observed, that things which had belonged to one sick or dead of the disease, if touched by some other living creature, not of the human species, were the occasion, not merely of sickening, but of an almost instantaneous death. Whereof my own eyes (as I said a little before) had cognisance, one day among others, by the following experience. The rags of a poor man who had died of the disease being strewn about the open street, two hogs came thither, and after, as is their wont, no little trifling with their snouts, took the rags between their teeth and tossed them to and fro about their chaps; whereupon, almost immediately, they gave a few turns, and fell down dead, as if by poison, upon the rags which in an evil hour they had disturbed.

7   In which circumstances, not to speak of many others of a similar or even graver complexion, divers apprehensions and imaginations were engendered in the minds of such as were left alive, inclining almost all of them to the same harsh resolution, to wit, to shun and abhor all contact with the sick and all that belonged to them, thinking thereby to make each his own health secure. Among whom there were those who thought that to live temperately and avoid all excess would count for much as a preservative against seizures of this kind. Wherefore they banded together, and dissociating themselves from all others, formed communities in houses where there were no sick, and lived a separate and secluded life, which they regulated with the utmost care, avoiding every kind of luxury, but eating and drinking moderately of the most delicate viands and the finest wines, holding converse with none but one another, lest tidings of sickness or death should reach them, and diverting their minds with music and such other delights as they could

devise. Others, the bias of whose minds was in the opposite direction, maintained, that to drink freely, frequent places of public resort, and take their pleasure with song and revel, sparing to satisfy no appetite, and to laugh and mock at no event, was the sovereign remedy for so great an evil: and that which they affirmed they also put in practice, so far as they were able, resorting day and night, now to this tavern, now to that, drinking with an entire disregard of rule or measure, and by preference making the houses of others, as it were, their inns, if they but saw in them aught that was particularly to their taste or liking; which they, were readily able to do, because the owners, seeing death imminent, had become as reckless of their property as of their lives; so that most of the houses were open to all comers, and no distinction was observed between the stranger who presented himself and the rightful lord. Thus, adhering ever to their inhuman determination to shun the sick, as far as possible, they ordered their life. In this extremity of our city's suffering and tribulation the venerable authority of laws, human and divine, was abased and all but totally dissolved for lack of those who should have administered and enforced them, most of whom, like the rest of the citizens, were either dead or sick or so hard bested for servants that they were unable to execute any office; whereby every man was free to do what was right in his own eyes.

8   Not a few there were who belonged to neither of the two said parties, but kept a middle course between them, neither laying the same restraint upon their diet as the former, nor allowing themselves the same license in drinking and other dissipations as the latter, but living with a degree of freedom sufficient to satisfy their appetite and not as recluses. They therefore walked abroad, carrying in the hands flowers or fragrant herbs or divers sorts of spices, which they frequently raised to their noses, deeming it an excellent thing thus to comfort the brain with such perfumes, because the air seemed be everywhere laden and reeking with the stench emitted by the dead and the dying, and the odours of drugs.

9   Some again, the most sound, perhaps, in judgment, as they were also the most harsh in temper, of all, affirmed that there was no medicine for the disease superior or equal in efficacy to flight; following which prescription a multitude of men and women, negligent of all but themselves, deserted their city, their houses, their estates, their kinsfolk, their goods, and went into voluntary exile, or migrated to the country parts, as if God in visiting men with this pestilence in requital of their iniquities would not pursue them with His wrath wherever they might be, but intended the destruction of such alone as remained within the circuit of the walls of the city; or deeming perchance, that it was now time for all to flee from it, and that its last hour was come.

10   Of the adherents of these divers opinions not all died, neither did all escape; but rather there were, of each sort and in every place many that sickened, and by those who retained their health were treated after the example which they themselves, while whole, had set, being everywhere left to languish in almost total neglect. Tedious were it to recount, how citizen avoided citizen, how among neighbors was scarce found any that shewed fellow-feeling for another, how kinsfolk held aloof, and never met, or but rarely; enough that this sore affliction entered so deep into the minds of men and women, that in the horror thereof brother was forsaken by brother, nephew by uncle, brother by sister, and oftentimes husband by wife: nay, what is more, and scarcely to be believed, fathers and mothers were found to abandon their own children, untended, unvisited, to their fate, as if they had been strangers. Wherefore the sick of both sexes, whose number could not be estimated, were left without resource but in the charity of friends (and few such there were), or the interest of servants, who were hardly to be had at high rates and on unseemly terms, and being, moreover, one and all, men and women of gross understanding, and for the most part unused to such offices, concerned themselves no

further than to supply the immediate and expressed wants of the sick, and to watch them die; in which service they themselves not seldom perished with their gains. In consequence of which dearth of servants and dereliction of the sick by neighbors, kinsfolk and friends, it came to pass—a thing, perhaps, never before heard of—that no woman, however dainty, fair or well-born she might be, shrank, when stricken with the disease, from the ministrations of a man, no matter whether he were young or no, or scrupled to expose to him every part of her body, with no more shame than if he had been a woman, submitting of necessity to that which her malady required; wherefrom, perchance, there resulted in after time some loss of modesty in such as recovered. Besides which many succumbed, who with proper attendance, would, perhaps, have escaped death; so that, what with the virulence of the plague and the lack of due attendance of the sick, the multitude of the deaths, that daily and nightly took place in the city, was such that those who heard the tale—not to say witnessed the fact—were struck dumb with amazement. Whereby, practices contrary to the former habits of the citizens could hardly fail to grow up among the survivors.

11   It had been, as to-day it still is, the custom for the women that were neighbors and of kin to the deceased to gather in his house with the women that were most closely connected with him, to wail with them in common, while on the other hand his male kinsfolk and neighbors, with not a few of the other citizens, and a due proportion of the clergy according to his quality, assembled without, in front of the house, to receive the corpse; and so the dead man was borne on the shoulders of his peers, with funeral pomp of taper and dirge, to the church selected by him before his death. Which rites, as the pestilence waxed in fury, were either in whole or in great part disused, and gave way to others of a novel order. For not only did no crowd of women surround the bed of the dying, but many passed from this life unregarded, and few indeed were they to whom were accorded the lamentations and bitter tears of sorrowing relations; nay, for the most part, their place was taken by the laugh, the jest, the festal gathering; observances which the women, domestic piety in large measure set aside, had adopted with very great advantage to their health. Few also there were whose bodies were attended to the church by more than ten or twelve of their neighbors, and those not the honorable and respected citizens, but a sort of corpse-carriers drawn from the baser ranks, who called themselves *becchini* and performed such offices for hire, would shoulder the bier, and with hurried steps carry it, not to the church of the dead man's choice, but to that which was nearest at hand, with four or six priests in front and a candle or two, or, perhaps, none; nor did the priests distress themselves with too long and solemn an office, but with the aid of the *becchini* hastily consigned the corpse to the first tomb which they found untenanted. The condition of the lower, and, perhaps, in great measure of the middle ranks, of the people shewed even worse and more deplorable; for, deluded by hope or constrained by poverty, they stayed in their quarters, in their houses where they sickened by thousands a day, and, being without service or help of any kind, were, so to speak, irredeemably devoted to the death which overtook them. Many died daily or nightly in the public streets; of many others, who died at home, the departure was hardly observed by their neighbors, until the stench of their putrefying bodies carried the tidings; and what with their corpses and the corpses of others who died on every hand the whole place was a sepulchre.

12   It was the common practice of most of the neighbors, moved no less by fear of contamination by the putrefying bodies than by charity towards the deceased, to drag the corpses out of the houses with their own hands, aided, perhaps, by a porter, if a porter was to be had, and to lay them in front of the doors, where any one who made the round might have seen, especially in the morning, more of them than he could count; afterwards they

would have biers brought up or in default, planks, whereon they laid them. Nor was it once or twice only that one and the same bier carried two or three corpses at once; but quite a considerable number of such cases occurred, one bier sufficing for husband and wife, two or three brothers, father and son, and so forth. And times without number it happened, that as two priests, bearing the cross, were on their way to perform the last office for some one, three or four biers were brought up by the porters in rear of them, so that, whereas the priests supposed that they had but one corpse to bury, they discovered that there were six or eight, or sometimes more. Nor, for all their number, were their obsequies honored by either tears or lights or crowds of mourners, rather, it was come to this, that a dead man was then of no more account than a dead goat would be to-day.

The Collapse of Public Health

Ronald J. Glasser

1   Americans, we know, pay too much for their health care, and compared with other countries we receive a very poor return on our investment. The reasons are many, but they are not hard to understand: in essence, we have tended historically to view health care as a commodity like any other. But health is not a product; it is a public good. The evidence is clear that even when viewed through the reductive lens of purely economic self-interest, market-based, entrepreneurial medicine is a failure. Healing people after they fall ill is vastly more expensive than preventing the illness in the first place: every dollar spent preventing diphtheria, for instance, saves $27; every dollar spent on measles, mumps, and rubella saves $23. Yet policymakers have consistently preferred the most expensive and least efficient models of health care, proving once again that the apostles of privatization are motivated not by hard-nosed economics but by an incoherent ideology that is little more than a brittle mask concealing the most irrational species of self-interest.

2   For the last quarter century, especially after the election of Ronald Reagan and his declaration that government itself is the problem that afflicts us, the public-health infrastructure of this country has been eviscerated. Between 1981 and 1993, public-health expenditures declined by 25 percent as a proportion of overall health spending; in 1992, less than 1 percent of all American health care spending was devoted to public health. That trend has continued, even after the anthrax attacks of 2001, when politicians suddenly realized how vulnerable the nation was to biological attack.

3   Since then, it is true, the federal government has appropriated about $2 billion for bioterrorism response, an undertaking that if it were actually carried out would necessarily involve improving the public-health infrastructure. In theory, the bioterrorism money is channeled through the CDC, which distributes it to the states, which in turn disperse money to local health departments. Superficially, the gains are impressive: the CDC's budget for "public health preparedness and response for bioterrorism" increased from $49.9 million in 2001 to $918 million in 2002 and $870 million in 2003. Yet strangely enough, state and local public-health budgets have continued to decline. Public-health laboratories in California could lose 20 percent of their funding this year; the Alabama Department of Public Health expects to fire 250 people and to close regional labs and

cut back on its flu-vaccination programs. State funding for AIDS prevention in Massachusetts has been cut by 40 percent over the last two years. Larimer County, Colorado, where last summer 500 people contracted the West Nile virus, received $100,000 in federal funds but lost $700,000 in state money. Overall, thirty-two states cut their public-health budgets between fiscal years 2002 and 2003. Michigan cut its spending by 24 percent, Massachusetts by 23 percent, and Montana, which received more federal bioterror money per capita than New York, cut its public-health budget by 19 percent. Many states, facing huge budget deficits, apparently took the federal money and simply cut their own appropriations. This should come as no surprise: in 2003 the states collectively faced a $66 billion shortfall, and in 2004 state deficits are estimated to be $78 billion. Federal investment will do no good if state politicians, struggling to cope with the economic effects of other federal policies, use those funds to reduce their own deficits.

4   The Trust for America's Health (TFAH), a nonprofit group that monitors public-health policy, in December released a comprehensive study of what the state health departments have accomplished with their "increased" funding. TFAH found that only twenty-four states had spent at least 90 percent of their 2002 bioterror funds, and only seventeen states had passed at least 50 percent of the money along to local health departments. Much of the money is mired in bureaucracy. A February GAO report revealed that the states were not much better prepared for bioterrorism (and by extension, a natural epidemic) than they were in 2001.

5   Of course, state health departments can hardly be blamed for their inability to correct a quarter century of neglect with what amounts to a mere $2,000 for every staffed hospital bed in America. Bioterrorism funds are being used simply to keep the lights on, and no one who has carefully observed the Bush Administration would expect it to follow through with its promises to rebuild the public-health system. In fact, the President's 2005 budget proposal calls for a $105 million decrease in state and local bioterrorism funding. The new budget also cuts $1.1 billion from the "Function 550" account, which finances disease-prevention programs and other public-health initiatives, and the federal Public Health Improvements Programs were cut by 64 percent.

6   Secretary of Health and Human Services Tommy Thompson has claimed that preparing for bioterrorism will enable the government to respond to influenza and other infectious diseases; in fact, the reverse is true. Bioterrorism is a remote threat and a massive attack is very unlikely, but it captures the imagination of weak-minded politicians and a populace raised on movies starring Bruce Willis. The truly imminent biological threat, which all public-health experts agree will inevitably strike, is an influenza pandemic. The 1918 pandemic killed 550,000 Americans and 30 million worldwide. A virulent flu would thus be much worse than a bioterrorism attack, and it would strike every part of the country more or less simultaneously. These facts are well known and understood, yet TFAH found that only thirteen states have a plan or at least a draft of a plan to confront an influenza pandemic. Amazingly, the CDC itself has yet to release a federal plan for such a pandemic; nor does the CDC require states to report flu cases or even flu deaths.

7   Every year influenza epidemics emerge from areas such as the Guangdong region of China, where large populations of farmers, pigs, and poultry share their species' various strains of the influenza virus. When multiple strains of the virus infect the same host, they begin to share genes, creating new mutations; when a new strain emerges for which humans have no immunity, a pandemic can occur.

8   In response to a 1997, avian influenza outbreak that began to infect humans but stopped short, for some reason, of becoming an epidemic, the World Health Organization significantly expanded its flu-prevention activities and set up its Global

Agenda for Influenza Surveillance and Control, a program whose four main objectives are to monitor the spread of influenza in animals and humans, to identify each year's newest infective strain, to accelerate global pandemic awareness, and to increase usage and speed development of an effective vaccine. Each year the WHO surveillance program puts its infectious-disease teams along with its worldwide network of more than one hundred laboratories on alert, hoping to detect outbreaks before they spread around the globe. Such generalized surveillance is difficult and expensive, but the danger of emerging infections and the continuing influenza threat have left the world health community with little choice.

9   In February 2003 the WHO issued a report about a group of patients with severe influenza in Hong Kong. The index case was a physician from Guangdong province in China. A global alert was soon issued concerning similar illnesses in Singapore and Hanoi. The WHO sent Dr. Carlo Urbani, an Italian infectious-disease specialist, to Hanoi to investigate. Urbani swiftly determined that the disease was something unusual and that it was highly contagious and virulent. Unlike influenza, which always begins with a runny nose, waves of generalized aches and pains, and weakness, followed by days of fever and an increasing cough before the onset of pneumonia, this disease progressed almost immediately to severe pneumonia, respiratory collapse, and, for many, death. We now know that these alerts were describing the SARS outbreak, which nearly became a global pandemic. Working closely with the Vietnamese authorities, Urbani and other specialists from the WHO, the CDC, and Doctors Without Borders were able to contain the disease in Hanoi, though tragically Urbani himself contracted SARS and died in a makeshift isolation ward in Bangkok. It was not long before the disease spread to Toronto. By late March, 6,800 people there had already been quarantined, with another 5,200 health-care staff working "in quarantine" at facilities that public-health officials had quickly set aside for treating suspected SARS cases. In the United States public-health officials were simply holding their breath and hoping for the best. Not only have cutbacks stripped rural areas of their hospitals and clinics but even the major cities now lack the number of acute-care and infectious-disease beds—not to mention the nursing staff, technicians, and isolation units—to deal with a bad year of influenza much less a full-fledged disease with what appeared to be the staggering demands of SARS.

10   What happened next was unprecedented: researchers quickly determined that the disease was caused by a new type of virus and very rapidly isolated the cause as a previously unknown coronavirus that had apparently jumped from an animal species to humans. It was not lost on the world's infectious-disease experts that what had taken physicians and scientists almost four years in the case of AIDS was accomplished for SARS in less than four months. It is no exaggeration to say that the billions of dollars so reluctantly pushed into viral research as a result of the efforts of AIDS activists in the 1980s and 1990s enabled the WHO to quickly find the cause of another viral plague. And it was the ability to share accurate information in real time via email and the Internet that allowed the WHO to hold the disease in check.

11   In the midst of all the tracking of potential contacts, the increased hospitalizations, the thousands of people in quarantine, the disease simply vanished at virtually the same time all over the world. Coronaviruses thrive in cold weather, and, like influenza, they spread during the winter months, which accounts for the yearly outbreaks of colds and upper-respiratory infections. The realization that SARS is a cold weather virus is troubling, because it means that there has been no real victory, only a reprieve. It has to be assumed that SARS is still out there waiting for another winter.

12   The lesson of the SARS outbreak was that preparation, surveillance, and decisive action from public officials can prevent epidemics. The WHO response was exemplary—

training, staffing, equipment, and funding were all in place, ready for an emergency—but we still lack a truly global early-warning system. In the United States we continue to be without an effective national warning system. As *Lancet* editor Richard Horton writes in *Health Wars,* his scathing critique of contemporary medicine, "No single agency—CDC, WHO, the military, or a non-governmental organization (such as Médecins Sans Frontières)—currently has the resources, staff, or equipment to act as a rapid-response strike force during a civilian health emergency." If SARS had come to the United States, there is little hope that it could have been contained.

13   Today, we are no better prepared for a SARS epidemic than we were last year. "Homeland security," curiously interpreted to exclude the most plausible and deadly threats facing our population, has remained the priority. The massive smallpox immunization program in 2002 was little more than a distraction and waste of precious funds. Meanwhile, we are afflicted with a government that has waged war all across the world to avenge the deaths of 3,000 terror victims, far fewer than die of influenza in a mild year; a government that insists on spending $50 billion to build a missile-defense system that does not work, a military-industrial make-work project designed to meet a threat that does not exist. The war in Iraq consumes almost $4 billion a month, twice the amount we have largely squandered on bioterrorism since 2001. We have grown so foolish and so incompetent that perhaps we do not deserve to survive. Perhaps it is simply time to die.

CASEBOOK

Food Controversies

Everyone eats. Eating is among the few truly universal human experiences. It is also a subject that can be investigated through the lens of many disciplines, such as anthropology, popular culture, agriculture, nutritional science, chemistry, politics, and business. The readings in this section invite you to think about food from many different perspectives—from heritage to health—as you digest the writers' ideas.

From *Fast Food Nation*
Eric Schlosser

1   The taste of McDonald's french fries has long been praised by customers, competitors, and even food critics. James Beard loved McDonald's fries. Their distinctive taste does not stem from the type of potatoes that McDonald's buys, the technology that processes them, or the restaurant equipment that fries them. Other chains buy their french fries from the same large processing companies, use Russet Burbanks, and have similar fryers in their restaurant kitchens. The taste of a fast food fry is largely determined by the cooking oil. For decades, McDonald's cooked its french fries in a mixture of about 7 percent cottonseed oil and 93 percent beef tallow. The mix gave the fries their unique flavor—and more saturated beef fat per ounce than a McDonald's hamburger.

2   Amid a barrage of criticism over the amount of cholesterol in their fries, McDonald's switched to pure vegetable oil in 1990. The switch presented the company with an enormous challenge: how to make fries that subtly taste like beef without cooking them in tallow. A look at the ingredients now used in the preparation of McDonald's french fries suggests how the problem was solved. Toward the end of the list is a seemingly innocuous, yet oddly mysterious phrase: "natural flavor." That ingredient helps to explain not only why the fries taste so good, but also why most fast food—indeed, most of the food Americans eat today—tastes the way it does.

3   Open your refrigerator, your freezer, your kitchen cupboards, and look at the labels on your food. You'll find "natural flavor" or "artificial flavor" in just about every list of ingredients. The similarities between these two broad categories of flavor are far more significant than their differences. Both are man-made additives that give most processed food most of its taste. The initial purchase of a food item may be driven by its packaging or appearance, but subsequent purchases are determined mainly by its taste. About 90 percent of the money that Americans spend on food is used to buy processed food. But the canning, freezing, and dehydrating techniques used to process food destroy most of its flavor. Since the end of World War II, a vast industry has arisen in the United States to make processed food palatable. Without this flavor industry, today's fast food industry could not exist. The names of the leading American fast food chains and their best-selling menu items have become famous worldwide, embedded in our popular culture. Few people, however, can name the companies that manufacture fast food's taste.

4   The flavor industry is highly secretive. Its leading companies will not divulge the precise formulas of flavor compounds or the identities of clients. The secrecy is deemed essential for protecting the reputation of beloved brands. The fast food chains, understandably, would like the public to believe that the flavors of their food somehow originate in their restaurant kitchens, not in distant factories run by other firms.

5   The New Jersey Turnpike runs through the heart of the flavor industry, an industrial corridor dotted with refineries and chemical plants. International Flavors & Fragrances (IFF), the world's largest flavor company, has a manufacturing facility off Exit 8A in Dayton, New Jersey; Givaudan, the world's second-largest flavor company, has a plant in East Hanover. Haarmann & Reimer, the largest German flavor company, has a plant in Teterboro, as does Takasago, the largest Japanese flavor company. Flavor Dynamics has a plant in South Plainfield; Frutarom is in North Bergen; Elan Chemical is in Newark. Dozens of companies manufacture flavors in the corridor between Teaneck and South Brunswick. Indeed, the area produces about two-thirds of the flavor additives sold in the United States.

6   The IFF plant in Dayton is a huge pale blue building with a modern office complex attached to the front. It sits in an industrial park, not far from a BASF plastics factory, a Jolly French Toast factory, and a plant that manufactures Liz Claiborne cosmetics. Dozens of tractor-trailers were parked at the IFF loading dock the afternoon I visited, and a thin cloud of steam floated from the chimney. Before entering the plant, I signed a nondisclosure form, promising not to reveal the brand names of products that contain IFF flavors. The place reminded me of Willy Wonka's chocolate factory. Wonderful smells drifted through the hallways, men and women in neat white lab coats cheerfully went about their work, and hundreds of little glass bottles sat on laboratory tables and shelves. The bottles contained powerful but fragile flavor chemicals, shielded from light by the brown glass and the round plastic caps shut tight. The long chemical names on the little white labels were as mystifying to me as medieval Latin. They were the odd-sounding names of things that would be mixed and poured and turned into new substances, like magic potions.

7   I was not invited to see the manufacturing areas of the IFF plant, where it was thought I might discover trade secrets. Instead, I toured various laboratories and pilot kitchens, where the flavors of well-established brands are tested or adjusted, and where whole new flavors are created. IFF's snack and savory lab is responsible for the flavor of potato chips, corn chips, breads, crackers, breakfast cereals, and pet food. The confectionery lab devises the flavor for ice cream, cookies, candies, toothpastes, mouthwashes, and antacids. Everywhere I looked, I saw famous, widely advertised products sitting on laboratory desks and tables. The beverage lab is full of brightly colored liquids in clear bottles. It comes up with the flavor for popular soft drinks, sport drinks, bottled teas, and wine coolers, for all-natural juice drinks, organic soy drinks, beers, and malt liquors. In one pilot kitchen I saw a dapper food technologist, a middle-aged man with an elegant tie beneath his lab coat, carefully preparing a batch of cookies with white frosting and pink-and-white sprinkles. In another pilot kitchen I saw a pizza oven, a grill, a milk-shake machine, and a french fryer identical to those I'd seen behind the counter at countless fast food restaurants.

8   In addition to being the world's largest flavor company, IFF manufactures the smell of six of the ten best-selling fine perfumes in the United States, including Estée Lauder's Beautiful, Clinique's Happy, Lancôme's Trésor, and Calvin Klein's Eternity. It also makes the smell of household products such as deodorant, dishwashing detergent, bath soap, shampoo, furniture polish, and floor wax. All of these aromas are made through the same basic process: the manipulation of volatile chemicals to create a particular smell. The basic science behind the scent of your shaving cream is the same as that governing the flavor of your TV dinner.

9   The aroma of a food can be responsible for as much as 90 percent of its flavor. Scientists now believe that human beings acquired the sense of taste as a way to avoid being poisoned. Edible plants generally taste sweet; deadly ones, bitter. Taste is supposed

to help us differentiate food that's good for us from food that's not. The taste buds on our tongues can detect the presence of half a dozen or so basic tastes, including: sweet, sour, bitter, salty, astringent, and umami (a taste discovered by Japanese researchers, a rich and full sense of deliciousness triggered by amino acids in foods such as shellfish, mushrooms, potatoes, and seaweed). Taste buds offer a relatively limited means of detection, however, compared to the human olfactory system, which can perceive thousands of different chemical aromas. Indeed "flavor" is primarily the smell of gases being released by the chemicals you've just put in your mouth.

10   The act of drinking, sucking, or chewing a substance releases its volatile gases. They flow out of the mouth and up the nostrils, or up the passageway in the back of the mouth, to a thin layer of nerve cells called the olfactory epithelium, located at the base of the nose, right between the eyes. The brain combines the complex smell signals from the epithelium with the simple taste signals from the tongue, assigns a flavor to what's in your mouth, and decides if it's something you want to eat.

11   Babies like sweet tastes and reject bitter ones; we know this because scientists have rubbed various flavors inside the mouths of infants and then recorded their facial reactions. A person's food preferences, like his or her personality, are formed during the first few years of life, through a process of socialization. Toddlers can learn to enjoy hot and spicy food, bland health food, or fast food, depending upon what the people around them eat. The human sense of smell is still not fully understood and can be greatly affected by psychological factors and expectations. The color of a food can determine the perception of its taste. The mind filters out the overwhelming majority of chemical aromas that surround us, focusing intently on some, ignoring others. People can grow accustomed to bad smells or good smells; they stop noticing what once seemed overpowering. Aroma and memory are somehow inextricably linked: A smell can suddenly evoke a long-forgotten moment. The flavors of childhood foods seem to leave an indelible mark, and adults often return to them, without always knowing why. These "comfort foods" become a source of pleasure and reassurance, a fact that fast food chains work hard to promote. Childhood memories of Happy Meals can translate into frequent adult visits to McDonald's, like those of the chain's "heavy users," the customers who eat there four or five times a week.

12   The human craving for flavor has been a largely unacknowledged and unexamined force in history. Royal empires have been built, unexplored lands have been traversed, great religions and philosophies have been forever changed by the spice trade. In 1492 Christopher Columbus set sail to find seasoning. Today the influence of flavor in the world marketplace is no less decisive. The rise and fall of corporate empires—of soft drink companies, snack food companies, and fast food chains—is frequently determined by how their products taste.

13   The flavor industry emerged in the mid-nineteenth century, as processed foods began to be manufactured on a large scale. Recognizing the need for flavor additives, the early food processors turned to perfume companies that had years of experience working with essential oils and volatile aromas. The great perfume houses of England, France, and the Netherlands produced many of the first flavor compounds. In the early part of the twentieth century, Germany's powerful chemical industry assumed the technological lead in flavor production. Legend has it that a German scientist discovered methyl anthranilate, one of the first artificial flavors, by accident while mixing chemicals in his laboratory. Suddenly the lab was filled with the sweet smell of grapes. Methyl anthranilate later became the chief flavoring compound of grape Kool-Aid. After World War II, much of the perfume industry shifted from Europe to the United States, settling in New York City near the garment district and the fashion houses. The flavor

industry came with it, subsequently moving to New Jersey to gain more plant capacity. Man-made flavor additives were used mainly in baked goods, candies, and sodas until the 1950s, when sales of processed food began to soar. The invention of gas chromatographs and mass spectrometers—machines capable of detecting volatile gases at low levels—vastly increased the number of flavors that could be synthesized. By the mid-1960s the American flavor industry was churning out compounds to supply the taste of Pop Tarts, Bac-Os, Tab, Tang, Filet-O-Fish sandwiches, and literally thousands of other new foods.

14   The American flavor industry now has annual revenues of about $1.4 billion. Approximately ten thousand new processed food products are introduced every year in the United States. Almost all of them require flavor additives. And about nine out of every ten of these new food products fail. The latest flavor innovations and corporate realignments are heralded in publications such as *Food Chemical News, Food Engineering, Chemical Market Reporter,* and *Food Product Design.* The growth of IFF has mirrored that of the flavor industry as a whole. IFF was formed in 1958, through the merger of two small companies. Its annual revenues have grown almost fifteenfold since the early 1970s, and it now has manufacturing facilities in twenty countries.

15   The quality that people seek most of all in a food, its flavor, is usually present in a quantity too infinitesimal to be measured by any traditional culinary terms such as ounces or teaspoons. Today's sophisticated spectrometers, gas chromatographs, and headspace vapor analyzers provide a detailed map of a food's flavor components, detecting chemical aromas in amounts as low as one part per billion. The human nose, however, is still more sensitive than any machine yet invented. A nose can detect aromas present in quantities of a few parts per trillion—an amount equivalent to 0.000000000003 percent. Complex aromas, like those of coffee or roasted meat, may be composed of volatile gases from nearly a thousand different chemicals. The smell of a strawberry arises from the interaction of at least 350 different chemicals that are present in minute amounts. The chemical that provides the dominant flavor of bell pepper can be tasted in amounts as low as .02 parts per billion; one drop is sufficient to add flavor to five average size swimming pools. The flavor additive usually comes last, or second to last, in a processed food's list of ingredients (chemicals that add color are frequently used in even smaller amounts). As a result, the flavor of a processed food often costs less than its packaging. Soft drinks contain a larger proportion of flavor additives than most products. The flavor in a twelve-ounce can of Coke costs about half a cent.

16   The Food and Drug Administration does not require flavor companies to disclose the ingredients of their additives, so long as all the chemicals are considered by the agency to be GRAS (Generally Regarded As Safe). This lack of public disclosure enables the companies to maintain the secrecy of their formulas. It also hides the fact that flavor compounds sometimes contain more ingredients than the foods being given their taste. The ubiquitous phrase "artificial strawberry flavor" gives little hint of the chemical wizardry and manufacturing skill that can make a highly processed food taste like a strawberry.

17   A typical artificial strawberry flavor, like the kind found in a Burger King strawberry milk shake, contains the following ingredients: amyl acetate, amyl butyrate, amyl valerate, anethol, anisyl formate, benzyl acetate, benzyl isobutyrate, butyric acid, cinnamyl isobutyrate, cinnamyl valerate, cognac essential oil, diacetyl, dipropyl ketone, ethyl acetate, ethyl amylketone, ethyl butyrate, ethyl cinnamate, ethyl heptanoate, ethyl heptylate, ethyl lactate, ethyl methylphenylglycidate, ethyl nitrate, ethyl propionate, ethyl valerate, heliotropin, hydroxyphenyl-2-butanone (10 percent solution in alcohol),

α-ionone, isobutyl anthranilate, isobutyl butyrate, lemon essential oil, maltol, 4-methylacetophenone, methyl anthranilate, methyl benzoate, methyl cinnamate, methyl heptine carbonate, methyl naphthyl ketone, methyl salicylate, mint essential oil, neroli essential oil, nerolin, neryl isobutyrate, orris butter, phenethyl alcohol, rose, rum ether, γ-undecalactone, vanillin, and solvent.

18   Although flavors usually arise from a mixture of many different volatile chemicals, a single compound often supplies the dominant aroma. Smelled alone, that chemical provides an unmistakable sense of the food. Ethyl-2-methyl butyrate, for example, smells just like an apple. Today's highly processed foods offer a blank palette: whatever chemicals you add to them will give them specific tastes. Adding methyl-2-peridylketone makes something taste like popcorn. Adding ethyl-3-hydroxybutanoate makes it taste like marshmallow. The possibilities are now almost limitless. Without affecting the appearance or nutritional value, processed foods could even be made with aroma chemicals such as hexanal (the smell of freshly cut grass) or 3-methyl butanoic acid (the smell of body odor).

From *Food Politics: How the Food Industry Influences Nutrition and Health*
Marion Nestle

1   Like much else in nutrition, fortification has an eventful history. The very first techno-foods were fortified or enriched. To explain the difference: vitamins and minerals are added to white flour to compensate for the loss of nutrients that occurs when whole grains are milled. For example, unfortified white flour contains 25 percent or less of vitamin B_6, magnesium, and zinc and less than 10 percent of the vitamin E found in the whole grain. The white flour sold in stores is considered fortified because vitamins (thiamin, niacin, riboflavin, and, more recently, folic acid) and one mineral (iron) are added at *higher levels* than those found in the original grain. In contrast, enrichment is the restoration of nutrients to their *original level* in the unprocessed food. Despite these technical distinctions, the term *fortification* usually refers to any addition of vitamins or minerals to food.

2   As a public health approach, fortification was designed to overcome widespread deficiencies of certain key nutrients in the diets of the general population. The practice dates to the early 1830s, when a French chemist advocated the addition of iodine to table salt to prevent goiter (enlarge thyroid glands). Europeans began adding iodine to salt in the early 1900s, but large-scale additions of other nutrients did not become possible until later in the century when scientists identified vitamins and learned how to purify and synthesize them in large quantities. In the United States, a 1918 survey found one-third of the population of Michigan (where soils are particularly deficient in iodine) to have enlarged thyroid glands; in some areas, the prevalence exceeded 60 percent. Within just ten years from the time iodized salt was introduced in 1924, officials were iodizing more than 90 percent of the salt sold in Michigan. The happy result was that goiter had all but disappeared, in Detroit, for example, the prevalence of goiter fell from 47 percent to 2 percent among school children and to about 1 percent among adults.[1]

This remarkable achievement encouraged the use of iodized salt throughout the country and virtually eliminated iodine deficiency as a public health problem.

3   Vitamin D was first added to milk in 1931, but fortification truly took off just prior to World War II when the FDA established a *standard of identity* for enriched flour that went into effect in 1942. A standard of identity is a recipe for the nutrient composition of a specific food such as enriched bread; the food must contain each of the elements of that recipe in order to be marketed under that designation. The FDA soon established standards of identity for other foods: cornmeal and grits in 1943, pasta in 1946, enriched bread in 1952, and rice in 1958.[2]

4   In the 1950s, manufacturers began to fortify cereals with additional vitamins, minerals, and protein at levels higher than in the original foods. The initial purpose of fortifying cereals and grains was to raise the intake of the four nutrients then considered most deficient in the diets of the population: thiamin, niacin, riboflavin, and iron. To ensure adequate intake, the standard specified higher amounts than in the original grain. Even though losses of all of the other vitamins and minerals in whole grains were just as substantial, nutritionists considered those nutrients less critical to public health. As a public health strategy, fortification and enrichment ("nutrification") seemed to make good sense because they were "the most rapidly applied, the most flexible, and the most socially acceptable intervention method of changing the intake of nutrients without a vast educational effort and without changing the current food patterns of a given population. The principle of nutrification challenges a long-standing belief that the consumer must consciously desire and be involved in nutritional change."[3]

5   Fortification strategies especially appeared to make sense because nutrient deficiencies occurred most commonly among low-income populations without enough money to buy a variety of foods or enough education to make the most nutritious choices. Because nutrient deficiencies were still observed in areas with much poverty, the 1969 White House Conference on Food, Nutrition, and Health strongly recommended the accelerated use of fortification, particularly of breakfast cereals and other foods likely to be basic sources of calories for ethnic, cultural, socioeconomic, and regional groups at especially high risk of inadequate nutrient intake.[4] In response, the FDA raised the levels of thiamin, niacin, and riboflavin in the standard of identity for grain foods and more than doubled the iron standard. The amounts of these nutrients in the food supply immediately increased. Indeed, the availability of iron rose so quickly that health officials began to be concerned that the food supply contained too much of it; the FDA reduced the standard, but then increased it again some years later. During the 1970s, various groups used data indicating that a significant proportion of the population was deficient in one or more nutrients as a basis for proposals to expand enrichment formulas to include up to ten vitamins and minerals, but the FDA rejected these out of fear that they might lead to excessive, unbalanced, and potentially harmful intake of essential nutrients.[5]

Folic Acid Fortification: Panacea or Techno-Fix?

6   The interweaving of the scientific and commercial issues that arise in any discussion of fortification is best exemplified by the addition of folic acid to grain products. In 1996 the FDA announced that it would require food companies to add this vitamin, which is also known as folate, to enriched grain products by January 1998.[6] The objective was to reduce the number of infants born with seriously debilitating brain and spinal cord defects (such as spina bifida) that result from incomplete closure of the neural tube during the first month of fetal development. Studies had revealed that mothers who consumed adequate amounts of folic acid and other vitamins during early pregnancy

reduced the odds that they might bear a child with a neural tube defect by 50 percent or more. Although the doses used in the studies varied by more than ten-fold, and few studies distinguished the benefits of folic acid from those of other supplementary vitamins, most (but not all) experts viewed this research as definitive evidence of the need for women of childbearing age to consume more of this vitamin. Because risk factors for neural tube defects are poorly understood, and because the fetal neural tube closes before a woman might have any idea that she was pregnant, the FDA chose fortification—rather than advice to eat better diets or take supplements—as the method most likely to raise folic acid intake among women "at risk" of pregnancy.

7   Unlike the other nutrients used in fortification, which were added to the food supply to prevent deficiencies in large segments of the population, folic acid was expected to prevent about half of the 4,000 cases of neural tube defects that occurred each year, a very small proportion of the 3 million or so babies born in the United States annually. To prevent these few—albeit devastating—cases, fortification would be likely to raise the folic acid intake of 260 million Americans, among them many who were already obtaining adequate amounts of the vitamin from foods. Indeed, raising folic acid intakes would produce one additional benefit: it would reduce blood levels of homocysteine, a by-product of protein metabolism associated with higher rates of coronary heart disease and stroke. The potential benefits, however, would need to be balanced against a possible hazard. Excessive amounts of folate interfere with the ability to diagnose deficiencies of vitamin B_{12}, a problem noted with increasing frequency among the elderly. Overall, the benefits of fortification were expected to outweigh the risks, but many questions remained unanswered.[7]

8   At the time the FDA called for folic acid fortification, the incidence of neural tube defects had been declining at a steady rate for many years and was already quite low. If the incidence declined further, it would not be obvious whether it did so as a continuation of ongoing trends or as a result of an increase in intake of the vitamin. Thus, in this one respect, folic acid fortification could be considered a techno-fix likely to promote the proliferation and consumption of more expensive processed foods, and not necessarily by the people who needed them most. As a member of the FDA Food Advisory Committee at the time, I saw this particular situation as a missed opportunity for developing a nationwide education campaign to encourage everyone to eat more fruits and vegetables—the primary dietary sources of folate as well as of so many other health-promoting nutrients and components. Federal officials considered this idea unrealistic, however, not least because of the substantial cost of such a campaign. I also was concerned that the masking of vitamin B_{12} deficiency might lead to yet another techno-fix: the addition of vitamin B_{12} to the standard of identity for enriched grains. To skeptics, myself among them, folic acid fortification was almost certain to lead to calls for the addition of larger numbers of essential nutrients—whether needed or not—to the general food supply.[8] As explained later in this chapter, subsequent evidence supports some benefits of folic acid fortification but leaves questions about other possible benefits unanswered.

Notes

1. Markel H. "When it rains it pours": endemic goiter, iodized salt, and David Murray Cowie, MD. Am J Public Health 1987;77:219–229.

2. Sebrell WH. A fiftieth anniversary—cereal enrichment. Nutrition Today January/February, 1992:20–21. Leveille GA. Food fortification—opportunities and pitfalls. Food Technology 1984;38(1):58–63.

3. Lachance PA, Bauernfeind JC. Concepts and practices of nutrifying foods. In: Bauernfeind JC, Lachance PA, eds. Nutrient Additions to Food: Nutritional, Technological and Regulatory Aspects. Trumbull, CT: Food & Nutrition Press, Inc., 1991:19–86. Quotation: p. 49.

4. White House Conference on Food, Nutrition and Health. Final Report. Washington, DC, 1970.

5. FDA. General principles governing the addition of nutrients to foods: notice of proposed rulemaking. Federal Register 39:20900–20904, June 14, 1974.

6. Chemical note: Foods and tissues contain the vitamin in the folate (reduced) form, which is metabolically active but unstable. Supplements provide it as folic acid (oxidized), which is stable and inactive but is readily converted to folate in the body. The terms are often used interchangeably.

7. Lindenbaum J, Rosenberg IH, Wilson PWF, et al. Prevalence of cobalamin deficiency in the Framingham elderly population. Am J Clin Nutr 1994;60:2–11. Tucker KL, Mahnken B, Wilson PWF, et al. Folic acid fortification of the food supply: potential benefits and risks for the elderly population. JAMA 1996;276:1879–1885.

8. Oakley GP. Let's increase folic acid fortification and include vitamin B-$_{12}$. Am J Clin Nutr 1997;65:1889–1890. But see: Gaull GE, Testa CA, Thomas PR, Weinreich DA. Fortification of the food supply with folic acid to prevent neural tube defects is not yet warranted. J Nutrition 1996;126:7730–7805.

You Want Fries with That? Review of *Fat Land: How Americans Became the Fattest People in the World* by Greg Critser

Michael Pollan

1   Add another to the string of superlatives wreathing the world's greatest power. Americans are now the fattest people on earth. (Actually a handful of South Sea Islanders still outweigh us, but we're gaining.) Six out of every 10 of us—and fully a quarter of our children—are now overweight. Just since 1970 the proportion of American children who are overweight has doubled, a rate of increase that suggests the fattening of America has a specific history as well as a biology. "Fat Land," a skinny book about this big subject, is the journalist Greg Critser's highly readable attempt to reconstruct that history.

2   At least from a business perspective, the fattening of America may well have been a necessity. Food companies grow by selling us more of their products. The challenge they face is that the American population is growing much more slowly than the American food supply—a prescription for falling rates of profit. Agribusiness now produces 3,800 calories of food a day for every American, 500 calories more than it produced 30 years ago. (And by the government's lights, at least a thousand more calories than most people need.) So what's a food company to do? The answer couldn't be simpler or more imperative: get each of us to eat more. A lot more.

3   Critser doesn't put it quite this way, but his subject is the nutritional contradictions of capitalism. There's only so much food one person can consume (unlike shoes or

CD's), or so you would think. But Big Food has been nothing short of ingenious in devising ways to transform its overproduction into our overconsumption—and body fat. The best parts of this book show how, in the space of two decades, Americans learned to eat, on average, an additional 200 calories a day. In the words of James O. Hill, a physiologist Critser interviewed, getting fat today is less an aberration than "a normal response to the American environment."

4   Some of the credit for creating this new environment belongs to an unheralded businessman by the name of David Wallerstein, the man Critser says introduced "supersizing" to America. Today Wallerstein is an executive with McDonald's, but back in the 1960's he worked for a chain of movie theaters, where he labored to expand sales of soda and popcorn—the high-markup items that theaters depend on for their profitability. Wallerstein tried everything he could think of to goose sales—two-for-one deals, matinee specials—but found he couldn't induce customers to buy more than one soda and one bag of popcorn. Why? Because going for seconds makes people feel like pigs.

5   But Wallerstein discovered that people *would* spring for more popcorn and soda—a lot more—as long as it came in a single gigantic serving. Thus was born the Big Gulp and, in time, the Big Mac and jumbo fries. Though Ray Kroc himself took some convincing: the McDonald's founder had naïvely assumed that if people wanted more fries they'd buy another bag. He didn't appreciate how social taboos against gluttony (one of the seven deadly sins, after all) were holding us back. Wallerstein's dubious achievement was to devise the dietary equivalent of a papal dispensation. Supersize it!

6   Now, you might think people would stop eating and drinking these gargantuan portions as soon as they felt full, but it turns out hunger doesn't work that way. Citing studies in the "growing field of satiety"—the science of human satisfaction—Critser writes that people presented with larger portions will eat up to 30 percent more than they otherwise would. Human hunger is apparently quite elastic, which makes excellent evolutionary sense: it behooved our hunter-gatherer ancestors to feast whenever the opportunity presented itself, thereby storing reserves of fat against future famine. Researchers call this trait "the thrifty gene." The problem is that in an era of fast-food abundance, the opportunity for feasting now presents itself 24/7.

7   What makes supersizing such an effective business strategy is the cheapness of basic foodstuffs in America. Since the raw materials of soda and popcorn, French fries and even hamburgers represent such a tiny fraction of their retail price (compared with labor, packaging and advertising), expanding portion size becomes a way to multiply sales without adding much to costs.

8   Critser, to his credit, is more interested in ferreting out the political history of "overnutrition" in America than indulging in the usual pseudopsychology or sociology of fat. So "Fat Land" begins at the beginning, with the 1971 arrival in Washington of Earl Butz. Butz, you'll recall, was Richard Nixon's secretary of agriculture, a blustering, quotable and foulmouthed agricultural economist from Purdue. The early 70's marked the last time food prices in America had climbed high enough to generate political heat. Bad weather, a grain shortage and soaring costs for agricultural inputs (fuel, chemicals, equipment) were squeezing farmers; at the same time consumers were protesting the high costs of basic foods like sugar, cheese and, perhaps most sensitively, meat. Beef, that American entitlement, had suddenly become a luxury good.

9   Recognizing the political peril of cranky consumers and restive farmers, President Nixon dispatched Butz to re-jigger the American food system. The Sage of Purdue promptly loosened regulations, beat down trade rules and expanded subsidies. By 1976, when a racist joke he told on a plane cost him his job, Butz had largely succeeded in

driving down the cost of food and vastly increasing the output of America's farmers. Say what you will about the problems of a heavily subsidized industrial agriculture, the cost of food is no longer a political issue in the United States.

10   Now we find ourselves confronted with the unintended consequences of cheap and abundant food, foremost among them the epidemic of obesity. Critser takes us on a brisk tour, by turns funny and depressing, of a society learning to accommodate itself to its new dimensions: restaurants adding square inches to their seats; government agencies relaxing their weight, fitness and dietary guidelines; Seventh Avenue recalibrating clothing sizes to make for happier visits to the dressing room. Less amusing is what our weight is doing to our health, and Critzer is sure-footed and clear in describing the science of obesity, especially the precise mechanism by which our diet has led to an epidemic of Type 2 diabetes. What used to be called adult onset diabetes now afflicts millions of children as well as adults, and costs America's health system billions of dollars a year.

11   In the last year or so, there have been signs that the fattening of America is emerging as a political issue. A grass-roots parents' movement to get fast food and vending machines out of the schools is gathering steam, and several lawsuits have recently been filed by obese customers against fast-food chains, seeking to hold the companies liable for health problems. The suits seem absurd on their face (no one's forcing people to eat this stuff), but then so did the early suits against the tobacco companies. There does seem to be at least one area in which the tobacco analogy is apposite: the ethics of marketing unhealthy products to children.

12   Indeed, the question of responsibility looms large in the growing debate over obesity, and it is here that Critser loses his footing a bit. While "Fat Land" does an excellent job connecting the dots between government and corporate policies and the fattening of America, by the end of the book the problem has largely, and somewhat inexplicably, been redefined in terms of personal responsibility. Critser expresses the hope that "the food industry might . . . take it upon itself to do something" like resize portions, but nothing that has come before gives us reason to think the industry would ever do any such thing.

13   George W. Bush has defined this as "the era of personal responsibility" and finally it is under this banner, so congenial to business, that Critser marches, seemingly in spite of himself and his best journalism. So instead of seriously entertaining any public solutions to what he has so convincingly demonstrated is a public problem, Critser ends by imploring us to eat less, get off our duffs and, incredibly, bring back gluttony as a leading sin. Personal responsibility is all to the good, but everything else in "Fat Land" suggests it is probably no match for the thrifty gene and the Happy Meal.

From *Seeds of Contention: World Hunger and the Global Controversy over GM Crops*
Per Pinstrup-Anderson and Ebbe Schioler

1   *Can the poor benefit from genetically modified foods?* Let's look at three short stories that illustrate the difference between the picture of genetic engineering that has been painted in the industrialized world and what researchers are actually doing.

- A top-ranking athlete is tested for performance-enhancing drugs after yet another victory, and the result is positive. The media milk this piece of news for all it's worth. Some weeks later, after a series of cross-checks and double-checks, it turns out a mistake was made. The athlete is completely exonerated, a fact that receives little attention in the press. Well, that's the way the cookie crumbles, some would say. But the athlete finds it hard to get his career back on track after being run through the media wringer.

- Great-grandmother's antique crystal glasses have been brought out for a family celebration. While washing the dishes, Dad almost drops one of the glasses on the floor. There are only eleven left as it is, so right then and there he is made to swear that he will never, ever break one of those precious glasses.

- It's a risky business being an electrician in Europe, where every wire carries a jolt of 220 volts. European electricians are trained in how to administer heart massage and mouth-to-mouth resuscitation just in case a worker accidentally comes in contact with a live wire. In the United States, where 110 volts is the norm, the risks are not quite so great, but the voltage is adequate to provide light and run most appliances. Doesn't it seem a bit bizarre for Europe to have opted for such a dangerous voltage?

We have here three rather silly anecdotes. Yet they serve to highlight some of the elements that GM crops are up against in the public debate. Here are a few examples that parallel these stories.

2   Several tired old chestnuts concerning the dangers of GM plants crop up again and again in the debate about genetic engineering. We have heard that a diet of GM potatoes killed rats in a laboratory in Scotland; that GM crops could kill harmless insects, even the beautiful monarch butterfly; and that GM soybeans carrying a gene from Brazil nuts contained a substance that could cause severe allergic reactions in consumers. As we have noted in earlier chapters, for all these stories either the results have been disproved by extensive research or the potential problem died a natural death during routine checking procedures. But one doesn't have to read too many letters to the editor or too many home pages on the Web to find that these stories are still doggedly making the rounds.[1] As the athlete in our first anecdote found out, retractions never have quite the same impact as hot news.

3   Many of our actions involve an element of risk, and not many things come with a lifetime guarantee—the only way a family can guarantee that no harm will come to its heirloom crystal is never to use it. Most forms of progress necessarily carry some risk. Of course, we weigh the risks and benefits and do everything we can to reduce the risks. And this is the understanding with which research on genetic modification is carried out, whether designed to solve medical, agricultural, or other problems. Refusing to embark on anything new until an official guarantee can be given that all the risks have been eliminated, as some parties would have it for GM plants,[2] is tantamount to bringing progress to a grinding halt. Such insistence on an ironclad lifetime guarantee ("our tests have confirmed that genetic modification will never, in any way, involve any element of risk whatsoever") runs counter to a simple, basic rule of science (and for that matter of life itself): it is impossible to prove a negative thesis. This assumes, of course, that we all agree that the debate surrounding a scientific subject should be conducted using arguments with a solid scientific foundation.

4   The system for supplying electricity in Europe treads the line between efficiency and risk. Making electric power completely safe is impossible, and attempts to do so would be hugely expensive, requiring massive restructuring of the national grids and a

radical redesign of machinery and appliances. The resulting electricity bills would put a serious strain on the household budget. And potentially dangerous high-tension power lines would still be needed to distribute electricity to consumers. In the ongoing debate on GM plants, no evidence has been produced of any harm done. But many people do not even want the current switched on, no matter how many layers of insulation are wrapped around the cables.[3] Better to do without, they say.

Wanted: Some Dynamic Thinking at All Levels

5 Why is the debate on GM foods, pro and con, so heated? A major reason is that things seemed to happen so fast: GM plants entered the market so quickly and are already an irrefutable fact of life. (Another reason, a general distrust of new technology and of the competence and integrity of both government authorities and private companies, is discussed in Chapters 6 and 7.) While GM plants are having an enormous impact on certain crops and on the agricultural supply in some countries, in others they are seen as a threat. Genetically modified soybeans are the chief GM crop, accounting for 90 percent of all the soybeans sown in Argentina and 50 percent in the United States in 1999. Soybeans accounted for 54 percent of all GM crops under cultivation in the world in 1999, maize 28 percent, and rape and cotton 9 percent each.[4]

6 And why have GM crops become so widespread in such a short time? These crops have fulfilled their promise. They provide robust yields with less work for the farmer and require smaller supplements of insecticides and pesticides that are friendlier to the environment than those used in traditional farming. All parties except the insecticide producers have profited: farmers, for whom the new crops mean lower costs or higher yields; consumer, because of less concern about pesticide residues; and manufacturers of seeds and herbicides, through larger sales and greater profits.

7 Looking at the specific qualities targeted in the first wave of GM plants, one might ask with good reason whether the new features made enough of a difference to the consumer to merit all the time and effort put into developing them. But then one could easily have asked the same question when the first ballpoint pens appeared on the market in the late 1940s. They were appallingly ugly, made of plastic in mottled tones of dishwater gray; they left ink stains on the pockets of men's white shirts; and they cost about one-and-a-half week's wages for, say, a delivery boy. As we know, though, both ballpoints and plastic were here to stay, improving in quality and dropping in price. Or think of people's first attempts to fly: weird contraptions were tried out with varying degrees of success on available patches of flat ground everywhere from the clover fields of Denmark to the prairies of North America. Sheer lunacy, respectable citizens were quick to agree. In comparison with these trial-and-error efforts, GM plants emerged as clear winners right from the start. The GM products already marketed have presented few problems, and those farmers who are looking for just what these plants have to offer get value for their money. Product development does not stop here, of course. Other crops, with fresh attributes and other combined benefits, will be forthcoming as quickly as laboratory experiments can be carried out, findings checked, and trials completed.

8 And herein lies the main obstacle to a constructive discussion of GM crops. Much creative, dynamic thought goes into discussion of the risks entailed in the new plant varieties. Granted, no ill effects have been proven, but it is not inconceivable that problems could arise. Or to put it another way, which reflects the arguments one hears so often, "Things may be going pretty well at the moment, but in the long run. . . ." All too rarely does the same dynamic come into play when looking at the beneficial effects: "There may not be much to shout about at the moment, but in the long run . . ." would be a reasonable parallel line of argument.

9   Having seen such a high degree of success with relatively new techniques in such a short time, we can fully expect a steady flow of results from this young branch of science as it develops in the coming years. This is particularly important for poor farmers and consumers in developing countries, who stand to gain very little from currently available genetic engineering technology. As the technology is developed, even more safeguards against ill effects will be incorporated—prompted, of course, by a healthy self-interest, since any evidence of serious errors or major problems would prove both expensive and disastrous for private and public investors in genetic modification. When the private corporation Aventis sold to farmers GM maize seed approved for livestock feed only, they failed to foresee that the GM maize (called StarLink) might end up in human food, for which it was not approved. According to informal sources, the cost to Aventis of this miscalculation, as of March 2001, has been in excess of a billion U.S. dollars, and the bills are still coming in.

Apparent Agreement on Many Points

10   At a conference on biotechnology and biosafety held by the World Bank in 1997 and attended by representatives of a number of U.N. organizations, research institutes, foreign aid systems, and developing countries, a short list was drawn up of some of the things that need to be done to make farming in the developing countries more productive. Most people would probably agree that this list goes at least some way toward covering the necessary agenda.

- Apply intensive farming techniques over a wider area, including, in some areas, increased fertilizer use.

- Conserve soil and water, with special priority to combating erosion.

- Maintain biodiversity.

- Improve pest control.

- Expand irrigation and make it more efficient.

- Improve livestock management.

- Develop new crop strains that are higher yielding, pest resistant, and drought tolerant.

- Reduce dependency on pesticides and herbicides.

The authors of this agenda, which won general endorsement at the conference, stated that genetic engineering seemed like a good means for fulfilling some of these goals: "At their best, the bioengineering techniques are highly compatible with the goals of sustainable agriculture, because they offer surgical precision in combating specific problems without disrupting other functional components in the agricultural system."[5]

11   There are no promises that genetic engineering will solve all ills, of course. From the days of the Wild West comes the myth of the cowboy hero's magical silver bullet, which never missed its mark and wiped out all the bad guys. In the debate surrounding genetic modification, few promise that this technology is a silver bullet. In fact, the disavowal of any such claims has become almost routine.[6] But not uncommonly, critics assume that such empty promises are being made.[7] Clearly, the debate is not well served by one side ascribing to its opponent patently unreasonable arguments to which all right-thinking individuals would take exception.

12   One of genetic modification's truly interested parties, a representative of one of the multinationals involved in seed production, who has a vested interest in profiting from

this business, takes a sober view of what can be achieved. On the basis of the predicted population and its calorie requirements in 2025 and using figures provided by the FAO, he estimates that traditional plant breeding, increased use of fertilizer, and better irrigation systems could do 70 percent of the job; the other 30 percent will have to be fulfilled by various forms of biotechnology, including a good helping of genetic modification.[8] Thirty percent may not sound all that drastic, but it represents the extra calories that, for millions of families in the developing world, mean the difference between regularly going hungry and having enough to eat every day. And after 2025, agricultural production in the developing countries will have to go on increasing in order to cover the expected increases in the population.

Different Priorities

13   Even such a conservative goal as securing 30 percent of the growth in food supply over a twenty-five-year period through biotechnology may well prove difficult to attain. The private companies that are the major players in this field have not geared their research toward yield increases in developing countries but toward solving the problems of farmers in the wealthy countries. The explanation is very simple: this is where the money lies. So public research must do all it can to exploit the research potential of biotechnology to solve some of the high-priority problems in the developing world. Though the agendas of private and public research institutes differ, this does not mean that findings produced on one side cannot be absorbed or adapted by those working on the other. The substantial limitations and pitfalls of a constructive and close collaboration between private and public research are discussed in Chapter 6.

14   Research work can be classified in many different ways, depending on the interests involved: private versus public, industrialized world versus developing world, farmers versus consumers. These are not necessarily conflicting categories; a fair amount of overlap in potential benefits is possible for all those involved. But for simplicity's sake, we are considering here the research findings from a industrialized-world versus developing-world perspective, keeping in mind that to a large extent both sides have a common interest in furthering the development of robust high-quality agricultural plant material.

Big Hits in the Industrialized World

15   The first priority for agricultural biotechnology research in the industrialized world was to find a way to render crops resistant to the milder forms of weed-killer chemicals, so farmers could spray the weeds without damaging the crops. This accomplishment was environmentally sound because the milder forms of pesticides did little or no damage to the environment. This was a success with farmers, however, primarily because it eliminated tedious and time-consuming weeding close to plants and helped increase profit by cutting back on labor costs. It was also a smart way of turning a profit for the agro-industrial companies that sold the plant seeds, especially if they also happened to own the factories that manufactured the weed-killer chemicals. The breakthrough in this particular piece of research came about largely because the whole operation was technically feasible—the capacity for herbicide resistance being governed by a single gene.

16   The development of plants with a built-in pesticide was another high research priority that proved achievable. It is popular with farmers in the industrialized countries because it cuts back on the costs of industrial pesticide and the labor for spraying it. It benefits consumers by reducing pesticide residues in food. By reducing frequent, copious spraying, it also benefits the environment. And it is as beneficial financially for the

seed growers. The next logical research step, now under way, is to combine these two qualities in the same plant: resistance to pests and to weed killers.

17   Another front on which some progress has been made involves "shutting off" genes in crops—in fruit, for example, so that it ripens later and stands up better to transportation and storage, thus cutting back on waste. This could benefit farmers and wholesalers in the developing and industrialized countries.

18   More important from the consumers' point of view is the possibility of eliminating from crops both natural toxins and a predisposition to fungal infection, which would make the produce safer to eat. Research is also being carried out to reduce the allergenic effects of certain plants, such as wheat, peanuts, and soybeans. The allergenic tendencies of these plants cannot be effectively controlled through organic farming or bred out using conventional propagation methods.

19   The really big news in plant breeding today is the offensive now being mounted to improve the health-giving properties of plants. Vegetable oils containing a greater proportion of unsaturated fatty acids—better for human health—are in the offing. What better argument could there be for accepting GM foods than a vegetable oil marketed with the slogan, "Reduce your cholesterol with this oil." This type of advance is just around the corner. Another example is potatoes with a higher starch content—a real step forward nutritionally if they also happened to absorb less fat during cooking, so that people would be eating lower-fat French fries. Fruits could be developed to have a better aroma and greater sweetness, and no doubt more color could be added to the paler varieties—not directly health-giving properties, but perhaps encouraging consumers to eat more fruit.

20   Farmers are pleased to hear that in a few years seed producers will be able to offer them improved feed grains. Work is progressing nicely on development of a maize with kernels containing double the oil content of current varieties, increasing the oil from 3 or 4 percent to more than 6 percent. This means that farmers can give cattle, pigs, and poultry less feed concentrate, making them easier and cheaper to raise. And this will minimize the need to import feed grains, some of which come from the developing countries. This represents both a plus and a minus for the developing countries, of course: farmland now used to grow feed grains will be freed for growing human food, but exporting countries will lose revenue. Until recently, all attempts to increase the oil content of maize resulted in a drop in yield. Thanks to breeding work based on the mapping of the maize genes—not genetic modification as such, but a valuable spin-off from investment in new technology—this improvement can now be made without any loss in yield. Other properties in grains will also be improved, among them increases in amino acids (giving us more and better protein in bread grain, for example) and micronutrients.[9]

21   Consumers and farmers are already reaping the benefits of the shift toward more environmentally friendly herbicides, and work is progressing on the development of plants capable of withstanding common plant diseases and insect attacks. This will lead to less use of pesticides and thus lower concentrations of agrochemical residue. Advances in this area could be of great help to farmers in developing countries.

22   Looking only at what private companies have in the pipeline, one would be hard put to see how current research provides any solution to the world's food supply problems. No significant effort has been made to raise the yield ceiling of the major crops, simply because the main objective of private industry is to win a share of the market in the industrialized world, where food is plentiful and relatively inexpensive. The failure of the real heavyweights in the field to invest resources in trying to break down the biological barriers to greatly increased yields is disappointing. This state of affairs has come

under fire, and rightly so. Critics point out that promises made at the time of the first biotechnological breakthrough in the early 1980s have gone by the board in favor of lucrative—and easy—solutions to the profit-making agricultural concerns of the industrialized world. The first generation of results has left very few people convinced that the GM plants currently available are the solution to world food problems.[10]

NOTES

The following abbreviations are used in the notes: CIMMYT, Centro Internacional de Mejoramiento de Maiz y Trigo (International Maize and Wheat Improvement Center); IFPRI, International Food Policy Research Institute. Short titles are used for cited works after the first citation.

1. Mae-Wan Ho, *Genetic Engineering Dream or Nightmare? Turning the Tide on the Brave New World of Bad Science and Big Business* (London: Continuum, 2000).

2. Lord Melchett, "GM Crops Worse Than N-waste," *Guardian* (Manchester), September 6, 2000.

3. Robert B. Shapiro, *The Welcome Tension of Technology: The Need for Dialogue about Agricultural Biotechnology*, CEO Series no. 37 (St. Louis, Mo.: Center for the Study of American Business, Washington University, 2000).

4. Nuffield Council on Bioethics, *Genetically Modified Crops: The Ethical and Social Issues* (London: Nuffield Foundation, 1999).

5. "Gener Spredes i Naturen [Genes are spreading in the wild]." *Politiken* (Denmark), September 12, 1999.

6. Mira Shiva and Vandana, "India's Human Guinea Pigs: Human vs. Property Rights," *Science as Culture* 2 no. 10 (2000): 59–81.

7. Christina Aid, "Selling Suicide," at <www.christian-aid.org/nk/reports/suicide/summary> accessed September 23, 1999.

8. Ibid.

9. S. Rampton and I. Stanber, *Trust Us, We're Experts: How Industry Manipulates Science and Gambles with Your Future* (New York: Jeremy P. Tarcker/Putnam, 2000).

10. Cyrus G. Ndixitu, "Biotechnology in Africa: Why the Controversy?" in *Agricultural Biotechnology and the Poor*, ed. G. J. Persley and M. M. Lantin (Washington, D.C.: Consultative Group on International Agricultural Research, 2000).

Progress Is Killing Us, Bite by Bite
Gregg Easterbrook

1 Your great-great grandparents would find it hard to believe the Boeing 747, but perhaps they'd have a harder time believing last week's news that obesity has become the second-leading cause of death in the United States. Too much food a menace instead of too little! A study released by the federal Centers for Disease Control ranked "poor diet and physical inactivity" as the cause of 400,000 United States deaths in 2000, trailing only fatalities from tobacco. Obesity, the C.D.C. said, now kills five times as many Americans as "microbial agents," that is, infectious disease.

2   Moon landings might seem less shocking to your great-great grandparents than abundance of food causing five times as many deaths as germs; OutKast might seem less bizarre to them than the House passing legislation last week to exempt restaurants from being sued for serving portions that are too large.

3   Your recent ancestors would further be stunned by the notion of plump poverty. A century ago, the poor were as lean as fence posts; worry about where to get the next meal was a constant companion for millions. Today, America's least well-off are so surrounded by double cheeseburgers, chicken buckets, extra-large pizzas and super-sized fries that they are more likely to be overweight than the population as a whole.

4   But the expanding waistline is not only a problem of lower-income Americans who dine too often on fast food. Today, the typical American is overweight, according to the C.D.C., which estimates that 64 percent of American citizens are carrying too many pounds for their height. Obesity and sedentary living are rising so fast that their health consequences may soon supplant tobacco as the No. 1 preventable cause of death, the C.D.C. predicts. Rates of heart disease, stroke and many cancers are in decline, while life expectancy is increasing—but ever-rising readings on the bathroom scale may be canceling out what would otherwise be dramatic gains in public health.

5   O.K., it's hard to be opposed to food. But the epidemic of obesity epitomizes the unsettled character of progress in affluent Western society. Our lives are characterized by too much of a good thing—too much to eat, to buy, to watch and to do, excess at every turn. Sometimes achievement itself engenders the excess: today's agriculture creates so much food at such low cost that who can resist that extra helping?

6   Consider other examples in which society's success seems to be backfiring on our health or well-being.

Productivity

7   Higher productivity is essential to rising living standards and to the declining prices of goods and services. But higher productivity may lead to fewer jobs.

8   Early in the postwar era, analysts fretted that automation would take over manufacturing, throwing everyone out of work. That fear went unrealized for a generation, in part because robots and computers weren't good at much. Today, near-automated manufacturing is becoming a reality. Newly built factories often require only a fraction of the work force of the plants they replace. Office technology, meanwhile, now allows a few to do what once required a whole hive of worker bees.

9   There may come a point when the gains from higher productivity pale before the job losses. But even if that point does not come, rapid technological change is instilling anxiety about future employment: anxiety that makes it hard to appreciate and enjoy what productivity creates.

Traffic

10   Cars are much better than they were a few decades ago—more comfortable, powerful and reliable. They are equipped with safety features like air bags and stuffed with CD players, satellite radios and talking navigation gizmos. Adjusted for consumers' rising buying power, the typical powerful new car costs less than one a generation ago.

11   But in part because cars are so desirable and affordable, roads are increasingly clogged with traffic. Today in the United States, there are 230 million cars and trucks in operation, and only 193 million licensed drivers—more vehicles than drivers! Studies by the Federal Highway Administration show that in the 30 largest cities, total time lost to traffic jams has almost quintupled since 1980.

12   Worse, prosperity has made possible the popularity of S.U.V.'s and the misnamed "light" pickup trucks, which now account for half of all new-car sales. Exempt from the fuel-economy standards that apply to regular cars, sport utility vehicles and pickup trucks sustain American dependence on Persian Gulf oil. A new study in the Journal of Risk and Uncertainty showed that the rise in S.U.V.'s and pickup trucks "leads to substantially more fatalities" on the road.

13   So just as longevity might be improving at a faster clip were it not for expanding waistlines, death rates in traffic accidents might show a more positive trend were it not for the S.U.V. explosion.

14   The proliferation of cars also encourages us to drive rather than walk. A century ago, the typical American walked three miles a day; now the average is less than a quarter mile a day. Some research suggests that the sedentary lifestyle, rather than weight itself, is the real threat; a chubby person who is physically active will be O.K. Studies also show that it is not necessary to do aerobics to get the benefits of exercise, a half-hour a day of brisk walking is sufficient. But more cars, driven more miles, mean less walking.

Stress

15   It's not just in your mind. Researchers believe stress levels really are rising. People who are overweight or inactive experience more stress than others, and that now applies to the majority. Insufficient sleep increases stress, and Americans now sleep on average only seven hours a night, versus eight hours for our parents' generation and 10 hours for our great-grandparents'.

16   Research by Bruce McEwen, a neuroendocrinologist at Rockefeller University in New York, suggests that modern stress, in addition to making life unpleasant, can impair immune function—again, canceling out health gains that might otherwise occur.

17   Prosperity brings many other mixed blessings. Living standards keep rising, but so does incidence of clinical depression. Cellphones are convenient, but make it impossible to escape from office calls. E-mail is cheap and fast, if you don't mind deleting hundreds of spam messages. The Internet and cable television improve communication, but deluge us with the junkiest aspects of culture.

18   Americans live in ever-nicer, ever-larger houses, but new homes and the businesses that serve them have to go somewhere. Sprawl continues at a maddening pace, while once-rustic areas may now be grid-locked with S.U.V.'s and power boats.

19   Agricultural yields continue rising, yet that means fewer family farms are needed. Biotechnology may allow us to live longer, but may leave us dependent on costly synthetic drugs. There are many similar examples.

20   Increasingly, Western life is afflicted by the paradoxes of progress. Material circumstances keep improving, yet our quality of life may be no better as a result—especially in those cases, like food, where enough becomes too much.

21   "The maximum is not the optimum," the ecologist Garrett Hardin, who died last year, liked to say. Americans are choosing the maximum, and it does not necessarily make us healthier or happier.

Prayer to the Sockeye Salmon

Anonymous (Kawakiutl, nineteenth century)

Translated by Jane Hirshfield

Welcome, o Supernatural One, o Swimmer,
who returns every year in this world
that we may live rightly, that we may be well.
I offer you, Swimmer, my heart's deep gratitude.

5 I ask that you will come again,
that next year we will meet in this life,
that you will see that nothing evil should befall me.
O Supernatural One, o Swimmer,
now I will do to you what you came here for me to do.

Fruit Plummets from the Plum Tree

Anonymous (China, c. 600 B.C.)

Translated by Tony Barnstone and Chou Ping

Fruit plummets from the plum tree
but seven of ten plums remain;
you gentlemen who would court me,
come on a lucky day.

5 Fruit plummets from the plum tree
but three of ten plums still remain;
you men who want to court me,
come now, today is a lucky day!

Fruit plummets from the plum tree.
10 You can fill up your baskets.
Gentlemen if you want to court me,
just say the word.

Hansel and Gretel

Anne Sexton

Little plum,
said the mother to her son,
I want to bite,
I want to chew,
5 I will eat you up.
Little child,
little nubkin,
sweet as fudge,
you are my blitz.
10 I will spit on you for luck
for you are better than money.
Your neck as smooth
as a hard-boiled egg;
soft cheeks, my pears,
15 let me buzz you on the neck
and take a bite.
I have a pan that will fit you.
Just pull up your knees like a game hen.
Let me take your pulse
20 and set the oven for 350.
Come, my pretender, my fritter,
my bubbler, my chicken biddy!

Oh succulent one,
it is but one turn in the road
25 and I would be a cannibal!

Hansel and Gretel
and their parents
had come upon evil times.
They had cooked the dog
30 and served him up like lamb chops.
There was only a loaf of bread left.
The final solution,
their mother told their father,
was to lose the children in the forest.
35 We have enough bread for ourselves
but none for them.
Hansel heard this
and took pebbles with him
into the forest.
40 He dropped a pebble every fifth step
and later, after their parents had left them,
they followed the pebbles home.
The next day their mother gave them

each a hunk of bread
45   like a page out of the Bible
and sent them out again.
This time Hansel dropped bits of bread.
The birds, however, ate the bread
and they were lost at last.
50   They were blind as worms.
They turned like ants in a glove
not knowing which direction to take.
The sun was in Leo
and water spouted from the lion's head
55   but still they did not know their way.

So they walked for twenty days
and twenty nights
and came upon a rococo house
made all of food from its windows
60   to its chocolate chimney.
A witch lived in that house
and she took them in.
She gave them a large supper
to fatten them up
65   and then they slept,
z's buzzing from their mouths like flies.
Then she took Hansel,
the smarter, the bigger,
the juicier, into the barn
70   and locked him up.
Each day she fed him goose liver
so that he would fatten,
so that he would be as larded
as a plump coachman,
75   that knight of the whip.
She was planning to cook him
and then gobble him up
as in a feast
after a holy war.

80   She spoke to Gretel
and told her how her brother
would be better than mutton;
how a thrill would go through her
as she smelled him cooking;
85   how she would lay the table
and sharpen the knives
and neglect none of the refinements.
Gretel
who had said nothing so far
90   nodded her head and wept.
She who neither dropped pebbles or bread
bided her time.

The witch looked upon her
with new eyes and thought:
95 Why not this saucy lass
for an hors d'oeuvre?
She explained to Gretel
that she must climb into the oven
to see if she would fit.
100 Gretel spoke at last:
Ja, Fräulein, show me how it can be done.
The witch thought this fair
and climbed in to show the way.
It was a matter of gymnastics.
105 Gretel,
seeing her moment in history,
shut fast the oven,
locked fast the door,
fast as Houdini,
110 and turned the oven on to bake.
The witch turned as red
as the Jap flag.
Her blood began to boil up
like Coca-Cola.
115 Her eyes began to melt.
She was done for.
Altogether a memorable incident.

As for Hansel and Gretel,
they escaped and went home to their father.
120 Their mother,
you'll be glad to hear, was dead.
Only at suppertime
while eating a chicken leg
did our children remember
125 the woe of the oven,
the smell of the cooking witch,
a little like mutton,
to be served only with burgundy
and fine white linen
130 like something religious.

A Handful of Dates

Tayeb Salih

1 I must have been very young at the time. While I don't remember exactly how old I was, I do remember that when people saw me with my grandfather they would pat me on the head and give my cheek a pinch—things they didn't do to my grandfather. The strange

thing was that I never used to go out with my father, rather it was my grandfather who would take me with him wherever he went, except for the mornings when I would go to the mosque to learn the Koran. The mosque, the river and the fields—these were the landmarks in our life. While most of the children of my age grumbled at having to go to the mosque to learn the Koran, I used to love it. The reason was, no doubt, that I was quick at learning by heart and the Sheikh always asked me to stand up and recite the *Chapter of the Merciful* whenever we had visitors, who would pat me on my head and cheek just as people did when they saw me with my grandfather.

2   Yes, I used to love the mosque, and I loved the river too. Directly we finished our Koran reading in the morning I would throw down my wooden slate and dart off, quick as a genie, to my mother, hurriedly swallow down my breakfast, and run off for a plunge in the river. When tired of swimming about I would sit on the bank and gaze at the strip of water that wound away eastwards and hid behind a thick wood of acacia trees. I loved to give rein to my imagination and picture to myself a tribe of giants living behind that wood, a people tall and thin with white beards and sharp noses, like my grandfather. Before my grandfather ever replied to my many questions he would rub the tip of his nose with his forefinger; as for his beard, it was soft and luxuriant and as white as cotton-wool—never in my life have I seen anything of a purer whiteness or greater beauty. My grandfather must also have been extremely tall, for I never saw anyone in the whole area address him without having to look up at him, nor did I see him enter a house without having to bend so low that I was put in mind of the way the river wound round behind the wood of acacia trees. I loved him and would imagine myself, when I grew to be a man, tall and slender like him, walking along with great strides.

3   I believe I was his favourite grandchild: no wonder, for my cousins were a stupid bunch and I—so they say—was an intelligent child. I used to know when my grandfather wanted me to laugh, when to be silent; also I would remember the times for his prayers and would bring him his prayer-rug and fill the ewer for his ablutions without his having to ask me. When he had nothing else to do he enjoyed listening to me reciting to him from the Koran in a lilting voice, and I could tell from his face that he was moved.

4   One day I asked him about our neighbour Masood. I said to my grandfather: 'I fancy you don't like our neighbour Masood?'

5   To which he answered, having rubbed the tip of his nose: 'He's an indolent man and I don't like such people.'

6   I said to him: 'What's an indolent man?'

7   My grandfather lowered his head for a moment, then looking across at the wide expanse of field, he said: 'Do you see it stretching out from the edge of the desert up to the Nile bank? A hundred feddans. Do you see all those date palms? And those trees—sant, acacia, and sayal? All this fell into Masood's lap, was inherited by him from his father.'

8   Taking advantage of the silence that had descended upon my grandfather, I turned my gaze from him to the vast area defined by his words. 'I don't care,' I told myself, 'who owns those date palms, those trees or this black, cracked earth—all I know is that it's the arena for my dreams and my playground.'

9   My grandfather then continued: 'Yes, my boy, forty years ago all this belonged to Masood—two-thirds of it is now mine.'

10   This was news to me for I had imagined that the land had belonged to my grandfather ever since God's Creation.

11   'I didn't own a single feddan when I first set foot in this village. Masood was then the owner of all these riches. The position has changed now, though, and I think that before Allah calls to Him I shall have bought the remaining third as well.'

12   I do not know why it was I felt fear at my grandfather's words—and pity for our neighbour Masood. How I wished my grandfather wouldn't do what he'd said! I remembered Masood's singing, his beautiful voice and powerful laugh that resembled the gurgling of water. My grandfather never used to laugh.

13   I asked my grandfather why Masood had sold his land.

14   'Women,' and from the way my grandfather pronounced the word I felt that 'women' was something terrible. 'Masood, my boy, was a much-married man. Each time he married he sold me a feddan or two.' I made the quick calculation that Masood must have married some ninety women. Then I remembered his three wives, his shabby appearance, his lame donkey and its dilapidated saddle, his djellaba with the torn sleeves. I had all but rid my mind of the thoughts that jostled in it when I saw the man approaching us, and my grandfather and I exchanged glances.

15   'We'll be harvesting the dates today,' said Masood. 'Don't you want to be there?'

16   I felt, though, that he did not really want my grandfather to attend. My grandfather, however, jumped to his feet and I saw that his eyes sparkled momentarily with an intense brightness. He pulled me by the hand and we went off to the harvesting of Masood's dates.

17   Someone brought my grandfather a stool covered with an ox-hide, while I remained standing. There was a vast number of people there, but though I knew them all, I found myself for some reason, watching Masood: aloof from the great gathering of people he stood as though it were no concern of his, despite the fact that the date palms to be harvested were his own. Sometimes his attention would be caught by the sound of a huge clump of dates crashing down from on high. Once he shouted up at the boy perched on the very summit of the date palm who had begun hacking at a clump with his long, sharp sickle: 'Be careful you don't cut the heart of the palm.'

18   No one paid any attention to what he said and the boy seated at the very summit of the date palm continued, quickly and energetically, to work away at the branch with his sickle till the clump of dates began to drop like something descending from the heavens.

19   I, however, had begun to think about Masood's phrase 'the heart of the palm'. I pictured the palm tree as something with feeling, something possessed of a heart that throbbed. I remembered Masood's remark to me when he had once seen me playing about with the branch of a young palm tree: 'Palm trees, my boy, like humans, experience joy and suffering.' And I had felt an inward and unreasoned embarrassment.

20   When I again looked at the expanse of ground stretching before me I saw my young companions swarming like ants around the trunks of the palm trees, gathering up dates and eating most of them. The dates were collected into high mounds. I saw people coming along and weighing them into measuring bins and pouring them into sacks, of which I counted thirty. The crowd of people broke up, except for Hussein the merchant, Mousa the owner of the field next to ours on the east, and two men I'd never seen before.

21   I heard a low whistling sound and saw that my grandfather had fallen asleep. Then I noticed that Masood had not changed his stance, except that he had placed a stalk in his mouth and was munching at it like someone surfeited with food who doesn't know what to do with the mouthful he still has.

22   Suddenly my grandfather woke up, jumped to his feet and walked towards the sacks of dates. He was followed by Hussein the merchant, Mousa the owner of the field next to ours, and the two strangers. I glanced at Masood and saw that he was making his way towards us with extreme slowness, like a man who wants to retreat but whose feet insist on going forward. They formed a circle round the sacks of dates and began examining them, some taking a date or two to eat. My grandfather gave me a fistful, which I began

munching. I saw Masood filling the palms of both hands with dates and bringing them up close to his nose, then returning them.

23 Then I saw them dividing up the sacks between them. Hussein the merchant took ten; each of the strangers took five. Mousa the owner of the field next to ours on the eastern side took five, and my grandfather took five. Understanding nothing, I looked at Masood and saw that his eyes were darting about to left and right like two mice that have lost their way home.

24 'You're still fifty pounds in debt to me,' said my grandfather to Masood. 'We'll talk about it later.'

25 Hussein called his assistants and they brought along donkeys, the two strangers produced camels, and the sacks of dates were loaded on to them. One of the donkeys let out a braying which set the camels frothing at the mouth and complaining noisily. I felt myself drawing close to Masood, felt my hand stretch out towards him as though I wanted to touch the hem of his garment. I heard him make a noise in his throat like the rasping of a lamb being slaughtered. For some unknown reason, I experienced a sharp sensation of pain in my chest.

26 I ran off into the distance. Hearing my grandfather call after me, I hesitated a little, then continued on my way. I felt at that moment that I hated him. Quickening my pace, it was as though I carried within me a secret I wanted to rid myself of. I reached the river bank near the bend it made behind the wood of acacia trees. Then, without knowing why, I put my finger into my throat and spewed up the dates I'd eaten.

Text Credits

Chapter 1: *Page 6:* Marcia R. Carlisle, "What Made Lizzie Borden Kill?," *American Heritage*, July/August 1992. Reprinted by permission of *American Heritage* Magazine, a division of Forbes, Inc. © Forbes, Inc., 1992; *Page 13:* Ann Jones, "Laying Down the Law," from *Women Who Kill*. Copyright © 1996 by Ann Jones. Reprinted by permission of Beacon Press, Boston.

Chapter 4: *Page 107:* Courtesy of The City University of New York; *Page 108:* Courtesy of The City University of New York; *Page 108:* Courtesy of The City University of New York; *Page 113:* Reprinted by permission of LaGuardia Community College; *Page 114:* © EBSCO Publishing. All rights reserved; *Page 114:* © EBSCO Publishing. All rights reserved; *Page 115:* Reprinted with the permission of LexisNexis.

Chapter 5: *Page 133:* Introductory paragraphs to "Lorraine Hansberry, 1930–1965" bio, from *Contemporary Literary Criticism*, Gale Research, p. 182. Reprinted by permission; *Page 133:* Brooks Atkinson review of "A Raisin in the Sun," *New York Times*, March 12, 1959. Copyright © 1959 by the New York Times Co. Reprinted with permission; *Page 152:* William J. Broad, "Faulty Rivets Emerge as Clues to *Titanic* Disaster," *New York Times*, January 27, 1998. Copyright © 1998 by the New York Times Co. Reprinted with permission; *Page 154:* Screenshot, reprinted by permission of iParadigms, LLC.

Chapter 6: *Page 181:* Screen capture, reprinted by permission from Microsoft Corporation.

Chapter 7: *Page 186–189:* Excerpt from Wyn Craig Wade, *Titanic: End of a Dream*, Penguin, 1986, pp. 286–291. Reprinted by permission of the author.

Chapter 9: *Pages 247–248:* Three screen captures, copyright © 2005 by the American Psychological Association. Reprinted with permission.

Casebook—The *Titanic* Disaster: *Page 294:* Wyn Craig Wade, *Titanic: End of a Dream*, Penguin, 1986, pp. 286–291. Reprinted by permission of the author; *Page 291:* William J. Broad, "Faulty Rivets Emerge as Clues to *Titanic* Disaster," *New York Times*, January 27, 1998. Copyright © 1998 by the New York Times Co. Reprinted with permission; *Page 298:* From *Down with the Old Canoe: A Cultural History of the* Titanic *Disaster*, by Steven Biel. Copyright © 1996 by Steven Biel. Used by permission of W. W. Norton & Company, Inc.; *Page 304:* "Another Belfast Trip" from *A Night to Remember* by Walter Lord. Copyright © 1955, 1976 by Walter Lord. Reprinted by permission of Henry Holt and Company, LLC.

Casebook—Issues in War and Peace: *Page 311:* Jonathan Schell, "The Empire Backfires." Reprinted with permission from the March 29, 2004, issue of *The Nation*. For subscription information, call 1-800-333-8536. Portions of each week's *Nation* magazine can be accessed at http://www.the nation.com; *Page 316:* Arlo Guthrie, "Alice's Restaurant." Copyright © 1966 (renewed) by Appleseed Music, Inc. All rights reserved. Used by permission; *Page 323:* "The Death of the Ball Turret Gunner" from *The Complete Poems* by Randall Jarrell. Copyright © 1969, renewed 1997 by Mary von S. Jarrell. Reprinted by permission of Farrar, Straus and Giroux, LLC; *Page 326:* "Waiting for the Barbarians," by Constantine Cavafy, translated by Edmund Keeley, *Selected Poems*. © 1992 by Edmund Keeley and Philip Sherrard. Reprinted by permission of Princeton University Press; *Page 327:* Agyeya, "Hiroshima," translated by Agyeya and Leonard Nathan, *Signs and Silence*. Delhi: Simant, © 1976. Reprinted by permission of the author; *Page 328:* Anonymous, from *The Book of Songs*, "The Great War Dance" translated by Constance A. Cook. Reprinted with permission; *Page 329:* "The Inaugural Poem" from *Blues: For All the Changes* by Nikki Giovanni. Copyright © 1999 by Nikki Giovanni. Copyright © 1999 by Nikki Giovanni. Reprinted by permission of HarperCollins Publishers Inc.; *Page 322:* "The Lost Pilot" from *The Lost Pilot* by James Tate. Copyright © 1978 by James Tate. Reprinted by permission of HarperCollins Publishers Inc.

Casebook—Global Health: *Page 332:* Larry Kramer, excerpt from *The Normal Heart*. Copyright © 1985 by Larry Kramer. Reprinted with the permission of Grove/Atlantic, Inc.; *Page 336:* Lara Jakes Jordan, "United States: Bush Administration Weighs Condom Warning," AP, March 12, 2004. Copyright © The Associated Press. All rights reserved. Reprinted with permission. For reorders call Valeo IP, Inc.; *Page 337:* Julie Davidow, "Washington: Safe Sex the 'Norm' among Seattle Gays," *Seattle Post-Intelligencer*, March 12, 2004. Reprinted by permission; *Page 337:*

World Health Organization: "Fact Sheet No. 104: Tuberculosis," Revised August 2002. Reprinted by permission; *Page 340:* Penn State, "Medieval Black Death Was Probably Not Bubonic Plague," April 15, 2003. Adapted from a news release issued by Penn State. Reprinted with permission from *Science Daily,* http://www.sciencedaily.com/releases; *Page 345:* Ronald J. Glasser, "The Collapse of Public Health." Copyright © 2004 by *Harper's Magazine.* All rights reserved. Reproduced from the July issue by special permission.

Casebook—Food Controversies: *Page 349:* Excerpt from *Fast Food Nation* by Eric Schlosser. Reprinted by permission of Houghton Mifflin Company. All rights reserved; *Page 353:* Marion Nestle, excerpt from *Food Politics: How the Food Industry Influences Nutrition and Health.* Berkeley: University of California Press, 2002, pp. 301–304. © 2002 The Regents of the University of California. Reprinted with permission; *Page 356:* Michael Pollan, "You Want Fries with That?" Book review of *Fat Land: How Americans Became the Fattest People in the World* by Greg Critser, *New York Times,* January 12, 2003. Reprinted by permission of International Creative Management, Inc. Copyright © 2003 by Michael Pollan. First appeared in the *New York Times; Page 358:* Per Pinstrup-Anderson and Ebbe Schioler, excerpt from *Seeds of Contention: World Hunger and the Global Controversy over GM Crops.* Baltimore: Johns Hopkins University Press for the International Food Policy Research Institute (IFPRI), 2000, pp. 86–95. Reprinted by permission; *Page 364:* Gregg Easterbrook, "Wages of Wealth, All This Progress Is Killing Us, Bite by Bite," *New York Times,* March 14, 2004. Copyright © 2004 by The New York Times Co. Reprinted with permission; *Page 367:* "Prayer to the Sockeye Salmon" from *Women in Praise of the Sacred* by Jane Hirshfield, editor. Copyright © 1994 by Jane Hirshfield. Reprinted by permission of HarperCollins Publishers Inc.; *Page 367:* Anonymous, "Fruit Plummets from the Plum Tree," translated by Tony Barnstone and Chou Ping. Original translation. Reprinted with the permission of Tony Barnstone; *Page 368:* "Hansel and Gretel," from *Transformations* by Anne Sexton. Copyright © 1971 by Anne Sexton. Reprinted by permission of Houghton Mifflin Company. All rights reserved; *Page 370:* "A Handful of Dates," by Tayeb Salih from *The Wedding Zein and Other Stories* (copyright © Tayeb Salih 1968) is reproduced by permission of PFD (www.pfd.co.uk) on behalf of Tayeb Salih.

Photo Credits

Chapter 1: *Page 1:* Collection of Fall River Historical Society; *Page 3:* Public domain; *Page 3: New York Times,* 1892.

Chapter 2: *Page 33:* Courtesy of Marian Arkin.

Chapter 3: *Page 74:* Beinecke Rare Book and Manuscript Library, Yale University.

Chapter 4: *Page 100:* Smithsonian American Art Museum, Washington, DC / Art Resource, NY.

Chapter 5: *Page 131:* Copyright © Bettmann / CORBIS; *Page 141:* Courtesy of Research Services, Duke.

Chapter 6: *Page 165:* Frederick Douglass National Historic Site, National Park Service.

Chapter 7: *Page 183:* Copyright © National Gallery of Ireland.

Chapter 8: *Page 210:* Library of Congress.

Chapter 9: *Page 242:* Courtesy pm.London.org.

Chapter 10: *Page 260:* Courtesy of Marian Arkin; *Page 260:* Library of Congress; *Page 261:* Library of Congress; *Page 261:* Library of Congress.

Casebook—Issues in War and Peace: *Pages 320–321:* From *Maus I: A Survivor's Tale / My Father Bleeds History* by Art Spiegelman, copyright © 1973, 1980, 1981, 1982, 1984, 1985, 1986 by Art Spiegelman. Used by permission of Pantheon Books, a division of Random House, Inc.

Index